THE WIZARD'S GOWN

-REWOVEN-

BENEATH THE GLITTER OF MARC BOLAN

BY TONY STRINGFELLOW

THE WIZARD'S GOWN

~REWOVEN~

BENEATH THE GLITTER OF MARC BOLAN

BREEZE HAYWARD PUBLISHING

Special Edition First Published 2007.

© 2007 TONY STRINGFELLOW. Drawings ©Tony Stringfellow. All Photographs © Peter Sanders.

Tony Stringfellow has asserted the Author's right under the Copyright, Designs and Patents Act 1988 to be identified as the Author of this work.

© All rights reserved. Tony Stringfellow 2007. The complete contents of this work are protected under copyright and may not be copied or reproduced, in whole or part, in any way or form without the prior knowledge and consent of the originator and publisher.

ISBN 13: 9798685245113

A catalogue record of this book is registered at the British Library.

Published by Breeze Hayward Publishing

E-mail: breeze.hayward@virgin.net OR ts@tonystringfellow.com

This book is dedicated to my children.

Marc Bolan: Drawn by Tony Stringfellow in 1970 at the age of 13yrs.

ABOUT THE AUTHOR

Now livingin Tywyn, Wales, Tony Stringfellow was born and educated in Wolverhampton, attending St. Chad's Grammar School. A well-known and respected artist/sculptor, working in the entertainment business for over 20 years. He has written books, many short stories and articles, and has been writing his own poetry since he was 13yrs old.

Author of the original *'From Beneath the Wizard's Gown -Marc Bolan Unglittered'* and this Special Edition, **'The Wizard's Gown – Rewoven – Beneath the Glitter of Marc Bolan'**, also has a book of his own poetry available. In his own collection of poetry, **'Silent Solitudes',** he gives a sense of awareness for the truth of life, which is sometimes too readily ignored. You cannot be untouched by his words!

A second collection **'Cracks in the Shell'** is soon to be published. And an audio CD of Tony Stringfellow reciting his work, '**Naked Therapy'**, is also available.

www.tonystringfellow.com

CONTENTS

Chapter 1. Just a Man?

Chapter 2. Mythical Landscapes.

Chapter 3. Anointment.

Chapter 4. Dove Dancing.

Chapter 5. Citadels of Truth.

Chapter 6. Witch Songs.

Chapter 7. Sun Seals and Moon Eels.

Chapter 8. Pebble Dance.

Chapter 9. The Swan Kings Legacy.

Chapter 10. In the Eyes of a Child.

Chapter 11. Gods and Men.

Chapter 12. Gurus and Dreams.

Chapter 13. In the Shadow of the Wizard.

Chapter 14. Talking with a Wizardly Mentor.

Acknowledgements.

From Beneath the Wizard's Gown

Completely absorbed by the concept of Ego,

The wizardly elf stood alone by his throne

Taller than the moon shadows

He had once looked up to.

He wore a gown to protect his soul

That was woven from the Runes of Time.

The winds of the Earth Lords

Rippled the mysterious fabric

Causing star drops of meaning

To escape from beneath its heavy hem.

The whirling words wandered the ears of mortals,

Enchanting them with beguiling images

From a magical world.

The wizardly elf was no longer alone

For his words had found friends.

By Tony Stringfellow

1. **Just a Man?**

Four o'clock Saturday morning outside the Odeon in Birmingham, England. A line of overly pubescent teenage girls have been spawned with a condition known as T-Rextasy and were forming a queue six hours before the box office was due to open. They had hours to wait in the cold of the morning before they would be rewarded with their prize, tickets to see the bopping elf himself, Marc Bolan.

On the 9th of June 1972 every dusty crevice of the old cinema would creak and groan as the highly decibelic screams of those young fans would challenge the sound systems of the day, screams and scenes that had been widely reported as being reminiscent of Beatlemania, Bolan was-a-rollin. Telegram Sam, had eventually fallen out of the Top 40, spending two weeks in the number one slot and 12 weeks riding the charts, Metal Guru had followed it to number one and remained there for 4 weeks. Marc Bolan had successfully morphed into a 'Pop Icon'. The magical elf endeared himself to his relatively newfound audience by charismatically bopping and boogie-ing through an already impressive catalogue of hits in a truly embryonic mixture of Glam rock and Punk. The irony, though, lay within the magnanimous highlight of the gig, one song that he had only recently performed live, an unknown entity to most of his fans, for it had yet to be released on 'The Slider' album. The band left the stage; Bolan grasped his acoustic guitar and for a few moments, brashly discarded the glitter and the makeup. He sat cross-legged upon the stage encircled by one lone spotlight, the remainder of the stage in darkness. One tiny man, a mass of dark corkscrew hair and his guitar, in solitude upon the stage. There was a silence beyond the emphatic silence of Simon and Garfunkle, until the first chord, the first phrase "I'm just a man". The female content of the audience erupted into spasms of ecstasy but then the silence prevailed as Bolan caressed them within the spell of 'Spaceball Ricochet'. The performance was simple but magical. At this point the 'Wizard' was still alive and well, bathing his leaves in the sun light but his roots were soon to perish.

Mark Feld was born in 1947, he was to have just three decades to ascend the ladders of musical accolade and acquire the status of Legend. With a change of identity Marc Bolan served his artistic apprenticeship on the streets during the late fifties and early sixties, becoming the face about town, he strove to nurture his musical and mystical talents, initially playing in a semi-skiffle group with Helen Shapiro at the tender age of ten. By 1967 he had progressed significantly having already made a number of recordings, although none had been of any commercial success. He had also gained the attention of Simon Napier-Bell who placed him in Johns Children after a few recording attempts failed to follow through. Marc was on a constant learning curve absorbing all around him, music, image and personality were all under constant development. According to Marc his ethereal development even encompassed a period living with a wizard in Paris an early example of Marc's ability to 'embroider' events to enhance his image. Simon Napier-Bell believes this to be a story enriched by his imagination, "I seem to remember he went to Paris when he was just over 16, and met some old queen, who picked him up and took him home for the weekend, who was a magician and did some conjuring tricks, and Marc dreamed up the rest and was back in London by Monday writing his song." (The Wizard).

At the end of a tour with John's Children, supporting The Who, Simon took the band to see Ravi Shankar in Luxembourg the influence of which resulted in Marc leaving John's Children and forming Tyrannosaurus Rex with Steve Peregrin Took. "Marc was unbelievably impressed and four weeks later had given up all idea of playing with a band. Instead he was playing acoustic guitar (and singing) sitting cross-legged on a rug surrounded by joss sticks and with just a bong player to accompany him - Tyrannosaurus Rex." Simon Napier-Bell.

Ravi Shankar was born in the Holy City of Varanasi, city of temples and learning, in 1920. India's leading sitar player and cultural ambassador he has influenced many, from Yehudi Menuhin to George Harrison, so it is little surprise that he had such an effect on the young sponge-like Marc Bolan. There are obvious musical influences in the early albums, possibly extending to Marc's later work, Metal Guru and onwards.

In 1968 the first album 'My people were fair and had sky in their hair... but now they're content to wear stars on their brows' was released; not the shortest of titles but Bolan was already impressing the right people with his significant talent, the reading of a children's story on the album and a short transcript on the sleeve by John Peel, who embraced every opportunity he could to champion the Elf's music, a music that was unique. Marc Bolan took the influences of the 'Hippie' folk music of the sixties, skiffle and every myth and legend from as many cultures as he could absorb to forge an amalgamation of mystical incantations, each song a wealth of magical symbolism, with strange titles such as 'Frowning Atahuallpa' and 'Dwarfish Trumpet Blues'. This debut album possessed a rawness that was a little brash but a new world had been born and Bolan went on to enhance his mystical image with a second album, 'Prophets Seers and Sages, the Angels of the Ages' and a third in 1969 'Unicorn'. In 1970 Bolan opened the album 'A Beard of Stars', with an electric instrumental and Steve Peregrin Took had been replaced by Micky Finn. Still highly acoustic in its overall production, the album brought a new musical dimension to the mystique of Tyrannosaurus Rex.

Although Marc had played a very 'naïve' electric guitar with John's Children, his new found electrification was a significant development and despite not being generally thought of as a leading guitarist, this album and the two that followed showcased a wealth of extremely imaginative musicianship, having had the benefit of a few lessons from Jimmy Page. 1970 was to be another stepping-stone in Bolan's career; Tyrannosaurus Rex became T-Rex with the release of the like named studio album, commonly referred to as the 'brown album'.

There was an occasional sense of humour that would creep through his passionate devotion to music, in the lyrics or in the dedications on each sleeve, 'Prophets' being dedicated to 'The Memory of Kahlil Gibran, the hill of Youth and Dandy the Beano-Seller'. The title of 'Prophets' was clearly inspired by Kahlil Gibran, the Lebanese poet/philosopher, 1883-1931 whose best known work 'The Prophet' was (and likely still is) essential reading for all aspiring hippies. Ironically the 'brown album' was to be the last to carry a dedication for quite a time, which may have been symbolic of a change in attitude towards his music by the enigmatic Mr. Bolan and to the majority of the cult following that he had amassed to whom he was soon to lose his crown of mysticism.

In the year that 'Let it Be' roamed the charts for just ten weeks, peaking at number two, an uncharacteristic chart topper, narrating tales of Druids and the 'People of the Beltane' tore the pop world apart and rode a Swan through the charts for twenty weeks, also peeking at number two. 'Ride a White Swan' was Bolan's first commercial success, and despite never appearing on any original studio album, remains a classic refrain, poking the finger at the 'Love Me Do' approach to chart success. The Wizard had landed.

Much to the disdain of his loyal fans, Bolan discarded his Wizard's gown for a satin jacket, make-up and sequins. The bopping pop idol was born and needless to say the fans that had grown to believe in his ethereal dedication, struggled to adjust to his blatant commercialisation. There was no cause for concern within the Jurassic camp for the long lost Mr. Mark Feld had seduced a fresh farmyard full of pulsing fans and would scarcely notice any decline in artistic recognition.

Early in 1971 'Hot Love' gave Bolan his first number one, to be followed by his sixth album 'Electric Warrior' from which a further two songs would top the charts, 'Get It On' and 'Jeepster' reaching number 1 and 2 respectively. 'Electric Warrior' became Marc Bolan's first number one album and can undoubtedly be categorised as a classic album but the commercial influences are obvious and although the earlier mysticism was still prevalent in the lyrics, musically Bolan had adopted a more soulful and almost bluesy approach. In one interview Marc described 'The Electric Warrior' as some type of musical superhero, which it proved to be as a remarkable train of hits followed. Bolan had found a formula, which appealed to the mass of teenage T-Rextesses who hung on his every sequin.

'The Slider' followed, another excellent album, but a safer album than any before, settling into the formula of popularity he had carved. The album was well received by the critics and the fans, with a number of exceptional songs and peaked at number four in the charts. The next three albums, however, formed a gradually downward slide of credibility, 'Tanx' still reached number four in the charts and whilst not a bad musical work, marked the beginning of the decline. The make-up was fading and by 1974 his popularity was beginning to wane. 'Zinc Alloy and the Hidden Riders of Tomorrow' failed to impress and 'Bolan's Zip Gun', his tenth album saw Marc Bolan, described by one critic as 'the spangled dwarf', at the bottom of his pit.

The T-Rextesses were growing up, Bolan's lyrics had now become truly nonsensical and he was struggling to cope with the pressure of a waning success; drink drugs and rock 'n' roll were taking their toll upon the fading wizard and he was crumbling. The fans that he had initially nurtured with his Druid spells had long since turned their back on his commercial ramblings. Bolan had lost his way.

Elton John, Bowie, The Stones, The Beatles have all stumbled along the yellow brick road of success but this stumbling tortured Bolan, he remained prolific, producing song after song but there was an overwhelming shallowness and during 1974 Bolan found himself being cast aside by even the closest of people, his marriage failed and he was separated from his wife June. Micky Finn, Bill Legend and even Tony Visconti stepped down from the T-Rex train. He had become an extremely self-centred egotist, overwhelmed by drink and drugs, living as the ghost of his past success.

There was a light that had begun to shine; a relationship had developed between Marc and his backing vocalist Gloria Jones. Nine years his senior, Gloria had joined the band as a backing singer also playing keyboards and was an artist in her own right, a respected songwriter having written for Marvin Gaye and Diana Ross and recorded the original 'Tainted love' and 'Heartbeat'. '"When I met Gloria it solved my problem of loneliness." Marc had once said and on September 26th 1975 she gave birth to their son, Rolan. This was his motivator; he now had purpose and a newfound focus of determination.

'The Futuristic Dragon' was an album of consolidation and he was beginning to shed the skin of sequins and mature into his music but he had a steep hill to climb for he had alienated all but the most diehard of fans and critics.

His twelfth album 'Dandy in the Underworld' was to be the last Bolan recorded and the Wizard was truly regaining his steps with the album climbing to 26 and 'I Love

To Boogie' reaching number 13 in the singles chart but Bolan was no longer concerned with re-attaining his old chart success, musical recognition was his agenda, to regain the respect he once enjoyed. 'Dandy in the Underworld' certainly turned the heads of the music world back in Bolan's direction and critics who had spent the past two years condemning and beheading the magical elf, were now beginning to trumpet his return to form; he was poised to regain his credibility. Sadly, with a twist of irony, he would never reap from the crop he had sewn. Marc Bolan died in a road accident before that credibility could be replenished.

He had given us a decade of mystical music, his imaginative approach to lyrics, music and style laid the paths to many different doors, glam rock, punk rock and artists such as Elton John and David Bowie all walked from Bolan's footprints. Over the years he suffered condemnation from the critics yet Bolan was the seventies most successful pop star, in retrospect he was conceivably the most innovative rock star ever, to quote Tony Howard (Bolan's business manager) "He was probably one of the best rhythm guitar players to come out of this country."

Although his music, lyrics and poems where saturated with influences, that it is a part of the growth of intellect; each word written has been written before and all artists are influenced by their peers and predecessors, Bolan took those influences and stirred them in a cauldron of imagination; there has been no one else who could have pulled so much from that cauldron and ride the charts on a giant White Swan.

Beneath the façade of make-up that was the pop icon, there had lingered an intellect that poured imagery into overflowing cups of music lyrics and poems. Some seemed to be nonsensical but when you don the gown of Marc Bolan there is a fascinating world to be found within his words, which he desperately held on to through all his commercial success. In an interview with Steve Wright in March 1976 Marc said, "I want to revert back to Marc Bolan 1969, which was Tyrannosaurus Rex." Meaning he wanted to get back to his roots, the period when his imagination was at its strongest and most ethereal, when he penned his feelings and dreams without the compromise of commercial pressure. He still wanted the accolade of success but had become aware that he had become a predictable music factory, reproducing a tried and tested formula, which, inevitably, was becoming more and more dissolved. He needed to put the magic back, to top up the potion with the all-important ingredient that made everything Bolan special, his soul. He had a spiritual side that was expressed within his lyrics, but not one portraying conventional religions. Although from Jewish origins, Bolan did not adhere to the accepted, established 'norms' of religion, whilst considering himself spiritual, like the rest of his persona, individuality was paramount, to the point of creating his own Godly character 'Rarn'. His beliefs being an amalgamation of all he had absorbed from his traditional upbringing to the works of Kahlil Gibran.

Cladding himself in an array of lame costumes, did he himself become a true metal Guru? He sold the song and the image so well, believing strongly in himself. He once said that Marc Bolan was not an image, he was real, he dressed in the same clothes and projected the same persona in daily life as when he was in the full view of the eyes of the media and his fans. There was a twist of truth within the package he delivered, that this mortal man who was fully aware he would die young, foretelling his death in lyrics and songs and visibly uncomfortable in interviews when his mortality was questioned, was an enchantment from an ethereal place, the images he created not being of this world. Yet perhaps they were and Marc Bolan possessed an extraordinary sense of magic that allowed him to convey those images musically and linguistically. His brother, Harry Feld, once said "He had such a vivid imagination", with respect to Harry, this is such an understatement, Marc Bolan was imagination, he created endlessly, from dawn to dusk, his image, his voice, his music, his character, his poetry and words, spilling from him constantly in one form or another. Where did all that creativity originate? From within his mind! He had a need to create and gave us much more than a few pop hits, Marc Bolan gave us a world of fantasy to slip into whenever we wish, a world that he conjured and controlled. From an early age he became very self aware and honed himself and his imagination with everything that was within his reach. From the childhood books about fairies to the latest adolescent craze on the streets. Although he was not academically accomplished he had the ability to absorb all he needed to develop his world, whether it was the manipulation of the media, a manager, a few guitar chords or the English language. His book of poetry, 'Warlock of Love', published in March 1969, was a best seller, in fact he became the best selling poet of the time and in his own words "Not bad for a street punk from Hackney."

Since his death, a mass of material has been unearthed, that had been previously filed away or discarded. The poetry within these pages having being hidden until now, is the largest complete collection of his poetry to be published since 'Warlock of Love' and it reveals an uncanny depth of imagination and imagery, some disturbingly gory, some enchantingly beautiful, all intriguing and beguiling revealing a depth to Marc Bolan not generally appreciated. Most of his words have been perceived as being meaningless but some had a strong depth and a defining meaning: *'Hold the glove of gold behind you Love the glove of truth.'* To call them meaningless would depend on their intention, it is perhaps more fitting to describe them as abstract. It has somehow become acceptable for us to appreciate the pop art of Andy Warhol, the cubism of Pablo Picasso and the surrealism of Salvador Dali and to embody them with academic credibility, yet the words of Marc Bolan, which as paintings would fit into most categorisations, have been given little tenability. Did Dali consider himself an artist? He was certainly not an artist from the mould of Renoir. Marc Bolan was not from the mould of Wordsworth (despite attending a school of the same name) yet he regarded himself a poet. Can he be considered as a poet? The definition of a poet is a person possessing high powers of imagination and expression. Can Marc Bolan be denied the wearing of that mantle?

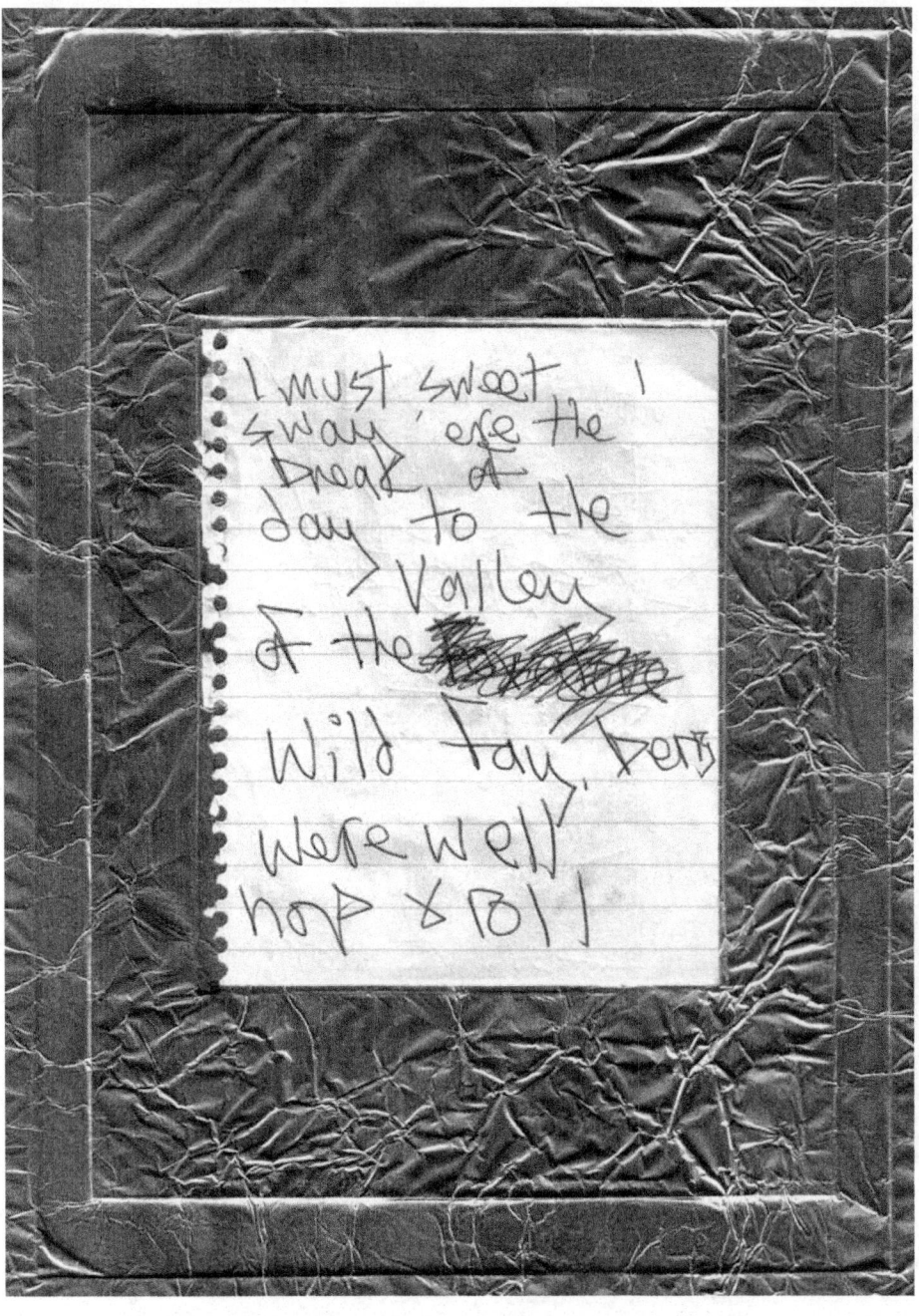

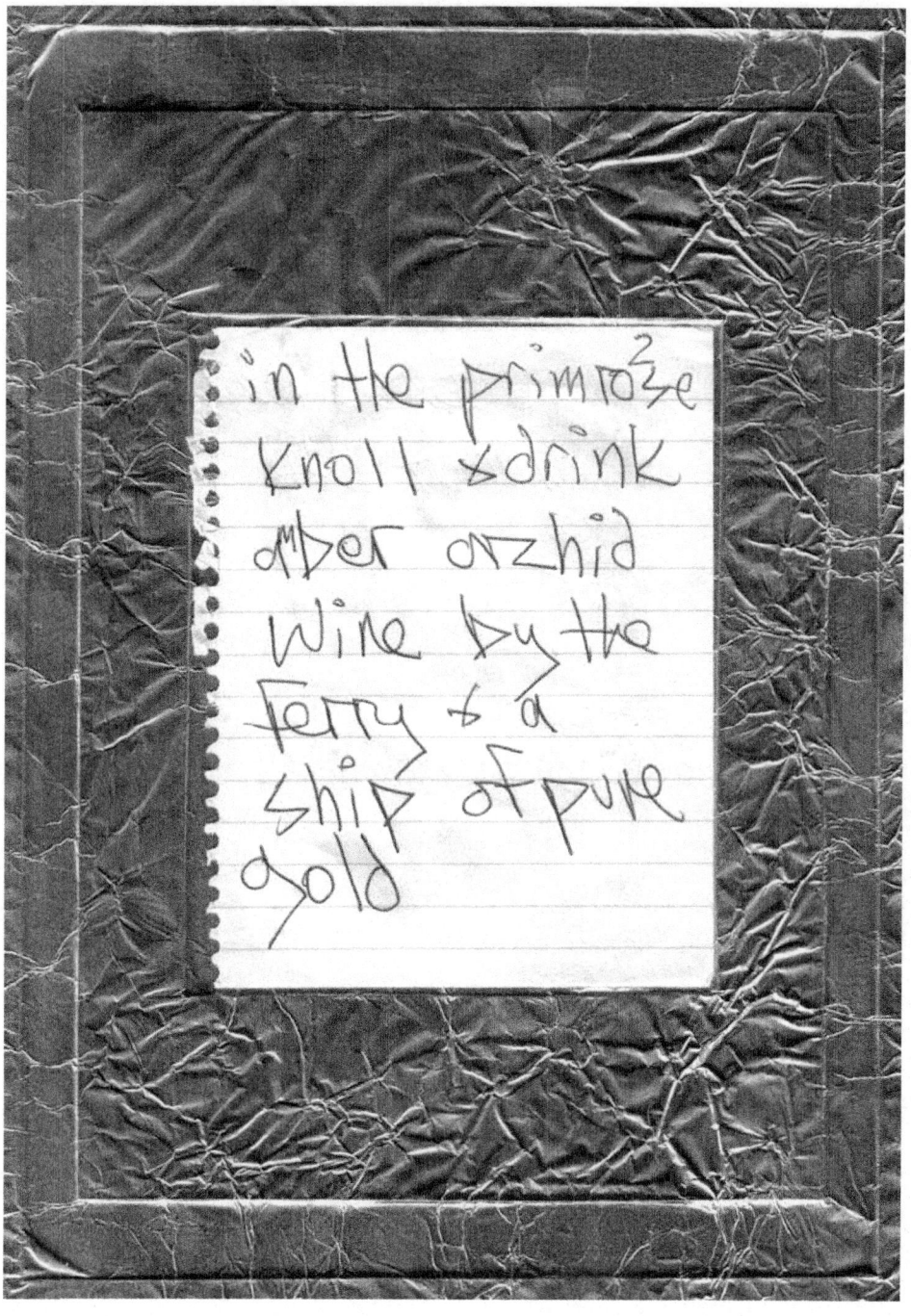

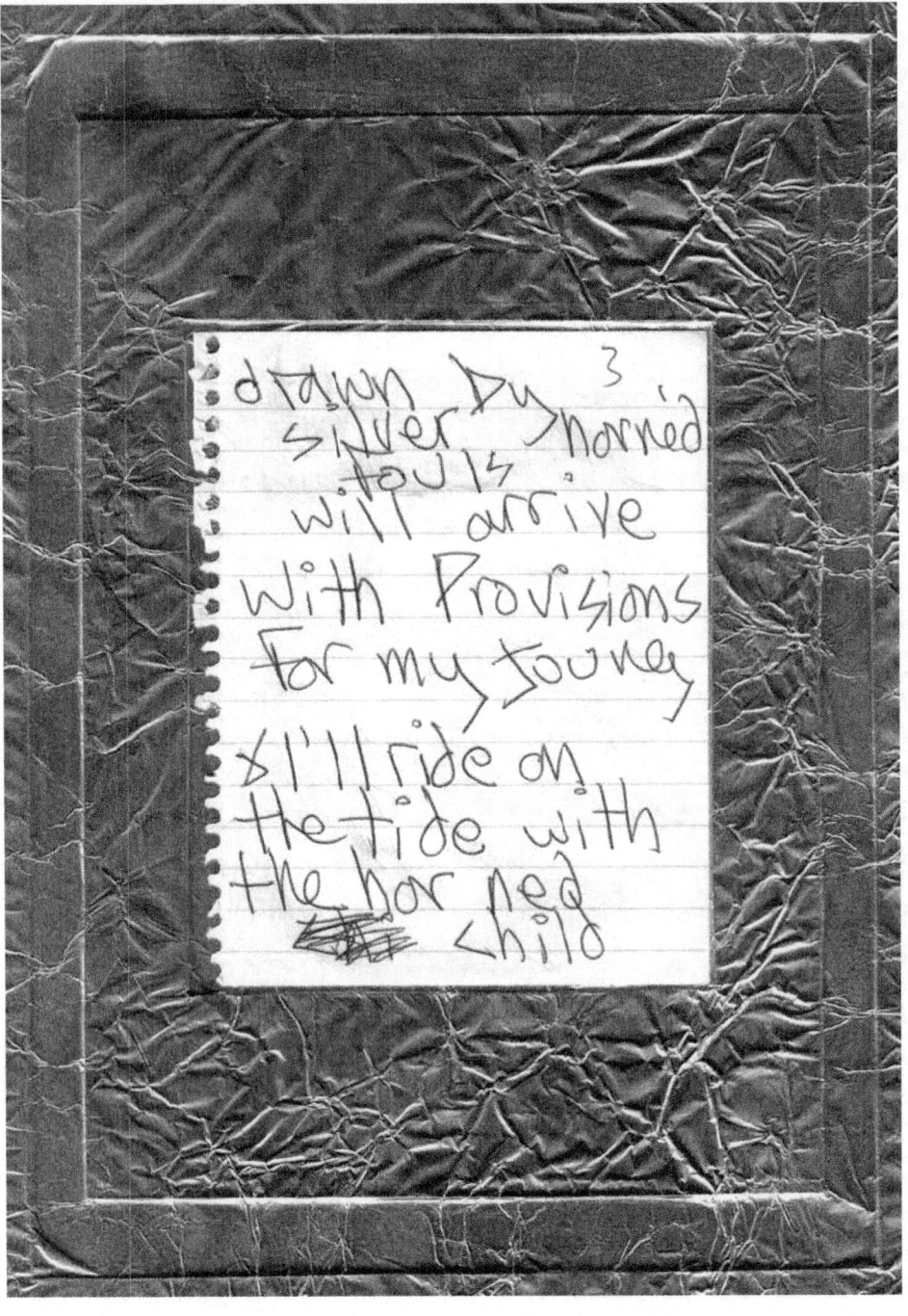

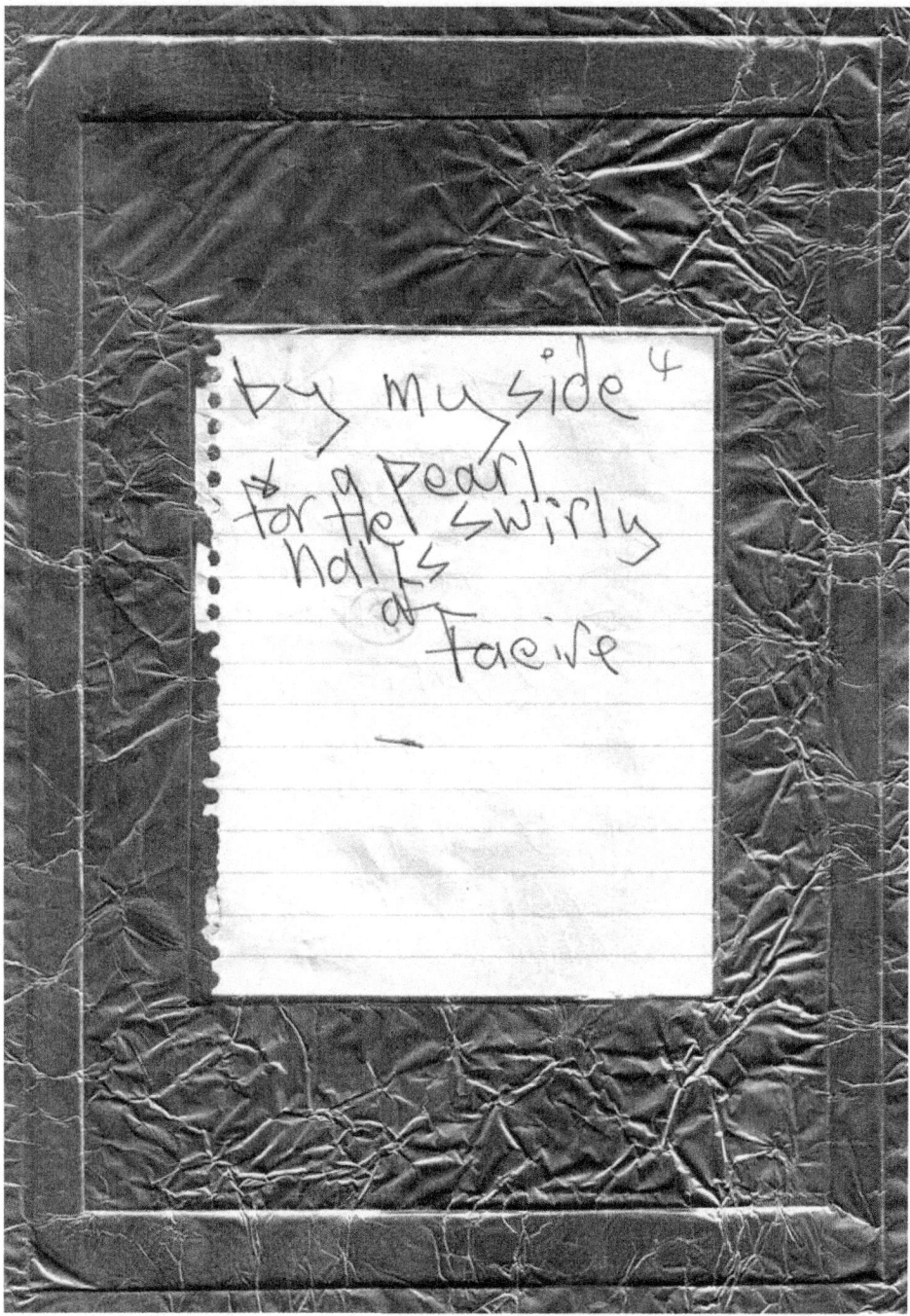

2. **Mythical Landscapes**

"It's really…kind of visionary poetry. Slightly mystical in a way…I used mythical landscapes… I didn't use this planet as a media to base it on." Marc Bolan 1972.

I must sweet sway

'Ere the break of day

To the valley of the wild Fay berry,

Where we'll hop and roll

In the primrose knoll

And drink amber orchid wine

By the ferry

And a ship of pure gold,

Drawn by silver horned foals,

Will arrive with provisions for my journey

And I'll ride on the tide

With the horned child by my side

And a pearl for the swirly halls of Faerie.

An image is set, where a curly haired elf saunters down to the valley, swaying as he goes, to where the fairy berries grow, 'fairy' being the definition of 'Fay'. Fay berries (or Feaberries) are a type of gooseberry and the first apparent definition appears in 1597. Although it is clear from the original text that the initial thought was a foxglove, which was also known as 'Witches gloves' and 'Dead men's fingers' but it has been scribbled out, either because its 'image' was not as romantic or that it simply did not rhyme with 'ferry' and 'faerie'. While there 'I' becomes 'we' and there is a suggestion of a love interest within the lines 'Where we'll hop and roll - In the Primrose knoll - And drink amber orchid wine', and the unmistakable reference to 'rock and roll', which has been given a mystical twist with the substitution of the word 'hop' for 'rock'. 'Hop' being an American colloquialism for an informal style of dance. The lovers drink wine and dance while they wait for the ferry, which brings all that is needed for the journey to

Faerie…Fairyland. The word 'Faerie' is believed to have originally been used extensively by Edmund Spenser (1552-1599), the renaissance English poet, author of 'The Faerie Queene', a poetical epic of chivalry comprising of 72 cantos divided into six books of virtues: - Holiness, Temperance, Chastity, Friendship, Justice and Courtesy, first published in approximately 1590 (the word Fay berry also first appeared around 1590). Despite Spenser's Elizabethan vocabulary there are obvious influences on some of Bolan's poetry, and although it is doubtful that Marc read the entire work, he has clearly read or heard extracts from Spenser's questful text and you do not have to read far into the epic to see the potential influences on Marc's work.

'Vpon a great aduenture he was bond,

That greatest Gloriana to him gaue,

That greatest Glorious Queene of Faerie lond

To winne him worship, and her grace to haue,

Which of all earthly things he most did craue;

And euer as he rode, his hart did earne

To proue his puissance in battell braue

Vpon his foe, and his new force to learne;

Vpon his foe, a Dragon horrible and stearne.

Whereas Marc's' work is incommensurable to Spenser's, the later being dedicated to Queen Elizabeth 1 and an allegorised historical account of the period, interwoven with a tale of chivalrous fantasy, he undoubtedly absorbed some of the imagery and lyrical 'flow' of Spenser's style of writing. It would be ambitious to compare Bolan's treasured gift for the halls of Faerie to Sir Walter Raleigh's gifts of treasure to his queen, as it would be to compare the depth of Spenser's work to Marc's, beyond the parallels already drawn, there is a gigantic difference in the nature and magnitude of the quests undertaken and it is not necessary to delve any deeper into the work of Edmund Spenser, but the Bolanesque quest is clear and simple, to deliver a pearl to the sacred halls of Fairyland, maybe as a form of offering to gain a mystical blessing for the love interest inferred.

Another feasible influence to Marc's poetry and lyrics also manifests itself in this short poem; a reference to the 'horned child' may easily be dismissed as another rambling or creation from the crazy mind of a pop icon, aspiring to be a credible poet, simply becoming lost in his own fantasies who having already talked of 'silver horned fouls' has plainly extended the horned image. When linking to the drinking of 'Orchid wine' and a number of more direct references and the almost rewriting of ancient tales, which will become evident in other poems in this book, it is surely justifiable to draw a parallel with the 'horned child', brought into this surreal scene by Marc, and Dionysus. This comparison takes us a long way from the streets of Hackney and will undoubtedly open a door of ridicule but the connections with Greek mythology will become plainer in later poems. Of course the young Unicorns themselves are of Homeric origins.

Dionysus is one of the numerous sons of Zeus, and is a Greek god, one of his many roles being the god of wine. Born from the bonding of Zeus and his daughter Persephone, he became a religion in his own right in the Greek Mediterranean regions and there are many tales about Dionysus, some of which are contradictory but most have similar threads, particularly the story of him being ripped apart by the Titans who then cooked and ate him leaving just his heart. Zeus banished the Titans back to the underworld and rescued Dionysus' heart, enabling him to bestow upon his son a rebirth.

Dionysus is the subject of 'The Bacchae' a Greek drama by Euripides, which also depicts the tearing apart of a human, Pentheus a young king who has denied Dionysus as a god, and is entrapped by Dionysus who reveals him to the Maenads. The Maenads being the women under the ecstatic spell of Dionysus, in their delirium they attack the king, gruesomely killing him. The re-enacting of the Titans act of cannibalism became a religious ritual in many regions, although a goat or a calf would be used.

This is one of the shortest of the poems enchantingly describing a brief scene of fantasy, yet it has already revealed numerous influences, it is an ideal opening example of Bolan's work, with no references to the real world that we inhabit, 'Horned foals' (or baby Unicorns) 'And a ship of pure gold', such magical images so simply placed conjuring an aura of a special world that we are generally not privy too, but Marc Bolan certainly appeared to be.

Marc took his poetry seriously, but not in a classical, academic or even political way, as Dylan may be depicted; generally he did not continually give us deep underlying meanings beneath his words, more he used the words to paint images in our minds, attempting to relay the pictures he held in his own mind, but where did those images come from?

Marc Bolan seems to have had a mind overloaded with strange visions and concepts, both musical and lingual that are far from this world and generally not recognised by most, but if you take time to allow yourself to be absorbed by his magic you will be carried off on a ship of gold to a dreamscape where the most beautiful is possible. You will be led to a land that is an amalgamation of fantasies, myths, legends, religions and music.

In an interview around the period of 1971, Marc is asked how much of an escapist he is and whether he is losing touch with the real world? He responds with a Socratic argument, posing two basic options and questioning both, logically arguing each point with credibility, ultimately leading to the conclusion that the so defined fantasy world, which resides in our imaginations, is more real than the perceived material exterior. He uses an example of the tape recorder the interviewer is using, stating that it would not exist if someone had not designed it and to design it they had to imagine it in their mind, consequently their imagination became reality. He also uses an example closer to home; when under pressure for another number one hit single, a new song has to be recorded but from where? He has to conjure up all his inspirational imagination in the form of lyrics and music to formulate the new song. From the corner of his mind, where linger the mythological fantasies of Greece and the writings of C.S Lewis, images are born, lyrics are spawned and notes erupt from the silence. The delusion becomes a vision, make believe becomes invention, the fanciful notion becomes a wish and the chimera becomes a Metal Guru. From the mind to the mouth and hands, to the microphone and guitar, to the tape. It all now becomes tangible, the fantasy is pressed into vinyl, marketed and the accountants count the reality. But which is the reality, without the imagination the record would not exist, the tape would not exist, and the accountant's maths would not exist. Conclusively fantasy and imagination are an essential part of what is perceived as reality, if reality itself is not a part of our imagination? The only thing we know resolutely is that which is in our minds, and that which we allow into our minds, ergo the strongest reality must dwell there, with our fantasies.

Marc argues the point along these lines, so convincingly that the interviewer concedes and confesses to having a friend who is researching solid state physics, expecting to be able to prove that there is no solid world, to which Marc replies "I'm sure, I'm positive!"

"It's really…kind of visionary poetry."

Marc does not mean this in the context of his poetry being philosophical or harbouring any foresight as the parables and poems of Kahlil Gibran, or even the words of Dylan, but in the context of imagery, although it is reasonable to conclude that he held aspirations for his words to hold a depth of meaning on occasions, which he achieved in some of his poems and lyrics, particularly the later ones; most, though, are simple observations of life around him, and the bizarreness of its reality or pure fantasy. The song 'New York City', for example, is no more than an observation of the madness of the city, the absurdity of the reality that within the hustle and bustle of one of the largest, busiest cities in the world and all its' commercial and financial enterprises, which many depict as the 'real world', an old woman is casually walking its streets carrying a frog, oblivious to the contrast she portrays. The song is no more than an observation or a comment on the eccentricities and peculiarities of city life, and seeks to be no more. So to attempt to read more into the simplicity of the song would be futile, it makes it's plain statement of observation so well; an artist does not have to fill a page with charcoal to create a picture, what is not drawn is as important as what is drawn and likewise, more can sometimes be said with less words.

Marc's approach to his writing was to create images with his words for us to observe, linguistic paintings of scenes from his imagination. In earlier works his linguistic brush strokes could be laborious, as he would attempt to 'fill the page' with an abundance of similes and metaphors lavishly detailing the image, as the Renaissance artists would photographically reproduce their subject. It is essential that an artist is capable of reproducing photographically so he is qualified to judge and evaluate what may be omitted. As Marc progressed with his juggling of words and images he soon developed the art of Impressionism and in the song 'New York City' Minimalism. A true writer also needs to be able to appreciate when to use excessive vocabulary and when to be minimalistic and be capable of adjusting his style and output to convey the drama of the image he wishes to portray with his words. Marc had this capability, as can be seen from this first short poem in comparison to the last poem in this book, 'Gods and Men' which is the longest and tells an almost epic story, whereas the first gives us a complete scene and implies a depth of possibilities within a few lines. Marc displayed this ability in his songs too; 'New York City' compared to 'Dandy in the Underworld', the first being as described, a simple statement of observation, and the second an almost biographical musical drama. He also exhibited this instinct in performances, for example when performing 'Get it on' it would be a lavish performance with dramatic solos and a fully camped persona projected by Marc with the entirety of his musical and 'glam' excesses, yet when he performed 'Spaceball Ricochet' he would be alone, cross legged on the stage, with his acoustic guitar like a mystical wandering minstrel. Marc Bolan knew when to shout and when to whisper.

The title of 'Dandy' clearly also had its inspirations in Greek mythology, an adaptation of 'Orpheus in the Underworld', confirmed by the sub-title of the title track on the album sleeve, 'A Bolonic revision of Orpheus descending'. Parallels can be drawn in the lyrics between the story of Orpheus and Bolan's life, the story contained within the song being a modern amalgamation of the two. Another key comparison is that Orpheus was the god of music, enchanting people with his songs and poetry and one of the chosen few, an Argonaut having quested, under the leadership of Jason, in the search for the Golden Fleece. Orpheus is also credited in some circles as being the introducer of the cult of Dionysus. At the time of the release of 'Dandy', Marc was being heralded as the Godfather (or the introducer) of Punk Rock, primarily by himself, mainly because he had always referred to himself as a 'street punk', so to imply that he was, with a light hearted arrogance, depicting himself as a modern Orpheus, is not unreasonable, but what was Bolan's fleece?

Orpheus descended into the underworld to regain his wife, Eurydice 5, who had been killed by a serpent, and then returned from that underworld; if Marc was making a connection between himself and Orpheus it could be that he saw his past few years of self abuse by overindulgence in drink and drugs as his discention into hell, also having lost his wife. It is probable that his portrayal of 'Dandy' was an affirmation that he had returned, having refocused himself and overcome his addictions, reasserting himself as the 'god' of music and poetry. It cannot be denied that Marc saw himself as the 'Dandy', a man overwhelmingly devoted to style, fashion and appearance, and the opening line of the song *'Prince of players, pawn of none'* is a real statement of just how Marc perceived himself; the prince of the music industry and his peers, totally un-beholding to any record company, not in any conceivable way a pawn in anyone else's game, he had been to his hell and returned, in control and stronger than ever. Just as Orpheus had journeyed to Egypt to learn more about the gods and their mystical ceremonies, so Marc Bolan had roamed the music and literary world to enhance his creativity, even his untimely death had orphetic undertones. Although there are a number of versions telling of Orpheus's demise, the favourable comparison is that he was struck down by Zeus for revealing too many of the gods mystical mysteries to man.

There are many other comparables between Marc and Orpheus and with extensive correlations it would almost be possible to prove that Marc was a reincarnation of Orpheus but that would presume that Orpheus was more than a legend. Marc Bolan has certainly ascended to a similar status as Orpheus in regard to his songs, poetry and charisma and possibly in another two thousand years he will equal the mythical status of the Greek god but for the present it is sufficient to conclude that Marc had had to attain extensive knowledge of Orpheus and his contemporaries in order to make the accurate references within his work and to confidently cast himself in the metaphoric role.

"I am like thee, O, Night, dark and naked; I walk upon the flaming path which is above my day-dreams, and whenever my foot touches earth a giant oak tree comes forth."

"So I lay for one day in the way of the spray, where my knowledge becomes like a spring tree and takes root. With the adornment of shadows upon my waning back, my silk self grows the torturous knowledge of a misty century."

Two extracts, but only one was written by Marc Bolan, which one?

Marc Bolan could not be described as an academic in the classic sense of the word, he did not in any way excel at school, he could see no point in what he was being taught, it held no purpose for him, he was not being taught anything that he deemed as useful, this should not, however, be a reflection of his intellect, many acclaimed minds and talents did not excel in the realms and constraints of an education system; Marc said that he was expelled at the age of fourteen, basically because he never went to school but an old friend Wendy Wilchenski who spent a lot of time with Marc recalls that it was when he was about twelve or thirteen, and that she was nearly expelled with him, "He was only ever interested in music and clothes." She said.

Marc did, however, register with the Hillcroft School in Tooting when his family moved to Summerstown in 1962. Marc was fifteen at the time and must have therefore been reinstated into the school system. Actor Christopher Chittel, who plays Eric Pollard in Yorkshire Television's serial drama Emmerdale, remembers Marc well, recalling that it was Marc who suggested he went into modelling and acting. He also remembers Hillcroft as being a 'rough school' and there being one particular gang there at the time called 'The Clan' who dominated most of the schools population, but generally left himself and Marc alone. According to Chris, Marc was quiet, always very well dressed and confident, yet different, outstandingly individual. He also described Marc as a loner, but in the sense that he didn't need anyone else, he didn't need to be a part of the *clan*, he was always ahead of the crowd. It is understandable that he was perceived as being quiet at the Hillcroft School because he was out of his domain, away from the familiar turf where he had already made his mark and he knew he would not be there for long, so he simply kept his head down.

There is an irony in the fact that a 'street punk from Hackney' who was expelled from the William Wordsworth School should become a poet and even more a bestselling poet, but in truth he possessed the essence of a poet, although he did not conform to the educational requirements and indoctrinations of the time he had a hunger for knowledge, but on his own terms and to meet his own requirements, he became a graduate of the streets, of modern culture. Marc's' wife, June, said "He was completely self taught, he read a lot." And "He was extraordinarily well read." And it is clear that he did read extensively, despite Tony Visconti's supposed comment to the contrary, "He didn't read much at all, books had to be read to him." It is reflected in his writings, and to refer back to the two extracts above, the second is by Marc (appearing in its entirety in a later chapter) the first is from a piece by Kahlil Gibran, 'Night and the Madman' from 'The Madman' first published in 1918. There is an undeniable feel of similarity between the styles of the two extracts although the complete pieces are very different; the consideration being that Marc had had to absorb the methodology of Gibran's writing at some point for him to be able to emulate it within his own works. It is clear that Marc did this with 'prophetic' quotes appearing on the covers of 'Prophets Seers and Sages', 'Unicorn' and to some degree 'A Beard of Stars' and the 'brown album', the dedication in 'A Warlock of Love' also displaying Gibranistic tendencies. Two books of Kahlil Gibran's can be seen in the cover photographs by Peter Sanders on 'Unicorn', 'The Prophet' and 'The Broken Wings'. The metering and rhythmic style of many of Marc's poems is very similar to Kahlil's open style.

'And they say the eagle and the vulture

Dig their beaks into the same carcass,

And are at peace, one with the other,

In the presence of the dead thing.'

From '*Love*' by Kahlil Gibran.

Strong similarities can also be drawn between the imagery of the two writers, although Marc's imagery generally adorned more of a mystical guise, when his subject matter was of a philosophical character he adopted a more naturalistic form of imagery as Gibran. This is more evident in the second poem at the beginning of chapter three and in some of the poems and dedications, such as in 'Warlock' and the other previous examples, also in lyrics when Marc adopts his prophetic pose he uses more earthly images, his famous simile comparing 'our lives' to 'trees of possibilities' being a fine example. Again, though, it would be over ambitious to compare the work of Marc Bolan to the works and philosophies of Kahlil Gibran as a whole, beyond that of the influences outlined, as Marc did not aspire to being a philosopher, although his work proves to hold more philosophical meaning as it matures with time.

Comparable parallels can be drawn with the works of Dylan Thomas, C. S. Lewis and even Tolkien, although Bolan himself admitted that he didn't really 'get into' 'The Lord of the Ring's' having only read it once when he was about thirteen. He did, however, claim to have read 'The Chronicles of Narnia' four times (although that was probably one of Marc's' renowned exaggerations) and to have 'got off' on it. There is an undeniable air of Kahlil Gibran to the early Tyrannosaurus Rex albums, as there is an equally undeniable 'Narnian' air, with dedications made to both.

Marc shared similar literary stimulations as C.S.Lewis who also enjoyed the mythologies of ancient Greece as well as the tales of Beatrix Potter and her talking animals, drawing from both and more for his inspirations. The image of the character Mr. Tumnus is undeniably Pan like. Marc has commented that he had a liking for Pan (there is a photograph with Marc holding a statue of the god, not included in this book), who was half man half goat and him being the Greek god of fertility always depicted playing 'panpipes' is probably why Marc expressed an interest in him, many of Marc's words, lyrics in particular being of a sensual nature. The whole concept of slipping into an alternative adjacent world has a very Olympian feel and an air of post war escapism. Ironically the fantasy world which the four war torn children in C.S.Lewis's Chronicles escaped into held as many, if not more, trials and tribulations than the real world. 'The Chronicles of Narnia' was a very contemporary work to Marc Bolan, the first book, 'The Lion the Witch and the Wardrobe' first being published in 1950, the other six books in the collection being published over the following six years, completing the collection by 1956. At around the same time J.R.R. Tolkien, a fellow professor at Oxford and a close friend to C.S.Lewis, published 'The Lord of the Rings', another escapist epic.

As previously mentioned, Marc did not take to Tolkien's Hobbit tale, despite his earlier works being described by many as Tolkienesque (even in the first pages of this book), yet there are little if no Tolkien references in Bolan's work but he did embrace Lewis' Narnia, as is clearly evident on 'My people were Fair' with the children's story read by John Peel. It evokes a question as to why Marc did not take to the tales of middle earth when he was so heavily into anything of a fantasy or 'other worldly' nature. It may be that the Hobbit tale was of a more academic approach by the linguistic professor who did in actual fact create a completely independent world with no obvious ties or links to the world we know... the real world. Man is a part of the trilogies' adventures but there is nothing to link Tolkien's man to the world we inhabit, not even with distant historic threads. In the Narnian tales the wardrobe forms a portal back and forth between the real world and Narnia, where the children find their escape from their wartime refuge, as in most of Marc's influences, there was always a safety line.

The Greek myths and legends have a constant link to the real world of their time, the Olympian gods forever playing games with the fates of their mortal underlings, the legends interwoven with Greek history, outlining the gods' supposed influences. Edmund Spenser's 'Faerie Queene' is an allegoric tale threaded with the reality of Elizabethan history. All of Kahlil Gibran's poems and parables, regardless of their slightly outlandish similes deal with very real issues and morals. The works of Hans Christian Anderson, which were undoubtedly part of Marc's library of children's fairy tales as he refers to them quite knowledgably in at least one interview, always have a foot inside the door of reality along with their profound parable style. Even the fairy tales of the Brothers Grimm keep a root in reality. Marc was clearly well read in both of these as they reveal themselves in his work, 'One Inch Rock' being an amalgamation of 'Tom Thumb', 'Thumbelina' and rock and roll. If we follow Marc's earlier 'Socratic' argument concerning fantasy and reality, he links the two, declining to draw a definitive line between them, but overlapping them. Marc read so keenly to fuel his imagination with other worlds, giving him substance to draw on, but there always needed to be a portal to bring the fantasies back to reality. 'The Lord of the Rings' does not have such a portal, which is probably why Marc did not 'get off' on it. This is, in probability, too deep an analysis but it is curious that Bolan did not embrace the Tolkien tales as he did everything else of a fantasy nature.

Within the stories of Hans Christian Anderson, we can find a further link with the opening poem. 'The Last Pearl' is a short story about the birth of a child and the death of a mother, although the two are not directly related. The two angels (also referred to as fairies in the tale) of the newborn in the house, go in search of the one pearl missing from the set of pearls given to the new baby by the angels/fairies; the pearls of health, wealth, fortune and love, the pearl missing is sorrow, without which the others would have no meaning. Which one of these five pearls is being delivered by the subject of Marc's poem? Could it be Love?

Marc's work would definitely fit into the category of romanticism, and changed quite radically over a relatively short period of time. The highly descriptive, flowery nature of the poems in this collection and 'Warlock', and other work of the same period, and the move to an ethereal, prophetic style, coinciding with the same outward projection through his music, his attire and even his persona, is in stark contrast to his earlier writings. This linked to his profound 'name dropping' of classic poets such as Lord Byron and Lord Tennyson in interviews implies that he went through a purging process on literature. Marc certainly learnt little at school, as confirmed by his school friend Wendy Wilchenski, who recalls that they spent most of their time at a café near Marc's home in Stoke Newington Common Road that had a jukebox and the 2i's café or hanging around the stage door of the Hackney Empire while 'Oh Boy' was being filmed. Regardless of attending The William Wordsworth school Marc barely learnt to read and write there, his agenda was not focused on academic knowledge at that point, but he did have a mind that searched for knowledge and when he needed to learn he learnt. Once he had found a direction for his life Marc went about acquiring the knowledge he required. This is evident in the progression of his work. There are few complete samples of Marc's earlier writings available, most have been dispersed amongst his fans and sold at auctions, mainly as individual pages. One collection, currently owned by an American fan, David Reginold, and known as the 'Big Top' purely because that is the name of the type of notebook used, is quite interesting. It is mainly a short diary giving an insight into Marc's life at the time, unfortunately Marc did not date any of the pages but it is quite easy to establish an approximate date from the content of the text. Firstly it is written under the name of Marc Feld, 'Author, poet & folk singer & actor & hung up crazy cat' with the notable 'c' instead of 'k' at the end of Marc, indicating that he has begun his transition to Marc Bolan. Marc makes a strong reference to Manfred Mann who made their initial impact in1964, their first hit being 5-4-3-2-1 in January, he also tells of buying the new Jesse Fuller album 'San Francisco Boy Blues', released in 1964 and a poem '2000yrs & green with age' has a note 'inspired by the movie "She" ', which starred Ursula Andress and was also released in 1964. Marc also makes a sarcastic reference to his Tooting penthouse, which indicates that it precedes him moving in with Allan Warren at his Kensington address in what has been estimated to be October of 1964. There is also a poem entitled 'Riggs O'Hara' who was a friend of Marc's around this time, 'The Wizard' written by Marc in the early part of 1965 was a result of him going to Paris with Riggs O'Hara and supposedly encountering a conjurer, although the truth of 'The Wizard' will be revealed in a later chapter. The second part of this collection does not contain as many helpful clues but it is easy to estimate that it is from the summer 1965 because of the adoption of the full name Marc Bolan and there is also one of the few references to Tolkien in one of the poems in this collection,

'Tiped for stardom, by goblin unknown,

Knowin maybe, I'd seen some ring

(But don't worry 'cos Gandalf sees all)

Marc moved in with Mike Pruskin towards the end of the summer of 1965 and Mike is reported to have said that Marc was always reading and that one of his favourite books at the time was 'The Hobbit' by Tolkien where Gandalf the wizard makes his first appearance.

It is also interesting to note that in another of these poems Marc uses the terms *'Scene Seeker'* and *'Purple picture'* which is the first evidence of his word and idea playing, which will ultimately develop into *'Scenescof'* and *'Pictures of Purple People'* discussed later in this chapter.

The lady was a Scene-Seeker

Her mind was distorted to a purple picture.

She loved the artist (any old artist)

The lady was a Scene-Seeker still

Till she dies- I'll smile secretly.

The next collection, which is more extensive and signed and dated by Marc between April and May 1966, when he was almost 19, shows strong glimpses of his imagination breaking through but the writings are extremely adolescent and vulgar in parts. The language and style is very much a reflection of the street language of the period and Marc wrote as he would have probably spoken. In an interview he likens these early writings to the work of the American novelist 'Jack Kerouac', which when compared to 'On the Road', Jack Kerouac's renowned beat novel written in a slightly diaretic style as it happened, is a legitimate comparison albeit faintly over ambitious; Marc was clearly familiar with Kerouac's work but it is unlikely that he was really influenced by Jack Kerouac, if he was only fleetingly.

Some of these early writings can loosely be described as poems but are more like thoughts or observations jotted down, with no real direction, form or flow. They are quite erratic and there is little of the romantic descriptiveness of his later poetry. They tended to be quite dark observations of life around him, randomly picked from his day. 'Subway Scene', for example, is written as if Marc is thinking aloud, observing *'a huge fat man clutching a new shinin' kettle'*, you can almost imagine Marc sitting on the subway scrawling into his notebook, whilst looking around for something or someone else to inspire him. There are few overpowering or unusual influences and references detectable in these early scribblings, there is a mention of 'Blue Suede Shoes', Napoleon, Joan of Arc, Dylan and Flash Gordon, just as would be expected from a young 'street punk from Hackney'. They do, however, develop quite rapidly over the period in which they were written, which was less than a month. The last few in the set containing blatant references and beginning to show signs of a poetical form. It could be surmised that 'A Maniacs Statement' is a direct result of Marc reading 'Howl' by the American poet Allen Ginsberg, the opening line of which being *'I saw the best minds of my generation destroyed by madness,'* there being a reference to Ginsberg in Marc's poem '*...recited his mad Ginsberg voice'*. A poem written a few days later, May 11th 1966, confirms this having the opening line *'I was digin' a Ginsberg poem'* and the final line *'good ole Allen Ginsberg'* along with the contents of the poem being a clear reflection on Ginsberg's 'Howl'. It is also interesting to note that Allen Ginsberg was an early friend and contemporary of Jack Kerouac, both being essential reading for the beat generation.

These writings are the first real evidence of Marc embarking on a literary journey and coincide with the beginning of his musical career, having already had a few recording sessions, and are of the period when he was following the 'Bob Dylan' trend, who was the probable influence for him choosing Allen Ginsberg, Dylan himself being a fan of the poet. This is also the time when Bolan recorded 'San Francisco Poet' which shared the same inspiration, the lyrics containing references to beatniks.

This selection is likely to be Marc's initial serious attempts at writing and as he progresses it becomes obvious that he has expanded his bank of literary resources. The style of the second batch is very different to the style of the 'Big top' collection which is a little naïve although revealing a strong street awareness it has little structure or rhythm and the imagery is extremely weak. In the 'Kerouac/Ginsberg' collection there is much more of an edge to his words, they are quite violent and aggressive in parts, the imagery being considerably stronger and even grotesque in places, the difference seeming to confirm his emulation of Kerouac and Ginsberg, although it may only have been subconsciously. It is evidence of the young writer within Marc, having decided to write, experimenting with the medium, playing with styles and formats, on the first steps of the journey to discover and formulate his own style.

'Pictures of Purple People', written in the latter half of 1966 (recall the earlier mentioned poem), along with the track of the same name, is exceedingly more advanced, having much more depth and development of content than his initial embarkations into penmanship. It is in the style of a short play and there are two known versions that tell the story of a number of hippies getting high on a batch of purple sweets given to the main character, Jerry, by a wizard/tramp figure. In the earlier version the wizard is described as a 'ragged old man' who transforms from a blackbird in true Edgar Allen Poe tradition. In the second draft the blackbird metamorphoses not into a ragged old man but into a 'wizardly mulatto' the rest of the second draft is more prevalently embroidered with images and influences. It is less crude and more elaborately written than Marc's earlier work and is speckled with constant references, almost in an attempt to adorn himself with credibility. Among the references are Bob Dylan, Donovan, Orson Wells, Chuck Berry, Marlon Brando, Pan, even Alice in Wonderland and many other innocuous allusions. The story is plainly drug oriented and bridges the gap between reality and fantasy, the reality being based in the suburban dereliction of London, the fantasy somewhere in the newly fuelled imagination of Marc Bolan.

Whilst the other hippies indulge themselves in the fantasies invoked by the sweets Jerry battles the surreal world overthrowing and killing 'Scenescof', the fantasy world persona of the wizard. 'Scenescof' is Marc's first apparent attempt at word making, part of his consistent individualism, not content with the vast variety of vocabulary available, he has the need to expand the English language with his touch. If the meaning of the word is analysed it breaks down into two parts, 'scene' which means a place where events occur, whether real or fictional, or a section of a play. It was also a common 'in' term from the 1960s period, as 'Not my scene', 'Split the scene' or 'The music scene', all being slight twists on the original meaning. 'Scoff 'means to mock, to ridicule, to make fun of, it is therefore reasonable to contemplate the meaning of 'Scenescof' as being to ridicule the place where things occur, 'mocking the scene man'. Applying this definition enhances the allegory of the story; the supplier (Scenescof) arrogantly tries to ridicule the hippies and their culture (their scene) by exploiting them for his own entertainment and profit taking advantage of their vulnerability. The 'wizardly mulatto' is thus ridiculing where the hippies 'are at' by his name alone. Notably the name 'Scenescof' is also the title of a song on 'My People' and there is a chanted piece on the 'Prophets' album entitled 'The Scenescof Dynasty'. Embracing the opinion that 'Pictures of Purple People' is a drug based story it is reasonable to assume that the wizard character depicted is the 'supplier' and that the drugs supplied have opened a portal in the mind to a fantasy world, whilst in the fantasy world it could be deduced that the key character, Jerry, decides to kick the habit and battles with his demons, eventually defeating the source of his insanity, Scenescof. Marc, however, retains the idea of the fantasy world for future development. It is almost as if this story has formed a portal for Marc and his writing, enabling him to step from the real world (Depicted in the derelict London suburbs) to his world of imagination.

It has previously been concluded that there is no connection between the song 'Pictures of Purple People' and the play, but adopting the aura of the drug culture of the time, it could be deduced that the mirror in the lyrics of 'Pictures of Purple People' is a symbolic portal, representing the supplying and taking of purple sweets (Scenescof), initially the view of the world through the mirror, or the 'high' evoked being more beautiful, but as it transpires there is an ugliness beneath the false beauty reflected in the mirror, as there is in the pit of addiction and the mirror is broken to secure a place in reality. The mirror is a simple song representation of the wizard Scenescof and the purple sweets, also destroyed. The purple sweets providing the illusionary world are in reality Purple Hearts, a cocktail of amphetamine and barbiturate commonly taken during the sixties by the swinging generation, particularly Mods, a clan Marc had been affiliated to. Maintaining the drug related assumption, the lyrics of the song Scenescof can also be connected if 'Mister Scenescof' is seen as a combination of the 'supplier' and the Purple Hearts (as the mirror), then it can read that the subject has lost his 'babe' to the realms of addiction while not needing any form of fix himself. Thus the three pieces can be linked as indeed can the fourth 'The Scenescof Dynasty' being an extension of the fantasy world created, where the subject and his girlfriend, 'Suzie', engage in a joint trip into the mind of Scenescof, Suzie supplying the subject with the necessary drugs while they lay in bed, *'the key to the dark'*. 'The Dark' being the dark world of addiction, the world of Scenescof. They then roam the mind of Scenescof, depicted as a gruesome realm, until finally he is slain, cut from ear to ear, when it can be presumed they come down from the trip. The dynasty of Scenescof is overthrown and complete.

In summary Scenescof is a combination of the supplier and the drug/sweets, Purple Hearts, which/who opens the gateway into another world, within the mind of Scenescof where the subject embarks on a fantasy adventure until he battles and overcomes the influence of Scenescof. Establishing this connection between these four pieces makes it plausible to surmise that Marc may have intended 'Pictures of Purple People' to develop into a stage production of some type, incorporating the songs; when shown to Riggs O'Hara he felt it was written as a screenplay. All interesting scenarios considering that The Who made their first attempt at a short Rock Opera in 1966 with 'A Quick One While He's Away' on the album 'A Quick One' before their classic 'Tommy' in 1969 and 'Quadrophenia' in 1973.

'Pictures of Purple People' displays more depth and substance than Marc's writings from earlier the same year, demonstrating a rapid evolving of his penmanship as a form of expression, there are also stark differences between the first and second draft, the later being significantly more poetical and imaginative, the quality of the writing itself having improved dramatically. There is still an amateurish, adolescence to the work along with a definitive connection to the street culture of London in 1966 and it is clear that Marc is still searching for his natural style. The play was typed for Marc by his then publicist/manager, Mike Pruskin, who Marc shared a basement flat with in Manchester Street, near to Baker Street. Pruskin is known to have recalled Marc staying up all night playing his guitar and reading, also constantly writing reams of poetry, honing his new found art.

Upon examining a slightly later collection of Marc's poetry, which has only been published as a limited edition for fans, under the title of 'A Caged Thrush', more progression and development can be seen. The publisher's estimation for the date of these writings is around 1968, which is a reasonable estimate with the information they had available, but it is more likely that they are from a slightly earlier period, probably 1967. The subject matter of this collection still ebbs towards the Jack Kerouac style of Marc's earlier pieces. The first in the collection containing imagery that is quite palpable, the description being of a verisimilitudenous nature. The final piece in this collection, though, has an almost completely ethereal feel and the writings throughout the rest of the collection show a gradual progression from one to the other. There is also a steady degeneration in the quality of the handwriting, which is also evident throughout all of the work discussed, in the very first writings, considered earlier, Marc's hand writing is relatively neat, written in straight conformed lines, controlled and restrained in comparison to his later scribbles. A further sample of Marc's handwriting, a poem entitled 'Signs', published in 'Pictures of Purple People', shows only a slight degeneration, which is not significant. Marc dates both these selections as 1966. 'The Caged Thrush' collection is not dated but is considerably less controlled and the next samples of handwriting, published in 'The Krakenmist', follows on from the degeneration, becoming what is now generally known and recognised as Marc's handwriting style. 'The Krakenmist' has been dated by its publishers as 1968, due to some references made in adjacent texts to the album 'My People…'. Considering the handwriting and the subject matter of the work, which is now completely ethereal, this is a fair estimate.

It has been speculated that Marc was dyslexic but Jo Kapella from Shropshire, a specialist in learning difficulties, particularly Dyslexia, concluded, after extensive examination of Marc's handwriting from all the periods available, that there were no signs of Dyslexia. The untidiness of his later work is more evident of him frantically rushing his ideas to paper, and despite the untidiness it is quite legible. He does not make spelling mistakes of a Dyslexic nature; most mistakes evident are ones made commonly when writing hastily. There is more evidence pointing towards him not being Dyslexic with his ability to continue a train of thought and to keep his ideas focused, Marc could not have been such a prolific wordsmith, even creating his own words, if he had been Dyslexic, he had a fascination for words, and although he often used them with metaphoric twists it was always correctly. It is common for people to learn to cope as they get older hence any Dyslexic tendencies would have been more evident in his earlier writings, but there are none, Jo says of Marc's early diaretic writing, "They are written like song lyrics, as you would sing, in a form of slang, which is not Dyslexia."

It is more likely that the causes for the deterioration in Marc's handwriting was due to two key factors, firstly his outstanding proliferation of work and an urgency to get it all written down as quickly as possible, in between the studio and the gigs and the rehearsals and secondly the influences of various substances, such as drugs and alcohol, which can drastically effect handwriting. It is also plausible that Marc partly developed the rune like style to enhance his ethereal, mystical image, adding to his individuality even more.

In 'The Krakenmist' Marc has truly found his style, he has lost all portals and is absorbed in his Elysian world of Beltane, there is no sign of the earlier Jack Kerouac and Allen Ginsberg comparisons, the degenerate truth of the real world has been completely banished and Marc has created a world of a time before recorded time, when magic was the true power source of life. He has created characters, myths and legends of his own, building his own names and words when necessary in a truly individualistic style. He writes with confidence and conviction in his new kingdom, which is evident from the handwriting, itself evolving into an almost rune like symbolism. The style and descriptiveness adorns an array of ancient guises, which enhance, with conviction, the feeling that the author has hailed from these times. This piece tends to confirm that Marc has absorbed the works of the Romantic Poets with its almost excessive descriptive and flowery style with even the vocabulary adopting an air of romanticism. The original 'Kraken' being a poem by Lord Alfred Tennyson.

Below the thunders of the upper deep,

Far far beneath in the abysmal sea,

His ancient, dreamless, uninvaded sleep

The Kraken sleepeth: faintest sunlights flee

About his shadowy sides: above him swell

Huge sponges of millennial growth and height;

And far away into the sickly light,

From many a wondrous grot and secret cell

Unnumbered and enormous polypi

Winnow with giant fins the slumbering green.

There hath he lain for ages and will lie

Battering upon huge seaworms in his sleep,

Until the latter fire shall heat the deep;

Then once by men and angels to be seen,

In roaring he shall rise and on the surface die.

Although the Kraken is an ancient mariners' legend, it is more likely that Marc took his initial inspiration from Tennyson's poem, this coinciding with his adoption of a more 'romantic' style.

Unfortunately the piece is not complete and it is generally thought to be part of a larger work of Bolan's, other elements of which have been reflected in his music and lyrics. Marc had numbered the pages published from 89 to156 indicating that there are at least 88 previously completed pages missing. The title and theme of the larger work is common knowledge. 'Rarn' or 'Children of the Rarn', Marc had talked about many times and given musical hints of, which appeared on the 'Brown' album. Some of the poems in this book could be a part of 'Rarn' but it is impossible to deduce without more of Marc's original manuscripts being available.

To recapitulate, Marc's early writings from April 1966 are reasonably neat and controlled as far as handwriting, the subject matter being very adolescent and 'real', his later work, 'The Kraken' displays a scrawl-like handwriting, the subject matter being of a very 'unreal', surreal nature. All the known pieces in-between, in chronological order, depict a gradual transition from one to the other, in both handwriting style and content. This implies a number of things, firstly Marc's determination to absorb fuel for his imagination by his constant reading and to develop his own unique style, secondly a passionate urgency to get his thoughts and ideas down, hastily scribbling as he thinks, with little immediate regard for neatness, grammar or punctuation; the idea, the creation being the most important.

Within the first short poem at the beginning of this chapter, a number of influences have been revealed, also shedding light on Marc's approach to his writing of poetry, he understood that he could not create without a pool of knowledge to create from. A house cannot be built without bricks and materials, the architect can arrange those bricks and materials in a vast variety of ways but he must understand how to use them to the best advantage, understand their strengths and weaknesses. If the architect requires a certain style of window, he must go and source it so that his design is complete and can be realised. The architect does not, however, make the bricks, or the windows, but this does not detract from his talent to design an imaginative house. A brick is just a brick and of little use on its own, but when carefully arranged with others it can be many things, as can words. Marc did not find the word 'Faerie' or learn about 'The Horned Child' by lying in bed dreaming; he had to read and learn to give him the foundations and materials to build from. Marc took elements from everything he read, everything he experienced and built. Poems, lyrics and music, sometimes he built a garden shed, sometimes a lavish mansion, overall he constructed a city, filled with an assortment of buildings, each with a slightly different purpose but all strong and sturdy.

Marc had a great admiration for other artists, poets and writers and held aspirations of his own, not necessarily to be the best but to be considered among the best in each field of creativity he roamed. He had great respect for Bob Dylan, paying him homage in a number of songs, ('Telegram Sam' and 'Ballrooms of Mars') but despite one story claiming that the name Bolan was derived from Bob Dylan, he did not emulate Dylan's style for long, but absorbed it into his own (as, possibly, with the name).If the story of 'Bolan' being anagrammatic of Bob Dylan has any substance then there is a strong irony as Bob Dylan himself, christened Robert Zimmerman, adopted the name from the welsh poet Dylan Thomas.

With respect to the origins of the name 'Bolan', Riggs O'Hara, who Marc partly lived with for a while remembers an argument with the 'Likely Lads' actor James Bolam, who also shared the house. Marc had apparently decided on the name Marc Bolam, which James took exception to and ultimately Marc agreed to change the 'm' to an 'n'. This does not necessarily detract from the 'Dylan' theory as there may have been multiple reasons for Marc deciding on 'Bolan' and he did not actually change his name till at least six months later.

Bolan made no attempt to be as momentous or arrogant with his poetry and lyrics as Dylan, but more lyrical and mystical. He did, in his early Toby Tyler guise, become very Dylan-like in appearance and even recorded a Dylan track, but soon moved on in his own individualistic way. That is the heart of Marc Bolan, his craving to be an individual, to stand out in the crowd. Whereas he would be in contact and extremely aware of all around him, even wearing their shroud for a moment as he passed by, but this was more for the purpose of understanding rather than emulating. This was even evident in his youth when he was perceived to be 'The Face'' generally adorning the Mod attire but always adding his own individual badge.

'He was always different, always smart but always different from all the other boys' said Wendy Wilchenski. He took the essence of mod culture, mod fashion and reformed it in his own style.

There is an eternal irony in youth culture that as they strive to be different they become identical to all the other mods, teds, hippies, rockers, goths, beatniks and rappers or whatever clan they choose to adhere to; immediately adorning a uniform to identify them as being different, along with their thousands of peers but Bolan always moved one step ahead of the trends, taking a fashion and redefining it with his own touch. He applied this philosophy to everything that he did, his music and writing included. Marc never denied his influences, he was in fact quite open and blatant about them, even in earlier songs such as 'Desdemona' and 'A Midsummer Night's Scene', (songs written when he was with John's Children), clearly Shakespearian in origin, Desdemona being the oppressed wife of Othello, who he ultimately kills, believing her to have been adulterous after his jealousies had been fuelled by Lago. The lines in Marc's song *'Lift up your skirt and fly'* and *'Pick up your skirt and speak'* are almost instructions to oppressed women to get out and shout for their cause, the rest of the lyrics in the song embody a similar sentiment to other oppressed people. Desdemona, therefore, can be seen as a song symbolizing oppression. 'Midsummer Night's Scene' is a simple homage to 'Midsummer Night's Dream', Shakespeare's Greek comedy, as it states quite clearly in the chorus *'It's all down to a Shakespearean dream'* and the constant reference to 'Petals and Flowers' within the song confirms the inspiration for in Shakespeare's play the fairy Puck is instructed by the fairy king, Oberon, to pick flowers and use the juice from the flowers as a love potion on the eyelids of his sleeping queen, Titania. When she wakes she falls in love with the first thing she sees, which is Bottom who has been given the head of an ass by Puck, this gives credence to Marc's line *'Get her face there's a place disfigured with love'*. These blatant and accurate Shakespearian statements by Marc open another door for speculation, taking into account the chronology of the two songs, written and recorded while he was with John's Children early in 1967 and linking that with his writing of the play 'Pictures of Purple People' in the latter half of 1966, indicates that he had certainly read or been exposed to some of Shakespeare's works around that time period, namely 'Othello' and 'A Midsummer Night's Dream', and possibly as a result of the Bards inspiration aspired to be a playwright for a while. This is one of the more obvious literary influences on Marc's writing and whereas he never denied his influences they were sometimes more subtly disguised.

For example it is easy to allow the track 'Like a White Star, tangled and far, Tulip that's what you are' from the 'Unicorn' album, to wash over you as a pleasant love song but when the lyrics are examined more intimately there are clear references returning to the 'horned child' Dionysus with mentions of being '*In the Thunderbolt suit*' Dionysus was reborn from the thigh of Zeus, the thunderbolt throwing god, '*The Maenads of May*', The Maenads are the women who worshipped Dionysus and, according to one story, killed Orpheus, '*Silver Satyrs in parks*', Satyrs where the attendants of Dionysus, '*the Titans*' who killed Dionysus, according to one version of his death, and '*Vinyards spangled with love*', Dionysus being the god of wine; The whole song is in fact about Dionysus and confirms the original conclusion for the identity of the horned child mentioned in the poem at the start of this chapter. It is incredible that the shortest of poems should open so many doorways into the mind of Marc Bolan and can only enhance the belief in the depth of his imagination and intellect. He was undoubtedly well read even the name 'Tyrannosaurus Rex' which it would be natural to think of as having been inspired simply by the dinosaur was in fact inspired by a short story 'A Sound of Thunder' by Ray Bradbury, the American science fiction writer. It was probably how Ray Bradbury described the dinosaur as a tyrant lizard and the most incredible monster in history, that perked up Marc Bolan's ears to the name and it would undoubtedly live up to his ego's expectations of being the biggest rock/pop star ever; it would also appeal to Marc how the discovering and killing of the dinosaur in the story, had the outcome of changing the future, leaving its mark, whether justly acknowledged or not. In the Ray Bradbury story a company specialising in time travel offers the ultimate safari, travelling back in time to hunt dinosaurs. Eckles, the stories failed hero, loses his nerve and in fleeing from the thunderous Tyrannosaurus Rex steps on a butterfly killing it, not his intended mascot. Unaware of the butterfly stuck to Eckles' boot the hunting party return to the present to find a very different world, the result of the domino effect over billions of years caused by the butterfly's death. The moral being that no matter how small we may perceive our actions to be, they can have gigantic results and consequences. An apt inspiration for the young Marc Bolan, the small elf-like character who grew from the shadow of Tyrannosaurus Rex.

Marc certainly rode the beast to success with a monstrous determination; his hunger to fulfil his dreams was as deep and insatiable as the dinosaur's, fuelling that determination. With Marc's well-documented fascination for science fiction it is not surprising that he took his inspiration here, he often refers to science fiction, even saying that the role of pop star is 'quite a nice science fiction fantasy'. Some of his earliest heroes and role models were of the science fiction genre, such as 'Mighty Joe Young' and it would be with a sense of childhood pride that Marc would take the name of the largest, most vicious and unstoppable monster. He was obsessed with anything that was not real, not of the recognised 'real' world, the suggested criticism that he was an escapist and lived in a fantasy world was, therefore, quite true. The name Toby Tyler was even taken from the Disney film

'Toby Tyler. Ten weeks with a Circus' itself based on the book of the same name by James Otis about a boy who ran away to the Circus, which in a way is what Marc did, he ran away to the rock and roll circus, a world of make believe. The irony being that he became an incredibly real presence in the world that most of the critical people recognise as normal and decades after his death his artistic donation to that world is still very alive and a large contributor to the music industries bank balance, how real can he become, Marc Bolan the product! This only proves his hypothesis about which is the true reality, everything that came from his imagination is still here, still being listened to, still being played, still being read, still a part of many peoples' lives and still being talked about and dissected in an effort to understand his form of genius.

It is reasonable to conclude that Marc Bolan's attitude towards his writing was to absorb as much literary input as he could in order to feed his creativity and imagination from various genres; from that massive input his mind would anagrammatically rearrange the information, stories, legends, styles and words and spill forth a new Bolanesque world of fantasy into reality, creating his reality for us to indulge in. His writing was not like Shakespeare, Spenser, Kerouac, Bradley, Tennyson, Poe, Dylan, Homer, Euripides or any other, they were all merely the ingredients.

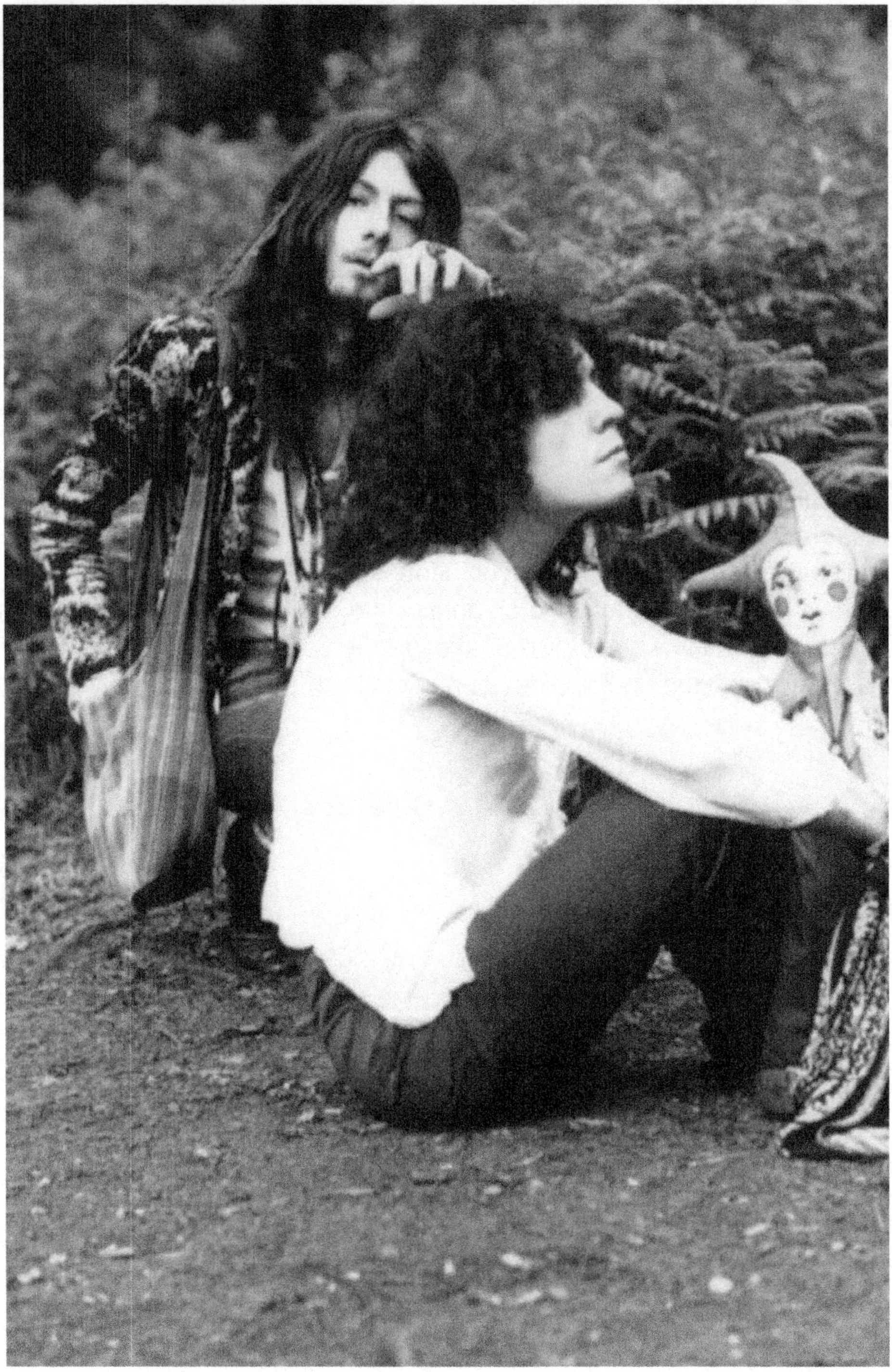

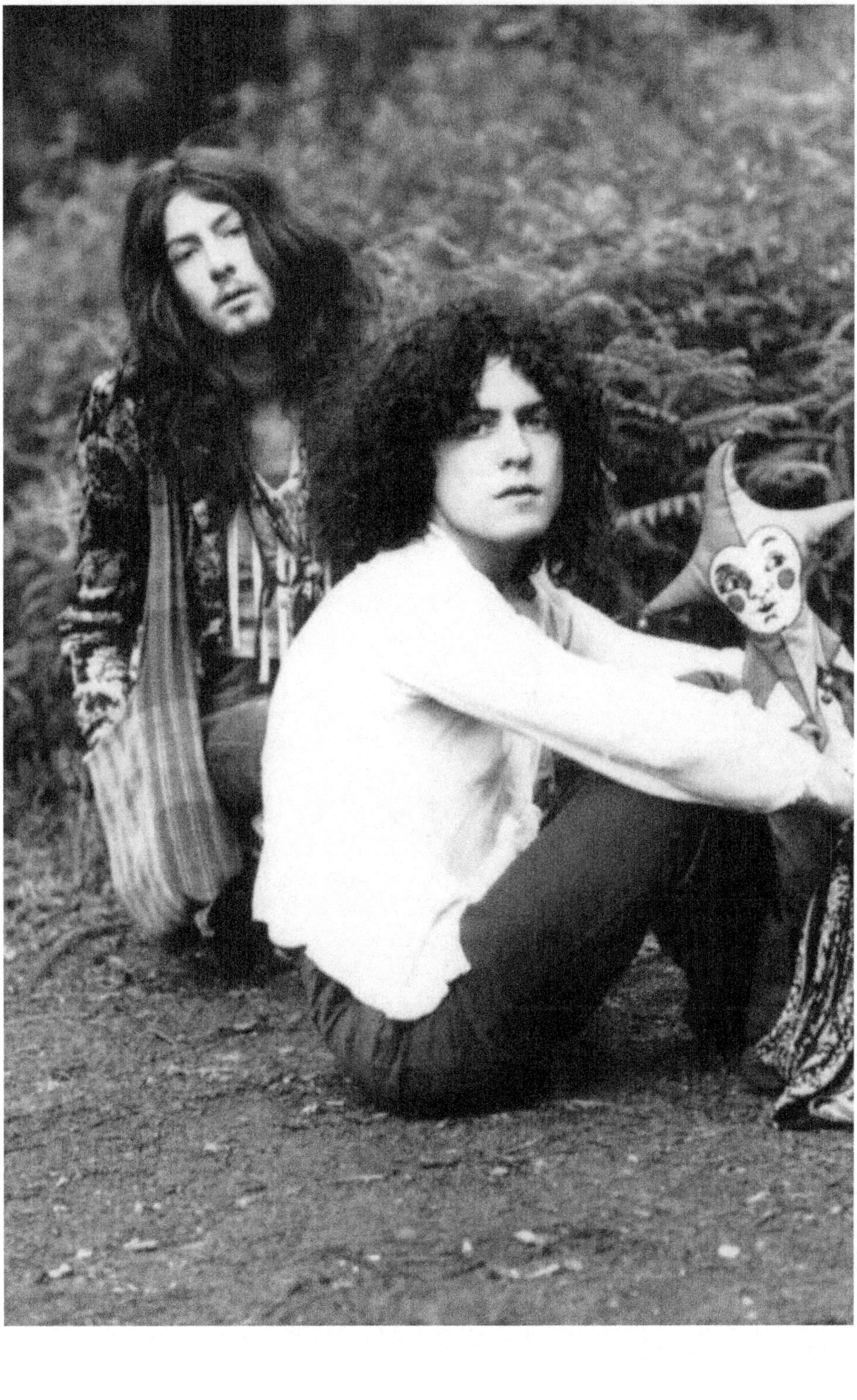

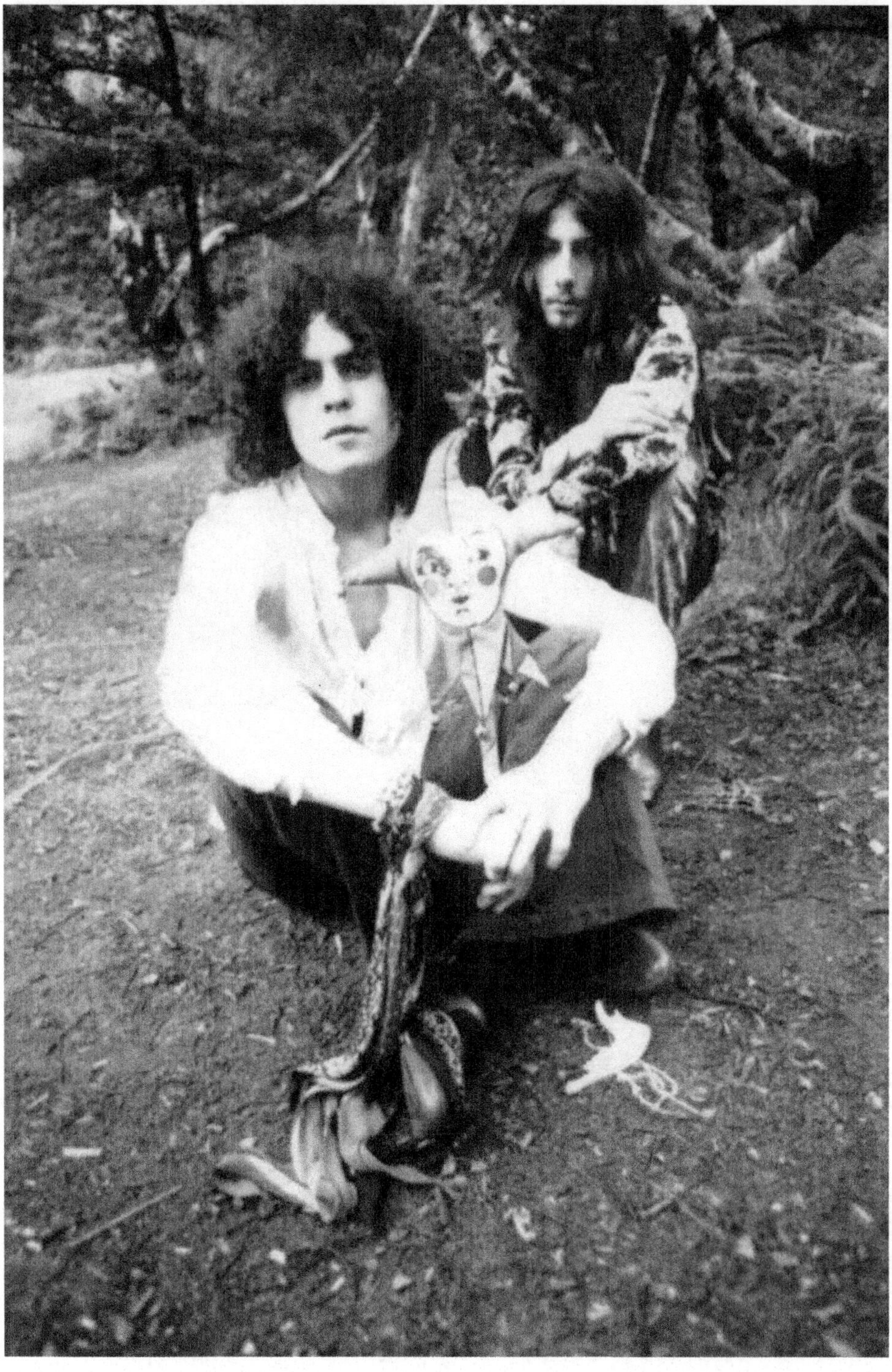

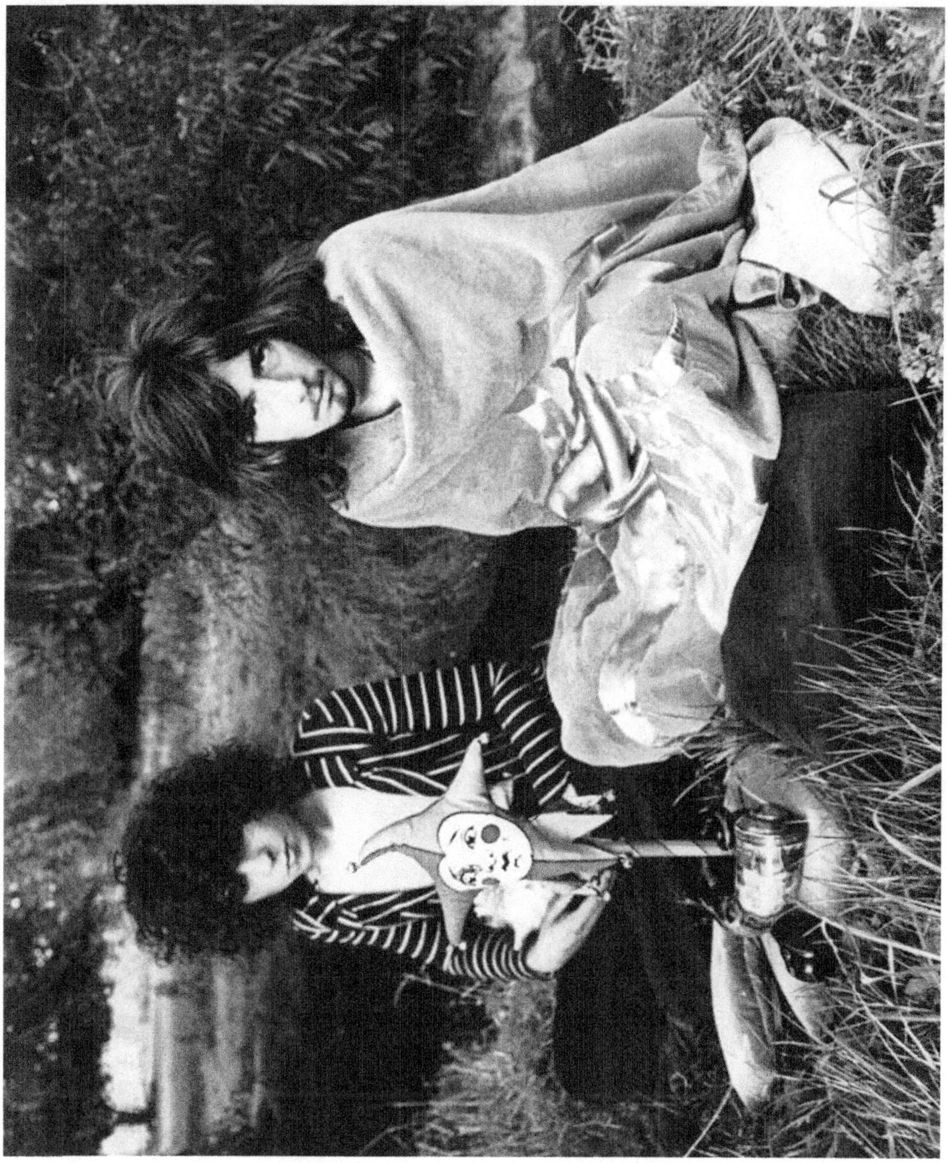

I annoint my head with
the blood of leaves to prevent
my skull from growing rusty.
as a knave in the tomb,
with a mouth like a womb,
all wiseness is stifled &
bled dry, so I lay for
one day in the way
of ~~the~~ pray, ~~of the dreamy stream~~, where my
knowledge becomes like
a spring tree and takes
root. with the adornment of
shadows upon the days
waning back my silk self grows the

tortured knowledge

a misty century. This magicment has been my own since the sons of Romana breathed deep of the winds on the hill. And caped as I am in driping saffronic yellows I'm a dancing soul, black bearded like the nomadic lords of our time

—

3. **Anointment**

"We are all splinters of God's head" Marc Bolan 1972.

I anoint my head with the blood of leaves

To prevent my skull from going rusty,

As a knave in the tomb

With a mouth like a womb,

All wiseness is stifled

And bled dry.

So I lay for one day

In the way of the Spray,

Where my knowledge becomes like a spring tree

And takes root.

With the adornment of shadows

Upon the days waning back,

My silk self grows the tortured knowledge

Of a misty century.

This magicment has been my own

Since the sons of Romana

Breathed deep of the winds on the hill

And caped as I am In dripping saffronic yellows.

I'm a dancing soul,

Black bearded like the nomadic lords of our time.

The first clues of meaning in this poem lie in one of its later lines '*Since the sons of Romana',* which does not refer to the companion of the BBC's Dr Who,

Romanadvoratrelundar. In fact Romana is one of two things, it is a term that was used when describing anything of Rome or it is the name given to the pre-Christian pagan religion of Rome, Marc could have meant it in either context here and it is not crucial to the overall meaning as to which. There is another part to the first clue in the word that has been scribbled out and replaced by *Romana*, the name *Solomon*. This tends to confirm the analysis and Marc's intent, although the name of *Solomon* was not completely fitting, which Marc obviously realised, it reveals the biblical theme. The second is in the next line

Breathed deep of the winds on the hill,

if that hill is Golgotha or Mount Calvary, the hill of skulls, then the theme of the poem becomes transparent. Firstly it has to be accepted that Mark Feld was primarily from a Jewish background, although his mother, Phyllis Feld, was not Jewish but Christian, Simeon, his father, was Jewish and Marc's family and friends and the community he lived and moved in were Jewish. Even though Marc Bolan was not a practicing Jew and had never had his Bar Mitzvah, he had those roots and having attended state schools in a predominantly Jewish community would not have necessarily absorbed much of the Christian interpretations and beliefs of the bible. Harry Feld, Marc's brother remembers their mother was an avid reader and constantly read with them as young children, so much so that they could both read and write before they went to school. As well as reading books such as 'The Water Babies' by Charles Kingsley, she also read the bible to them, but not in a religious context instead 'translating' the scriptures into stories of good and bad that the young brothers could relate to. Through his mother, Phyllis, Marc learned some of the Christian 'legends' but not their doctrinisms and was undoubtedly not pushed in any specific direction religiously. Harry recalls that they were more encouraged to keep an open mind and to ultimately find their own way whilst being taught right from wrong.

During the analogies being undertaken, it is important to remember that it is an understanding of Marc Bolan that is being attempted and that personal views are not being expressed. The comments and conclusions drawn are not intended to undermine in anyway the various viewpoints and beliefs of others. An attitude that Marc himself adopted with his ambiguous approach to religion in later years.

With the exception of his mother Marc's family, friends and the community circles he moved in were all Jewish and Jewish beliefs only acknowledge the Old Testament and do not accept Jesus as the Messiah. If acknowledged at all it is only as a learned man, so Marc would not have had the knowledge and respect of Jesus that is instilled into the Christians of the world, he would have seen him as no more than a special, learned man.

'He was a real funky stud' was Marc's description of Jesus in one interview. Considering all this it is acceptable that Marc would slightly misinterpret or be wrong on certain accepted Christian beliefs.

Standing before the sons of Romana, the Roman soldiers, as they breathed deep the winds at the top of Mount Calvary, would have been three crucifixes, upon one would have been Jesus. If this definition is embraced and applied to the rest of the poem then it can be seen that it is written from the perspective of Jesus and reflects his resurrection.

Returning to the beginning of the poem,

'I anoint my head with the blood of leaves

To prevent my skull from going rusty'

It was the custom at the time of Jesus to anoint the head with perfumed oil, or holy oil, it was part of the baptism ritual to be anointed with holy oil as well as water and the dying were also anointed. The name Christ means *the anointed one* and Christ was anointed many times but specifically for this appraisal, just a short time before his death.

"And while he was at Bethany in the house of Simon the leper, as he was reclining at table, a woman came with an alabaster flask of ointment of pure nard, very costly, and she broke the flask and poured it over his head. There were some who said to themselves indignantly, "Why was the ointment wasted like that? For this ointment could have been sold for more than three hundred denari and given to the poor." And they scolded her. But Jesus said, "Leave her alone. Why do you trouble her? She has done a beautiful thing to me. For you always have the poor with you, and whenever you want, you can do good for them. But you will not always have me. She has done what she could; she has anointed my body beforehand for burial. And truly, I say to you, wherever the gospel is proclaimed in the whole world, what she has done will be told in memory of her." Mark 14.

The holy perfumed oil could indeed be described as the blood of leaves, as it is made from the extracts or juices of many plants and there is one theory that the holy oil used for anointment contained cannabis, accounting for its calming properties in the casting out of demons, if those demons were seen to be of an epileptic nature. Therefore to anoint the head to prevent it from corroding or to preserve the mind was an understandable ritual.

As a knave in the tomb

His enemies considered Jesus a scoundrel, a troublemaker and a man from low social standing, a knave. To take another definition of knave, a servant, it could be read as the servant of God or man, again either definition is applicable.

With a mouth like a womb

A womb gives birth, hence *a mouth like a womb* would give birth too but to words, prophecies and parables, as was Jesus' undeniable role, constantly teaching the word of God.

All wiseness is stifled And bled dry.

Death comes and he is unable to speak.

So I lay for one day In the way of the spray,

He lay in the tomb on the stone table, arranged but motionless like a bunch of flowers. This is where Marc makes his mistake, if it can be deemed one, depending upon the religious standpoint. It is commonly believed by Christians that Jesus rose after the third day and Marc refers only to one day, and it is here that it has to be reasserted that Marc was not a Christian.

Where my knowledge becomes like a spring tree

And takes root.

Either his mind begins to grow again or the teachings he has spread through the people begin to grow from the seeds he has sewn.

With the adornment of shadows

Upon the days waning back,

Night comes and during the night

My silk self grows the tortured knowledge

Of a misty century

He begins his rebirth, his resurrection, his mind grows and his knowledge is restored. He has now passed through death and has encountered a spiritual transition and the magical experience of this transition has been his since the crucifixion.

This magicment has been my own

Since the sons of Romana

Breathed deep of the winds on the hill

And caped as I am

In dripping saffronic yellows

It was also a custom in biblical times to adorn the bodies with spices, saffron being the most precious spice and also gold cloth, (saffronic yellows) would indicate kingliness.

I'm a dancing soul,

This implies reincarnation, which Marc had, on a number of occasions, expressed a belief in and is quite clearly suggesting that he saw Jesus as a soul that 'danced' that was reborn, and would ultimately be reborn again, dancing from time to time. Marc had shown a consideration for reincarnation a few times, 'Cosmic Dancer' from the album 'Electric Warrior' was described by him as being about reincarnation.

Black bearded like the nomadic lords of our time.

Christ is always portrayed with a black beard, as are most of the prophets from many religions and most are nomadic wanderers, spreading their words far and wide and possibly in reincarnation they are nomadic through time. In this final line Marc places Jesus Christ in a collective with all the prophets, suggesting that there is a group of nomadic souls bestowing their wisdom upon the world.

Thus here is an insight into Marc's view of the resurrection of Christ and maybe his opinion of some of the orthodox prophets. For someone who proclaimed to holding no orthodox beliefs, to see the prophets of various faiths as 'dancing souls' is an interesting scenario, as consciousnesses placed in various time periods to guide the people of that period by adopting a persona that would best communicate with the masses of that era. This evokes the question as to what would be the most effective persona of the modern world that would be able to reach the masses efficiently?

Without the word 'Romana' providing the key to the meaning of this poem, it could elicit a variety of meanings, but the inclusion of those two lines pertaining to the sons of Romana help to focus the reader to the intended subject. Even then it is not immediately apparent, as Romana is not commonly used in contemporary vocabulary and it would be easy to overlook it's relevance and attribute the word to being a Bolanesque creation. It is not and was quite deliberately placed towards the end of the poem as if to clarify the mystery sketched out within the words. The form of this poem is very open, the first half flowing very quickly because of the four short rhyming lines (tomb-womb and day-spray) and the quickness of their rhythm but then there are no more rhymes and the rhythm slows to evoke the drama of the event, poising to contemplate the transition.

Stating that Bolan has written this from the perspective of Christ will undoubtedly raise objections from those who venerate Christ but it must be emphasised that Marc did not see Jesus Christ as the son of God, firstly because of his Jewish roots, and secondly because Marc appeared to be on a much broader spiritual journey which he had not reconciled. His interest in Greek Gods, witches, warlocks, white magic, as well as his delving into the writings of various philosophers such as Kahlil Gibran imply a form of searching. He did not embrace his Jewish roots, or even appear to pay them much heed, for example Jews do not write *God* in any form for fear it be defaced, yet Marc wrote *God* many times in songs and poems and he did not adhere to the Jewish customs, such as observing the Sabbath. It is realistic to conclude that he was like many, who although having their roots in a specific religion are not practicing in that religion but those roots have to have the effect of colouring their views, albeit subconsciously. And again like many, his root religion did not hold all the answers for Marc, so he looked elsewhere for those answers.

Peter Sanders was a leading music photographer of the late seventies, he photographed the Rolling Stones, Bob Dylan, the Doors, the Who, Jimi Hendrix and many more including Marc. Before becoming disillusioned with the rock world and enriched by eastern culture, eloping with his camera to India in 1970, Peter virtually shadowed Marc and was responsible for all the photos on Marc's earlier albums up until 'The Brown Album', even living in a flat just above him and June for a while. They had to spend a great amount of time together; as a result Peter developed a strong bond with Marc and was endeared to him as a person, although he admits he never really followed the music, especially when it became commercial.

Peter recalls Marc as being extremely intelligent and well read, always keen to learn. He also recalls Marc as being a very spiritual person and very aware that he was connected to something, 'tapped in' in some way. Although he recoiled from orthodox religions he had an overwhelming spiritual side and Peter agrees with the observation that Marc's interests seemed in some ways to be dominated by more pagan concepts. His apparent interest in white magic, witches and warlocks, Greek and Roman mythology, Celtic and early Druid mythology is boldly evident in his lyrics and poetry but to what depth those pagan interests influenced Marc's spiritual outlook can only be speculated. There are constant referrals to pagan values and beliefs in Marc's work, 'The Warlock of Love' being dedicated to the 'Woods of Knowledge', Druids revere trees, particularly the oak, the word 'Druid' itself means 'one with the knowledge of the oak' or 'wise person of the oak' (there is a dramatic irony in the fact that it was an oak tree that killed Marc), they also believe in being at one with nature, that all life is connected and in the spirit of nature. Many of the poems in the volume refer to trees in one context or another and they certainly portray an air of naturalistic spiritualism. They are almost an embodiment of Druidism; one poem (page 31 of the original volume) which begins by calling the daughters of love to unite could be easily read as an account of Beltane, the Pagan ritual of fire lighting to mark the coming of summer, traditionally a festival of fertility, of spring, a reference to which Marc made many times, notably in 'Ride a White Swan' and even white swans were held in reverence by ancient pagans, believing them to be holy women under enchantment, up until recent times it has been illegal to kill or harm a swan in Ireland, once punishable by death.

In the preface of 'Warlock' Marc bestows upon us a clue with regards to his spiritual development, where he describes the west as hiding behind the masks of the Orient because we find the lumbering shapes of the west (could these be the megaliths) fearful and spiritually under developed. He states that we long for legends, and look to the east for them, implying that we are not satisfied with our own spiritual culture. There is no intention here to depict 'Warlock' as a religious work, only to arouse an observation that Marc may have been exploring his inner beliefs and expressing this exploration within his writings, as many artists do. 'Stones for Avalon' from the 'Unicorn' album, is almost a pagan chant for the Isle of Avalon, an ancient spiritual centre for Druids, being home to a Druid college before Christianity. Stones are also of spiritual importance in Druidism, hence the megaliths, such as Avebury and Stonehenge, even stones on a smaller scale, such as pebbles, are revered. For centuries Avalon has been a spiritual centre for many, Buddhists and Christians alike, now also being home to the Glastonbury festival. Marc played Glastonbury Town hall in October 1968, then played the first festival in 1970, could the first visit have inspired or confirmed his interests in pagan beliefs, it certainly inspired the song 'Stones for Avalon'.

One of the key elements of Druidism is the strong belief in the importance of creativity and the personal evolution and growth of the creative aspects of the inner self. The Bards, although held in high esteem themselves, are the first phase in the training to becoming a Druid, and their main charge is to study the art of poetry, storytelling and song, so they may relate and bequeath their knowledge, through creativity, to others.

Oh hear the voice of the Bard

Who present, past and future sees

Whose ears have heard the holy word

That walked among the ancient trees.

William Blake- The First Song of Experience.

Creativity is as fundamental as nature to the followers of the pagan lifestyle as is their belief in reincarnation, the concept that death is a rebirth into another world, where we await rebirth back into this world, and that our souls are ever growing and learning, dancing from one world to the other.

Marc Bolan acculturated all of these philosophies, primarily through his creativity expressing all he absorbed through that creativity. 'Unicorn', which was released in May 1969, after Marc's visit to what is probably the most spiritual place in England, Glastonbury on the Isle of Avalon, contained a selection of songs that could be described as spiritual or religious which was not as obvious on his first two albums, although there were hints of spiritual themes on 'Prophets'. The aforementioned 'Stones for Avalon', 'Like a white Star' (Discussed in the previous chapter), which is about the Greek god Dionysus, 'The Seal of Seasons' and 'The Throat of Winter' could all be deemed as pagan songs, along with 'A Pilgrims Tale' and many of the others. 'Iscariot' has its roots in the Christian tale of Judas Iscariot but is not of Christian intent; again it has more of a paganistic content. The title of the album could itself be seen as spiritual, a unicorn being symbolic of purity and as legend tells, being drawn to the pure of heart. 'Nijinsky Hind' appears to be Marc's name for his unicorn and even that track relates back to our magical roots. The spiritual undertones continue through the next three albums with tracks such as 'A Day Laye', 'The Children of Rarn', 'Cosmic Dancer' and 'Girl' being the most obvious, although other songs have less distinctive spiritual properties, the spiritualism is underlying and plainly evident. 'Ride a White Swan' is not a hymn but is a transparently Pagan song with its references to Beltane and Druids, and in giving Marc his first hit along with the satisfaction of commercial success, it also marked the decline in his spiritual expression within his lyrics. Peter Sanders remembers Marc talking of putting his spiritual development on hold and that he would one day buy himself a private island where he would continue to pursue his spirituality. A dream he unfortunately never had the time to bring to fruition, unless there is a small island in the Bahamas bearing Marc Bolan's name.

Undoubtedly anyone of an orthodox religion will ridicule the references to magic and Druidism, yet all religions teach of magic in their accepted way, the resurrection of Christ could not be a more 'magical' event, along with his healings and all of his other miracles. Christ himself also taught that God is present in all things, the trees, the birds, the earth and all around us, and that we should look for him there, in nature. Marc, however, did not conform to the rigours of any orthodox religion; he appeared to take an overview of the whole and concluded his own interpretation of spirituality. In an interview on an American radio station in 1972 Marc discusses this spirituality and says how he considers himself to be a very religious, spiritual person, but cannot embrace any of the accepted religions. He clearly states that he believes in a supreme deity, an 'omnipresent strength' and the use of the word 'omnipresent' itself implies a depth of thought and inner belief of the subject. It is here that he discusses Jesus and describes him as a 'funky stud', one man of which there are many and he goes on to say that Jesus was a very strong soul that was totally evolved. Marc explains how he sees us all as splinters of Gods' head and that some of us have larger splinters than others and that Jesus and men like him allow those splinters to grow and take them over, like a good cancer.

His description of Jesus as a totally *evolved soul* along with his reference to him *being one of many* implicates the Druid theory of a soul growing and developing through death and rebirth between worlds. Presumably Marc would have included in the *man* Abraham, Moses, Mohammed, Buddha, Mahatma Gandhi and many others who could be described as evolved souls, all taking a humble road of spiritual dedication and bestowing upon others similar philosophies of good and evil. Marc continues in that interview to say he believes that what went wrong was the way they treated the churches (the way they are run), that Jesus did not want a Palomino stallion but an ass implying that the gold and opulence of the churches was not what Jesus preached, as with the other 'prophets', and we return to the notion of God being present in everything around us, even the wind that carries the seeds of life upon its breath, not in the gilded statues of the churches.

Marc was very prudent in this interview because although referring to Jesus calling himself the Son of God, he did not challenge that Christian belief, rather raised the consideration that we are all the sons and daughters of God and that apart from the exceptional evolution of his soul Jesus was no different to many. Having talked about Jesus in an articulate rock and roll style Marc concludes the interview by saying that the "...*Bible is a real funky book.*"

Marc was open to the exploration of various beliefs and as with his writing and music soaked up all he could before draining off the excess fluid leaving him with his own cocktail of belief and understanding; Harry said that if the Mormons knocked the door Marc was more likely to invite them in and 'talk the bum off them' and that it was his way of sapping all the knowledge he could from them. Peter Sanders remembered a meal at Marc and June's where Tony Visconti brought along a Tibetan Buddhist, Chime Rinpoche, who Marc had lengthy conversation and debate with but in contrast he also recalls a friend of Eric Clapton's that was 'from some Islamic group' who Marc was almost frightened of, although Peter cannot recount the reason for Marc's apparent apprehension.

'The Children of Rarn' is, according to Marc, a spiritual piece, Rarn being Marc's name for God, as he states in the previously mentioned American interview, also saying how sad he feels that a street punk like himself should have to devise his own name for God. The piece was, unfortunately, never completed, despite having an overwhelming potential, it was to be Marc Bolan's rock opera and was an idea he had originally conceived before The Who's 'Tommy' but apart from the short song on the 'Brown Album' and some demos with Tony Visconti, or, as Tony described, sketches, the project was shelved. It is possible that 'The Krakenmist' was to be a part of 'Rarn' but this can only be speculation, it is plain, however, that the content of the pieces of 'Rarn' available is very pagan and full of druidistic imagery. 'Futuristic Dragon' had a suggested air of druidism, in the title, the cover of the album and the title track that implies Marc toying with the notion of a return to his earlier ethereal mysticism but the rest of the songs on the album had no spiritual implications. 'Dandy in the Underworld' had no hints of druidism or spirituality but the lyrics are far more Bardic in their lamenting content than Marc's previous three albums. It would appear that he had put his spirituality on hold, preferring to play the role of the ancestor of punk until unfortunately meeting his oak of supreme knowledge.

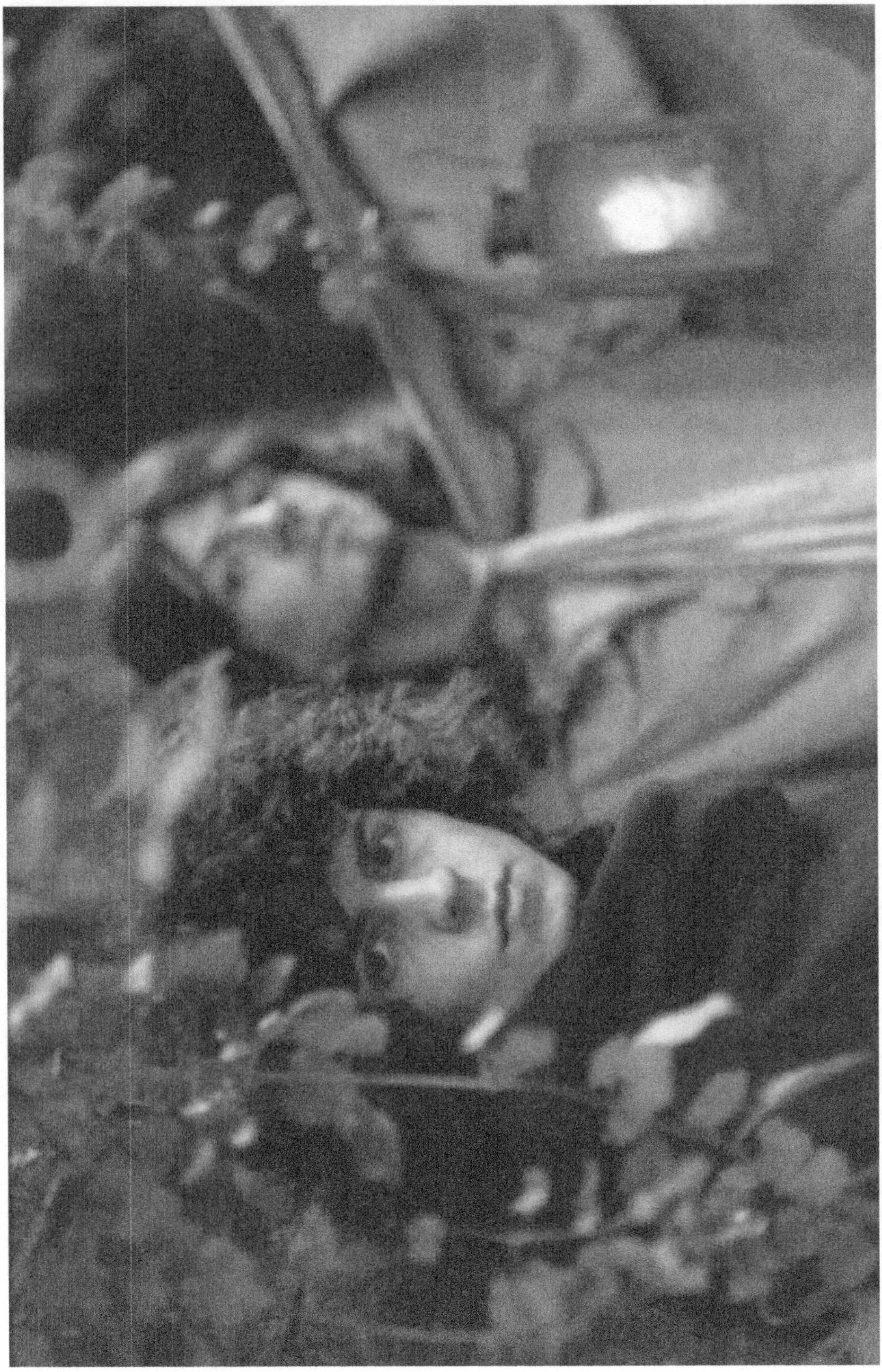

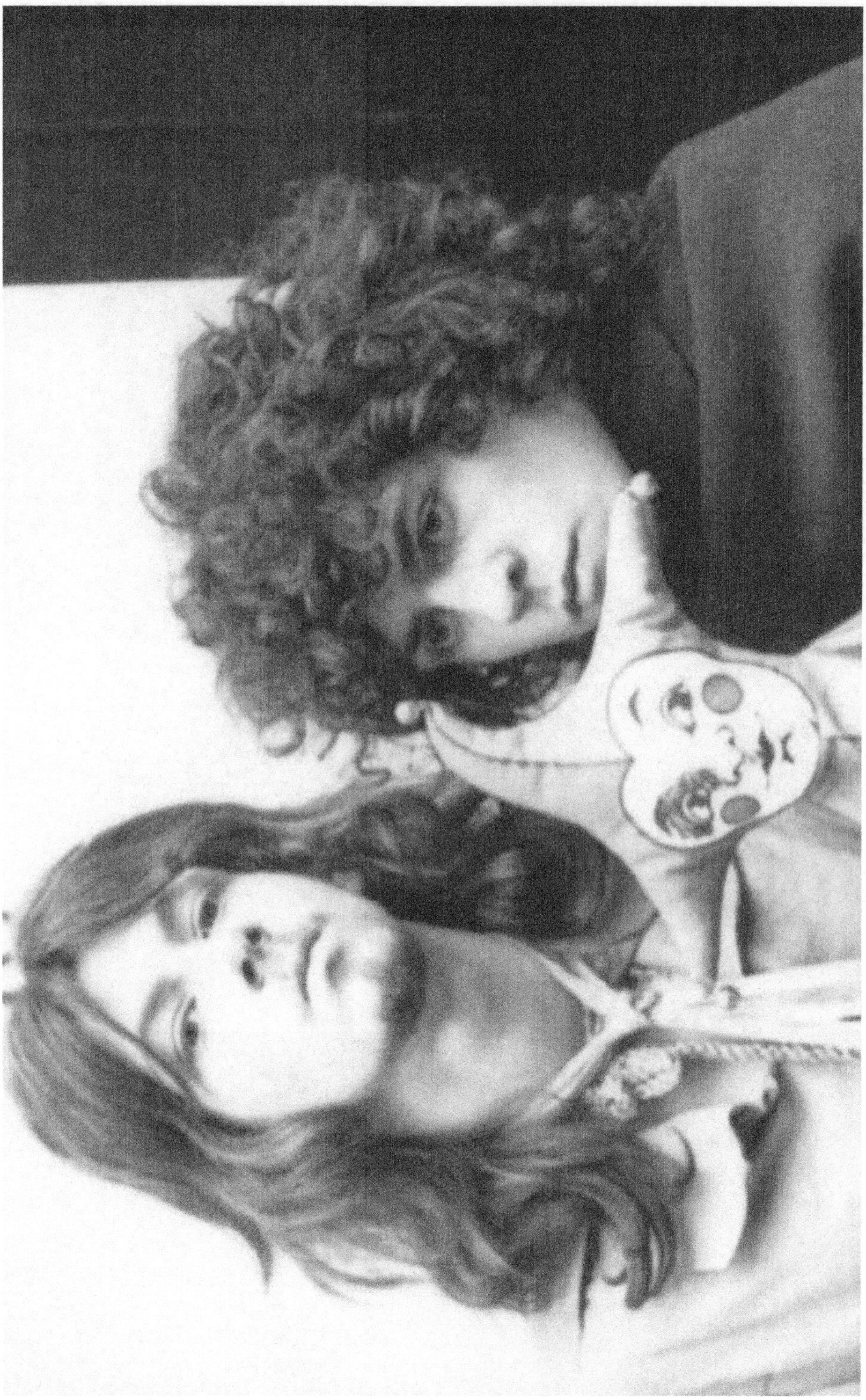

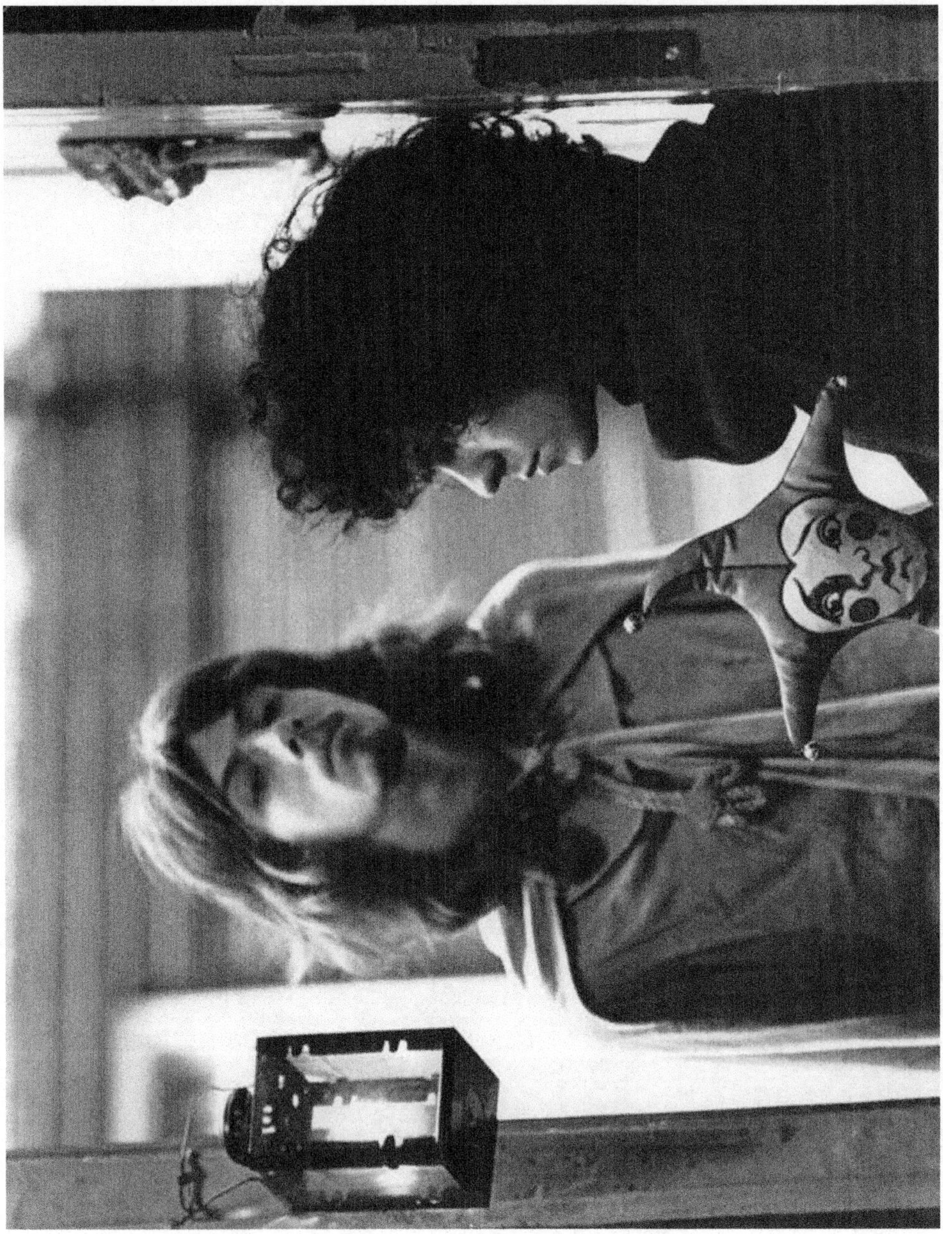

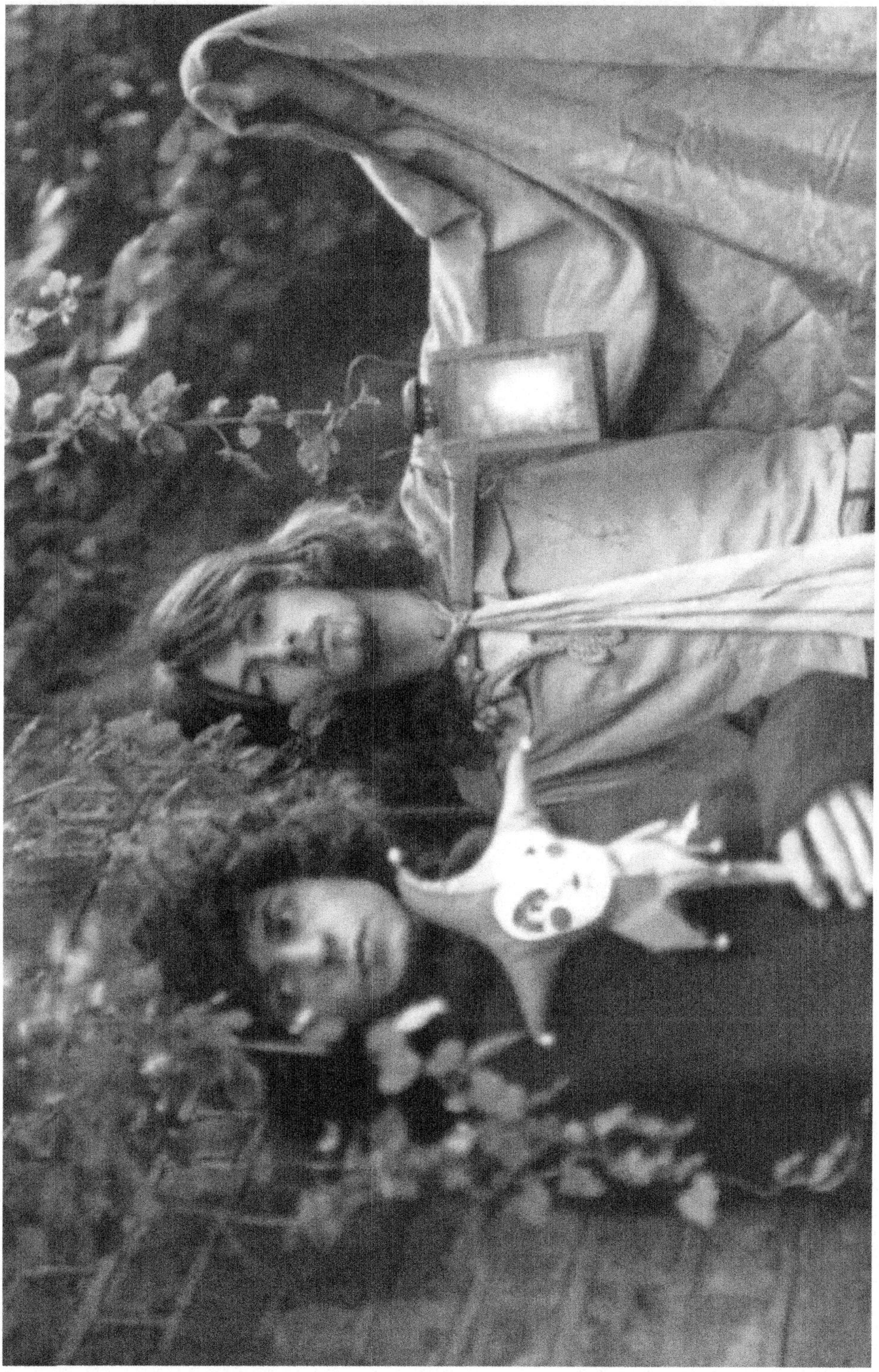

like a hush it seemed to me that I, dove danced upon the sea. my heart of winds blew wild & warm, night fleet, foot fled before the storm, a daunting of pinks & azure blue flowed like faith all on the few. who

virgiled thru the
vaulted night
free of the falcon
~~fools~~ ● fools of kite.
who ride the sky
in ~~vessels~~ ships of ice
& eat the frozen
hearts of lice & bed
in sheets that
the whipworm spun
& hide 'neath
our lys from
the light of
re:write the sun

4. **Dove Dancing**

"I mean doing in fact what one has always wanted to do, and finding out that it's altogether different from what one thought it would be. Probably because one never really knows what one wants to do, or knows what it's going to be like."
Marc Bolan 1972.

Like a husk it seemed to me

That I dove danced upon the sea.

My heart of winds blew wild and warm,

Night, fleet foot fled before my storm.

A dawn of pinks and azure blue

Flowed like faith all on the few

Who vigiled through the vaulted night,

Free of the Falcon fools of Kite

Who ride the skies in ships of ice

And eat the frozen hearts of lice

And bed in sheets that the Whip Worm spun

And hide 'neath our lies from the light of the sun.

Some poetry is written with a depth of meaning that it can be difficult to reach and even among literary academics it will cause huge debate, which in one respect is a positive achievement for the poet as it has the resulting effect of raising the attention of the reader to the possibilities and variability of the intended theme. However, if the poem has such a disguised meaning that it becomes oblivious to most readers then there is little purpose to the disguise as all that will be perceived is the mask itself. Many poems wear no mask and are completely unambiguous, simply being what they say. This applies to all art forms, poems, songs, sculptures and pictures; the bowl of apples is not always a statement on starvation, it is sometimes no more than a bowl of apples, although beautifully represented it is important to accept that that is all it is. If it were to be given any meaning it would be as an observation of the apples, of their moment in time but already the analysis is stretching beyond the image, they are just apples and we have to accept that is all the artist intended. As in Bolan's 'New York City' it is simply an observation of an absurd moment. Conversely some works have a depth and a 'subtleness' of meaning to intrigue and beguile the recipient, and there are many areas of grey between the two extremes. There is always the danger of attempting to assimilate meanings to works that were not intended or even conceived of by the artist or writer, which gives credence to the argument that the mask should not be too efficient a disguise and that it is the responsibility of the artist/writer to leave flaws, holes or clues in the camouflage that are accessible portals to the intended meaning, should there be one. This is sometimes a difficult responsibility for most creative talents to adhere to for their intended meaning is always conclusively apparent to them as the creator and they will revel in the ambiguity of their spawned piece and the debates it will induce, watching it being nurtured by the discussion. Some will even take pride in the confusion of meaning, as with 'Metal Guru', Marc alluded many times to a meaning of the song but permitted the debate to continue unresolved, ensuring its continuance. This can lead to the recipient only seeing a bowl of apples and, thus, no communication has been made; it can also lead to a state of general apathy towards a creators work if that work is continually too well camouflaged, although there may be a sense of satisfaction enjoyed by the creator at the achievement of the illusion. As if to add more confusion to this scenario, there is the possibility that the creator alludes towards an illusion that is to say that there is an implication of a sub-meaning to a piece when there is none. This would give the creator a false credibility but the act itself would be intriguing and warrant a form of credibility for its perceptive deception, as with the Sex Pistols. In order for there to be true creative credibility the responsibility, as stated previously, has to lie with the creator to allow enough to be seen of the intended meaning to be discovered, and in sufficient examples of their work.

The first poem simply narrates a scene, with a possible lovers undertone and unless it was intended as part of a larger work, which cannot be confirmed, scarcely holds any more depth than that, although a meaning could undoubtedly be reached if it were delved into deeply and imaginatively but it could not be thought of as a conclusive sub meaning as there are no apparent pointers. The second, however, has much more meaning, that is not evident on first reading but becomes plain when examined. The poem in this chapter falls into the grey area where it could hold more meaning than is initially visible. It is also possible to attribute meanings to this poem that may not have been intended, but can be read into its words by an individual reader depending on their experiences, perspective and agenda. It is essential, therefore, to remember who wrote this poem, his perspective, experiences and agenda and to attempt to read and understand it from that stance.

Marc said in an interview that his current poetry (1972) was 'more like street music' and about what was happening around him, he also said that he gave things alternative names, such as calling cars *sun stallions* and bad business men *chrome dragons*. A poem would therefore become a complete simile to describe a particular event, feeling, desire, experience, or even protest.

What lies beneath the mask of this poem is open to minimal speculation, unlike what lay beneath the mask of Marc Bolan.

Like a husk it seemed to me

That I dove danced upon the sea.

A husk is the dry outer skin of a seed or some fruits, the first thing that is seen of the seed or fruit, protecting and hiding the goodness within. The empty husk is then discarded as the content is either devoured or gives birth to new life. The husk of Marc Bolan is the pop star, the glitter clad image that was portrayed and exploited and that husk danced upon the sea of life or the sea of the media/music industry, like a dove, gracefully. A native American Muskogee (commonly known as Creek), who is also a dance master, related that doves and falcons are very strong figures in dance forms among many nations of native America; *Dove Dancing* is a term commonly used in America.

My heart of winds blew wild and warm,

Night, fleet foot fled before my storm.

It is said that you can hear songs upon the wind that it sings and from Marc's heart of winds songs blew wild and warm, like a storm of music, blowing the darkness of life before it, keeping night on the run before his storm of creativity, of presence.

A dawn of pinks and azure blue

Flowed like faith all on the few

Who vigiled through the vaulted night,

The colours could be a reference to Marc's flamboyant style and the joys of his newfound success, a dawn being symbolic of a new beginning. The spoils of this new era, which may be his music, will be enjoyed and rewarded to those who have stayed by his side through the dark struggling years that are now locked away (*vaulted night*).

Free of the Falcon fools of Kite

Who ride the skies in ships of ice

The Kite is a bird of prey that was almost extinct at the beginning of the 20th century and, although ornithologists will probably refute the observation, Kites are very similar to Falcons, also birds of prey. These birds of prey are allegories for record company executives riding the skies in their tall glass skyscrapers, feeding off the parasites of the music industry.

And eat the frozen hearts of lice

'Lice' being the parasites.

And bed in sheets that the Whip Worm spun

Definitively a 'whip worm' is also a parasite but it is not believed that to be Marc's intended meaning as they do not spin any type of thread, it is more likely that the term is a Bolanesque amalgamation of 'whipping boy' and 'silk worm', implying that the record executives are sleeping in the luxuries provided by their whipping boys, the artists.

And hide 'neath our lies from the light of the sun.

And in their bed of luxury they hide behind the lies of the images and marketing of the artists from the record buying kids whose adoration is the symbol of success and sunlight the artists bask in.

In summary the mask or perceived image of Marc Bolan dances in the world of the music industry, his music and creativity running before him keeping the darkness away. The few who have been loyal will also bask in the glory, whether it is the music or the spoils, now that they/he is free of the record industries controlling executives who feed off other people's talents, whilst keeping out of the limelight themselves.

If this analogy were correct then it would date the poem at around 1971-72 when Marc formed his own label. This is presuming that this poems mask is being worn by a hidden meaning, it may just be an empty husk but that is unlikely.

The poem has an easy flowing style with a simple A-B rhyming format although, as with all the poems in this book, the line-by-line layout and general form can only be guessed at because of the source materials un-groomed presentation. Marc was clearly not satisfied with the last line of this poem and had made a note to re-write it but there is no way to speculate what his discontentment was so the line has to be accepted as it is.

Marc had a strong sense of independence, whereas he was aware of the need for others around him and his need to feed off them, he had a yearning to be in control of his own work, hence the forming of his own record label, although there is an element of truth in the recognition of an egotistical motive, the main inspiration was control. He also had a tendency to discard those who had served their purpose, whether it be because they did not live up to his expectations or had become 'inefficient', as did Steve Took due to his excessive drug taking, or had ceased to be of use like John Peel who stopped plugging Marc as he gained commercial success with 'Ride a White Swan' and gave 'Get It On' what could only be described as a slaughtering review. There was also the element of people who became dispensable when he had learnt all he needed to know from them and bled them dry, managers, musicians, even his wife, June, had served her time along with Tony Visconti, two of the people who it would be thought to be indispensable. This is not to imply that Marc was heartlessly ruthless, his agenda was one of an artist, a creator who needed to communicate his art to as many people as possible, and that is all that really mattered to him, that was the core of his need in life, his purpose and furthermore is the reason that star status mattered so much to him. It is also why he was so prolific, he had so much to convey in a short time. There is no value in being a singer, a poet, a musician or a writer, if no one is listening, and no point if what you are saying is not being understood. To be heard you have to be where people can hear you, you have to become famous and what you say has to be credible. There are also many tools needed to attain that status, people were one of those tools, not in a conscious exploitation but more as one would eat of a meal until satisfied. Marc would simply take the nourishment he required from life for his objectives, his goals and his aspirations. His brother, Harry, described him as a 'reaper of information', which perfectly summarizes Marc's attitude to life, in every aspect. Although he could appear ruthless at times, the 'reaping' of knowledge/information characteristic is a necessary facet to anyone who needs to achieve and there is an element of that in everyone to varying degrees; everyone asks for a friend's advice or help, and has in turn been asked, it is by the trading of each other's knowledge and resources that we survive and develop, this is not, therefore, a criticism of Marc, more an appreciation of the intensity of his absorption, which could be described as his leading philosophy of life, to absorb, to take as much out of every aspect of life he could in order to regurgitate it in his own format.

The inbuilt drive of a creative individual to succeed in their ambition to be heard in which ever medium their creativity demands, can be overpowering and as previously stated, can appear ruthless but it is more likely that the host of the ambition is blinded by the intensity of that ambition, their work being a fundamentally integral part of their whole existence. In much the same way as most mothers are overwhelmed with devotion to their children and will sacrifice anything for their well being, in extreme cases appearing to be oblivious to the feelings and needs of others. Most people have a multitude of ambitions in the various categories of life and strive to balance them carefully against each other, a happy relationship, a good home, a reasonable career, healthy happy children and all the materialistic 'necessities' that the modern, commercial indoctrinations bestow upon us. To a creative person their work is their child, they give it birth, life, it is the spawn of their inner self, their soul, and is their passionate reason for existence. There is an inevitable conflict with the necessity to be a part of the world and to be heard that can lead to frustrations and impatience at having to deal with that world. Marc was fortunate for most of his career in having a good diplomat by his side, his wife June Child, who constantly mediated on his behalf, enabling him to be free to tend his children.

Marc Bolan secreted creativity from every pore of his existence and that secretion yearned to be fed, everything needs water to grow and survive and life was Marc's water in every aspect. The reaper of knowledge reaped constantly and although he may have appeared ruthless at times he was blinded by the necessity to nurture his children. When his offspring were well and growing, Marc was well, but when he felt they were safe he neglected them for a while, and they did as all children do, they misbehaved.

Up to the success that came with 'Ride a White Swan', 'Electric Warrior' and ''Slider' Marc Bolan constantly tended his creations and their source, the yearning to reach that goal of success being his predominant motivation but once there would have been a subconscious tendency to relax and enjoy the accolade his offspring received, and a feeling of security in the momentum they gathered. As when children leave home, the parent has a sense that the pressure is off, and although may champion the child's independence and achievements, forgets for a moment that there are a whole batch of new problems that the child must face and in that moment of relaxation, deservedly taken, the child will wander. This is what Marc Bolan did; he relaxed into the success of his creations and as he neglected them they became wayward, he fed them less healthily, drink and drugs was not their best diet and they lost their way. As soon as he realised and improved their diet then they began to respond.

He began to feed again off other people, off other music, absorbing the inspiration of the punk culture, which began to nourish his imagination, he had a new creative partner in Gloria and the musical banter between them quenched the thirst of his imagination and his agenda was broadened by the birth of their son.

The implication that Marc was ruthless is a harsh criticism; no one interviewed has described him in that way. He has been described as handsome, warm, gentle, charismatic, and a gentleman. Daralyn Gold (as she was in 1965) went to the William Wordsworth School and although she is five years younger than Marc and did not mix with him at school, she still remembers him and in particular being in the famous and relatively newly located Marquee Club in Wardour Street at the age of thirteen and finding Mark Feld standing beside her. She was at a Radio London show on a Saturday afternoon and got chatting to Marc. After the show he insisted on seeing her safely to the bus stop and even got on the bus with her to make sure she got home safely. "He was a really nice, genuine guy. He could have taken liberties...young girl...up the West End on her own...but he didn't. He wasn't like that at all. He was a very caring, sensitive person. It is such a shame that he died so young. I was terribly upset when he died."

There is another, extremely interesting revelation from this story, Daralyn recalls that while they were talking Marc was suddenly introduced and called up on to the stage to perform. She remembers it as being his first record and that he was still under the name of Mark Feld. It can be surmised that the song Marc performed was 'The Wizard'. This is all quite plausible as a man who moved in the same circles as Bolan, a young Davie Jones and the Manish Boys had already performed at the Marquee on November 4th 1964; Davie Jones was soon to become David Bowie and to gain a residency at the Marquee as David Bowie and the Lower Third in September 1965. Bowie's close friend, George Underwood designed Bolan's first album cover.

Marc had a real zest for life and everyone who came into contact with him describes him as magical and a pleasure to be around; he enjoyed being around interesting individuals and had a certain intensity of gratifying banter and debate. He was extremely articulate, a natural showman and performer, even in the private zone of the studio he would perform as if on stage. This bright, friendly, charismatic ambience that he carried through life endeared him to people and enabled him to draw them close so he could absorb their contribution to his crop. Even those who had been 'discarded' remained endeared to him, a common quote being 'It was a pleasure to have known him' and even his wife June, who he had hurt immensely, never lost her love for him, although she was as much a victim of Marc's absorption as anyone, "In the end I came to feel that I had nothing more to give him; I was drained; I was absolutely used up."

Each person who describes Marc draws on the same adjectives, one of the commonest being 'determined', he had a blind, driving determination to be successful and to get his words and music out but when he achieved that success there was an enigmatic aura as he relished the role, as if he had spent years journeying the world to find a new city, but when he reached his destination had no map and did not know where to go next, he was not prepared for the next part of his journey. Marc spent a while wandering the dark streets, lost, until he became familiar, with his new environment. This is not a suggestion that Marc was out of his depth, he wasn't, he had found his true role, his purpose in life…the Rock Star…the Rock Poet… and he indulged every moment but after a short while of gluttony at the banquette of stardom there would have been a sense of 'Well I'm here, what do I do now? Am I as good as I have said I am? Am I as good as they expect me to be? Can I deliver?'

And despite the outward façade of arrogant confidence and his constant self-promotion there would have been an inner well of insecurity growing in depth and when record sales finally began to wane and the critics turned the colour of their ink to a less favourable shade the well would have grown even deeper. Marc kept his external mask of make-up intact as much as he could, but the truth began to show as he not only hid behind the make-up but behind the drink and drugs, the make-up became thicker but camouflaged less and Marc Bolan became, for a while, the empty husk.

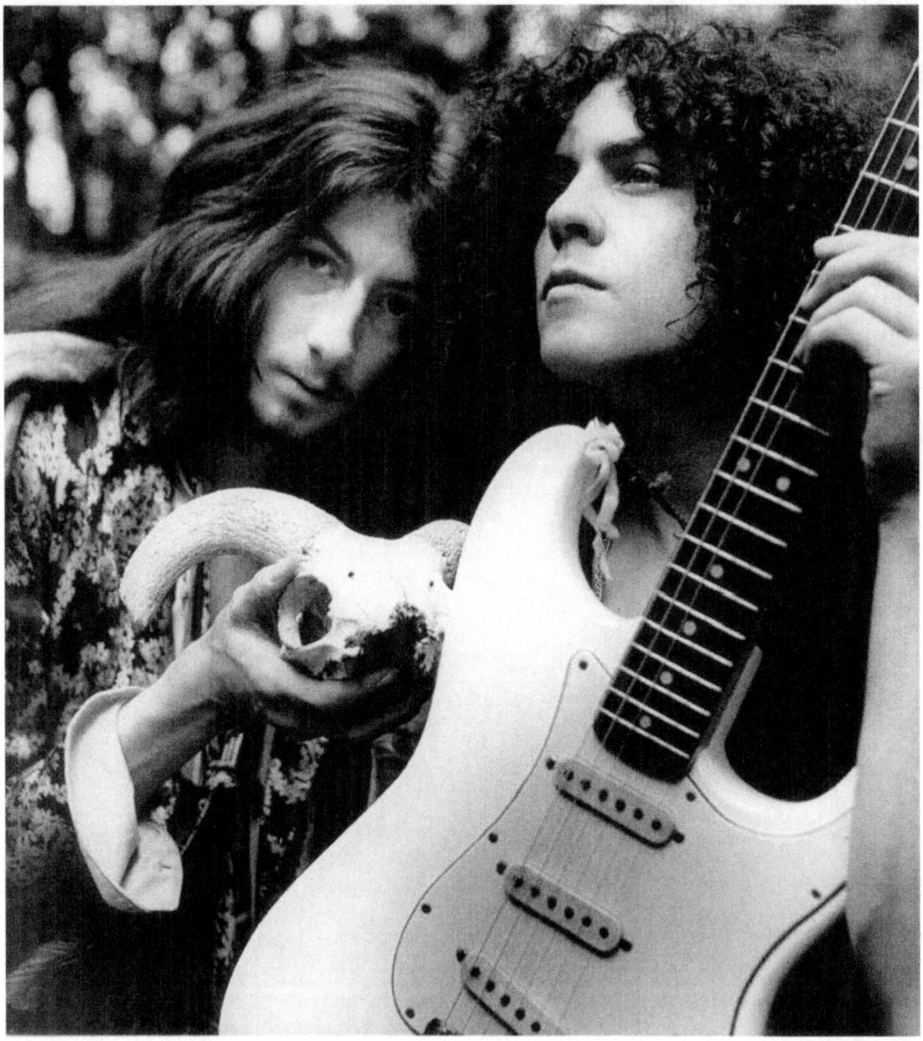

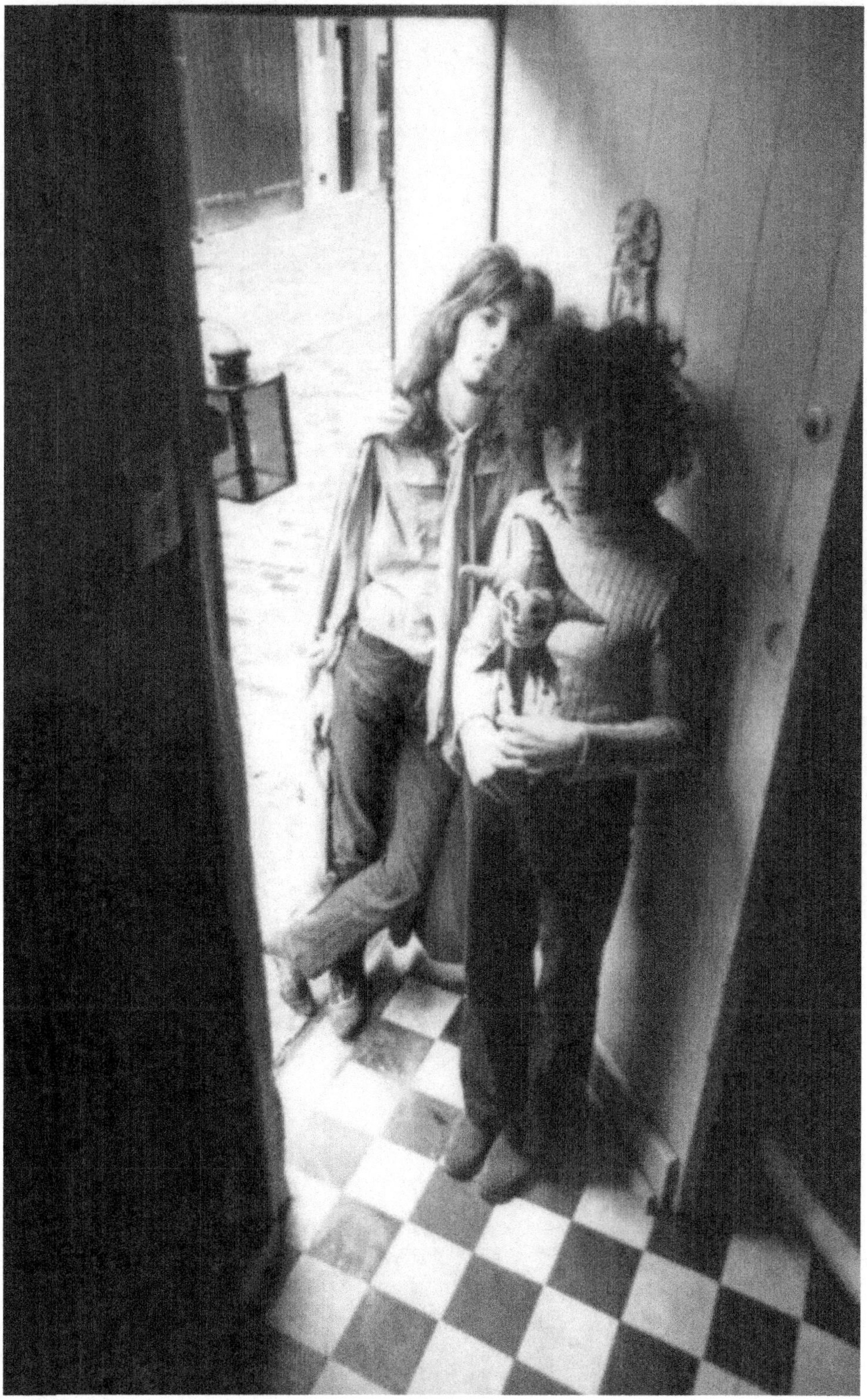

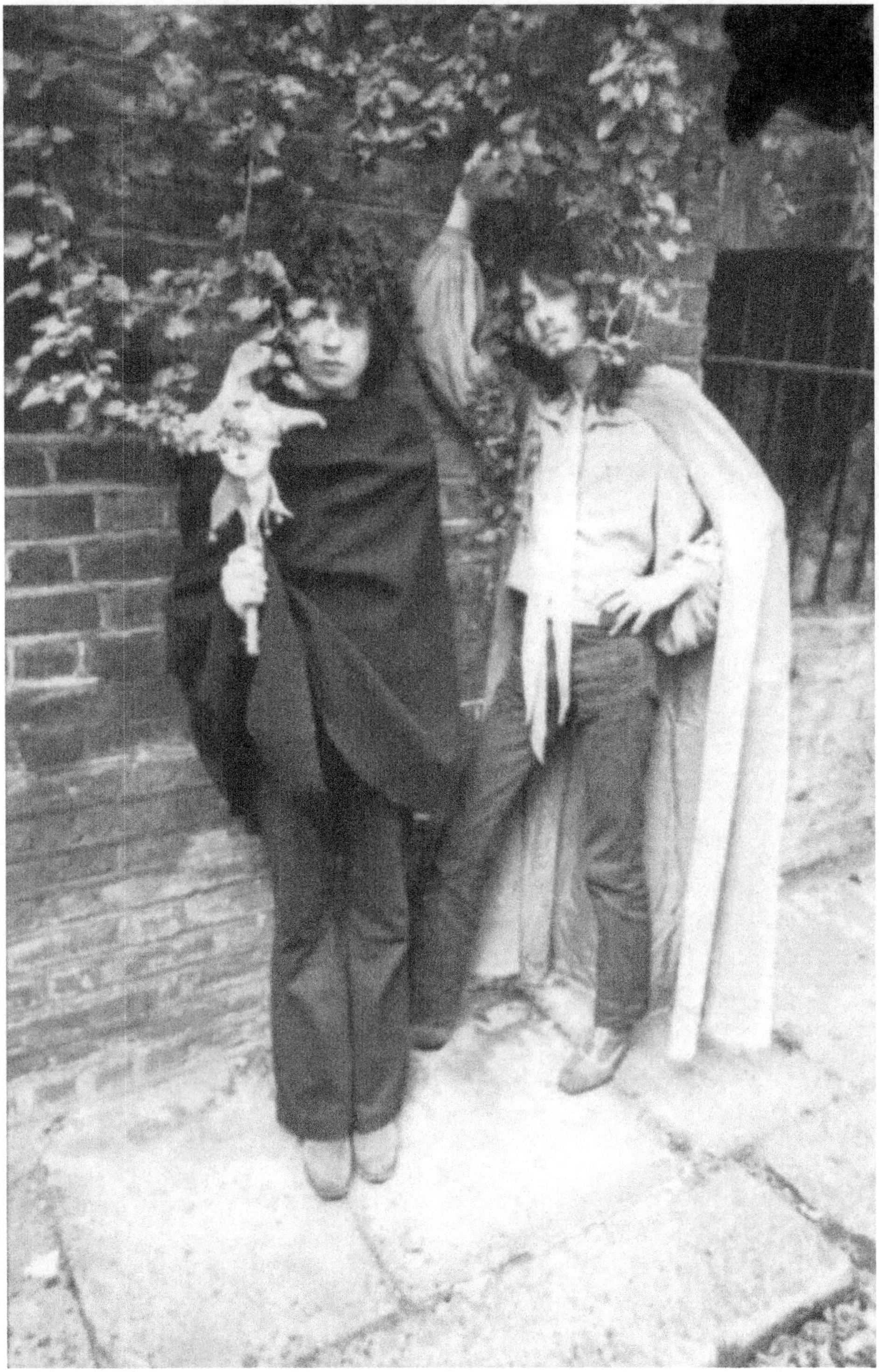

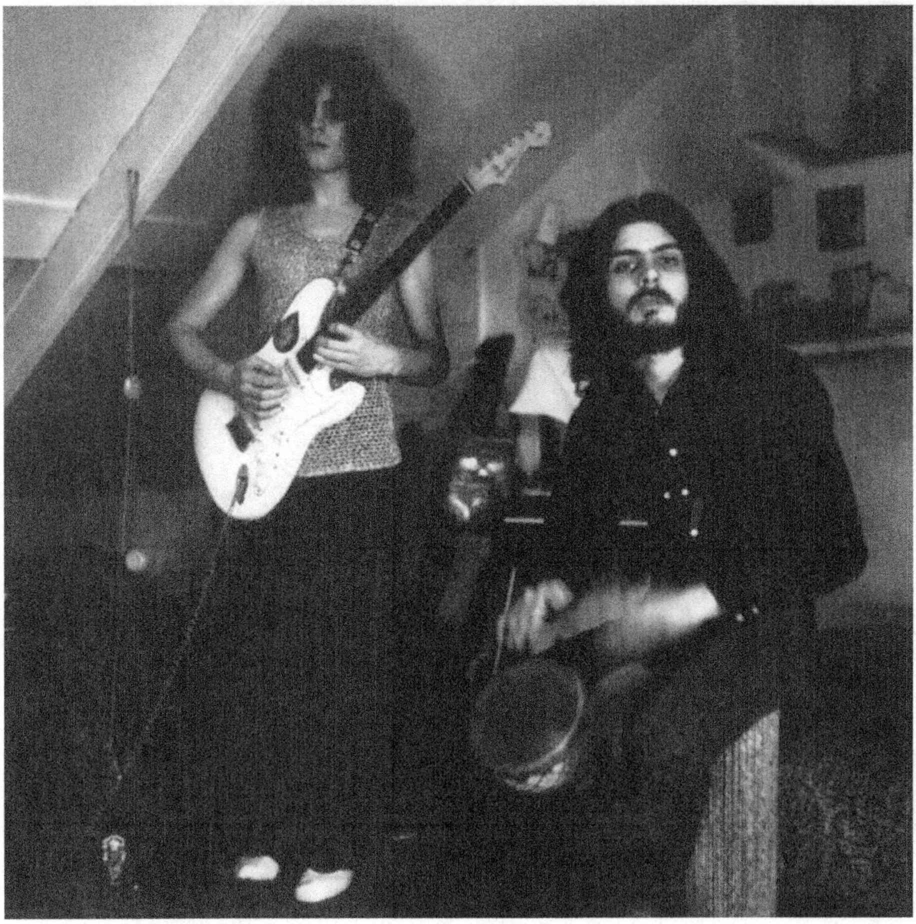

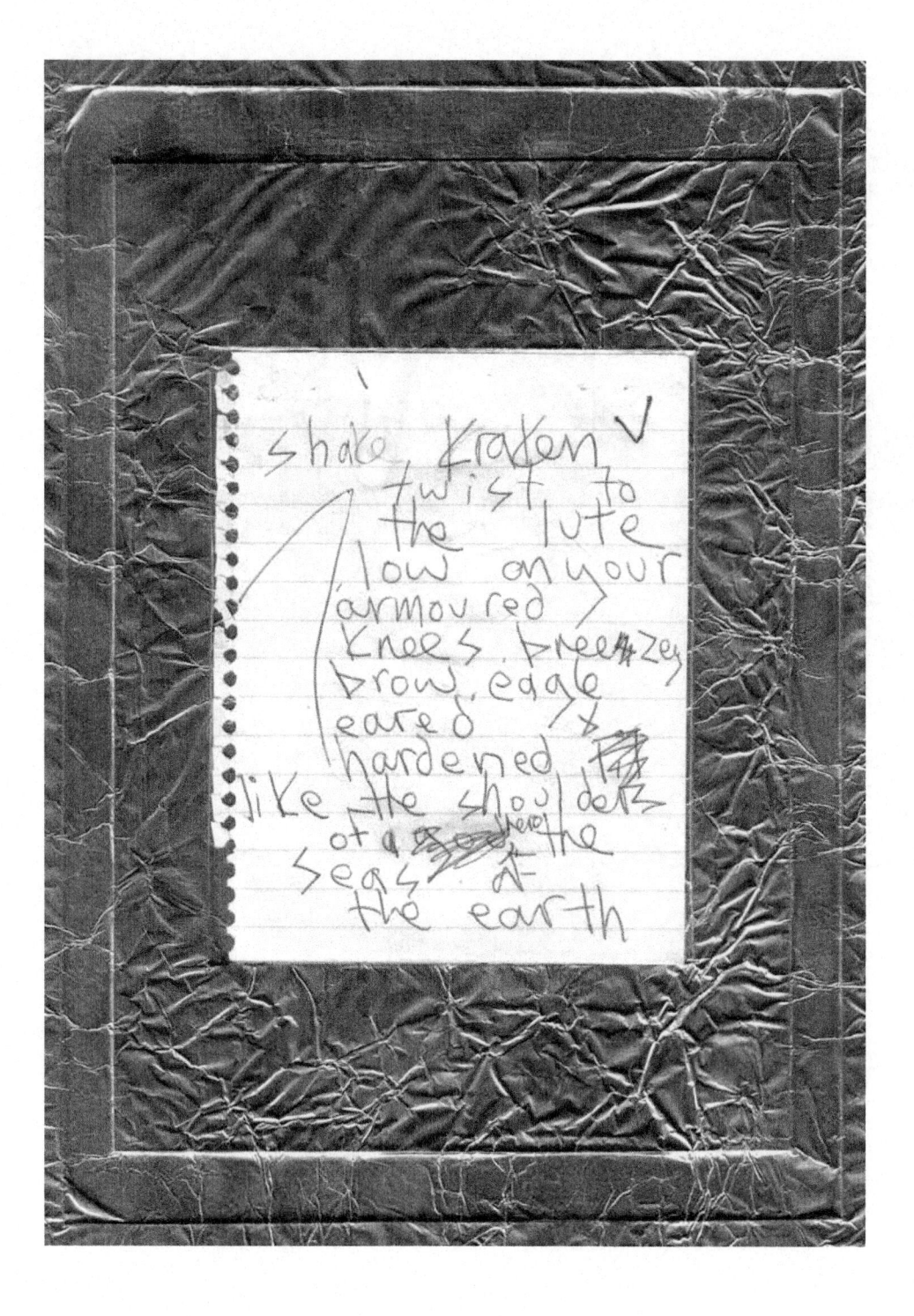

shake, kraken
twist to
the lute
low on your
armoured
knees, breezey
brow, edge
eared
hardened
like the shoulders
of a ~~soo~~ the
seas of
the earth

2

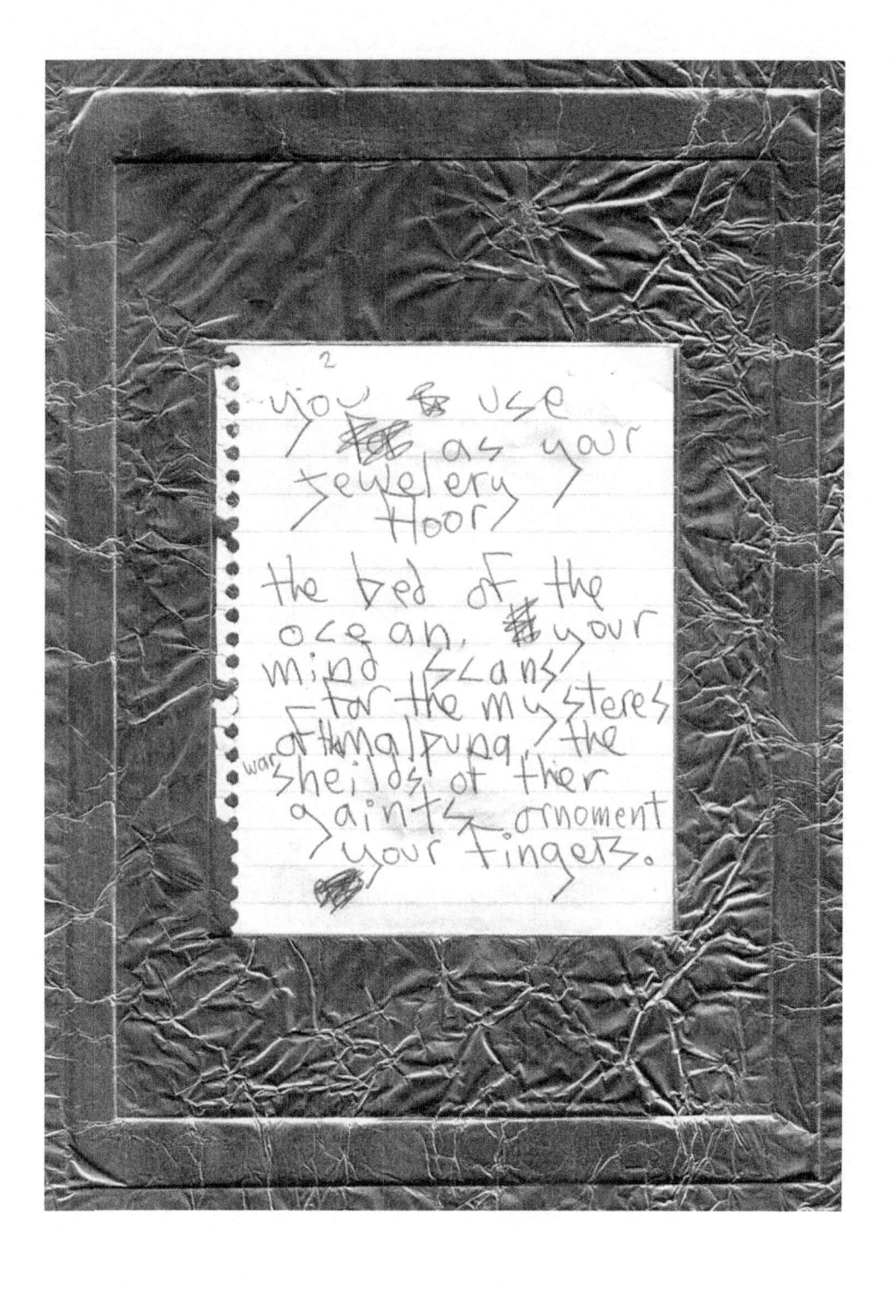

you use
as your
jewelery
floor

the bed of the
ocean, your
mind scans
for the mysteres
of Himalpuna, the
sheilds of ther
saints ornoment
your fingers.

3

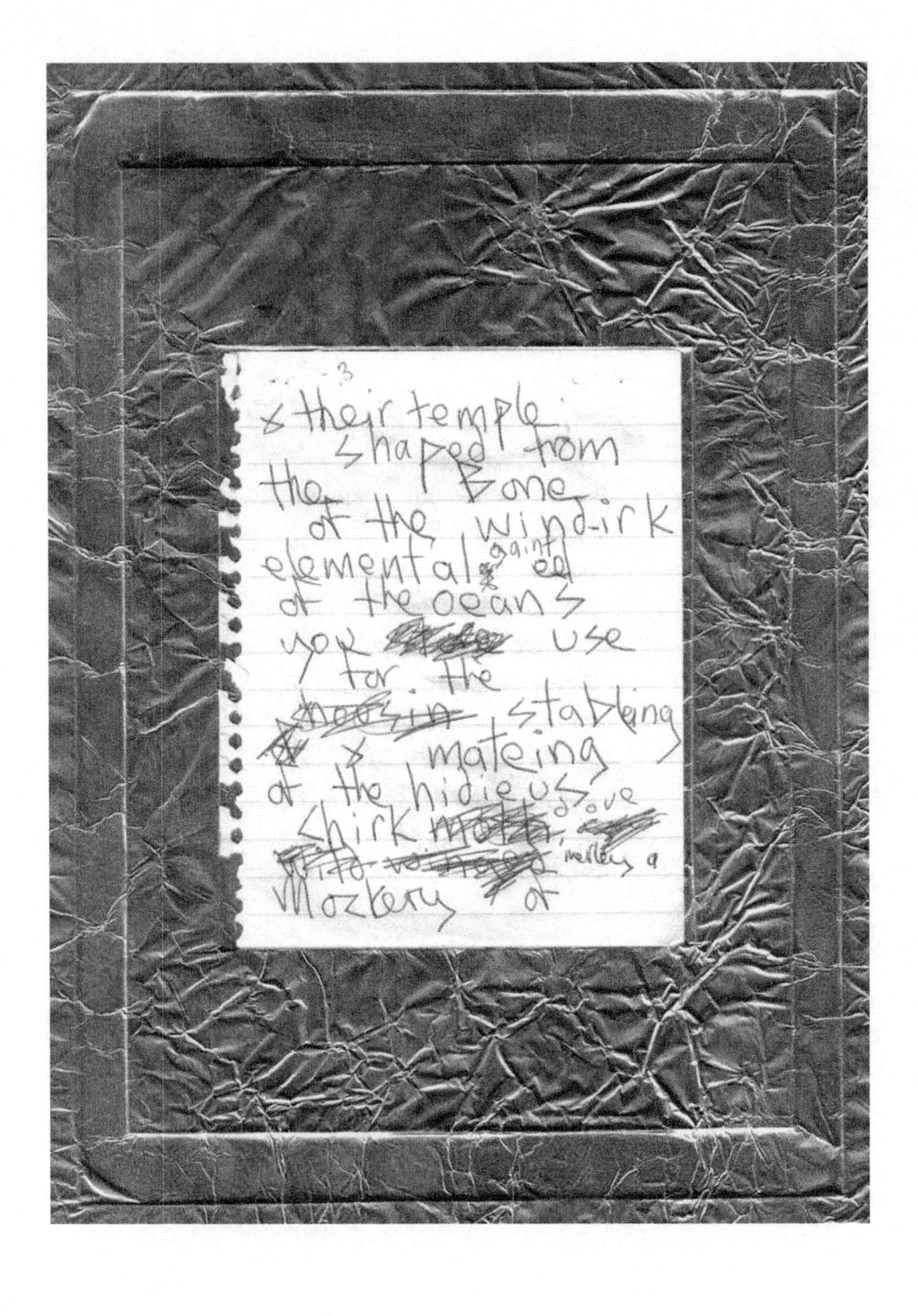

& their temple shaped from the bone of the wind-irk elemental against eel of the oceans you ~~rides~~ use for the ~~noesin~~ stabling & mateing of the hidieus dove shirk ~~moth~~ ~~into to these~~ meklay a mockery of

~~the flying~~

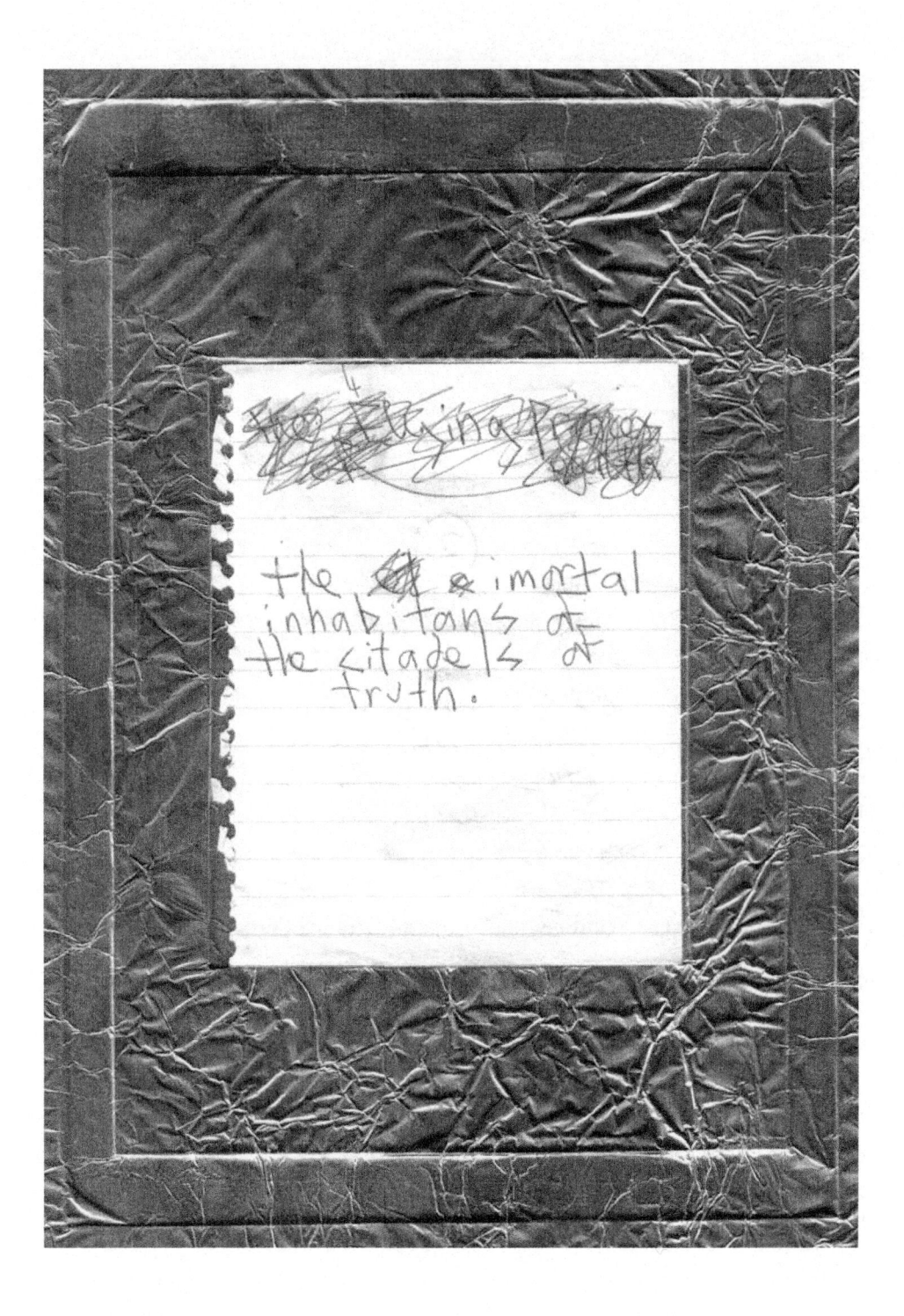

the imortal inhabitans of the citadels of truth.

5. **Citadels of Truth**

"Money is very important…it buys you freedom…it allows you to…if you want…to be a tramp." Marc Bolan 1972.

Shake Kraken,

Twist to the lute

Low on your armoured knees.

Breezy brow, eagle eared

And hardened like the shoulders of a hero,

In the seas of the earth

You use as your jewellery floor

The bed of the ocean,

Your mind scans for the mysteries of the Malpuna;

The war shields of their giants

Ornament your fingers

And their temple,

Shaped from the bone of the Wind-irk,

Elemental giant eel of the oceans,

You use for the stabling

And mating of the hideous Chirk dove,

Merely a mockery of the immortal inhabitants

Of the citadels of truth.

In contrast to the previous poem, this one wears no mask. It is a picture from Bolan's imagination, inspired by Lord Alfred Tennyson's 'The Kraken' and is of a similar length and form with parallels that can be drawn between the content of both pieces.

Below the thunders of the upper deep,

Far far beneath in the abysmal sea,

His ancient, dreamless, uninvaded sleep

The Kraken sleepeth: faintest sunlights flee

About his shadowy sides: above him swell

Huge sponges of millennial growth and height;

And far away into the sickly light,

From many a wondrous grot and secret cell

Unnumbered and enormous polypi

Winnow with giant fins the slumbering green.

There hath he lain for ages and will lie

Battering upon huge seaworms in his sleep,

Until the latter fire shall heat the deep;

Then once by men and angels to be seen,

In roaring he shall rise and on the surface die.

The Kraken by Lord Alfred Tennyson.

The Kraken is the subject of many ancient mariners' tales; a gigantic sea monster reputed to be able to overcome large ships, ravaging them to the depths. Henry Lee wrote an article for the International Fisheries Exhibition of 1883 dedicated to sea monsters, the Kraken being featured heavily in his work, tales of the beast being in abundance at the time, the following tale being included in his report,

"On the 6th Of July, 1734, there appeared a very large and frightful sea monster, which raised itself so high out of the water that its head reached above our main-top. It had a long, sharp snout, and spouted water like a whale; and very broad flappers. The body seemed to be covered with scales, and the skin was uneven and wrinkled, and the lower part was formed like a snake. After some time the creature plunged backwards into the water, and then turned its tail up above the surface, a whole ship-length from the head. The following evening we had very bad weather."

Henry Lee concludes that this tale relates to a giant squid like creature rather than a sea serpent, which is the assumption that Tennyson works under in his description *'Unnumbered and enormous polypi.'* Lord Tennyson himself has clearly found his inspiration in these stories and reports of his time (1809-1892), he would have been 74 when this particular report by Henry Lee appeared but the stories of the Kraken and similar creatures were quite bountiful and in common rendition at this time in history. Tennyson recounts that the creature of his poem sleeps at the bottom of the sea until the end of the world, *'Until the latter fire shall heat the deep'* and that it shall only be seen once before it dies on the surface of the sea *'Then once by men and angels seen, In roaring he shall rise and on the surface die'*.

Bolan's poem, however, relates more to the Kraken's history and how it has made its habitat on the floor of the ocean, the descriptions employed by Bolan giving an air of mythical depth to his particular narration of the monster. He gives it a past by implying its role in his version of mythology. Tennyson simply describes the creature's position at the bottom of the sea with little attention paid to the creature itself; the gloomy, desolate, stank isolation of its habitat being sufficient to evoke the dreary horror of the Krakens existence, employing the selfsame psychology used in horror films, not quite allowing us to see the monster, thus sustaining the intrigue.

In the film 'Clash of the Titans' the Kraken is the name given to the sea monster sent to kill Andromeda but the name has no true basis in Greek mythology and the film could not have influenced Marc Bolan in any way as it was not released until 1981. The film would have taken its influence from the same places as Marc, the mariner's tales and possibly

Lord Tennyson's poem. Bizarrely Ray Harryhausen's brilliantly animated Kraken bears an uncanny resemblance to Marc's description of the creature rather than the older tales of the sea goers, it has no squid like properties but towers powerfully above the water like a true Greek titan, a giant amongst monsters.

Marc opens his poem commanding the Kraken to shake, to twist to the sound of the lute whilst on its knees in submission; with the lute being a guitar like instrument, Marc is almost implying that he has the monster under control with his music.

Breezy brow, eagle eared,

Breezy used in this context means careless, carefree and almost defiant in the face of his dominator. He then goes on to describe it as rugged and strong like the shoulders of a hero, although Marc originally wrote

And hardened like the shoulders of a god

he has replaced god with what appears to be hero (whilst Nero is a possible interpretation of Marc's writing it would not make true sense so hero has been used).

Marc then describes the monsters habitat. The liberty has been taken to add the word "in" at the beginning of the next line in order to assist what is believed to be Marc's intended meaning.

In the seas of the earth

You use as your jewellery floor

The bed of the ocean.

The Kraken keeps his spoils, his treasures hidden in the depths of the oceans while his mind ponders the mysteries of the Malpuna. What is the Malpuna? No conclusive definition has been found, other than a word in the Tulu language meaning *doing* or *do,* which has no relevance to the poem. *Puna* has a number of definitions, it is a district of Big Island near Hawaii, it is a plateau of land between Peru and Bolivia, or with a moderation of significance, it is an island in the Gulf of Guayaquil in Ecuador. The Ecuadorian Punians were a warrior race who had lived under Inca domination but were overcome at the Battle of Puna by the Spanish in 1531, the Spanish going on to conquer the Inca Empire.

'Mal' means wrong or bad as in *malfunction* so it could be deduced that Marc's word play meant wrong *Punians* but this is desperately clutching at straws; it is without doubt that in Marc's imagination the *Malpuna* are a race of people defeated by the Kraken whose trophies he wears.

The war shields of their giants

Ornament your fingers

And whose temple

And their temple,

Shaped from the bone of the Wind-irk,

Elemental giant eel of the oceans,

he defiles with his pets,

You use for the stabling

And mating of the hideous Chirk dove,

Wind-irk and *Chirk dove* are creations of Marc, although 'irk' means to irritate, or is a river near Manchester and 'chirk' means to make cheerful or a shrill chirpy noise, or is a town on the welsh border with the famous Chirk Castle, none of these meanings have any real relevance beyond *irritating wind* and *shrill dove*, although it is known that Marc owned a cottage in Wales so may have taken some inspiration from the Castle or Chirk itself or it is likely they are just more examples of Marc's wordplay. Marc's portrayal of the Malpunan temple being fashioned from the bone of the *Wind-irk*, described as a giant eel of outstanding natural force (elemental), has a possible connection with the Incas of Peru. The Saksayuaman is an Inca temple, part fortress just north of Cusco described as a serpent because it winds back and forth for 600 metres until it reaches the Muiuparka, a structure at it's heart where the Incas performed various rituals; this link is in all likelihood coincidental, it is more probable that the Malpunan's temple is further creation of Marc's imagination.

The final lines

Merely a mockery of the immortal inhabitants

Of the citadels of truth

refers to a God and his entourage or Gods who survey the mortal world from their fortresses of righteousness, *truth*, and that the Krakens use of the Malpunan's temple to them is a contemptuous jest to their authority; the portrayal of the Kraken as a giant, evil monster with no regard or respect for anything is thus completed.

It was stated at the beginning of this chapter that this poem wears no mask and indeed it is felt that that is true, but as with most poems it could be possible to forge a meaning to fit. The Kraken could be regarded as symbolic for many things and Marc's apparent dominance of the character in the early lines a statement that he is in control, whether Marc's Kraken is drink, drugs, the music industry, life in general, money or the gigantism of T-Rex. There are no obvious keys in this piece to unlock any significant meaning, so there would be little point to the mask. It does, however, share inspiration with the afore mentioned and incomplete Krakenmist of Marc's. In this piece Marc also makes reference to Irks in a footnote where he describes Rark Stang, a grotesque monster, as having the hide of an Irk, they must therefore feature in a missing part of the fantasy to warrant the footnote. The Krakenmist is an invisible monster that attacks the warrior priest/wizard Agadinmar who, with the aid of Deene, the son of Rarn, conjures a spell that captures the Krakenmist in an onyx phial. Agadinmar then casts the phial into the sea, at the bottom of which the Krakenmist is doomed to lie forever. Marc gives us a suggestion that this may not transpire to be the end of the monster so it is plausible that the poem was intended as a part of the Krakenmist, which was not necessarily Marc's planned title for the whole work, more probably just a chapter, with the inclusions of Agadinmar and Beltane it is not unreasonable to presume that it is a part of 'The Children of Rarn'. It would appear from the poem that the Krakenmist duly escapes from his prison in a solid visible form, alternatively it could be a flash back to the monsters past, whichever the true analogy the creature had been there long enough to amass a wealth of treasure which it had hidden on the ocean floor far away from any taxmen, as indeed Marc Bolan appears to have done.

On 17th of November 1978, when the administrators were duly appointed to oversee Marc Bolan's estate, the gross value of his UK estate was £30870.59 , the equivalent value of £250,394.00 today. An amount that could not in anyway be described as large, even for the time, considering it was the estate of a rock star who had challenged the Beatles and up to the time of his death was the most successful artist of the seventies. It would be reasonable to expect that a man who worked so extensively at being in control of his career would be in control of the spoils of his work; it is likely that he was but the enigma of Marc Bolan's fortune remains unresolved. He had instigated, before his death, an offshore company, Wizard Bahamas, which to this day remains aloof but in control of his royalties. The true value of his estate and its recipients, therefore, is unknown and open to considerable speculation. The investigation and resolving of this particular aspect of Marc Bolan's life could be as dangerous and as mystical as the Kraken, leading to a book in its own right. More relevant is Marc's attitude to money and wealth; he could not be described as materialistic in any context of the word, not surrounding himself with ostentatious belongings, no fleet of flamboyant cars, extravagant holidays or excessive jewellery. This does not mean that he did not spend his money, he did lightly indulge in the bounties of his success, he had holidays, and he did have cars but not to the lavish, self-indulgent extent that most rock stars excel in spending, such as Elton John. It is more to say that this was not his motivation. Star status and the success of his music, his art were his motivation, money was a tool that gave him the freedom to concentrate on his art he would surround himself with the equipment he needed to perform his role to the best of his ability. In truth most of Marc's possessions were second hand, his three favourite guitars, the distressed Gibson Les Paul and the flying 'V' along with the white teardrop Stratocaster were all second hand; his 1957 white Rolls Royce was over ten years old, and all of the photos taken of Marc at home show him surrounded by 'old' things. It might be interpreted that he took some type of security in the feeling of nostalgia these items possessed, a comfort in the warmth of their history. As an old house has an atmosphere, that comes with its age, a maturity giving it a flavour of life like a vintage wine, as opposed to a new house which can feel clinical and cold. Intriguingly his poems and music carry endless references to the past, spreading from the ancient mythology explored in all of his earlier albums through to his last album, with the most obvious reference to Orpheus but also with the track *Jason B. Sad* being linked to *Johnny B. Goode* by the sleeve subtitle *A distant friend of Johnny B Goode* along with other hints in the lyrics.

There are confusing impressions that were portrayed by Marc about money and wealth. Many times, when he was asked about money in interviews, he appeared evasive, whilst on other occasions he was quite boastful. The truth is he was very candid about his finances and never revealed much, in one late interview he said that he'd taken a year off and spent the lot, but that does not really equate as nobody invests the time and money in buying an elaborate and secret safe if they have nothing to keep in it and Wizard Bahamas was just that an off shore company, set up to avoid the high levels of taxation payable in the UK in the seventies. 98% became payable if earnings exceeded £20,000 along with £2000 income from investments making a total in excess of £22,000 per annum, which is equivalent to over £178,000 today. This means that from current earnings of £178,000, £169,075 would have been payable in tax after the initial tax free allowance, leaving just £8925 for the artist, less other deductions this calculates as only £1100 in 1972. As a result of this excessive taxation many people, including rock stars became tax exiles or set up off shore companies. Simon Napier- Bell himself tells of his move to Spain in 1969 for tax reasons in his revealing book 'Black Vinyl White Powder'. Marc Bolan must have been earning these amounts to warrant the establishing of such an avoidance system.

On one hand Marc would give the impression that money was not of any importance to him, only in so far as it enabled him to buy the freedom he needed to for his art, he had stated that all he bought were records, books, studio time and guitar strings, but he would appear flamboyant with his eccentric wardrobe, although his clothes were a tool of his trade and thus a part of his art. It was as though in his apparent flamboyant extravagance he was playing the perceived role expected of him as a rock and roll star, but on the other hand he was quite frugal with his money and renowned for being hard in business matters. The other band members were notoriously poorly paid, as were many others in the T-Rex entourage. In conflict to this apparent hard business persona Marc appeared to be of a kindly, generous nature, and many people have described him as such, but that approach does not work in a business environment, Marc was mindful of this and knew he had to be in control and aware of his business affairs. After the departure of Tony Secunda in 1972 Marc and June put themselves in control, the stress of desperately trying to manage every aspect of his career and life was, inevitably, a huge strain on Marc Bolan and would have assuredly contributed to his inner struggle, the belief and yearning to be in control verses the practicalities of the reality. Whereas Marc was not classically materialistic he understood the importance of money and all that it enabled for him. This was a man who had with awesome determination, devoted every element of his life to becoming a rock star there was no room for failure, in any way. He had committed himself so completely, his appearance, personality, his self-belief and ultimately the act of becoming his own image that he would have seen the fruits of his success as his duly justified reward, his right! He would remember the days he'd spent as a busker, hustling to get through each day. The sacrifices he had made in devotion to his quest would have led to a sense of power he would have felt in being the epicentre of his own success.

This magnanimous position he had aspired to, empowered him, financially, to bestow his 'wisdom' and 'generosity' upon others, such as the Dammed and other up and coming punk bands, this would also have boosted his ego and whereas the money itself was not important to Marc Bolan, where money placed him, what it enabled him to do and achieve was.

Money was a cog in the gear box of the rock star machine that Marc Bolan had constructed; a cog that needed regular lubrication and maintenance for the machine to move at any speed, and without that cog, the machine would cease to function. Finding efficient mechanics had proved difficult so it became necessary for him to service the machine himself, with the aid of apprentices. There is a significant difference between the cog and the resulting finished product, which is the ultimate purpose of the machine. For many artists money is the resulting product; the music, the performing and the star role-playing are merely cogs in their machine, financial success being the sole purpose of the machine and they will do anything to attain that product. For Marc Bolan it was the opposite, to produce credible rock star status was his machines purpose, money was an essential part of that machine but along with many other essential parts.

This analysis is true for all roles in life, particularly the world of the arts. It is one thing to recognise the importance of money and its contribution to life and art as a tool but another to place money in the position of being the ultimate purpose. Outwardly the apparent appearance of difference in motive is subtle, but the true meaning of that difference is gigantic. If money is the ultimate motive then the art is shallow and holds little substance and will not sustain in its existence. The result in music is the 'one hit wonder' syndrome and an extensive catalogue of annoying songs that the whole world desperately tries to forget as soon as they have experienced their minute of fame. If money is kept firmly in its role as a tool then the resulting art has more depth of meaning and is more likely to be conceived with the DNA of credibility and substance, giving birth to a stronger, healthier art, which will survive into a natural longevity of respect.

From a rock star's perspective the extremes of the resulting difference is that of either being willingly forgotten as a quick money-spinning pawn of the music industry profiteers, like 'Mr. Blobby', or attaining a long standing 'legendary' status in the halls of rock fame, such as Jim Morrison, Jimi Hendrix, John Lennon, Roy Orbison and many others. As with all extremes there are various shades of grey along the connecting scale; Marc Bolan, with his approach and attitude, undoubtedly falls at the John Lennon, Jimi Hendrix end of the scale.

Peter Sanders fondly remembers Marc as being very mystical and spiritual, as do many people, and in no aspect materialistic, but does recall him saying that one day he would buy his own island, where he would resume his spiritual development, perhaps that was Marc Bolan's secret agenda and money was merely his tool for attaining that goal, or maybe he simply enjoyed the freedom to boogie.

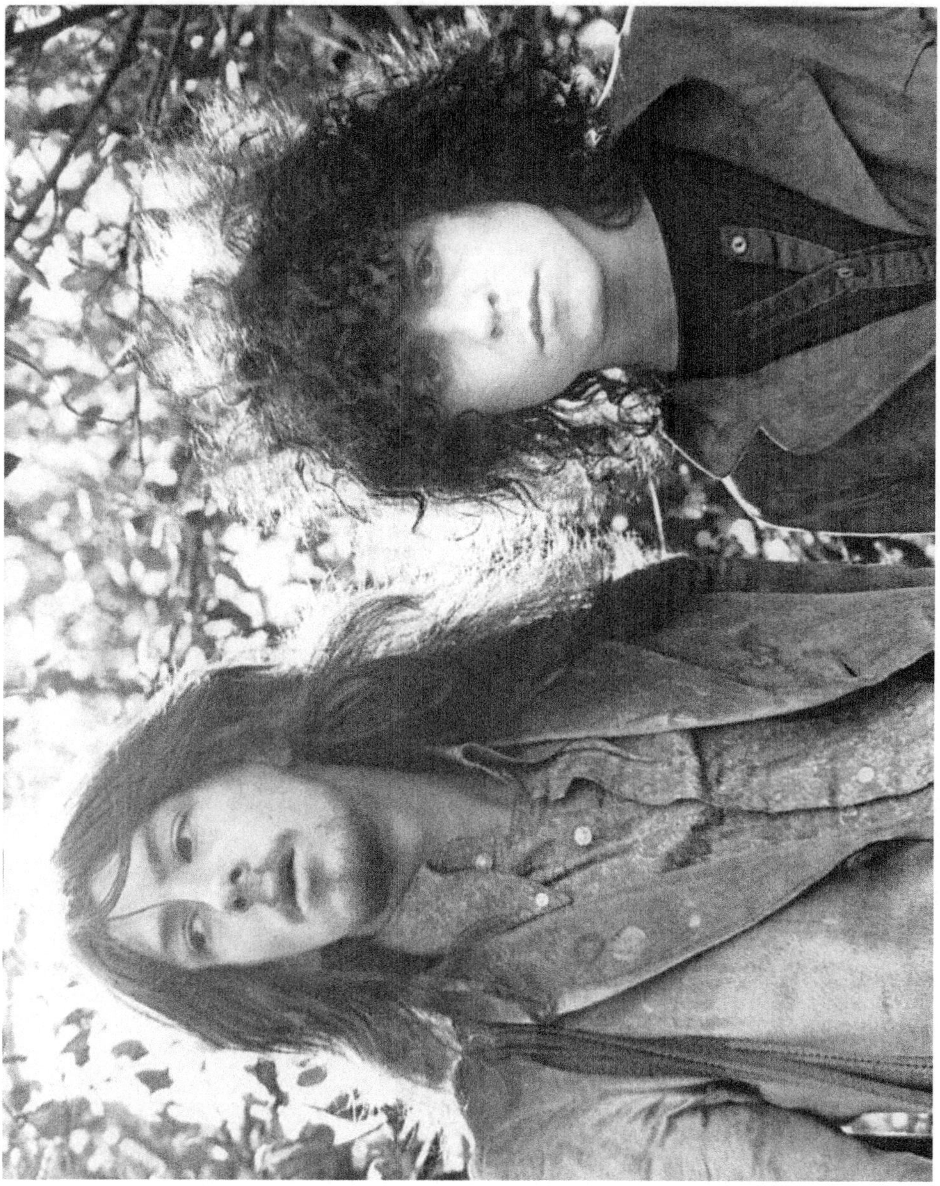

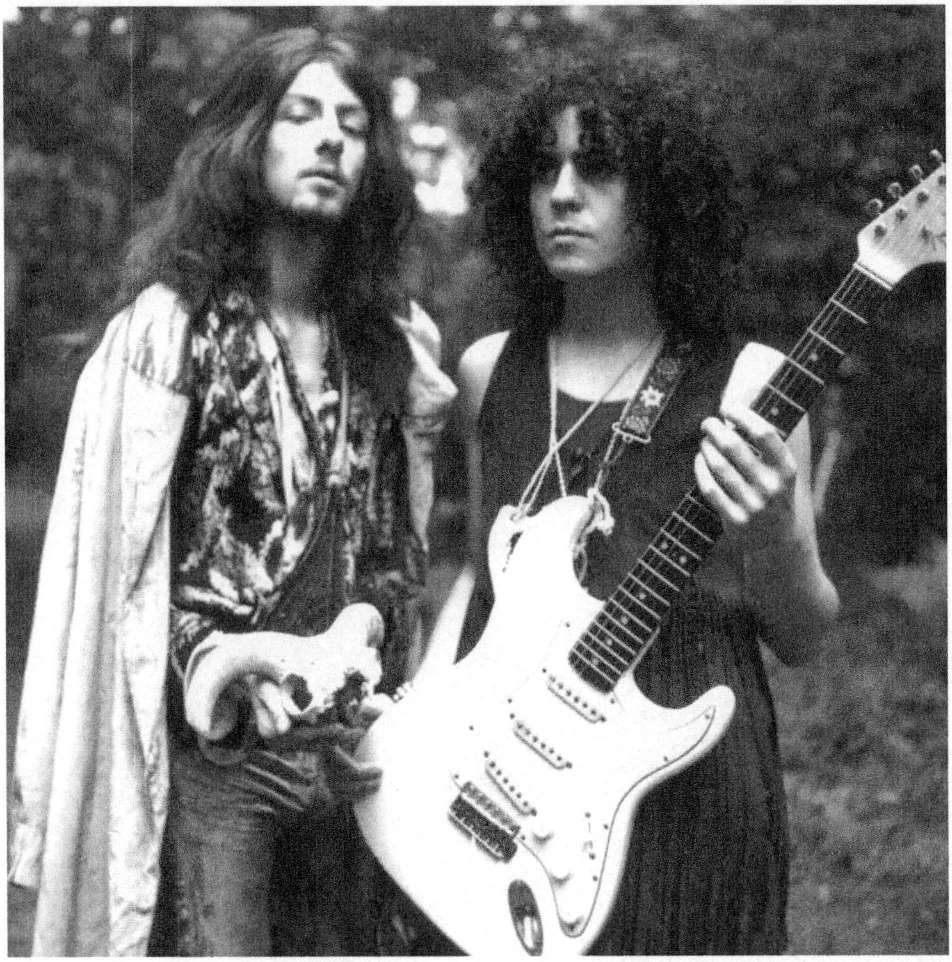

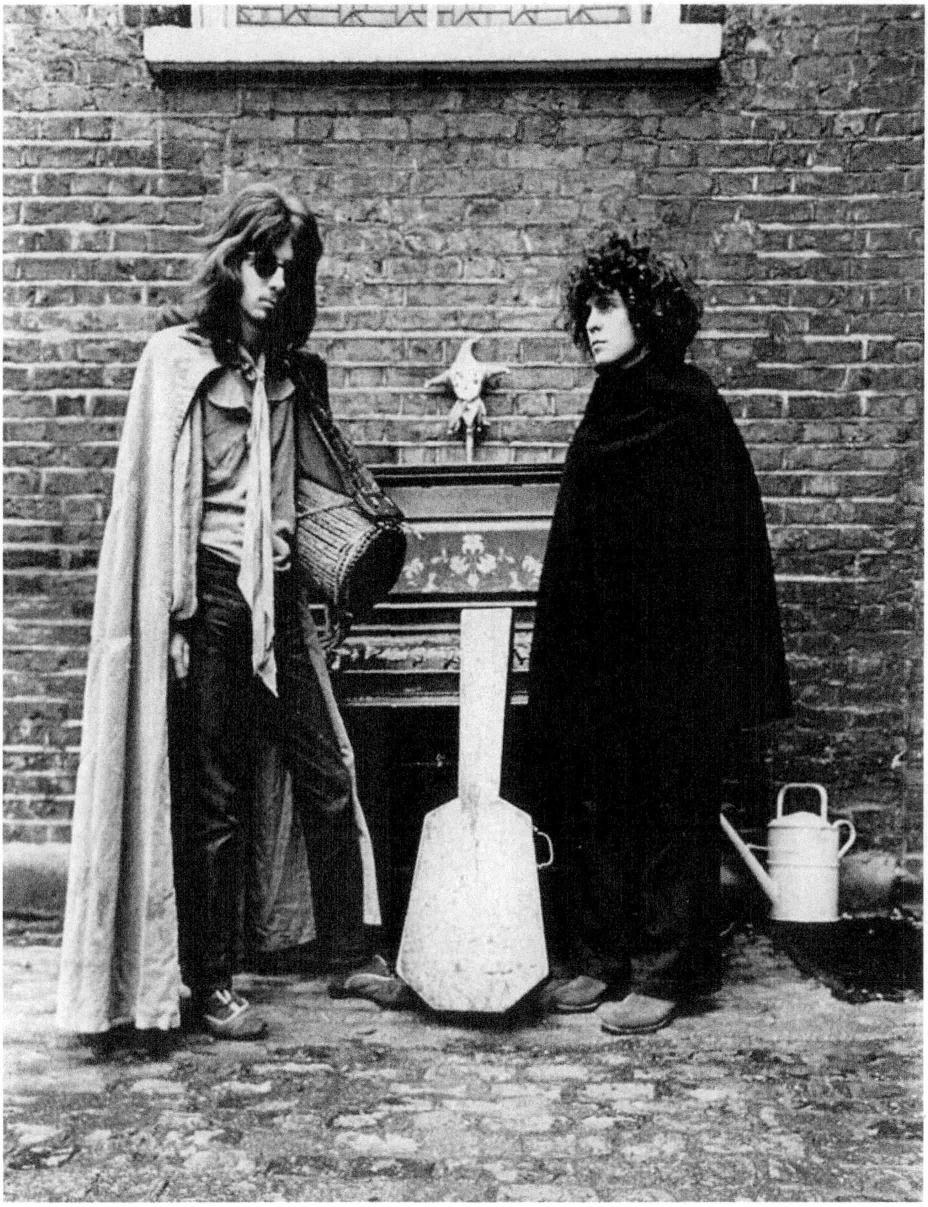

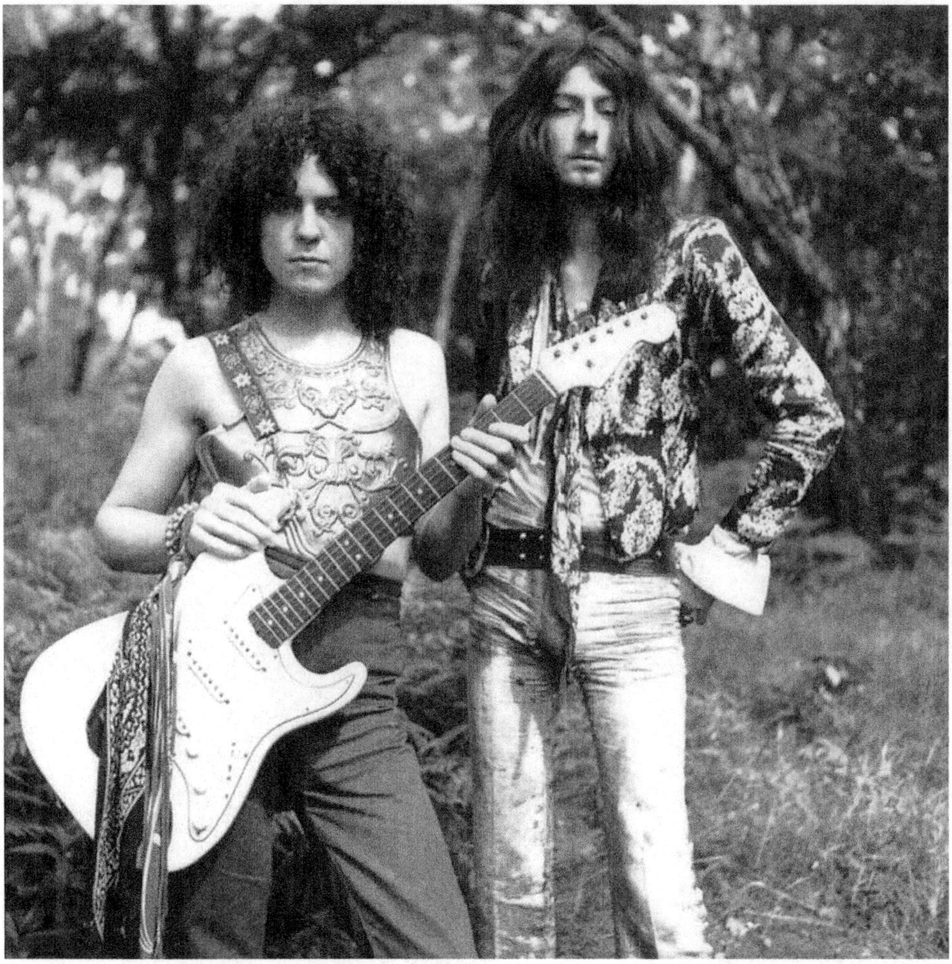

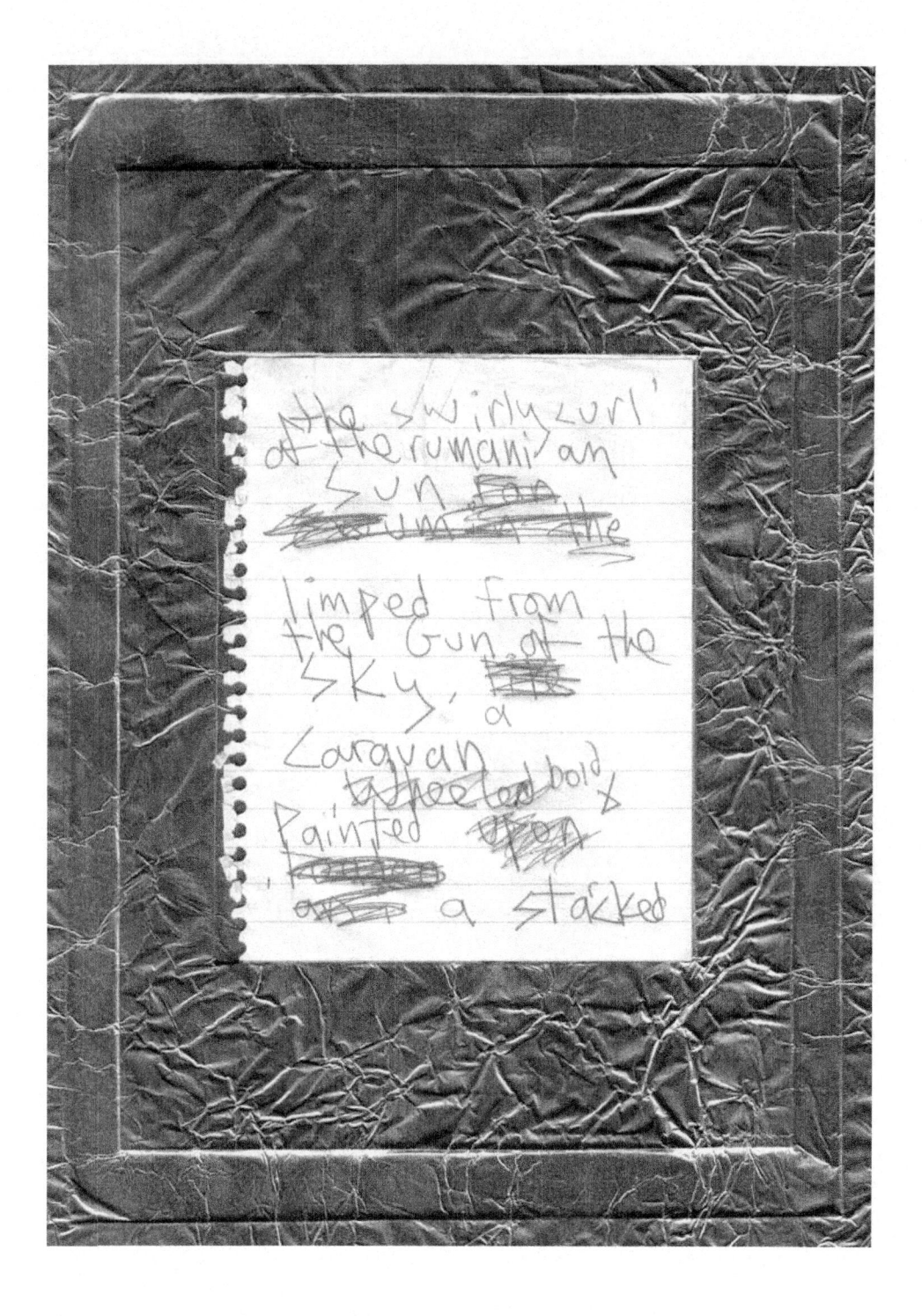

the swirly curl'
of the rumanian
sun ~~sun~~ ~~sound in the~~

limped from
the Gun of the
sky, a
caravan
~~wheeled~~ bold &
painted ~~pen~~
a stacked

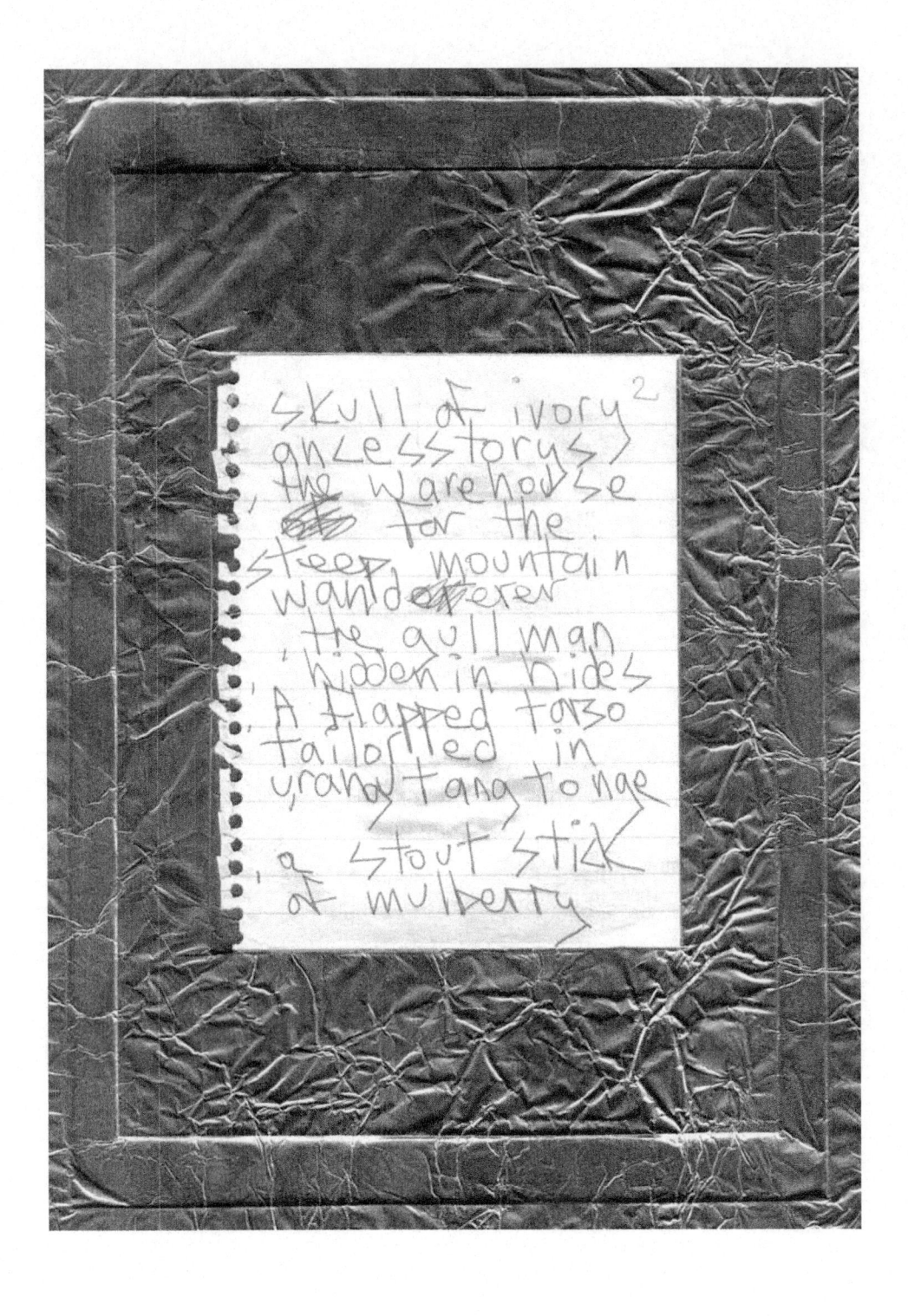

skull of ivory[2]
ancesstorys
the warehouse
~~as~~ for the
~~steep~~ mountain
wand~~erer~~
the gull man
hidden in hides
A flapped tarso
tailorted in
urangtangtonge
a stout stick
of mulberry

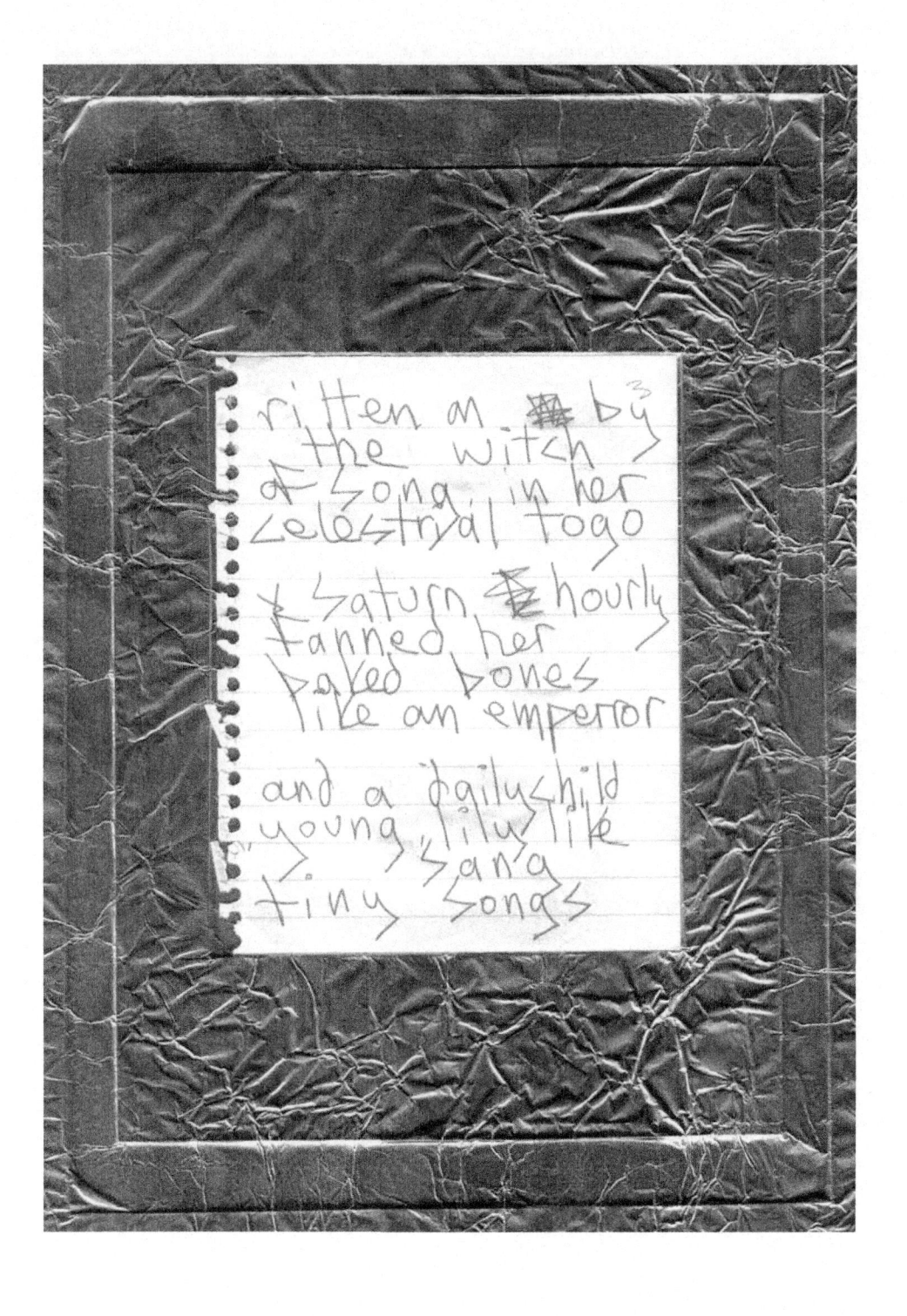

ritten on by
the witch
of song in her
celestrial toga

Saturn hourly
fanned her
baked bones
like an emperor

and a daily child
young lily like
sang
tiny songs

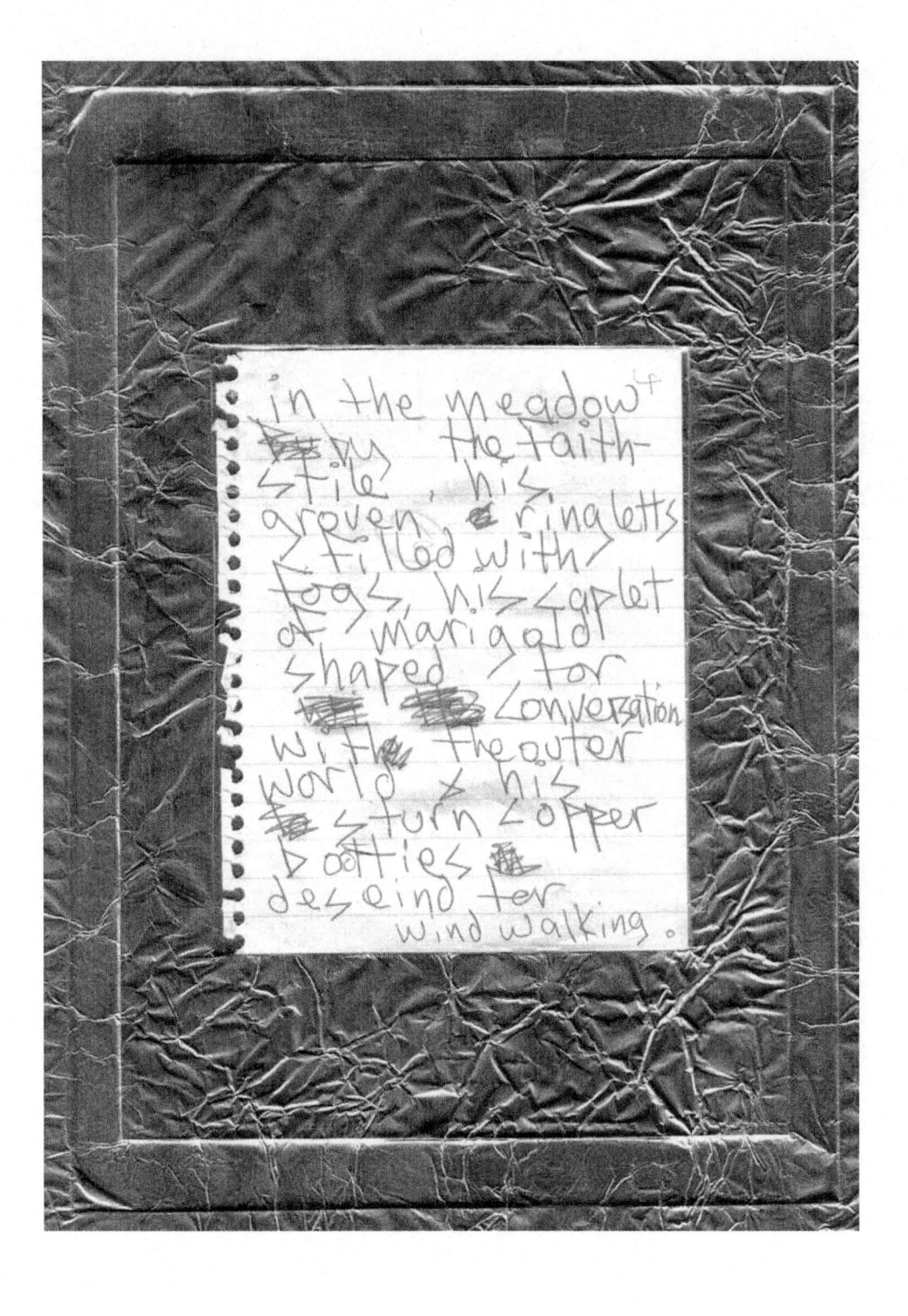

in the meadow
by the faith-
stile, his
groven ringletts
filled with
fog, his goblet
marigold
shaped for
conversation
with the outer
world, his
turn copper
botties
deseind for
wind walking.

6. **Witch Songs**

"I've only got one life, which is rock 'n' roll." Marc Bolan 1972.

The swirly curl of the Rumanian Sun

Limped from the gun of the sky.

A caravan, bold painted

A starked skull of ivory ancestors,

The warehouse for the steep mountain wanderer,

 The Gullman, hidden in hides,

A flapped torso

Tailored in Orang-utan tongue,

A stout stick of mulberry

Written on by the witch of song

In her celestial toga

And Saturn hourly fanned her baked bones

Like an emperor,

And a daily child,

Young lily like,

Sang tiny songs in the meadow

By the faith stile.

His groven ringlets filled with fogs,

His caplet of marigold

Shaped for conversation

With the outer world,

And his stern copper booties

Designed for wind walking.

It is essential to remember that the source of the poetry forming the nucleus of this book is from the notebooks of Marc Bolan and as every writer is fully aware, especially with poetry, notebooks do not necessarily hold the finished product. A trap that is easy to fall into is to believe that these are the finished versions, ready to go to print but that is not the case, they are versions of work in progress, there is not the luxury of being able to refer them to Marc for amendment and they have not been submitted by Marc for publication. He may have discarded some of them or totally re-written them before publishing, honing their form and content or used them as stimulation for something else. They are sketches in preparation for the final masterpiece, notes of the idea or inspiration, much akin to a demo tape which is far removed from the fully polished and produced song. Many works take on a completely different direction from their original form, being reworked to fit a new context or to become part of a larger piece. It will never be known what Marc's intentions were for the poetry housed here, educated assumptions can only be made.

All of the pages published are from a selection of loose sheets which have been torn from the notebook; some of the pieces may be incomplete and although every effort has been made to collate them correctly (all of the pages being numbered by Marc has assisted immensely in that respect along with the different coloured pens and pencils used), there may be pages missing from the ends of the poems which could place them in a completely different context or link them to another piece. However it is only possible to work with what is available and careful consideration has been made of each poem, although it is unfair to be too critical of the *unfinished* works. Evaluation is still justified provided that it is remembered that these are not necessarily Marc's finished versions.

The emphasis of this consideration is particularly relevant in evaluating this chapters poem, It has many interesting points and, as with most of Marc's poetry, a very magical, mythical descriptivety that is enriched with imagery of an outlandish nature. Unfortunately it has no direction, there is no purpose to this piece, no statement, no story, and even the picture painted is incomplete and disjointed. To such an extent that it would be conceivable to conclude that the poem has been collated wrongly, but it is the simplest of the selection to collate, because it is the only one to be written in red ink; the lines flow convincingly from one page to the next and the parts that appear to be disjointed fall mid-page so there is no possibility of any pages missing or any lost additions. Marc often added insertions or corrections on the back of the preceding page, linked by an arrow to their intended position in the piece, but there is no evidence of that here, nothing but the circled number six on the back of the last page, of which there is no apparent relevance.

The opening lines set the geography of the scene,

The swirly curl of the Rumanian Sun

Limped from the gun of the sky

which is the modern day Romania on what is described as a dull day, the sunlight limping from the gun of the sky, intimating that it is struggling to penetrate the clouds. This description evokes the image of the Sun being shrouded by misty, tumbling clouds giving the appearance of swirling rings of sunlight with odd rays breaking through the clouds, like shots from a gun.

Again there is the link to ancient mythology, the early inhabitants of Romania were the Dacians, Getae and the Thracians, all had close links and relations with the Greeks and Romans, sharing similar if not the same mythology and religions. This central European region has always been heavily populated, being environmentally conducive to life and Romania, being geographically central to a number of countries, has naturally absorbed a variety of cultures which have amalgamated to form it's own. Because of it's natural conduciveness, the area now known as Romania has a history of a human population preceding that of Greece and Rome, as does Bulgaria, formerly Thrace, just south of Romania. The roots of much of the commonly accepted Grecian mythology originate from these regions, Thrace itself playing an important role in Greek history. It is believed that Orpheus was born in the Rhodopi Mountains of Thrace and many Greek legends have encompassed these regions, including the previously mentioned Dionysus. It is certainly acceptable to describe the central areas of the now named Romania and Bulgaria as being under a Rumanian Sun as they were fairly nebulous in ancient times.

Almost immediately the poem becomes disjointed, reading like an inventory of mystical images and items. A caravan, a skull, the Gullman, a torso, a stick, a witch, a toga, Saturn, an emperor, and finally the daily child where the poem seems to find some direction.

A caravan, bold painted

A starked skull of ivory ancestors,

The caravan appears randomly from no apparent origin its only purpose to lead us to the Gullman. It is described as being boldly painted and made from the bare (starked) skull of a mammoth, *ivory ancestors* implying the ancestors of elephants. Mammoths were relatively common in central Europe up to 4000 years ago and the vision of the enormous skull of the large mammal being turned into a caravan is a surreal one. It is then portrayed as a storage vehicle for the mountain wanderer, the Gullman.

The warehouse for the steep mountain wanderer,

The Gullman, hidden in hides,

This area of Europe is fairly mountainous, from the Rhodopi Mountains, where Orpheus was born, in southern Thrace (Bulgaria) to the northern Balkan range, moving up to the Transylvanian Alps and finally reaching the Carpathian Mountains in the north east of Romania. Mountain wanderers were quite common place; also many characters of Thracian legends were part animal part human, the rendition of a mountain wandering Gullman is quite appropriate. Another possibility, and more probable, is an alias for the god Apollo, who in Greek mythology is the father of Orpheus, among others, and adopted the form of a swan and a variety of birds on many occasions; swans were sacred to Apollo, they encircled the island of his birth and there are stories of him riding on swans and his chariot being pulled by a flock of swans. (There is an obvious connection here to 'Ride a White Swan'). With the Greek Gods inhabiting Mount Olympus, he could also duly be described as a steep mountain wanderer. Another fascinating point being that Apollo is, amongst his many roles, the god of light, in other mythologies he is portrayed as the sun god, which is relevant to the opening lines of the piece. There is yet another potential concept, that of the souls of the dead being reincarnated in the form of birds, Orpheus chose to become a swan, Agamemnon an eagle, the Gullman and his warehouse could be discerned as the collector of those souls. Portraying him as being *hidden in hides* signifies that he is clothed in animal skins that are layered and sewn by a type of thread or leather lace made from the tongue of an Orang-utan.

A flapped torso

Tailored in Orang-utan tongue,

This is a peculiar concept, to make a thread from the tongue of any animal is perplexing, and to produce one from a creature that is so closely linked to humans has a disturbing air of cannibalism. Furthermore Orang-utans do not populate these regions; they are restricted to the Borneo and Sumatra, a considerable global distance from mid Europe. The probable reason for Marc's use of Orang-utan is it's rhythmic rhyming quality with tongue; it simply sounds good! If the Gullman were Apollo, the use of such a thread, which would be considered rare and precious by the gods, would be a symbol of his superiority.

A stout stick of mulberry

Written on by the witch of song

Another item appears on the list, a stick, assumedly the Gullmans' walking stick that has been inscribed by the witch of song. If we accept the Gullman as Apollo then it is reasonable to believe the witch of song to be Calliope, the eldest of the Muses, the goddesses of poetry and song, they sing to the Gods and it is believed they were led by Apollo. In Greek mythology Calliope married Apollo and bore Orpheus from their union; in Thrace mythology, however, Orpheus's father was Oeagrus, king of Thrace. As the picture starts to form it becomes clear that Marc has written this from the perspective of Greek mythology.

In many of his words, particularly his lyrics, Marc is very suggestive and sexual, giving sensual character to innocuous objects, making them phallic; it is therefore feasible that he intended the *stout stick* as symbolic of the sexual bonding of Apollo and Calliope. His following line relating to the *witch* of songs attire

In her celestial toga

confirms her status, the toga being the garment worn by the gods and the use of the word celestial, which means heavenly, divine, substantiates the theory that she is Calliope; there is further evidence in the next line.

And Saturn hourly fanned her baked bones

Like an emperor,

Saturn the god of time and agriculture, in many cultures, the original deity who was overthrown or banished, depending on the version read is often portrayed as, and the inspiration for the grim reaper, is a servant humbled to fanning her, likening her to royalty.

Then to the point of the poem, unobvious as it may be, the product of their bonding, the child.

And a daily child,

Young lily like,

Sang tiny songs in the meadow

By the faith stile.

Exactly what Marc means by a *daily child* is uncertain, the term daily usually refers to an event or happening that occurs every day with regularity or a domestic help, a cleaner. Either he is inferring that the child is a servant of some kind or that he is there every day, in the meadow singing his songs, this is his most probable intended meaning. He describes him as *lily like*, pure like white lilies and the portrayal of him singing by the *faith stile* conjures a spiritual image of the child as if his songs are prayers to the gods; the *faith stile* he goes to being equivalent to an alter.

His groven ringlets filled with fogs,

In this line Marc gives the child's hair the appearance of a grove, a small wood, filled with fogs, mists, bestowing him with even more of an ethereal presence.

His caplet of marigold

Shaped for conversation

With the outer world,

A caplet is a short cape, just covering the shoulders, the boys is orange and shaped or arranged in a pleasing way in order to make him approachable to talk to by the people of the world. Orpheus is reputed to have gone out into the world to teach mankind about medicine, writing and agriculture, travelling to Egypt to learn more about the gods, enchanting even the animals and trees with his songs and music on the way.

And his stern copper booties

Designed for wind walking.

Copper is a dark orangey brown colour, like leather; Marc is not saying that his boots are made of copper, but copper coloured of *stern* leather. Many times Orpheus had to cope with the wind, specifically when he joined Jason and the Argonauts on the search for the Golden Fleece, the northwest wind, Argestes carried the Argonauts from Assyria to the land of the Amazons. There is one belief that the god Boreus 1, the north wind, resides in Thrace, another reason for the need of wind walking. Is it necessary to point out the similarities between Marc and Orpheus that are displayed here?

This is the most difficult of Marc's poems, in this collection, to analyse. The flow and style is disjointed and confusing, misleading in some aspects. The imagery is inconclusive, and the connections between the various subjects of the piece are, on initial impressions, tenuous. It would not stand on its own and without the pre-knowledge of the other poems and an understanding of Marc's interest in mythology, it would be impossible to arrive at any form of valid comprehension. Therefore to conclude that it is about Orpheus may seem to be over ambitious, but all the elements tie in adroitly, the specific reference to a Rumanian Sun, giving not only the correct geography but also a pointer towards the identity of his father,

Apollo, and then the seemingly erratic mention of the witch of song in a celestial toga is a perfect description of his mother, Calliope. For Marc to then go on to depict the young boy singing songs and being diligently prepared to go out into the world to communicate, as Orpheus did is too coincidental to spurn. Coupling this with Marc's later references to Orpheus on his last album, 'Dandy in the Underworld', he was clearly extremely familiar with the character, even identifying himself personally with the father of songs.

Orpheus used his musical ability to control the world about him; he relied on its charm to hold even objects under his spell but ultimately his reliance on the beauty of his talent was his downfall. This could also be said of Marc Bolan, that the complacency he adopted in the musical formula he had evolved ultimately caused his demise.

Marc Bolan learnt many things to assist him in his climb to star status, and he did not learn them casually as he wandered his way through the music industry. He deliberately moulded his knowledge to fit his purpose, although there are those who have branded him shallow, even a fake in various areas, he was totally dedicated to his cause.

To level these types of accusations at Marc Bolan is completely unjust in view of the fact that from the age of eight years old, when his father Simeon erroneously bought home the Bill Haley record 'See You Later Alligator' instead of 'The Ballad of Davy Crockett' by Bill Hayes, he unreservedly fashioned himself into a rock star. Even his early childhood friends, Carol Shaw and Wendy Wilchenski, remember his obsession with music and his continual mimicking of his early heroes, Elvis and Cliff Richard. Wendy recalls that later they even managed to meet Cliff and his mother on at least one occasion and the young Mark Feld was so obsessed with music, he not only followed the artists but their managers and producers, pulling off the amazing feat for their age of securing invites for them both into after show parties on many instances, all in an effort to understand the workings of the industry, at a management and social level as well as the mundane marketing and hype aspects of image and style.

It was at the tender age of eight, when most children would be playing Cowboys and Indians or Moms and Dads that Mark Feld began to mould himself for his career. His mom bought him his first guitar at this time and it wasn't long before he was in his first group, Susie and the Hula Hoops with Helen Shapiro.

In the late fifties Joy Faulkner worked at the General Store owned by Roy and Roseanne Vincent, at 76 Fountayne Road, she remembers Marc 'dancing around the flower beds' with his guitar slung around his neck waiting to go into his music teacher, a Mrs. Agate, who lived next door to Joy. She recollects that Master Mark

Feld was always charming and confident, proclaiming even then that one day he would be a star, as he mimicked Cliff Richard. Roy Vincent remembers Marc stacking the milk crates together to form a street stage and standing on them playing his guitar for the girls, "He always had his guitar with him' and 'He was always surrounded by girls." said Roy.

Mrs. Agate did not teach the guitar but music and the piano and this is where Marc began to build his musical foundations, although classical music was not his goal, he knew he needed some musical training to help him in his development and dutifully attended Mrs. Agate's lessons. Every aspect of Marks' life, even then, was committed to being a rock star, he gave himself the experiences he needed to be capable of fulfilling the role he had cast for himself, he was never going to be anything else, and he was from the age of eight a rock and roll star. Marc Bolan did not accidentally fall into the limelight; he trained and fought through every element of the role. Simon Napier-Bell did not discover Marc Bolan, Marc Bolan sought him out, knocked on his door and forced his attentions upon Simon until he got what he wanted. In his book 'You Don't Have to Say You Love Me' Simon says "Marc really amazed me. He looked about fifteen yet he'd picked up more knowledge of the music business than seemed possible." He also says "Marc Bolan was the first rock singer I had anything to do with who lived up to being an artist. He had real inventiveness and individuality. He was his own creation." Both statements truly sum up Bolan and his approach to music reflected these attributes, he listened, learnt and absorbed all he could, he studied every aspect relevant to him and used it.

As a musician Marc Bolan was immensely more able than he was generally accredited, although it is true that his musical ability was limited, he was not a guitarist in the calibre of Eric Clapton, Jimmy Page or Hendrix, but he was far closer to those icons than is perceived. A friend of Clapton and Page at various points in his life, he learnt from both of them, taking lessons where he could, and milking their musical knowledge at every opportunity. His true ability was not housed in the knowledge of a thousand chords but in the imagination he employed in the playing of the ones he knew. In the early years with Steve Took, Marc created a magically mystical sound with a cheap guitar, bongos and a triangle, his imagination was strong enough to adapt to the limited resources at his fingertips. When he 'went electric' on 'A Beard Of Stars' the process was gentle, the two guitar instrumentals have a beautiful ethereal quality that overwhelms their simplicity, a magic that only Marc Bolan could capture. Eric Clapton could undoubtedly play the notes with more technical proficiency but the fairy dust would be missing. The closing track of the album, 'Elemental Child', still wears the ethereal guise but develops into a raunchy electric guitar explosion lasting almost six minutes, in true Hendrix style and employing many standard rock and roll techniques such as a three note progression to step up a key, warble, echo and the tremolo arm are all utilised as it builds to an almost sexual climax, the guitar gently and finally sighing as it orgasms.

Unfortunately most of the television footage of Marc's playing is from programs such as Top of the Pops, where because of the Musicians Union rules, artists were not permitted to actually play their music, they had to mime to recordings. In Marc's earlier TV performances of 'Ride a White Swan' he mimed well, but he developed an objection to not being allowed to play and made a point of miming badly along with his over pretentious 'camping it up' for the camera. This had the inevitable effect of diminishing the credibility of his musicianship. When listening to his albums carefully, the unused studio versions and demo's that have gradually come to light over the years since his death, or the limited footage of him *actually* performing and playing live, it is clearly evident that Marc Bolan was an extremely competent musician, a competence he required to be a rock star. However his competence was fuelled more by imagination than technical ability, that is to say, having an immense creative imagination that enabled him to utilise his ability to the extreme limits, he could bleed more emotion from one chord than most guitarists can draw from a hundred or more, in much the same way as Vincent van Gogh captured the passion of sunflowers with his fervent use of raw colour and bold, yet well placed brush strokes as opposed to the millions of pixels worth of detail encapsulated by artists like Michelangelo or Leonardo da Vinci. It is not that one approach is necessarily better or worse than the other, it is just that they are different; one is from the heart the other from the eye. Marc Bolan's musical approach came from the heart, he was passionate about his music, he loved and lived for music, listening intensely to, as well as dissecting and analysing the work of his predecessors and contemporaries in order that he understood completely how to best paint the song he pictured in his imagination. This can be most fittingly explained by comparing earlier songs, namely 'Debora' and 'By the Light of the Magical Moon' with later ones such as '20th Century Boy' and 'Children of the Revolution'. The earlier two are beautifully constructed songs, rich with intricate vocals relaying mystical words and lavished with all the acoustic instruments that were at hand, from Tabla to finger cymbals, Bolan even using his voice as an instrument. His imagination also utilises all the production techniques that were available (with the help of Tony Visconti), even reversing the track on Debora, strangely maintaining the melody of the song. The later two, however, are powerful riff based rocking numbers. They postulate their presence behind the raunchy guitar riff; there is no subtle tenderness to their sexually blatant musical pose.

An abundance of Marc Bolan's songs were sexual, or at least sensual in the mood that they set. 'Ride a White Swan' still holds some of the rich intricacies of his earlier work, with Marc's guitar taking a summery stroll behind his pagan lyrics, it cannot be described as erotic but it holds a romantic sensuality rising to another almost climatic chant at the end. 'Hot Love' is erotic, from the title itself and the lyrical content to the sultry bass riff that carries the whole song along, not forgetting the (again) sexually climatic guitar solo and vocal sigh midway along with the other vocal gesticulations Marc employs. 'Get it on' is uncompromisingly sexually explicit from the offset; lyrically it is transparently passionate with more sultry guitar work pouting under the periodic thrusting of the riff, it is anything but suggestive, it is brazen and obvious, even in its title.

It is surprising, therefore, that Riggs O'Hara relates Marc not being interested in sex and even more surprisingly that he does not remember him being particularly interested in music. Everyone who Marc came into contact with tells of how music was all he was interested in, but Riggs believed it was the fame and notoriety that Marc craved, to ascend to the legendary status he became; the music and the ambiguous sexuality he portrayed were merely tools to attain that goal. Simon Napier-Bell says in his book 'Black Vinyl White Powder' that record companies regarded songs and artists as no more than a means to sell their black vinyl, Riggs infers that Marc only saw his music and persona as a means to sell himself.

In slight contradiction Riggs told of paying for Marc's first recording session, although he could not definitively remember the studio name, Regent Studios seemed familiar to him and he was emphatic that no other guitarist was present at the session as previously speculated. Riggs also related a story of himself and Marc, two aspiring artists, watching Top of the Pops one evening when Marc proclaimed 'Anyone can do that' and then jumping up and wiggled his hips like Elvis, in mimickery of the act that was on 'But then he went and did it!' said Riggs.

Marc's utilisation of musically sexual innuendos, particularly in his singles, was clearly deliberate; he knew that the climatic riffs and vocals would seduce the subconscious of his pubescent fans. He had studied Elvis and Cliff in detail and seen their provocative performances arousing the passions of their fans, he took it one step further by putting the provocation in the music to an extent that had not been done before and without crudity. There was no swearing, no vulgarity but passion in the vocals and the riffs. Even when he courted the media he openly flirted with the camera and the interviewer.

To say that all of Marc's music was sexual would be ridiculous, it was not, many of his songs had completely different agendas and many were simply good old rock and roll, the key singles and songs, however, were sexual.

Contrary to Riggs O'Hara's recollections, it is well related that Marc had studied, bathed in and adored music from a very early age and it is more likely that the short time he spent with Riggs he used as a stepping stone in his stream of learning in order to accrue substance for his writing. Truly Marc Bolan desired fame, he made no secret of his yearning for stardom but it rode in tandem with his musical and poetical ambition. We are all multifaceted and reveal different aspects of ourselves to different people, who in turn see different aspects of us, depending on their own perceptions; these are not necessarily conscious portrayals but varied reflections depending on the angle of the mirror and equally they may be mixed with our conscious portrayals. Summarily, no one sees the whole of us except ourselves. In point, Marc Bolan was a complex individual, with many facets and in order to form a complete image it is essential to piece together all the mirrors he used. Riggs O'Hara was just one mirror, with one reflection.

If his only motivation was fame, Marc would not and could not have been as prolific. He wrote and composed almost constantly, in modern terms he would be described as a workaholic, his creativity was his soul. Fame was another tool, (as was money) for without fame there is nobody to listen and there is little point in writing if there is nobody to hear your words or music.

As previously stated, Marc dissected the work of his predecessors and contemporaries; he digested their music and their influences he regurgitated, embodying them in his own style. He did not record many cover versions, a mere handful, but he did borrow riffs and phrases from Chuck Berry, Howling Wolf and even Elvis, giving them his own distinctive interpretation, to the point where the 'borrowing' was totally eradicated. One example of flagrant borrowing was an early recording, which was never released by Marc, entitled 'Sally was an Angel'. It appears on the 'Beginning of Doves' compilation of Marc's early recordings and demos, it is a less than subtle working of 'Heartbreak Hotel', even steeling some of the original lyrics but it was more likely to have been a musical exercise for Marc, not blatant plagiarism. 'Jeepster' was based on the Howlin' Wolf song 'You'll be mine' and even the opening lines are almost the same 'You so sweet, you so fine' (Howlin' Wolf), 'You're so sweet, you're so fine' (Marc Bolan) and musically the song is very similar; it is well known that Marc did not want 'Jeepster' released as a single, possibly because he felt it was too similar. 'Get it on', however, is less blatant and although Marc has admitted it was based on the Chuck Berry song 'Little Queenie' the finished track bears little resemblance and even with Marc's final line paying lyrical homage to the original, 'And meanwhile, I'm still thinking' as opposed to Berry's 'Meanwhile, I was still thinkin'' the song is acutely different.

Marc was always open about his borrowed use of riffs and it is an inevitable necessity as there are only eight notes and limited permutations of those notes. Marc was not alone in taking inspiration from other sources, David Bowie's 'Starman' was written to the melody of 'Over the Rainbow', it is a trait all artists are guilty of, consciously or sub consciously: it is the extent of the reproduction of the inspiration that gives rise to concern in some cases when the 'inspiration' becomes a shameless copy. The whole combination of sounds, musically and lyrically makes a song different, the performance and production also contributing. It is a similar principle to the earlier theory discussed with regard to writing poetry and painting and a further extension of Marc Bolan's ability to absorb everything he came into contact with, ultimately giving it rebirth with his own touch of DNA.

These observations should not detract from or pollute the originality of Marc Bolan's work. The process is comparable to a chef choosing the best ingredients, the most succulent peppers and the tenderised beef in order to prepare the finest meal. When classical musicians perform the works of the Chopin or Mozart, re-arranging the piece to bestow their own signature upon it, they are not accused of plagiarism, but heralded for their imaginative interpretation. All musicians do the same, including rock musicians, the Rolling Stones, Eric Clapton and many more all have their heroes who have influenced them and that they emulate in their own work. When Marc took inspiration from 'Little Queenie' (interestingly from the Rolling Stones version of the song) and conjured up the sultry cuisine of 'Get it on' to titillate the taste buds, it became more than an interpretation, it became a song in its own right with its own life, a rebirth of the notes with a different personality, a child of Chuck Berry's original that itself was probably the spawn of one of Berry's heroes, Big Joe Turner or T-Bone Walker. Ultimately the evolution continues and 'Get it on' has gone on to inspire more artists, like Oasis and Supergrass, who in turn will inspire future artists.

Marc Bolan's abundance of imagination and creativity enabled him to develop a musical style that was completely unique, which, notwithstanding his influences, made him stand out on his own as an innovator. It cannot be said that the music of Marc Bolan 'sounds like' anyone else; he was alone in the propagation of the T-Rex sound and felt alone. He enjoyed musical debate and banter with his peers and despite the almost flippant image he had created, took it very seriously. There is a recording of a conversation between Marc and Roy Wood where he is obviously enjoying the raillery and is by far the most vocal; Roy Wood, one of the founder members of the Move who went on to form ELO with Jeff Lynne and then Wizzard, appears to be almost lost for words. It is also clearly visible on the excellently re-mastered version of 'Born to Boogie' that Marc is happily at home when performing with Elton John and Ringo Star. There is one point in the Wembley Empire Pool Concert during the performance of 'Baby Strange' where Marc mischievously smiles and shouts 'Back off Boogaloo' during the song, the title of Ringo's second solo single, which had not been released at the time of the concert but was to be shortly afterwards (the lyrics of Richard Starky's song are reputed to have been inspired by Marc Bolan); a conclusion that can be drawn is that Ringo must have been manning that particular camera and Marc was bantering with him. The point being that Marc relished the parrying with his musical allies and contemporaries, he was ecstatic at being included in the world he adored. Beguilingly he felt alone.

In much the same way as an athlete empathises with his peers and befriends them, they are ultimately competing against each other, Marc was competing with his peers and regardless of the perceived closeness there would always be a small moat of musical defence between each party. Ability, talent, imagination and inevitably ego all playing there part, it is not until an artist reaches maturity and can rest on the laurels of past success and acclaim that he can truly relax into banter with contemporaries as Sting, Bowie and Jagger are now fortunate to be able to do. This was not only a problem for Marc Bolan… Elton John, David Bowie, Rod Stewart and bands like Slade would all have had their moats and adopt a posture of modest defence when facing the musical castles of their confréres. Marc had been treading this path since the age of eight and yearned for the security of being able to spar with a like soul without being compromised. When his relationship with Gloria Jones flourished he had found that sparring partner, Gloria's soul roots being of further inspiration to him. His wife June, regardless of her long devotion, could not compete with the musical lovemaking they had embraced and disembarked from the train. Even though it would have broken her heart, June would have known Marc well enough to realise he had found the companion his creativity needed.

Marc had found new focus and direction, not only in the birth of their son but in the elation of finding a musical partner who was not threatening and would live within the boundaries of his moat, he is quoted as saying that he no longer felt alone when he met Gloria, and that would have been true for him, and it can only be speculated as to the roads their musical collaboration would have travelled. Orpheus had found his Eurydice.

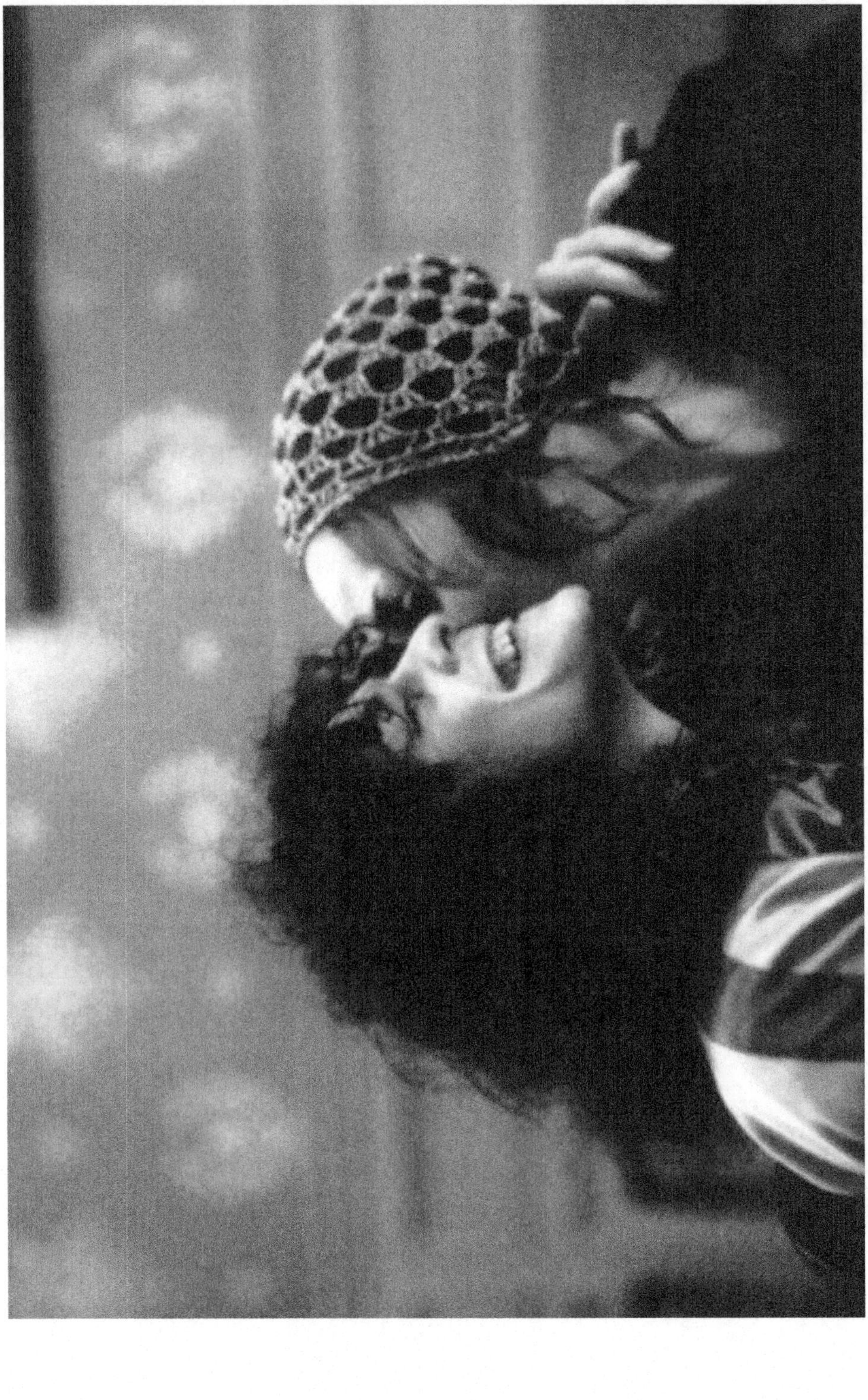

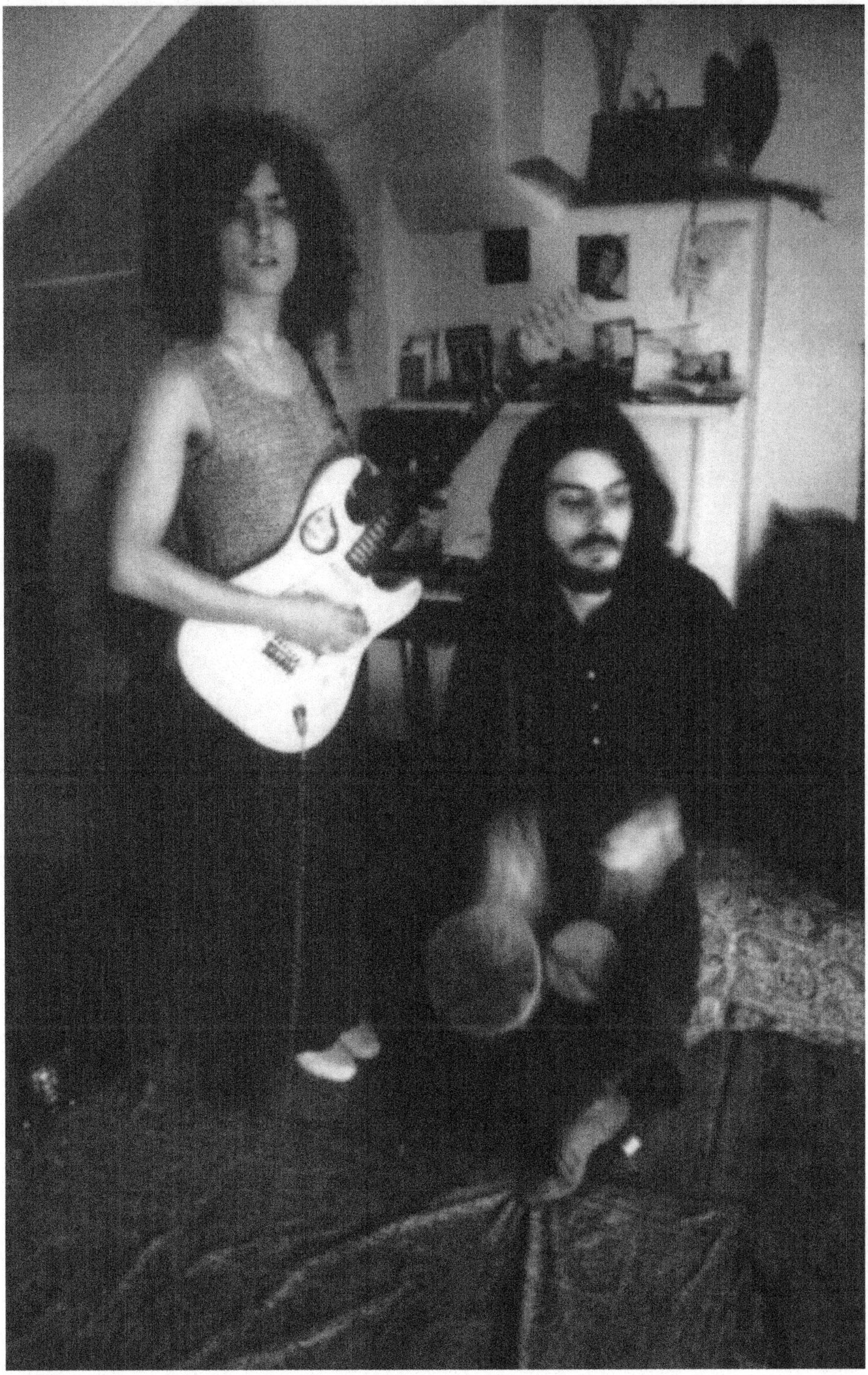

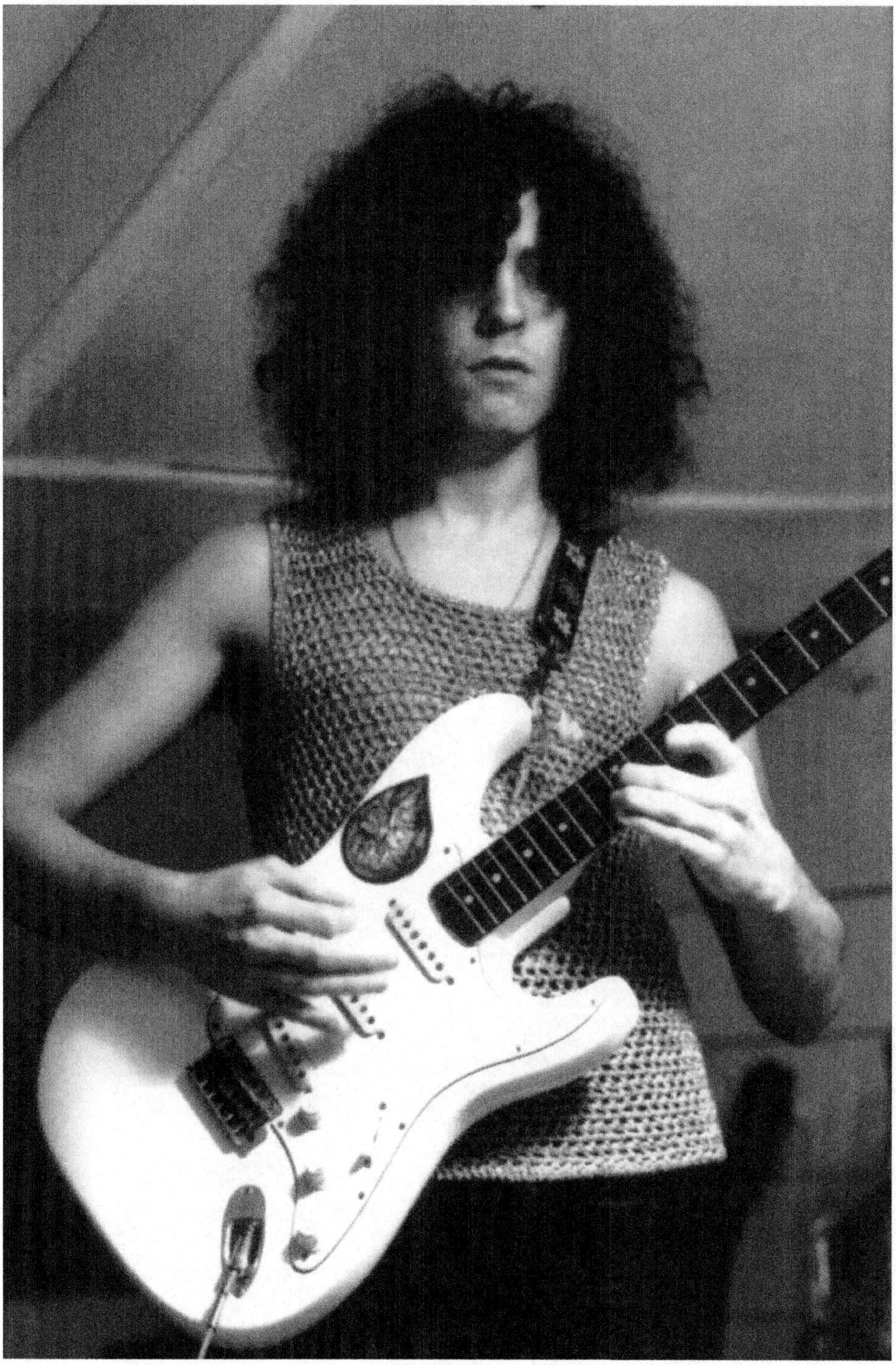

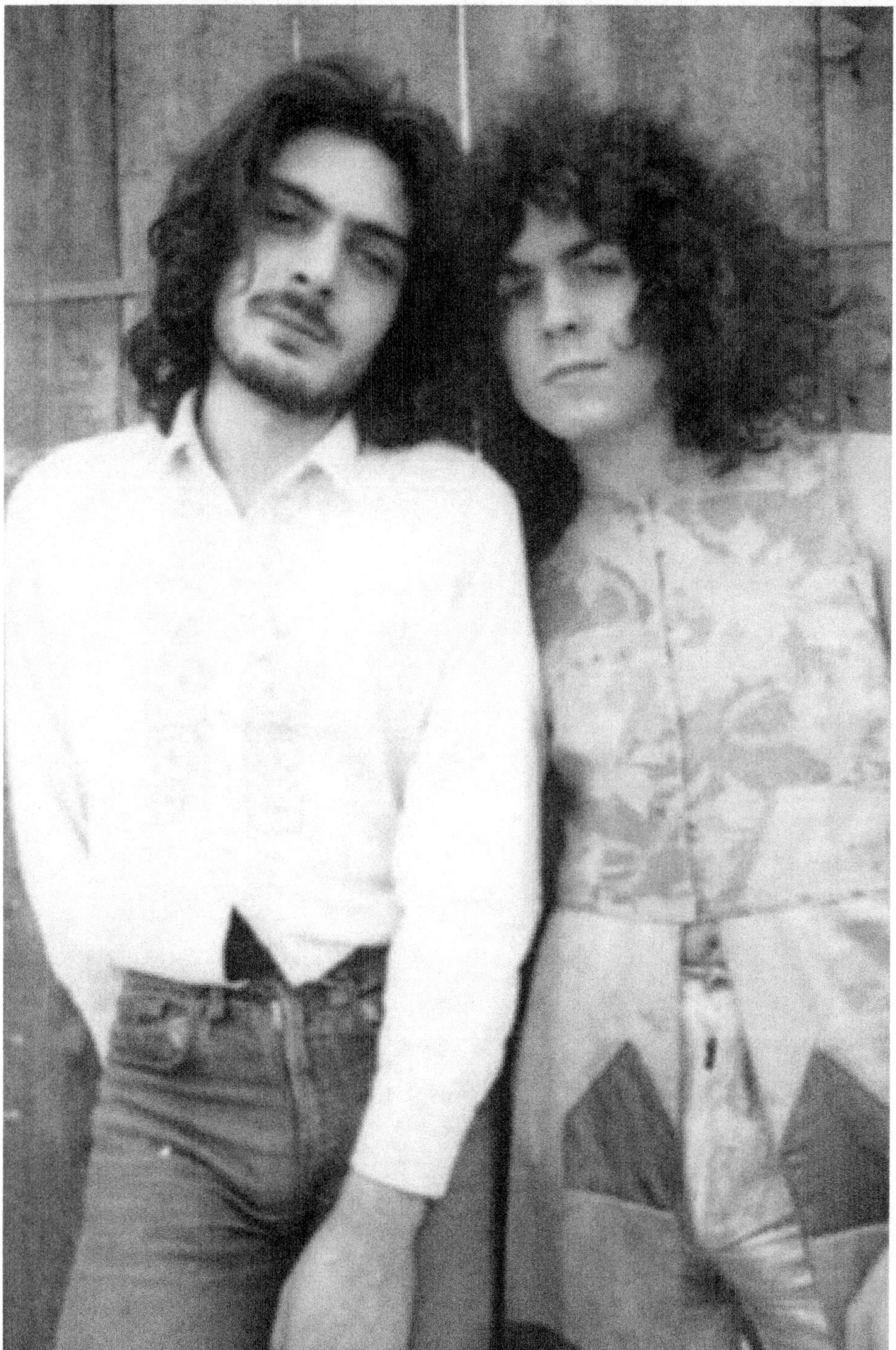

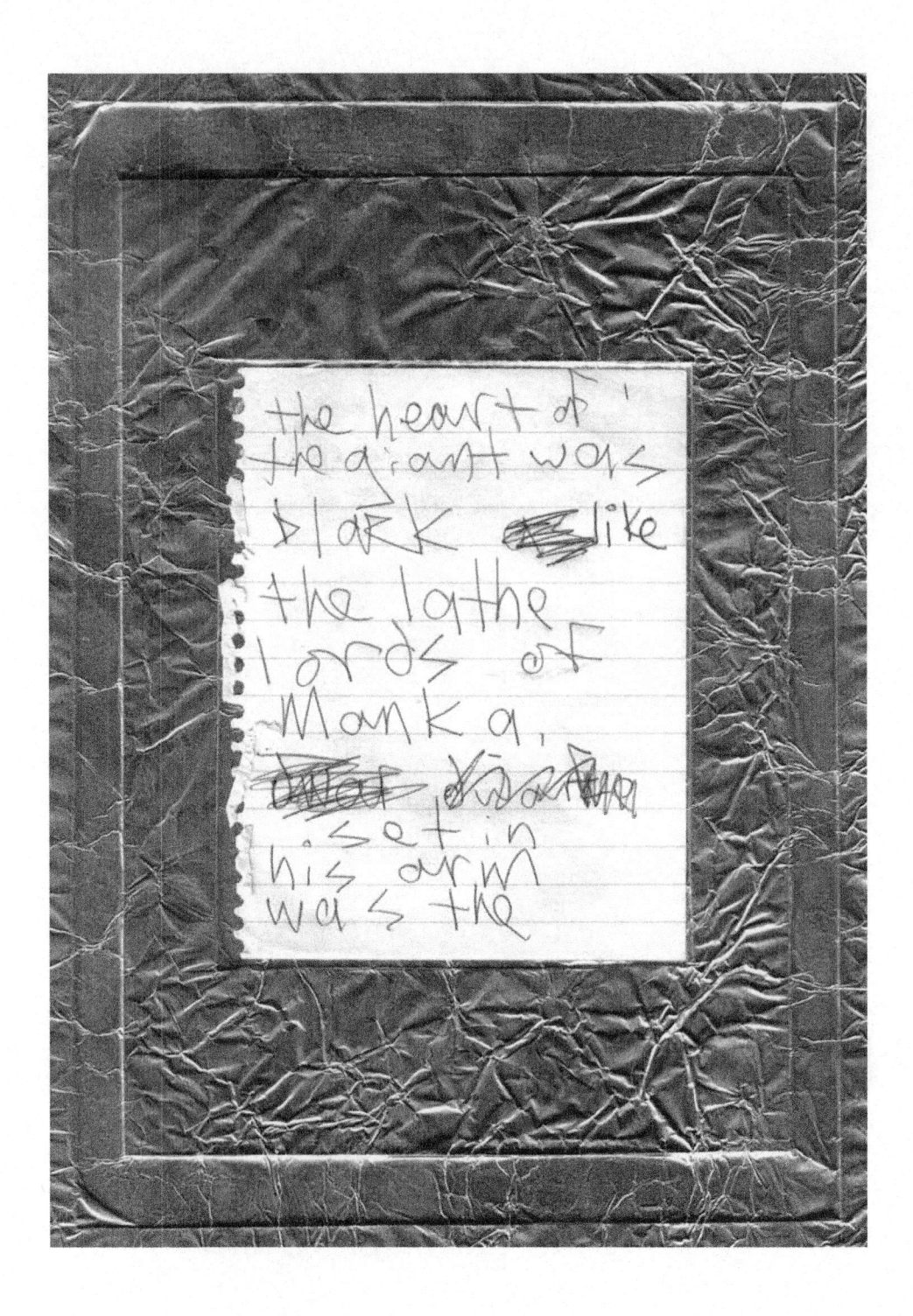

the heart of
the giant was
black ~~a~~ like
the lathe
lords of
Manka,
~~[scribbled]~~ ~~[scribbled]~~
set in
his arm
was the

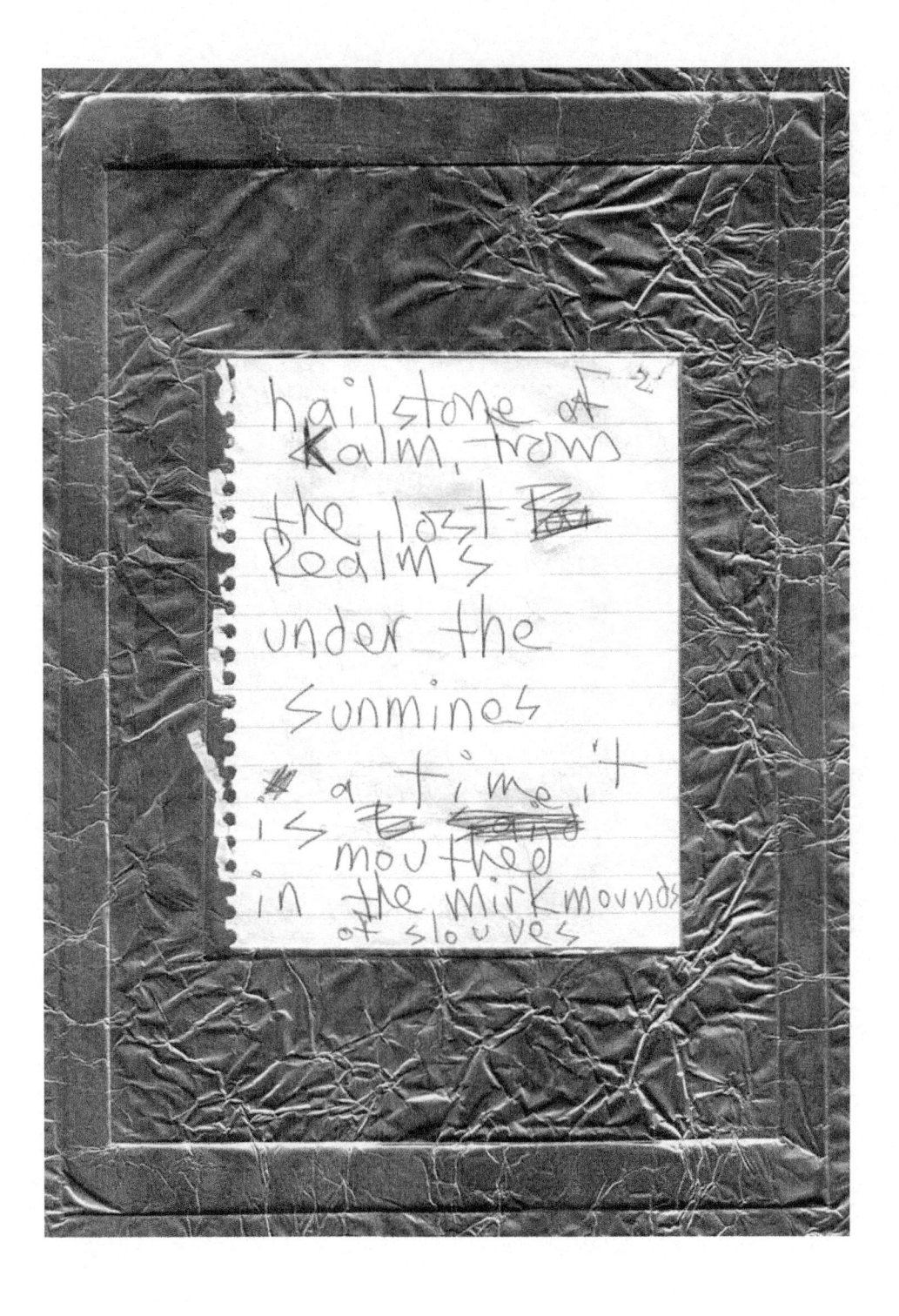

hailstone of Kalm, from the lost Realms under the sunmines # a time it is mouthed in the mirkmounds of slouves

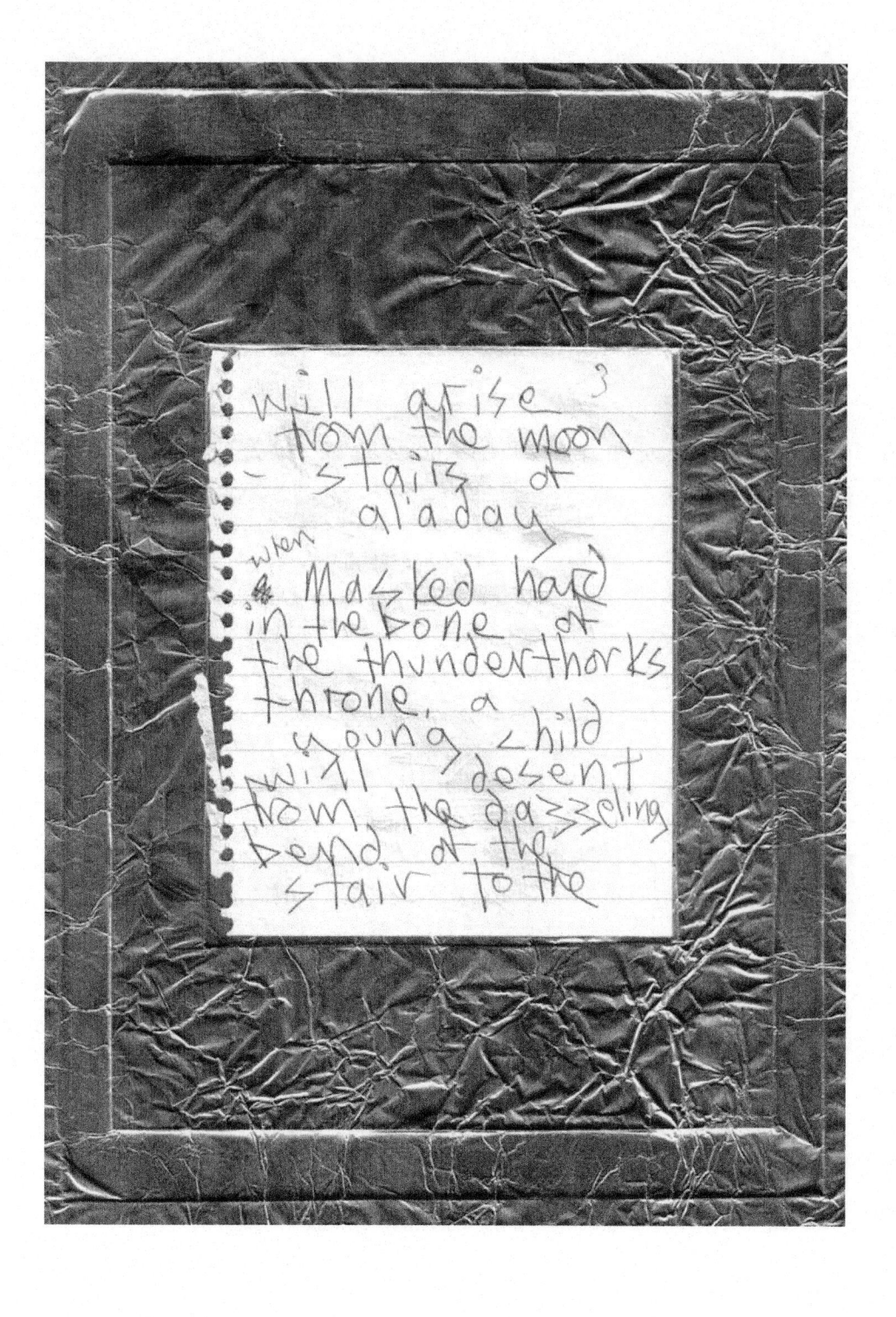

will arise
from the moon
stairs of
ala day

when
Masked hard
in the bone of
the thunderthork's
throne, a
young child
will desent
from the dazzling
bend of the
stair to the

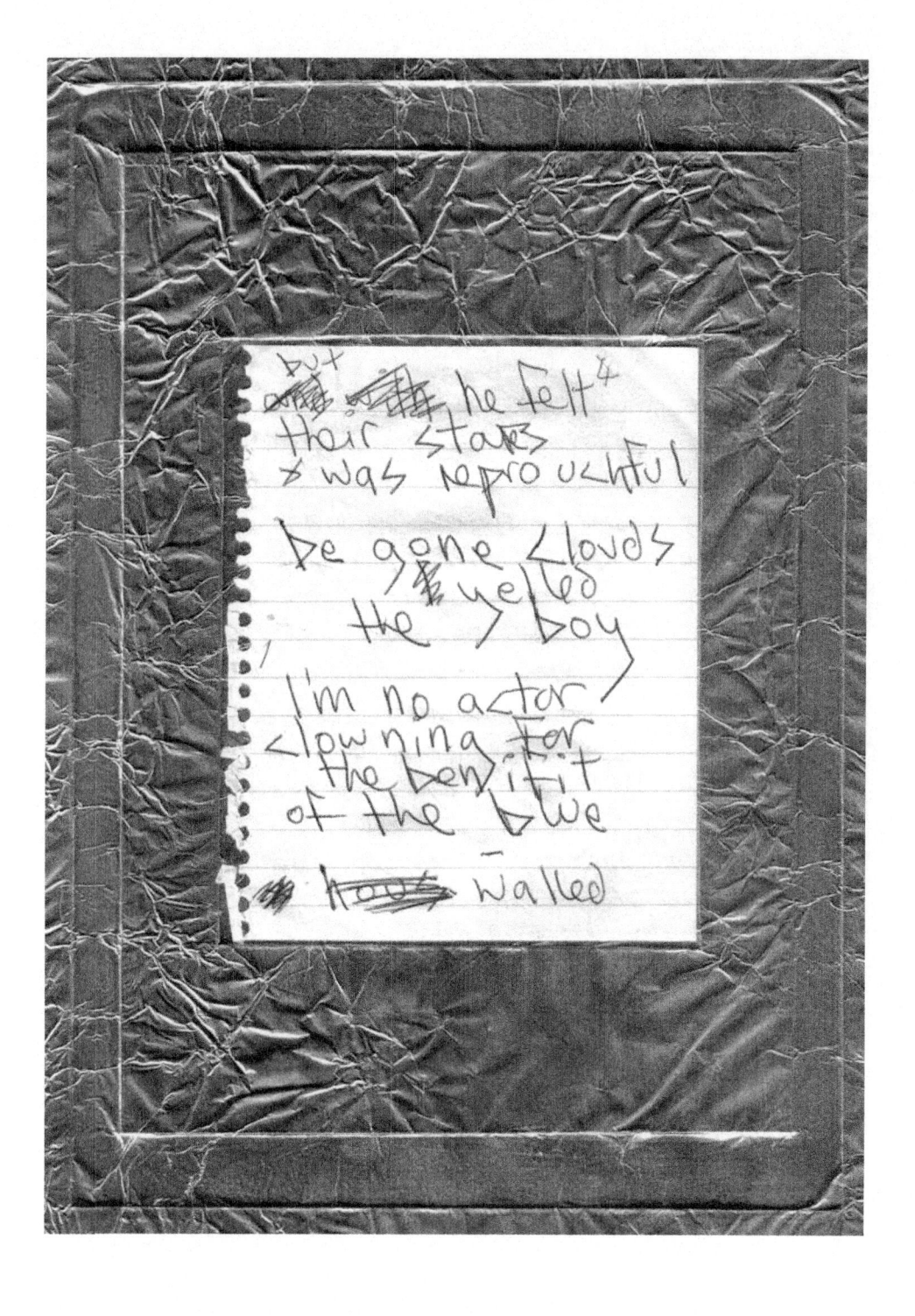

but
~~and~~ ~~and~~ he felt &
their stares
& was reprouchful

be gone clouds
~~&~~ yelled
the ~~>~~ boy

I'm no actor
clowning for
the benifit
of the blue

~~&~~ ~~kids~~ walked

the tweetings
~~to~~ ~~nice~~ ~~things~~
to ~~say~~ speak
nice things
to
the bloom kings

7. **Sun Seals and Moon Eels**

"I recently split with my wife. It wasn't very harassing. Mean, do I look heartbroken?" Marc Bolan 1973.

The heart of the giant was black

Like the Lathe Lords of Manka,

Set in his arm

Was the hailstone of Kalm

From the lost realms

Under the Sun mines.

A time, It is mouthed In the mirk mounds of Slouves,

Will arise from the moon stairs of all,

A day,

When masked hard in the bone

Of the Thunder Thorks throne,

A young child will descend

From the dazzling bend of the stair

To the Lair lay of Juniper

And recite from the night scrolls,

Exorcising the Bone Troll

And allowing the Sun Seals

To mate with the Moon Eels

And the Treelings

To speak nice things

To the Bloom Kings.

Who is the giant with the black heart? A particularly pertinent question in relation to this poem. The Bone Troll is the one exorcised and could be viewed as the giant focused upon by Marc's painting of the picture but on first impressions the real subject could be any number of things. There is no Greek mythology hidden in these words, it is instead populated with characters from Marc's own mind and possibly his life. Again it is feasible that this poem is an element of a larger piece, which could be given credibility by the fact that on initial reading there appear to be no references to anything external, except in the second line.

Like the Lathe Lords of Manka,

As with most of Marc's writing, one line gives the key to the tale, once that line has been 'decoded' the rest begins to fall neatly into place. Although *Manka* is a common surname in some parts of the globe the only other reference that could be found is a geographical one, which complies affably with the context of the line. The earliest area to be settled by farmers in Taipei, now the capital of Taiwan, was a district that became known as Manka. In November 1972 T-Rex toured Japan and again in October 1973, when they played and stayed in Hiroshima. Japan is just north of Taiwan, undoubtedly the reaper of knowledge harvested while he was there, inspiring the poem. It could be thought that the poem is about Taiwan, but it is not, it is about Japan itself.

If Manka is a reference to the early farm settlements in 1790 then *The Lathe Lords* also has relevance, as 'Lathe' is not only a wood turning tool but an ancient Anglo-Saxon measurement of land, in the same manner as an acre. *The Lathe Lords* would therefore be *the Land Lords of Manka*. The chronology now becomes relevant and remembering that this poem was written in approximately 1972 is important, no events between then and the present day can be taken into account and we have too be aware of the political, social and cultural climate of Japan and surrounding areas at this moment in history. There had been periods of political turmoil and following the Second World War, America had occupied Japan after unleashing two atomic bombs, forcing unconditional surrender from the land of the rising sun. Following Japans defeat, America secured it's control by entrapping the cooperation of Emperor Hirohito, despite cries for him to be tried for war crimes with him being described as the Hitler of Japan, the countries conduct during the war being equal to Germany's atrocities; instead he became America's pawn, enabling them to keep a disguised foot in the door of Japanese affairs long after their official occupation had ended. Japan was the Landlord of Taiwan and the giant was America.

The heart of the giant was black

Like the Lathe Lords of Manka,

The heart of America was black, like the heart of Japan. Marc is describing the hearts of the governments, not the people of the two countries.

Set in his arm

Was the hailstone of Kalm

From the lost realms

Under the Sun mines.

Set in the arm that the giant wields is a hailstone that keeps the calm, enabling him to keep control. Hailstones fall from the sky, as do atomic bombs, and America, having demonstrated the power of the bomb by dropping one on Hiroshima and one on Nagasaki, ended the war and took control of Japan. If there could be mines on the Sun at the bottom of those mines, in the core of our star, a mass of nuclear explosions would be found, an endless supply of Atomic bombs. *The hailstone of Kalm* is therefore the Atomic bomb.

A time,

It is mouthed

In the mirk mounds of Slouves,

Will arise from the moon stairs of all,

It is presumed that with the use of the word 'slouves', Marc has misspelled 'sloth's', which are slow, patient, 'laid back' animals that spend most of their life hanging almost motionless in trees, even when asleep. They could be thought of in a similar vein as a tortoise, slow, old and wise, they are also native to South America, but that has no real relevance. Therefore…It is said, in the dark gloomy homes of the wise, a day will come from the seas of time… *Moon stairs* referring to the tides of the sea and the waves, which are like steps in the water, both caused by the Moon's gravitational pull. They are governed by the cycles of the Moon, and it is upon the Moon's cycles that the original calendars were based. The seas waves/steps rise and fall like the ticking of Earths own clock, punctuating time.

A day

When masked hard in the bone

Of the Thunder Thorks throne.

Bone is the fundamental element of the skeleton, the framework that supports most living things. *The Thunder Thork* is Hirohito, Emperor of Japan through the Second World War until his death in 1989, consequently, having been hidden (masked) in the framework of the emperor's throne (the constitutional role of the sovereignty rather than the actual seat itself) a young child will appear

From the dazzling bend of the stair.

Having already described time as moon stairs, a bend in those stairs, a change in direction, would signify changing times. 'Dazzling' would imply bright or even enlightened times.

To the Lair lay of Juniper

Initially this line appears to be incongruous, the only meaning seeming to relate to the Japanese art of Bonsai. Marc Bolan, however, was a strong admirer of Donovan whose song 'Jennifer Juniper' reached number 11 in the British charts in February 1968. Donovan emerged from Japan in 1970, cutting short a tour and significantly a year of tax exile, much to the annoyance of his advisers. The line is Bolan's way of innocuously including one of his heroes; *The Lair lay* meaning the hiding place and *Juniper* referring to Donovan, the hiding place of Donovan was Japan.

And recite from the night scrolls,

Exorcising the Bone Troll

The night scrolls could be any form of ancient scriptures pertaining to Japan, possibly the Pali Canon the Buddhist scriptures, Buddhism being practiced by almost half of the Japanese people, the other half being Shinto. This is the native religion of Japan, which binds its beliefs by giving reverence to nature in a similar mythological style as the ancient Greeks, also entwined with many colourful gods, characters and stories, the key deity being the powerful sun goddess Amaterasu, hence the description of Japan as 'the land of the rising Sun'. The royal linage is, according to legend, descended from Amaterasu thus any child appearing from the royal line would look to and read from the scrolls of Japanese legend to banish the Bone Troll, which is America. The portrayal of America as a giant Troll feeding off the bones of it's defeated predator is not unreasonable, from a Japanese perspective. America had defeated and then occupied Japan, overseeing and prospering itself from Japan's post-war success; the Japanese would at this time have yearned for independence from America and to recapture their culture.

And allowing the Sun Seals

To mate with the Moon Eels

There are a few possible meanings to these two lines, *Sun Seals* definitely refers to the Japanese people, being the people of 'the land of the rising Sun' but whether it means them as a whole or as a part is not certain. It could allude to the Shinto element of the population; the *Moon Eels* would then be the Buddhist portion of Japanese society. The most likely analogy is that the *Sun Seals* are the Japanese people as a whole and the *Moon Eels* are the American people, America having first landed on the Moon in 1969 and then taking regular trips to our cosmic child in the years that followed.

And the Treelings

To speak nice things

To the Bloom Kings.

Treelings refers to the 'common' people of Japan who were always kept at a distance from the Royalty of their country and in relative ignorance of the workings of the Imperial Household, until recent years.

Bloom Kings, the final two words of the poem genuinely crown the definitive overview of the piece and confirm the analogy. Without that analogy it would be realistic to assume the final few lines to be elements of elfish rambling, the image of saplings having a magical chat to the flowers would proliferate an abundance of accusations about Bolan being high when he wrote this poem, or living in his fantasy world but the joke is on those who mock. The common name given to the Imperial throne of Japan is the Chrysanthemum Throne and the chrysanthemum is the coat of arms of the Emperor, truly the Bloom Kings!

The Emperor at the time Marc wrote this poem was Hirohito, incredulously his son, the current Emperor Akihito, had married Miss Michiko Shoda on April 10th 1959 making her the first 'commoner' or 'treeling' to marry into the Imperial family. He has also, since his ascension to the throne in 1990, become the most outward Emperor Japan has known, working hard to break down the barriers between Japan and the outside world, and between the Bloom Kings and Treelings.

This is an interesting poem by Marc, rich with allegories that almost lose the true meaning, but for one word that provides the key for unlocking his surreal code. It is intriguing on a number of levels, on first appraisal the reader could be forgiven for discarding it as a mere fantasy, and as previously said, possibly a part of his 'Beltane' but in truth it is a deep political observation of Marc's, it may almost be seen as a criticism of America.

Because of the complexity of the allegories employed it would help precipitate the clarity of the meaning by displaying the poem and 'translation' in the following manner:

The heart of the giant was black

Like the Lathe Lords of Manka,

Set in his arm

Was the hailstone of Kalm

From the lost realms

Under the Sun mines.

A time,

It is mouthed In the mirk mounds of Slouves,

Will arise from the moon stairs of all,

A day,

When masked hard in the bone

Of the Thunder Thorks throne,

A young child will descend

From the dazzling bend of the stair

To the Lair lay of Juniper

And recite from the night scrolls,

Exorcising the Bone Troll

And allowing the Sun Seals

To mate with the Moon Eels

And the Treelings

To speak nice things

To the Bloom Kings.

Translated....

The heart of America was black

Like the landlords of Taiwan (Japan),

To keep the peace

They had the Atomic bomb

Like the nuclear centre

Of the Sun.

A time, It is said In the homes of the wise,

Will arise from all time,

A day,

When having been hidden in the frame

Of the Emperors Throne,

A young child will come

From enlightened, changing times,

To the hiding place of Donovan (Japan)

And read from the scriptures,

Expelling American government

And allowing the people of Japan

To be friends with the people of America,

And the common people

To speak to the Kings of Japan.

And so it came to pass…

The marriage of America and Japan proved to be a prosperous one, Japan experiencing rapid economical growth, embracing certain elements of western culture and practices and opening up to the world. But the marriage was enforced by the dominant partner and parts of Japan felt suppressed. The blood lines of the eastern world were not from America, and although enjoying the freedom of enlightenment, Japan needed time on its own, to be itself. The suppressed partner would ultimately fight back, and has, having embarked on a strategy of economic war. America, as with most dominants, has failed to understand its partner and only looked to its own needs and expectations.

Global relationships between countries are extremely complex, a variety of differing political agendas, cultural disparities and fundamentally divergent outlooks on life itself lead to feelings of basic racism, and a love-hate relationship develops. Whereas it is enchanting to be mystified by the lore's and legends of other worlds, it is harder to take the time to understand them and countries, like people, tend to only view things from their own perspective, ultimately taking what they need from the relationship, leaving both parties feeling cheated.

Relationships between individuals bears comparison with those of countries, we fall in love with aspects of people that we admire and find alluring, and the elements of them that we need, albeit on a subconscious level. As individuals we can only truly perceive things from our own perspective, no matter how we may pontificate otherwise, any giving that we may do ultimately has its trade off. Successful, enduring relationships are those where the trade offs are mutual and balanced fulfilling the needs of both parties, whatever they may be. Time, events and circumstances can cause those needs to change and if the other party does not recognise those needs or cannot fulfill them then at least one of the party will be left wanting; animosity will grow and the relationship will ultimately flounder.

Marc Bolan was no different to anyone else in this regard. From an outsiders viewpoint he could almost be depicted as calculated and callous in his 'use' of people but that would be unfair as everyone spoken to described Marc as a warm, loving and caring person. He did, however, have an inner driving force that would sometimes blind him to the feelings of others, a common trait in successful people. The first person Marc loved, apart from his family, was probably Riggs O'Hara. Riggs, an actor from New York, was a year older than Marc, and recollected that they met in a mutual friends basement flat in Earls Court in 1963 when Marc was just sixteen. Riggs had gone to meet a friend and found Marc chatting to him. The two hit it off immediately and Riggs recalled rudely ignoring the friend before driving Marc home.

When first approached about Marc, Riggs' first words were "Oh what a lovely boy he was, so charming. Delightful boy." Which relays the affection he still holds for him but he was adamant that he did not love Marc in a romantic sense and their relationship was not a romantic one, certainly not from his point of view. Riggs made a lasting impression on the young Mark Feld but hurt him, as Marc's feelings were deeper than Riggs realised and that hurt was expressed later as he appears, in various forms, in Marc's poetry and songs. Marc did not make those feelings clear to Riggs at the time and their parting, he recalls, was strange.

'Hippy Gumbo', despite Simon Napier-Bells assumption of it being narcissistic, is actually about Riggs O'Hara, *Gumbo* being an American stew or soup is an allegory for the American actor and Marc singing 'He's no good, Chop him up for firewood' is evidence of the hurt he had felt. June revealed in an interview that the song was about a man Marc was in love with when he was about fifteen, although he was actually sixteen at the time of their relationship, it is clear that man was Riggs O'Hara. Riggs told of how the two young aspiring men lived in each other's pockets, going everywhere together, although he led the relationship, deciding where and where not they would go, Marc always following along.

Riggs O'Hara is an American actor, born in Brooklyn; he is confident and lovingly outspoken, extremely idealistic and opinionated. His knowledge of the literary arts is quite extensive, as are his associates in that world. He is a small man in stature but his personality portrays tall status, he predominates any conversation, as he must any relationship and it easy to see how Marc would have been drawn to him as a symbiotic host for knowledge. It is Riggs that introduced Marc to Shakespeare and the Greek tragedies and 'taught him to read' in the sense of what to read to expand his mind. They attended many plays together, including 'Othello' and 'Midsummer Night's Dream' and soaked up London's nineteen-sixties culture, with Riggs O'Hara as the guide. "Marc was always very keen to learn" said Riggs "If you knew something he wanted to know, he wouldn't give up until he'd got it from you."

The jobbing actor and the aspiring rock star went to Paris for a weekend on a cultural expedition, which spawned the tale of the 'Wizard'. Riggs recalls the weekend well, even the hotel they lodged in, Hotel Bourgogne Montana, rue de Bourgogne. There was, however, no wizard, no conjurer or mystical man in Paris and they were only there for the weekend, returning together on the Monday. Marc's embroidery of the expedition is pure fantasy for the purpose of hype. The true inspiration for 'The Wizard' was Riggs himself, his literary knowledge and worldliness being mystical to the young Marc Bolan, whose admiration and imagination conjured up a larger than life image of Riggs O'Hara.

When Marc realised that the relationship had run its course and they had both served their purpose to each other, the trade offs complete, he was gone, and Riggs never saw him again, apart from one brief meeting when Marc introduced him to Simon Napier-Bell. "It was remarkable really" said Riggs. Riggs had just been given his first part in a film, 'The Victors', and admitted he became self obsessed and mentally withdrew from the relationship, he became absorbed by the part and neglected Marc, with little thought for him and acknowledged that Marc must have felt hurt by his withdrawal. He recollected how one day when he was in the bath Marc came in and simply said, "I'll be going now." Then they both said goodbye and he left, there was no argument, no discussion and no pontificating, Marc quietly left and it was over.

On reflection Riggs believes that Marc knew that he was of no more use to him and maturely moved on, although astonished at the influence he had on Marc and genuinely unaware of the feelings Marc had for him, he remains resolute in the assertion that it was not a romantic relationship, although he regrets losing contact with Marc and wishes he had been there to influence him when he lost his way. Marc's writings imply a different perspective of the relationship. Riggs O'Hara went on to play parts in a number of films, 'Becket', 'Pigeons' and the role of Sinclair in 'Virgin Soldiers', which David Bowie also appeared in. He was also a member of the original cast of 'Joseph'.

Marc moved back in with his parents for a while, then embarked on a series of short gay relationships, most of which could be perceived as 'casting couch' encounters, including that with manager Simon Napier-Bell, before entering into his first real heterosexual relationship with Theresa Whipman.

Marc appeared to use his sexuality and was sexually quite open, Simon Napier-Bell recounts him coming round to his flat in the morning and climbing straight into bed with him, even when he was with Theresa. Yet in poetry and letters he proclaimed his undying love for Terry Mosaic, as she is credited on the 'My People' album. Marc appeared to have the ability to switch emotions almost instantly from one person to another, immediately discarding people who were no longer in favour, for whatever reason; he did it with Riggs and then with Terry when he met June. Regardless of the perceived view of Marc and Terry being close, when Marc met June Child they were living together within days, albeit in the back of a van, and their respective partners were forgotten. There was undoubtedly relevance in the fact that June worked for Blackhill Enterprises, Pink Floyds management. Marc and June's tradeoffs complimented each other extremely well and they were particularly close. Peter Sanders recalls them being very much in love, always holding hands, soul mates. As time progressed, though, Marc's needs changed and he yearned for someone he could parry with musically. Although he had had his indiscretions along the way, none were serious and June chose to 'ignore' them but when he met Gloria Jones there was an artistic bonding accompanying the emotional and sexual ones and June was of no more use, and she knew it, her tradeoffs were spent out. Gloria, however, had a purse full of tradeoffs to exchange with Marc. His emotional focus was instantly adjusted and June was almost forgotten, although they were never divorced.

Marc exhibited this trait of nonchalantly discarding people who were apparently close, quite frequently. John Peel is an excellent example, Marc and John were harmonious friends, until John neglected to include 'Get it on' in his play list, and his professional stance instantly dissolved the friendship, Marc had little more to do with him, he too was of no more use. John clearly felt bitter about the way Marc had treated him, which he made obvious through his artistic condemnation of Marc in the years that followed, even after Marc's death he struggled to bury the hatchet.

Marc's affections were shallow and flirtatious, with both men and women. He used his sexuality to gain peoples cooperation lulling them into a sense of closeness and familiarity, his girlish smile and glint of his eyes, the sweet giggly nature, and apparent vulnerability lured people in. It is a tactic that has been employed by women for centuries and Marc's androgynous-ness enabled him to exploit this ploy to the full.

This analogy seems harsh but is an obvious one when examining Marc's relationship progression and even people who loved him have concluded the same. It may not, however, have been a coldly calculated ploy as Marc Bolan had but one agenda, and one true love and relationship, to which he was devoted, dedicating his whole life to and never deviated from the bond and emotional closeness he felt with Rock and Roll. This sounds pretentious but it is nevertheless true, Marc Bolan's only true love affair was life long, he was completely faithful and lived in adoration of his love. He never betrayed her and never left her side, every element of his life was moulded to fit and revolved around the service he gave to her. He was always married to and deeply in love with Rock and Roll. As with all true artists the importance of their art surpasses every other sector of existence. It is the only true relationship that they experience and to Marc Bolan the trade offs were constant and well balanced. The love he felt for Rock and Roll can be clearly seen in the lovers sparkle that appeared in his eyes when on stage; he has the face of a lover whose love is reciprocated and he effervesces the excitement he feels; he is a lover elated.

As with all relationships there were highs and lows, moments of insecurity, worries of betrayal, of losing the love of your life, fears that were partly responsible for his wallowing in the realms of self pity, drink and drugs. He was, though, strong enough to realise that to keep his love he had to reassert his affections, and he did so, bringing himself under control to court his true love again.

All other relationships in Marc Bolan's life simply played lip service to his one true love, if they failed to fulfil their expectations in the role required, they were discarded. Perhaps a cruel assumption, but he was a man blinded by love.

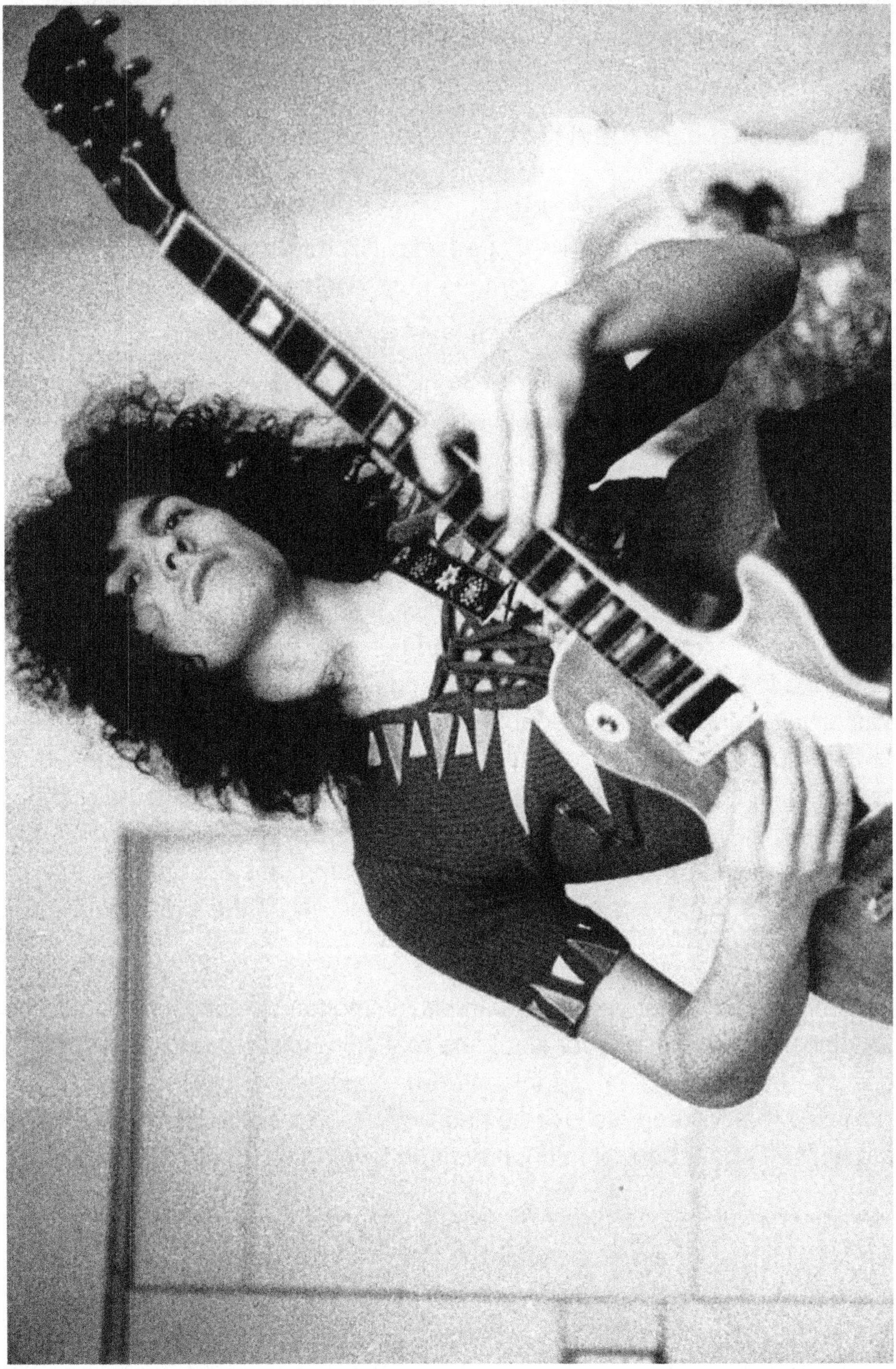

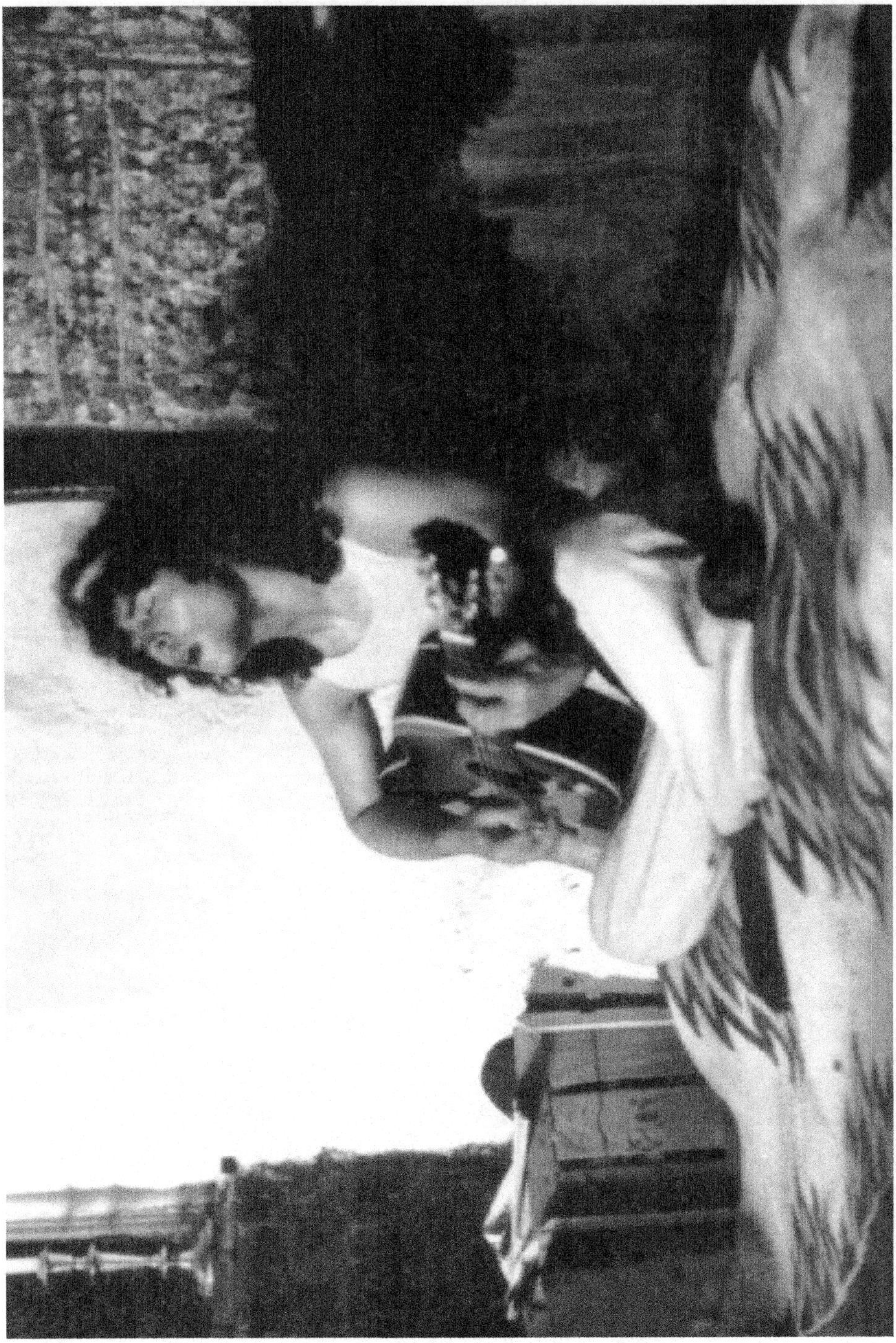

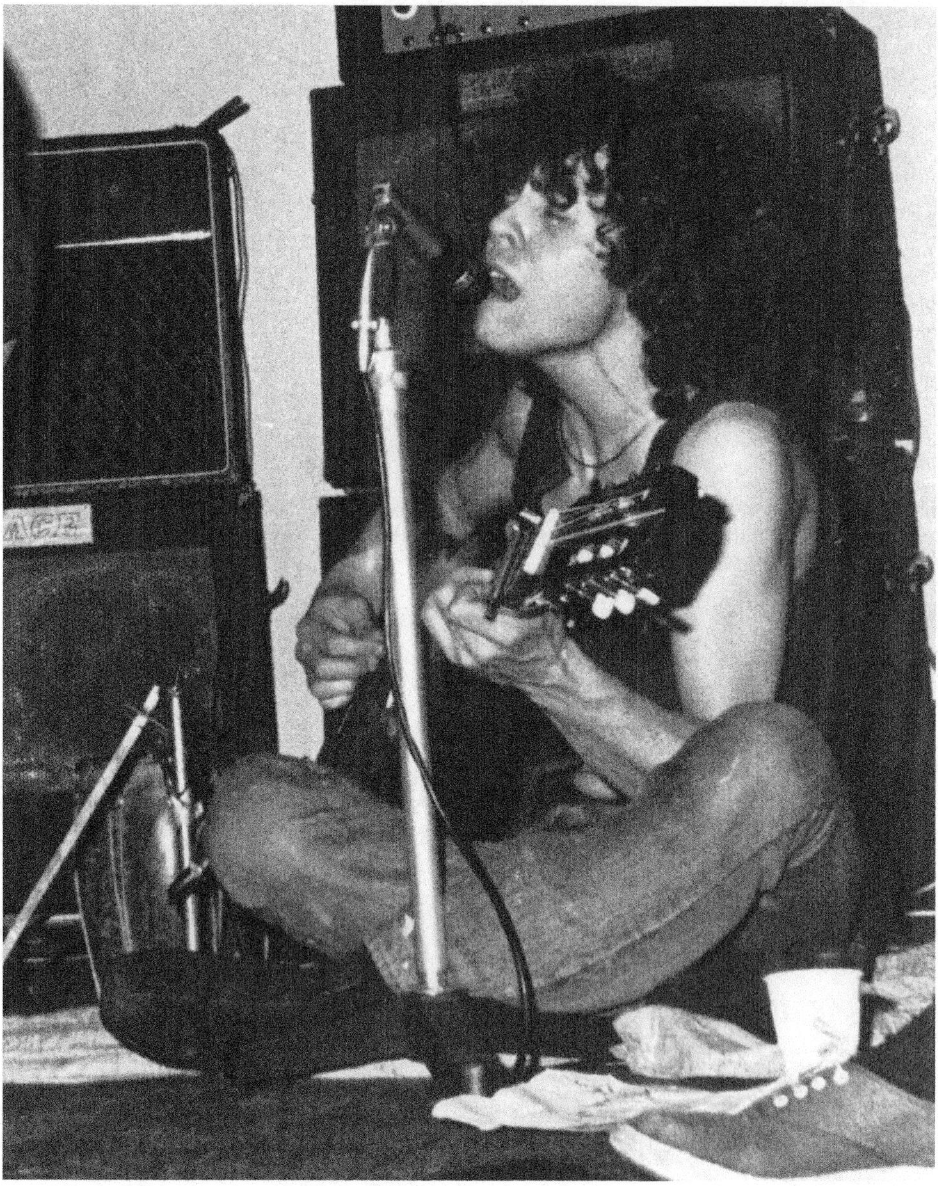

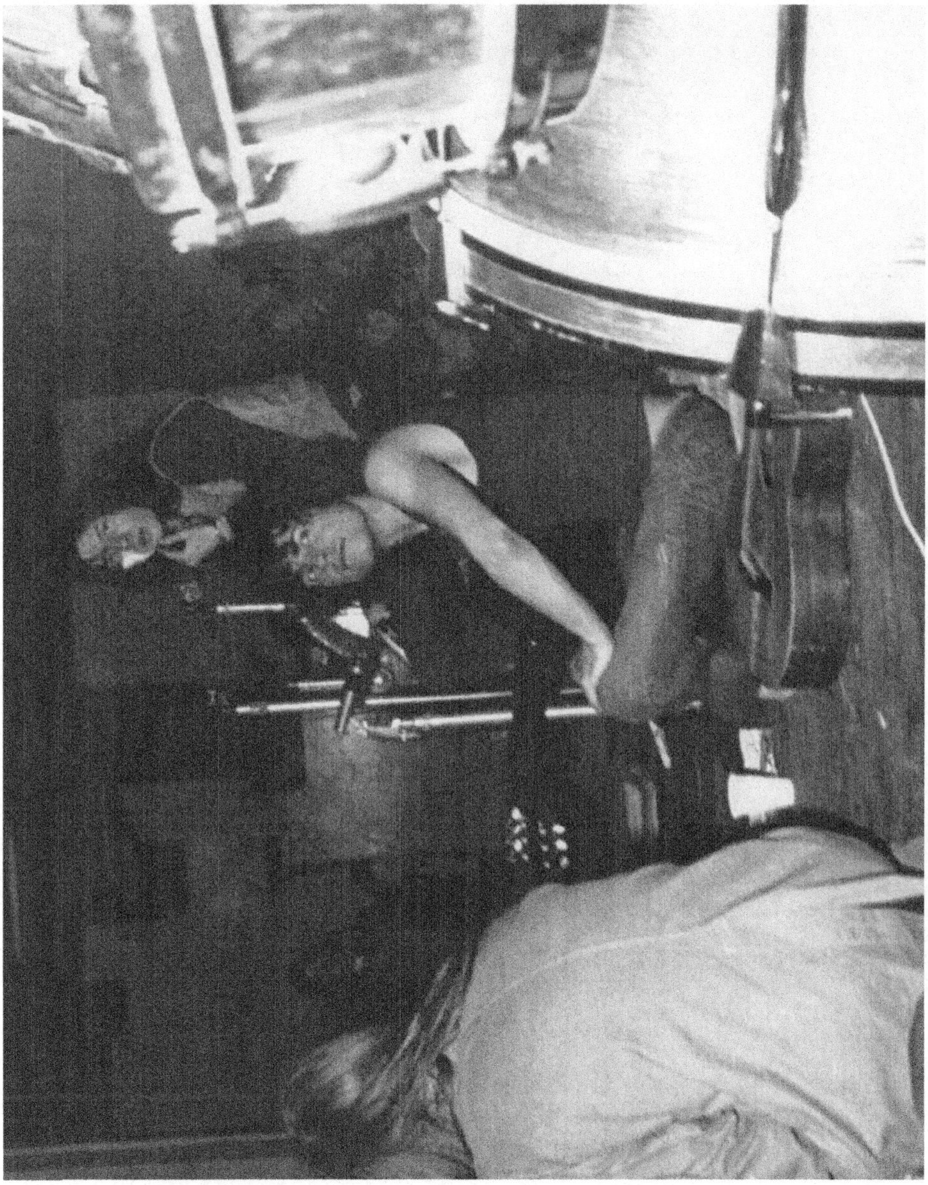

a boy barley 12 ①
~~So~~ Summers
Taped ~~the youngest~~
from the
Fall of fauns ✓

the rich liquids
~~cleansing~~ his
cleansing

head & shaping
his heart like
an orange

altho mutated, in
this ~~fu~~ crated
land he was
free from mockery

with his good
arm he
~~conducted the~~ made
his ~~peddles~~ dance

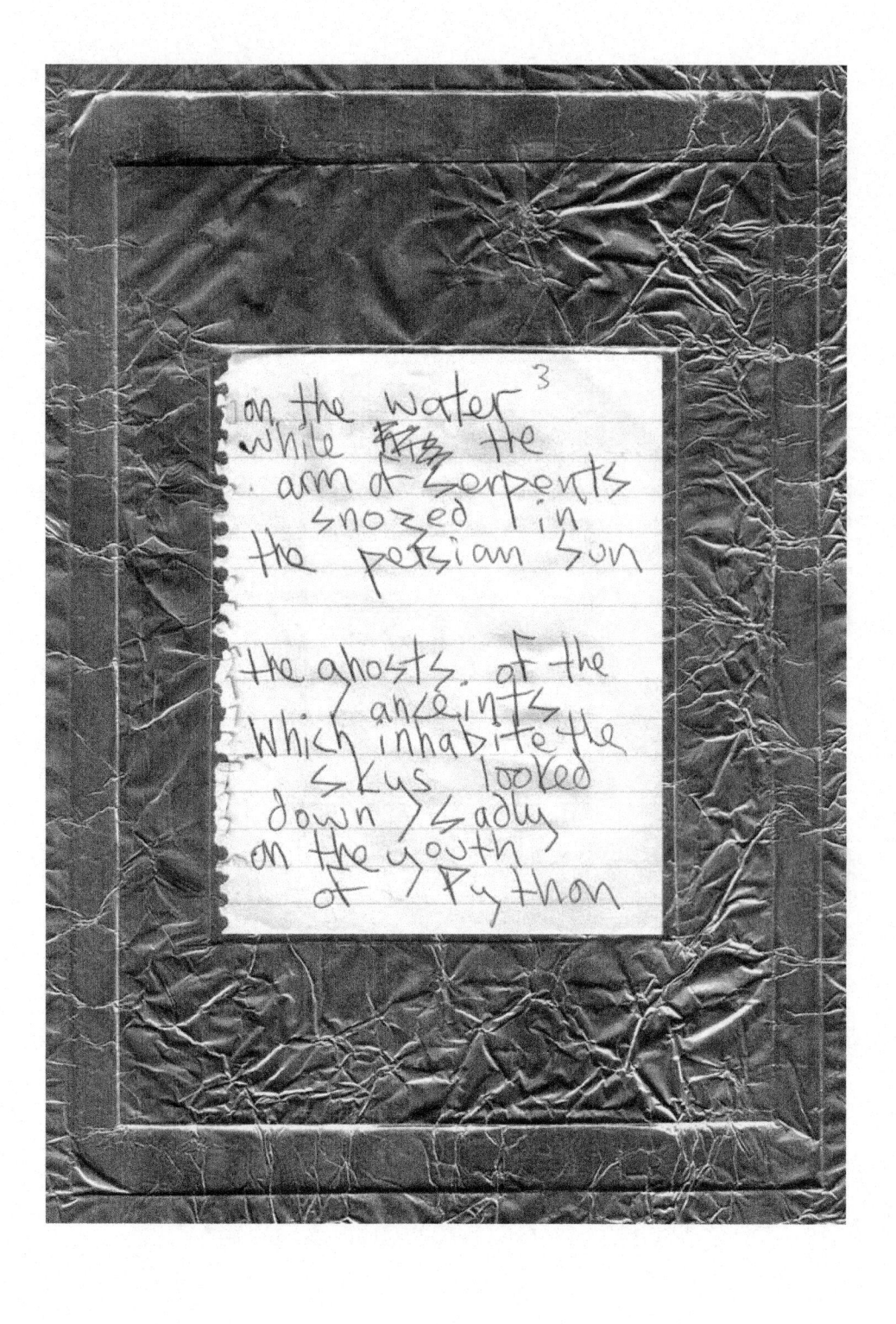

on the water [3]
while ~~the~~ the
arm of serpents
snozed in
the persian sun

the ghosts of the
anceints
which inhabite the
skys looked
down sadly
on the youth
of Python

but
~~and~~ ~~the~~ he felt ^&
their ~~stars~~
& was reproachful

be gone ~~clouds~~
~~&~~ yelled
the ~~>~~ boy

I'm no actor
clowning for
the benefit
of the blue

~~----~~ ~~hoes~~ wailed

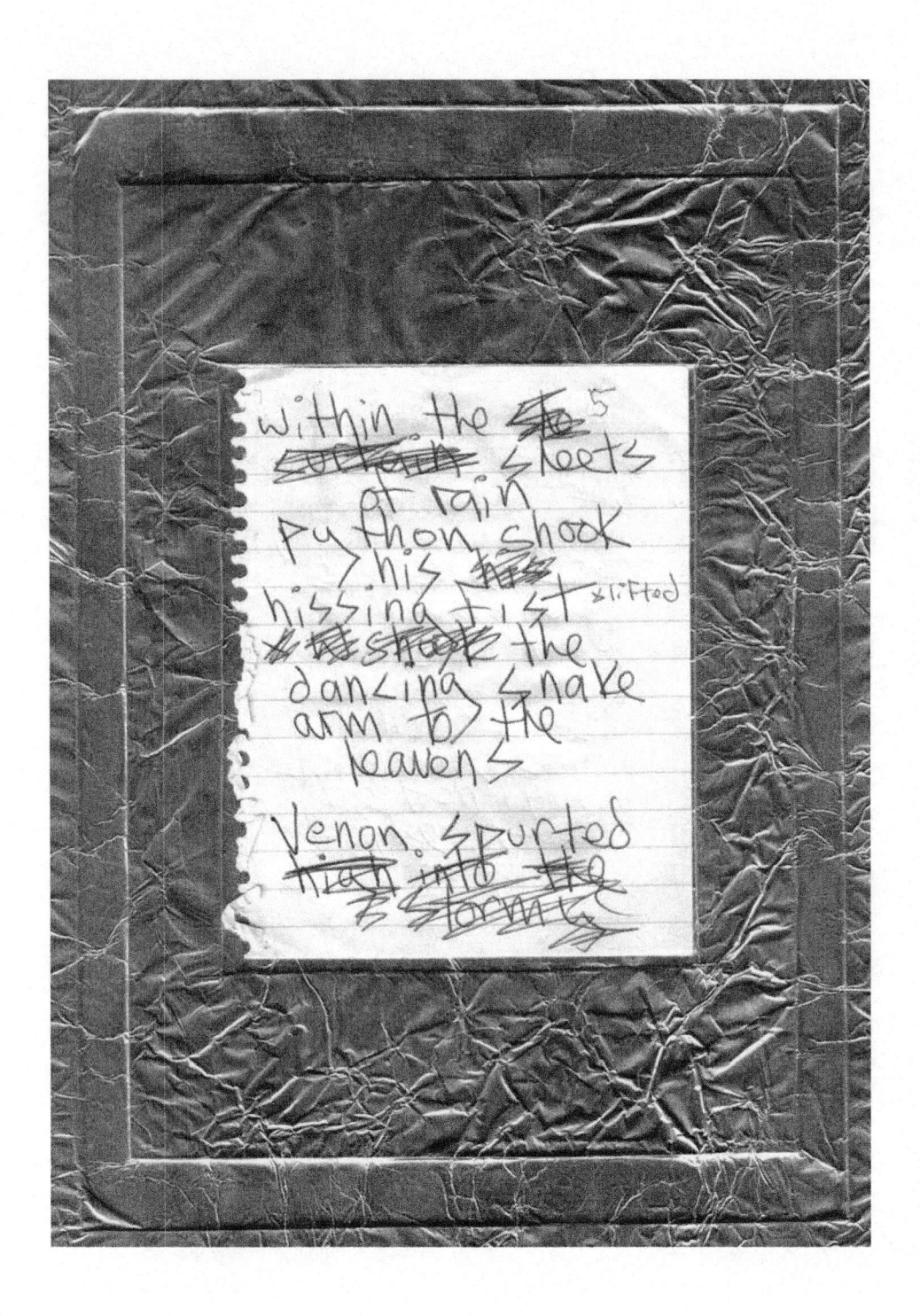

within the ~~so~~ sheets [5]
~~curtain~~
of rain
python shook
his ~~his~~
hissing fist ×lifted
×~~& shook~~ the
dancing snake
arm ~~to~~ the
heavens

venom spurted
~~high into the~~
~~storm~~

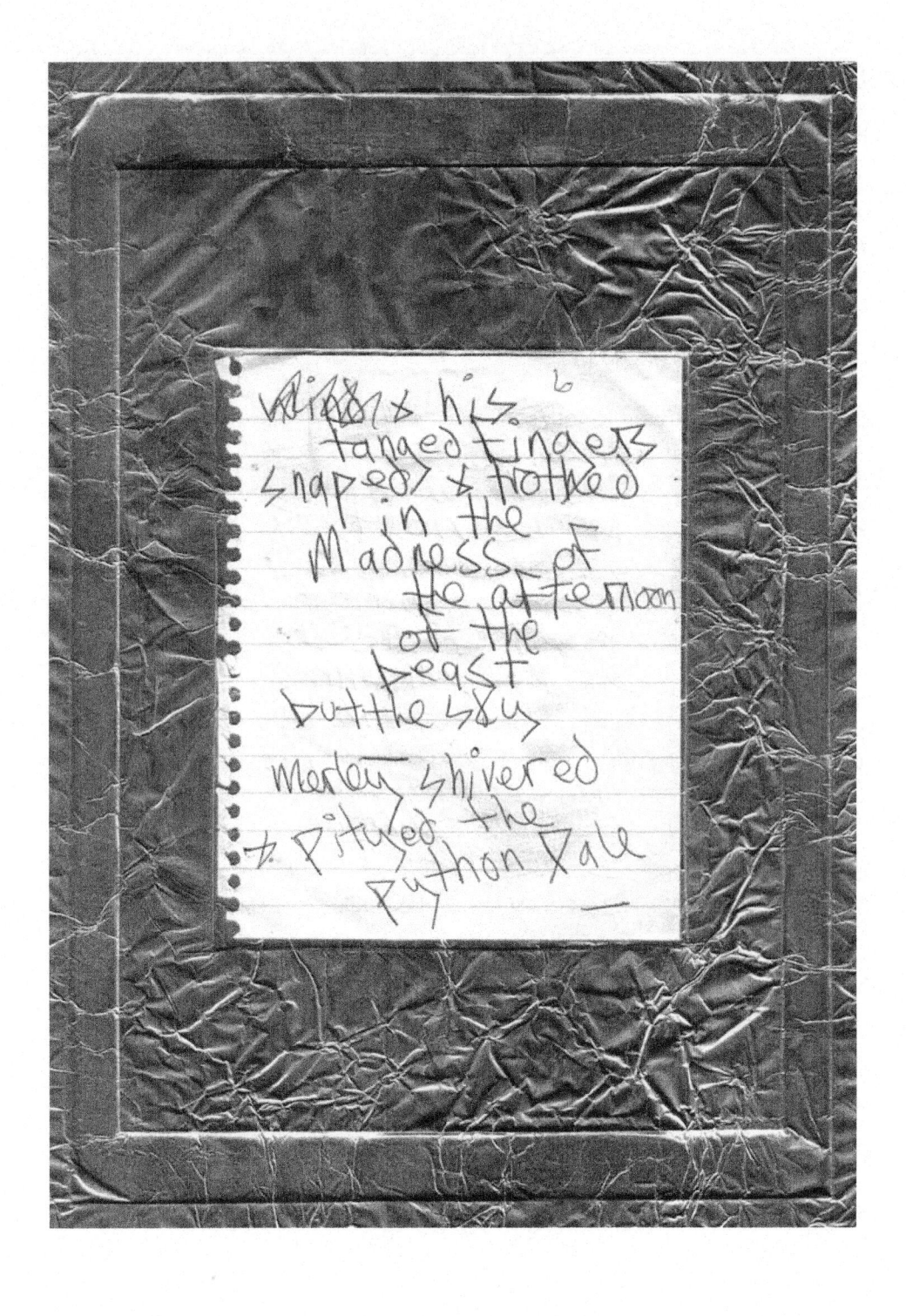

when & his
tangled fingers
snapped & frothed
in the
madness of
the afternoon
of the
beast
but the sky
merely shivered
& pitied the
python tale

8. **Pebble Dance**

"I feel the need, at the moment, to understand." Marc Bolan 1976.

<u>Python</u>

A boy, barely 12 summers,

Lapped from the Fall of Fauns,

The rich liquids cleansing his head

And shaping his heart like an orange.

Although mutated,

In this cratered land

He was free from mockery.

With his good hand

He made his pebble

Dance on the water,

While the arm of serpents

Snoozed in the Persian Sun.

The ghosts of the ancients,

Which inhabit the skies,

Looked down sadly

On the youth of Python

But he felt their stares

And was reproachful,

"Be gone clouds"

Yelled the boy,

"I'm no actor

Clowning for the benefit of the blue."

Walled within the sheets of rain

Python shook his hissing fist

And lifted his dancing snake arm to the heavens,

Venom spurted

And his fanged fingers

Snapped and frothed

In the madness of the afternoon of the beast.

But the sky merely shivered

And pitied the Python pale.

It should by now be growing clear that most of Marc's writing is allegoric, filled with symbolic representations of life and his life, akin to Edmund Spenser's 'Faerie Queene'. Some songs are singularly complete allegories, 'Metal Guru' being an excellent example, whereas others embody a variety of symbolic images, loosely connected. He always, however, enchants us with a clue, a tease to connect us to the reality masked behind his symbolism. In 'Telegram Sam', 'Bobbie's alright' refers to Bob Dylan, in chapter seven's poem 'The Lathe Lords of Manka' refers to Japan, In chapter six 'the Rumanian Sun' gives the clue to Thrace, in chapter three it was 'the sons of Romana' and in 'Python' it is the Persian Sun, but to where does this lead us? There is no reason for Marc to have used 'Persian', thus identifying the nationality of the scene; 'the warmth of the sun' would have sufficed, yet it was necessary in order to help the reader remove the poems make-up. But what lies beneath?

In 1935 Persia became Iran, under the leadership and request of Reza Shah Pahlavi; its current wealth and politics revolve around its oil fields but that has not always been the case, ancient Persia was rich with culture and it's empire was the envy of the world, particularly during the Achaemenid period. From this period rose one of the world's oldest monotheistic religions, Zoroastrianism, which has no connections to the masked swordsman, but revolves around the simplistic principle of the battle between good and evil, as opposed to the multitudinous gods of Greece and Rome. It's roots date back to 600BC, possibly further, and most of its philosophies were adopted by more modern religions. Zoroastrianism teaches that the sky was created first, which would complement the 'Big Bang' theory and opens up a door of debate that would take us far away from this poem, apart from its reference to the ancients inhabiting the skies. Persia is just one of three elements that give us the clues to the naked face below this poem. The second is the *Fall of Fauns*.

The *Fall of Fauns* implies a waterfall provided by, owned by or predominantly frequented by the Fauns. Initially it was thought that Marc had misspelled 'fauns' and meant 'fawns', pertaining to young deer, but that is not the case, he was deliberate in his spelling. *Fauns* are mythical creatures common to Roman and Greek legends, half man half goat, like Pan and C. S. Lewis' Mr. Tumnus, also the Satyrs, the attendants of Dionysus, were depicted as fauns. All of which have raised their heads before in Marc Bolan's mind.

The third element is the *Python* itself, the overall reptilian theme of the piece, *serpents, snake arm, venom* and *fanged fingers* all referring to the subject of the poem. Again serpents/snakes take many roles in mythology but to portray the subject as being deformed by having an arm like a snake, is a mythologically symbolic way of saying he is half man, half snake.

The question to resolve is what connects these three elements in the imagination of Marc Bolan, as an understanding of the workings of his mind, imagination and interests develops it becomes easier to draw the analogies.

Late in July 356 BC a young prince was born to a mother who was a keen follower of Dionysus, she was not, however, believed to have been impregnated by her husband but by the god Amun, who came to her in the form of a serpent. Because of this his countrymen did not view the prince as a pure heir to the throne nevertheless upon his earthly father's death he assumed the role of King at the young age of twenty and went on to become one of the most notorious characters in history, reigning for a mere twelve years before his premature death at the age of thirty two. During his reign he had conquered the Persian Empire and adopted much of its culture. The mathematic probability of all three prime elements being portrayed in one story is impossible to calculate as the potential numbers of variable elements are unknown, but given the nature of mythology and legend where almost anything is possible and likely, it would be extremely high. All three prime elements are here in this story along with more secondary allegories. It is interesting also to observe that there are certain similarities between this story and that of Jesus, however, that is another debate.

A boy, barely 12 summers,

Lapped from the Fall of Fauns,

Intriguingly, as with many lines in this poem there are two possible interpretations, but all relate quite conclusively to its subject. At the age of twelve Alexander the Great tamed a horse that was deemed un-rideable, impressing his father immensely. Being so impressed, not only with his horsemanship, but also his maturity and intellect, his parents, Phillip II and Olympias, recruited the service of Aristotle for his education, the Fall of Fauns, could thus refer to the pool of Grecian knowledge that Aristotle bestowed upon him. Alternatively the *12 summers* could refer to the twelve years that Alexander reigned as King and not his younger age, the *Fall of Fauns* would then allude to the life blood/water or lifeline of his home land, ancient Macedonia (now a part of Greece), which he fed from during his campaign across Central Asia.

The rich liquids cleansing his head

And shaping his heart like an orange.

Whichever interpretation of the waterfall is acknowledged it gave him a clear mind and a strong heart, with the conviction, belief and determination to lead his campaign.

Although mutated,

In this cratered land

He was free from mockery.

The mutation is symbolic of his considered impure breeding, as outlined in the brief synopsis; Alexander was believed not to be the son of his mother's husband, Phillip II, his earthly father. It was reported that she was visited by the god Amun, who came to her in the form of a serpent and that Alexander was thus the son of Amun and Olympias. As Amun was in the form of a serpent when he impregnated Olympias then it is reasonable to concur that Alexander was part snake. As a consequence he was mocked as the heir to the throne in Macedonia because he was not the true son of Phillip, but in Persia, the cratered land, he was free of such mockery and won his respect justly.

With his good hand

He made his pebble

Dance upon the water

His good hand would be his earthly half, the human part of him, and as a young human King he enforced his presence across the lands to secure his position as King. Alexander, upon the death of his father, quickly had any potential opposition of his ascension to the throne eliminated, dancing his pebble of assertion across the pool of his kingdom.

While the arm of serpents

Snoozed in the Persian sun.

His snake like mutated arm is representative of his godly half, as the son of Amun. To be the true heir to the throne of Macedonia Alexander had to suppress the speculations of his divinity, he therefore kept his godly half asleep, subdued until he had conquered Persia.

The ghosts of the ancients,

Which inhabit the skies,

Looked down sadly

On the youth of Python

Part of Alexander's agenda was to amalgamate the cultures of his conquered countries, to break down national barriers and homogenise the regions of the world. In order to affiliate himself with other lands he would adopt their style of dress, particularly Persian. This did not meet with favour in the hearts of the elders and traditionalists of Macedonia, which could be the allegory for the pity Marc bestows upon him. More likely it is that the *ghosts* of the ancients refers to the old gods such as Dionysus, who Alexander's mother worshiped, Zeus, the Olympians, their countless offspring and their ancestors, pitying the god trapped within the man, not being able to fully reveal himself.

Alexander rebukes them…

But he felt their stares

And was reproachful,

'Be gone clouds'

Yelled the boy

'I'm no actor

Clowning for the benefit of the blue.'

…telling them that he is not pretending for them.

Walled within the sheets of rain

This line refers back to the Fall of Fauns and suggests that despite his efforts Alexander was trapped in his Grecian roots.

Python shook his hissing fist

And lifted it up to the heavens,

Venom spurted

And his fanged fingers

Snapped and frothed In the madness of the afternoon of the beast.

Python raising his hissing fist alludes to Alexander stretching his army out across Central Asia, the *'spurting venom'*, the 'snapping' and the 'frothing' all refer to the battles he mercilessly raged along the way, in an almost mad obsession to conquer the world.

As Alexander's campaign progressed he became more assured of his own divinity, storming across Central Asia towards India, as if trying to prove his invincibility, his divinity, whilst still chained to his earthly roots, he began to believe he was a god.

But the sky merely shivered

And pitied the Python pale.

The gods paid little attention to the aspirations of a mere mortal, showing him only pity.

Ultimately Alexander the Great was not divine and following his premature death in Babylon his empire was torn apart by the conflicts of his successors.

When this poem is first read the make-up is so lavishly applied that it is almost impossible to see through the cracks. However, once they are found it becomes easy to reveal its true face; although during the course of the analogy there are sometimes doubts as to the truth of the character being revealed. Bolan adopts the allegories so convincingly that they develop a life and identity of their own, much like the rock star persona of Mark Feld. 'Python' becomes a character in his own right and the theme of the poem could simply and easily be pertinent to the turmoil of a disfigured boy, and the poem is valid in that guise, but in that guise Persia becomes irrelevant, as previously stated, and so does the identifying of the waterfall's source. To write of the allegoric character so convincingly, Marc would have had to believe in him, to be completely assured of his reality in order to relay that reality to the reader. As Alexander had to believe in the divine self he portrayed, else his soldiers would not have believed and bestowed their loyalty so willingly. And as Mark Feld had to believe in the character he portrayed, Marc Bolan. The allegories begin to mount and interweave as the make-up becomes the face.

It is intriguing to again find the links to Dionysus, not as openly apparent but nevertheless quite strong links. The mention of the *Fall of Fauns*, which is a portrayal of Dionysus' attendants, the Satyrs, is not as clear as indicated until it is understood that Alexander and his mother, Olympias, were strong followers of the god, and of Orpheus. Knowing of Marc's interest in these two characters makes the connection more apparent, along with Marc's interest in Greek mythology as a whole, of which Alexander the Great became a member. He indeed strived to become a part of the myths and legends he had learnt from the writings of Homer and the teachings of Aristotle, to become the legend was his true objective, his purpose and his reason for existence.

To attain legendary status a person has to display an unwavering dedication to the cause or subject they wish to exploit for the purpose. If two distinct yet completely differing legends are compared, the properties of their common denominators can be clearly seen.

Jesus Christ is undeniably the most successful legend of all time. The instant reaction in the conscious or subconscious would be to prepare for a debate into various religious philosophies but that is not the discussion being tabled. It is, instead, to examine the route taken to ascend to that status. In order to explain the purpose of the debate more clearly, so as not to cause any religious offence, let legendary status be portrayed as a building and for there to be two completely different buildings standing side by side, with two completely different functions. To construct both buildings the same processes would have had to be employed. Both need good foundations, both need strong walls laid brick by brick, both need good strong floors at different levels, windows, doors and a good roof, all built to accommodate their individual use, one is a cathedral and the other the war ministry.

Jesus Christ was born of an earthly mother with a divine father, his early years he spent learning his craft, the craft of godliness. When he was fully prepared he embarked upon his mission, his purpose, forsaking all other distractions in life, single-mindedly playing his role until death.

A short synopsis on the life of Alexander the Great would read in a similar fashion as would that of many legends, the predominant element of each being their single-minded determination and belief in their purpose, cause or reason right through to their death.

Marc Bolan had a fascination for legends, both mythical and real. Each of his poems in this book has drawn inspiration from a legend of some kind. Even America's dropping of its' bombs on Japan, rightly or wrongly, could be described as a legendary act. In his lyrics he pays homage to people who he perceives as legendary, such as Bob Dylan and John Lennon and respectfully he musically endorses people like Chuck Berry and Howlin' Wolf. As Riggs O'Hara stated, Marc Bolan yearned to become a legend and would have adored the status he has attained. In an interview in 1972 he said in response to a question asking how he would like to be viewed in two hundred years time, "I'd like them, if they ever found a record by Lennon or Chuck Berry, to think of me as one and the same."

It is doubtless that fame and legendary status were elements of his ambition along the with the respect which accompanies that status and it is certainly a part of the motivation that drove him, but motivation is hollow without a belief, purpose or reason, to what would he be motivated to do? For Jesus Christ it was the irrefutable belief in his divinity and the role he was playing in the salvation of mankind; for Alexander it was the conviction to unite the people of his empire. For Marc Bolan it was the belief that he had the power to communicate and entertain through his words and music, and that he had the talent to influence music and expand musical boundaries. From his youth that belief drove him, although when younger he was not sure of his reason himself, it all began to come into focus for him when he was sixteen and everything in his life revolved around his words and music. In one way or another every aspect of his life fuelled his reason for being. For any artist their art is their reason for existence.

Marc Bolan could never have been anything other than a rock star, every part of him was attuned for that role, his looks, his personality, his talent and his love for the part; this does not detract from his single- minded determination to succeed in his purpose and it is that determination of fulfilling his reason for being that makes him a legend.

Bill Legend said that Marc always had to be the main man and that he was always driven and almost pushing himself and everyone else to the limit, he commented on how quick and musically proficient Marc was in the studio, "On the ball!"

that he always appeared to have a very clear idea of what he wanted to achieve, although Bill complained about the lack of demos to help him prepare for new songs he also admitted that Marc was possibly looking for the spontaneity.

It has to be said that Bill's comments were made in a positive tone, and that he holds a great deal of admiration for Marc but what he describes of him would be perceived by many as arrogance, a trait attributed to Marc many times and a trait attributed to many legends. It is a fine line that distinguishes between arrogance and self-assurance, self-belief and the confidence and determination to assert that belief. If the belief is asserted and is right then a hero, a legend is born, if it is asserted and is wrong, then an arrogant fool is left to repent in ridicule.

Riggs described Marc as an opportunist, saying that he capitalised on and used every opportunity, just to become famous, and that he was lucky to find he had a talent when he got there, "It's usually the other way round, people who are famous generally have no talent!" he said.

When viewing the whole picture it is more conceivable that Marc was aware of his underlying talent quite early and that his period with Riggs was a part of his self-development, and yes in one respect Riggs is correct, Marc utilised the opportunity of spending time with Riggs to help structure his foundations, but music was his reason for forming those foundations. When Mark Feld stood on the milk crates outside Roy Vincent's store he knew where he was going, he knew his purpose, his reason for existing and he exploited every opportunity that would assist him in fulfilling that purpose. In his own words Marc Bolan was born to boogie and boogie he did until he died, never detracting from his self-belief and determination, his reason for being.

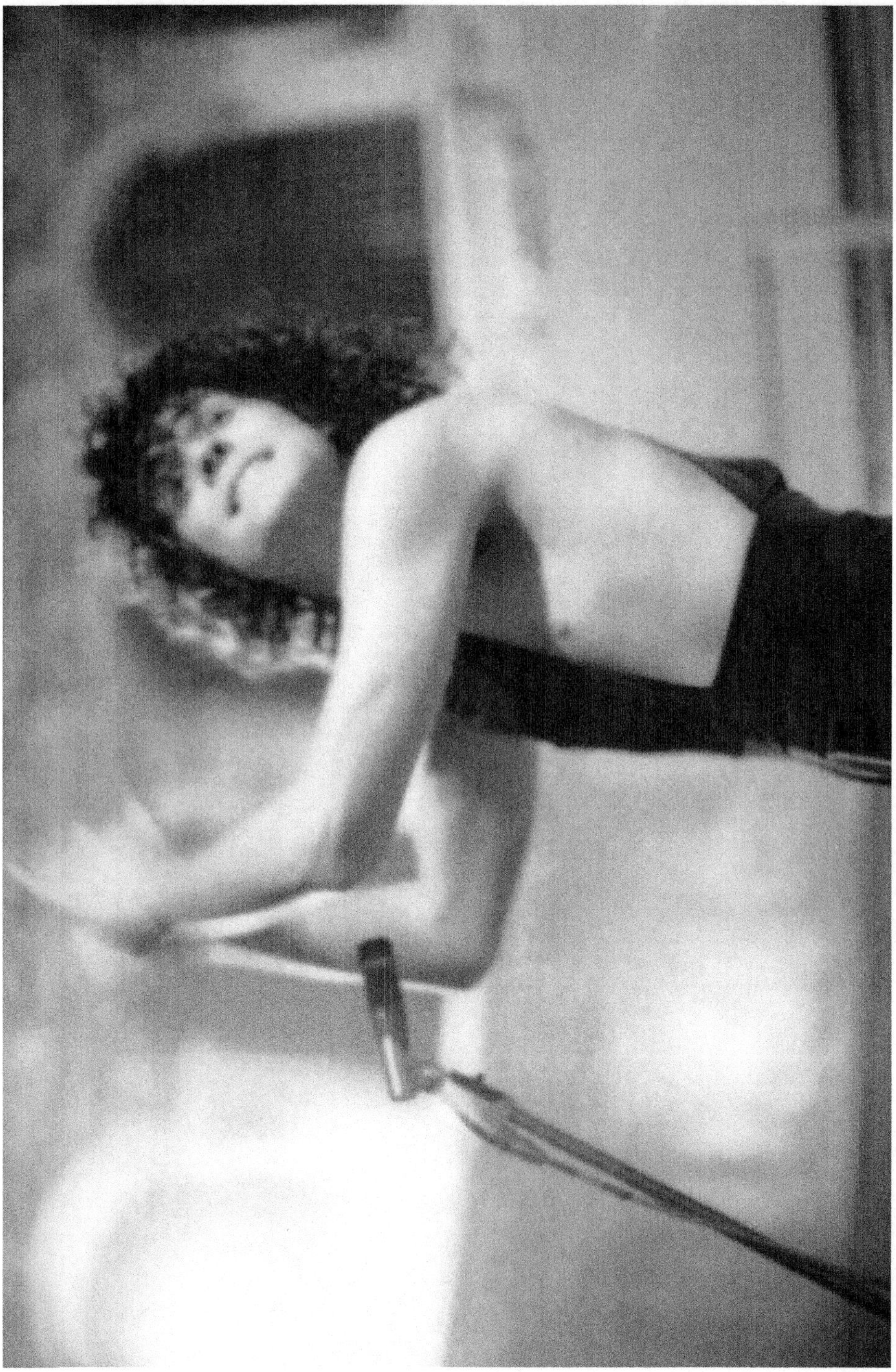

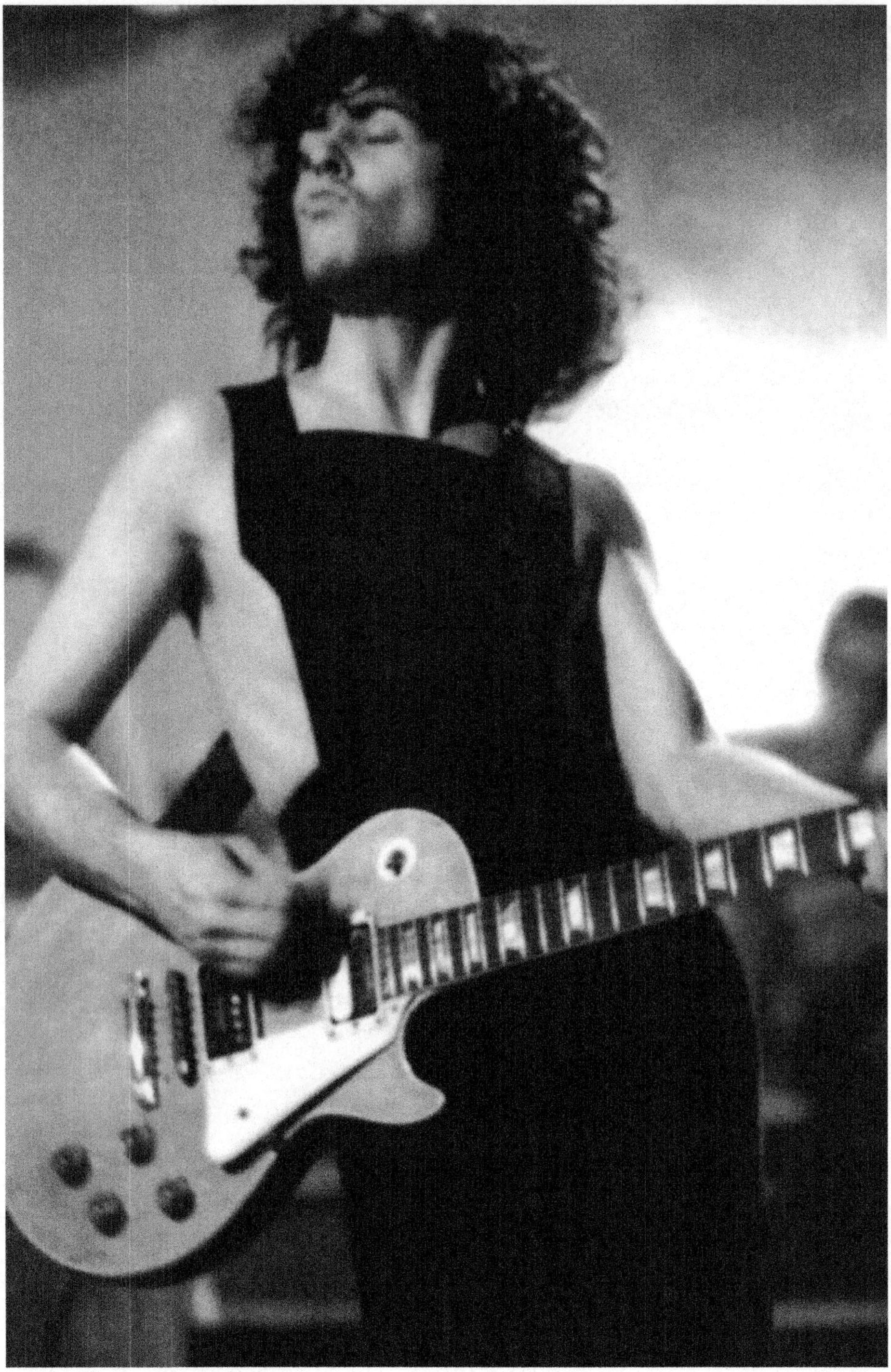

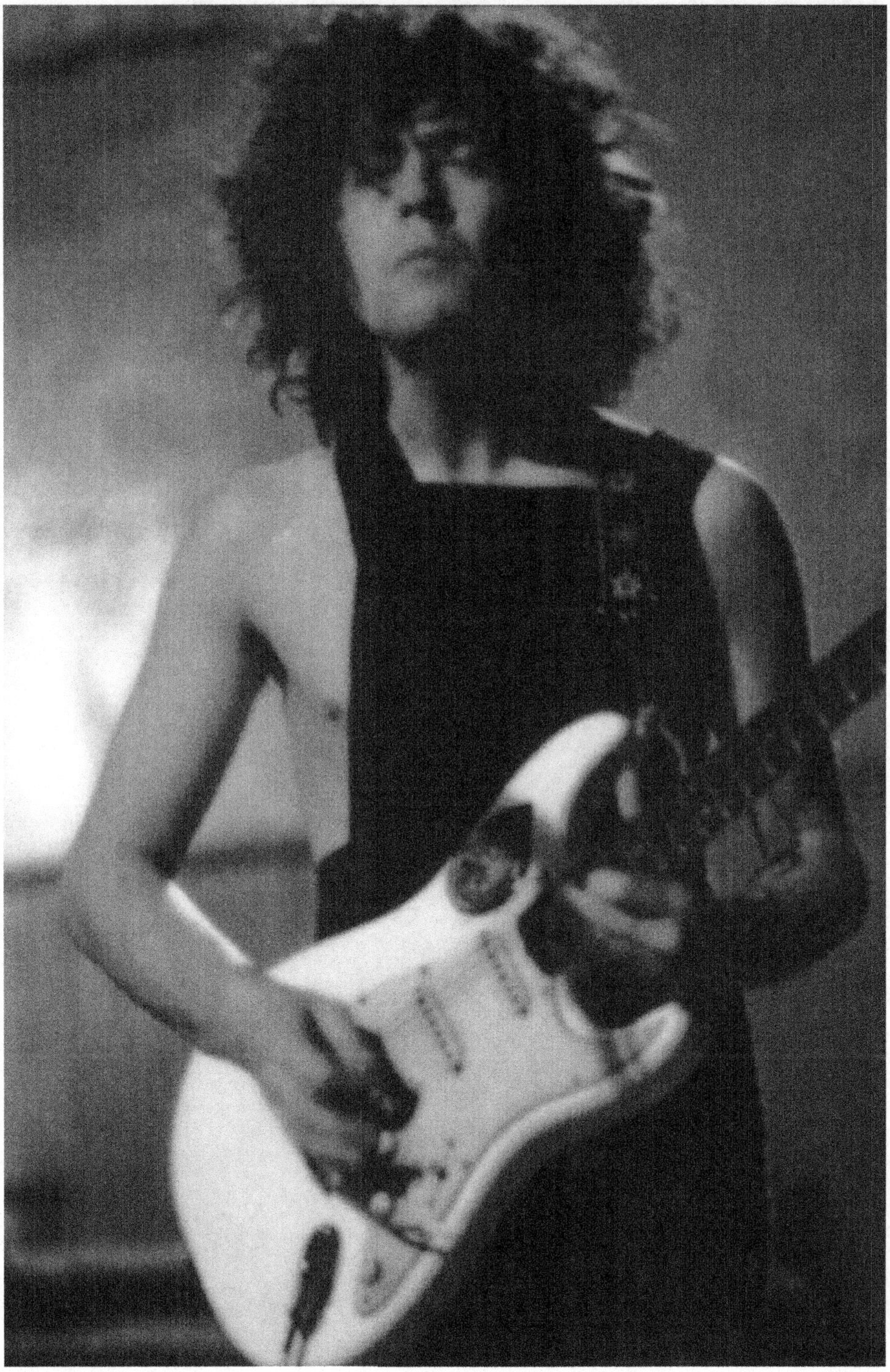

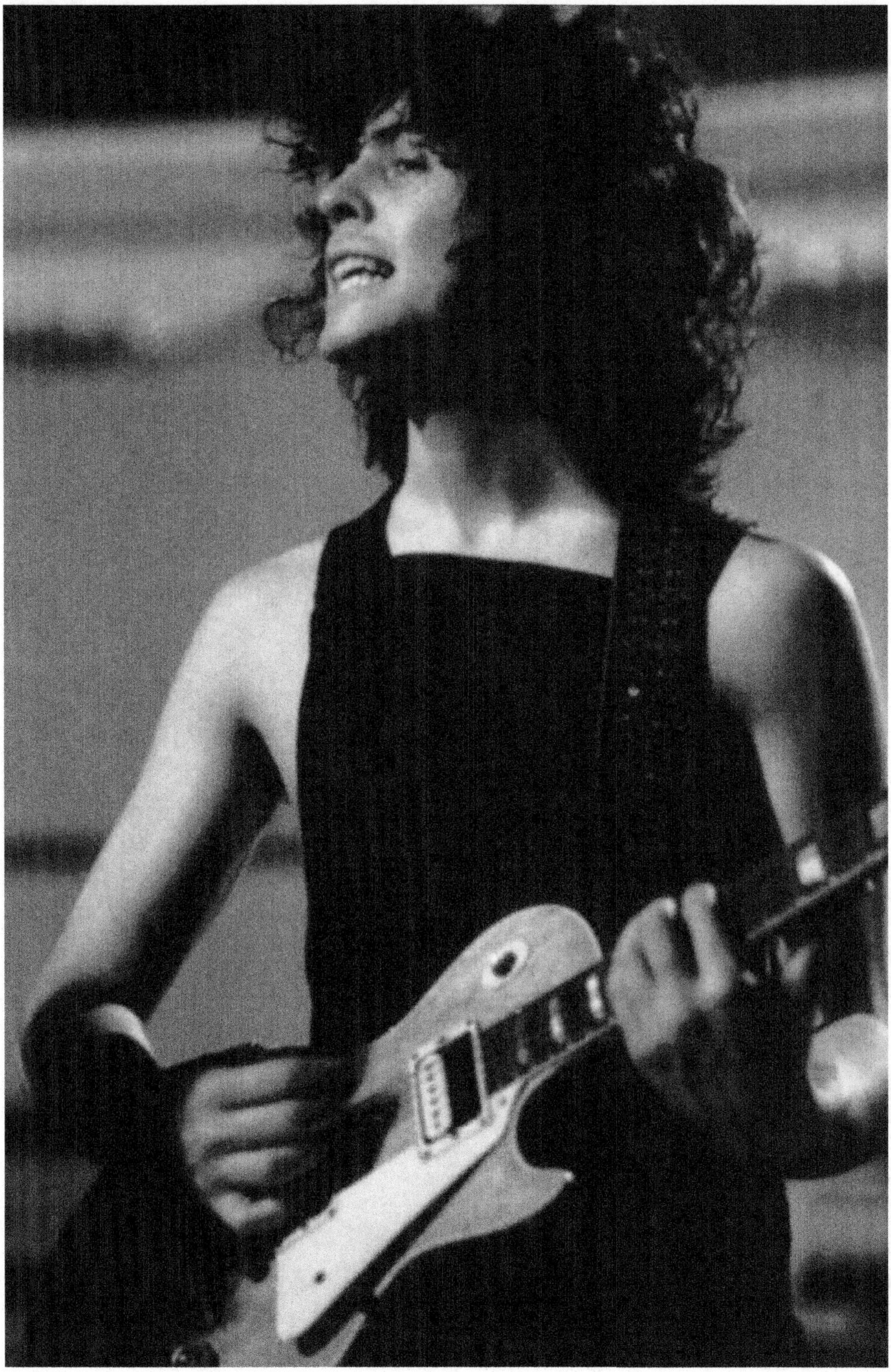

down the stairs
of wind he went

bent with
bolt of thunder
sword

with spike & sheild
of ~~lazuli~~ LAZULI
to battle with
the elder horde

the anceint brood
that ~~be~~ dig saw

with lust & greed[2]
earths fairy cave
with silver beards
& grimy hands

they long have
robbed ~~the~~
~~~~ lozallands
of topaz & stone
the gods have
grown,

on silver nights [3]
from many heights
with finger
green they d,tard
~~shake~~ s preen,

these things
were seen
in bygone days

when men had
eyes for things
of wonder,
now all that'

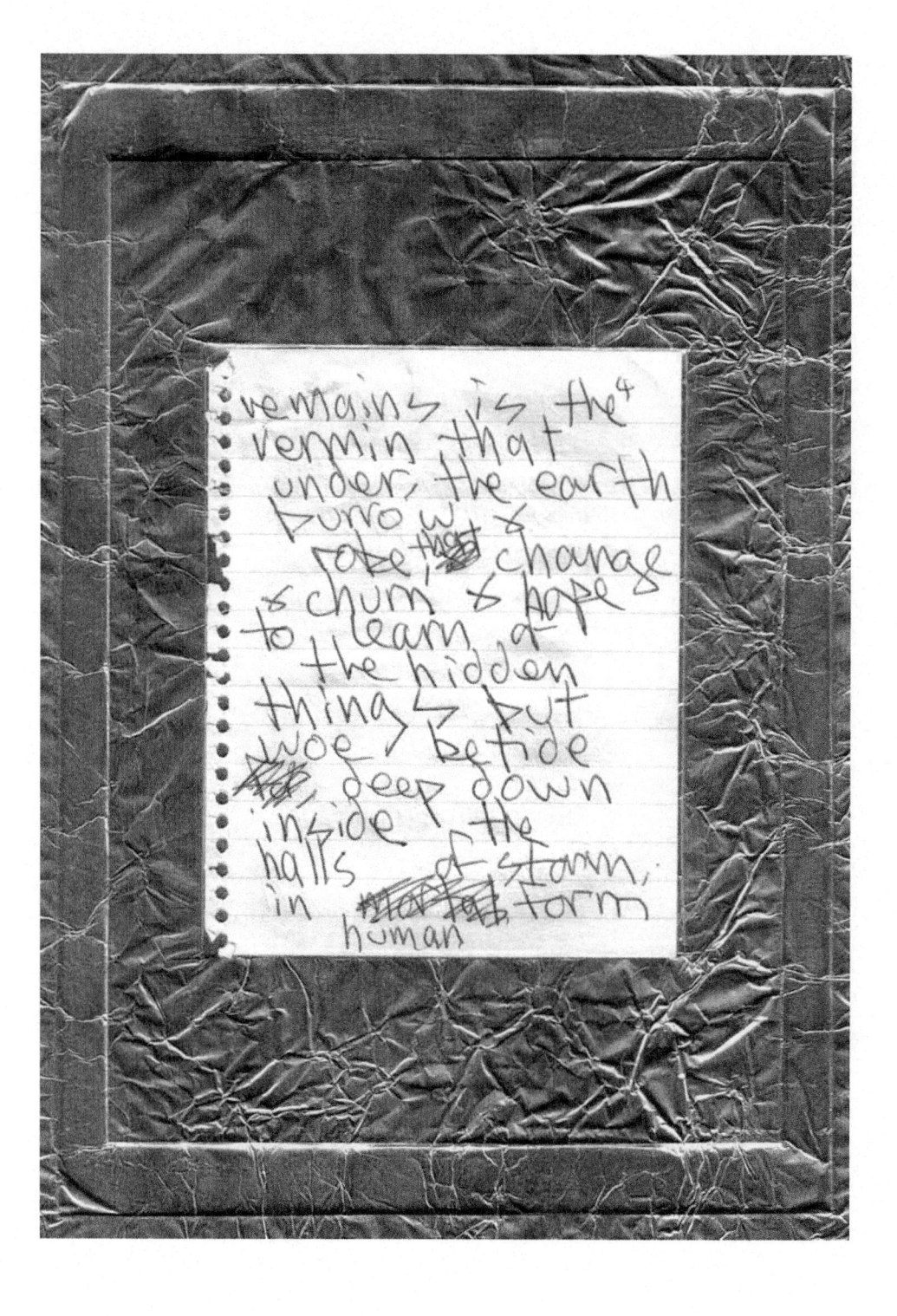

remains is the
vermin that
under the earth
burrow &
~~poke that~~ change
to churn & ~~hope~~
to learn of
the hidden
things, but
woe betide
~~it,~~ deep down
inside the
halls of ~~damn~~ ,
in ~~horted~~ form
human

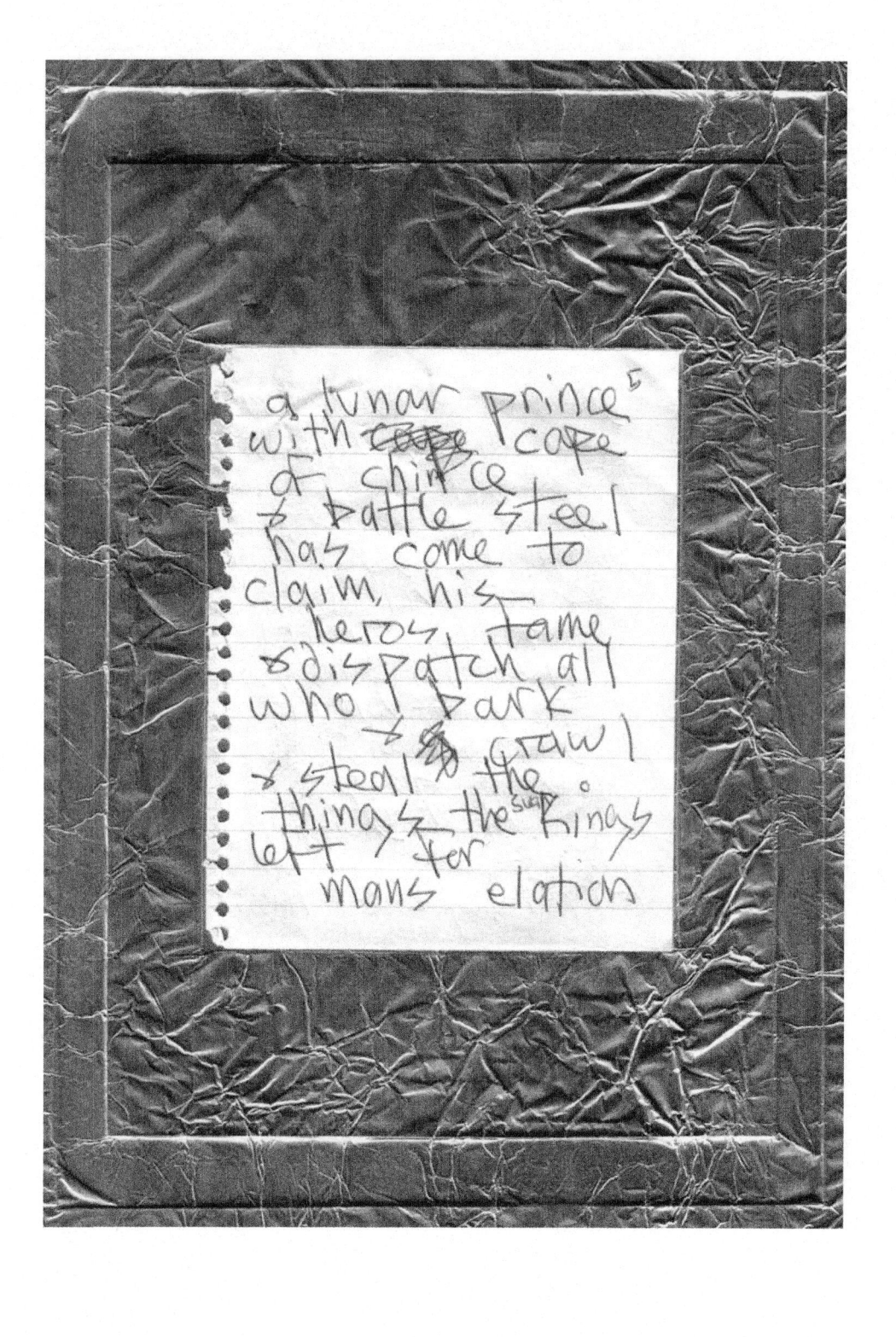

a lunar prince[s]
with ~~cape~~ core
of ~~china~~ battle steel
has come to
claim his
hero's fame
& dispatch all
who bark
& crawl
& steal the
things the[sup] kings[s]
left for
mans elation

"things to please 6
his sight,
so that they
might have
a bond, a hold
to reach him
by. For the
gods need
beauty, purity
or a fair thought
on which they
may enter
the hearts of
       men.

9. **The Swan King's Legacy**

"Somewhere one has to decide that everyone has a different head." Marc Bolan 1972.

Down the stairs

Of wind he went,

Bent with bolt of thunder sword

With spike and shield of Lazuli,

To do battle with the elder horde,

The ancient brood

That dig and gnaw

With lust and greed,

Earths' fiery cove.

With silver beards and grimy hands

They have long robbed the local lands

Of Topaz and stone

The Gods have grown,

On silver nights

From moony heights,

With fingers green

They'd tend and preen,

These things were seen

In bygone days

When men had eyes

For things of wonder.

Now all that remains

Is the vermin

That under the earth

Burrow and rob.

They change and churn

And hope to learn

Of the hidden things,

But woe betide

Deep down inside the

Halls of Storm,

In human form,

A Lunar Prince

With cape of chintz

And battle steel,

Has come to claim

His hero's fame

And dispatch all

Who bark and crawl

And steal the things

The Swan Kings

Left for man's elation,

Things to please his sight

So that they might

Have a bond,

A hold to reach him by.

For the Gods need beauty, purity

Or a fair thought

On which they may enter

The hearts of men.

When Riggs O'Hara read this poem he believed that it reflected their break up, mainly because of its opening line. He expressed an opinion that most of the poems shown to him contained references to elements of their relationship, although he hid his reasoning behind a cloak of privacy; this probably says more about Riggs than Marc Bolan and indeed any reader. There is a danger when reading poetry, although some would say that it is the essence of poetry and music, to place a meaning that resounds from our own agenda and experiences, neglecting those of the writer and it is certainly true that some writers, musicians and artists deliberately provoke and court these types of analogies, Marc Bolan was himself guilty of this. As previously discussed, it encourages debate and intrigue which extends the life of the piece, or increases the sales figures as people desperately try to decode the lyrics, to see behind the make-up. 'Metal Guru' is (again) an excellent example, Marc loved the game that he set with his lyrics, only he knew their true meaning and he teased with slightly insufficient clues. All he would ever say about 'Metal Guru' is that it was about someone he knew and indeed it is. The true subject of the song may be aware of the disguise because of what can be described as insider knowledge, but without confirmation in some form it may be impossible to reach a confident conclusion. That is unless the mind, thought processes, experiences and chronology of the writer can be first understood, only then will the true meaning of 'Metal Guru' be reached, if there is one to be reached?

If the writer makes the mistake of using plastic surgery instead of a mask or makeup then the original face of the poem will no longer be there to be seen, there would thus be little point to the disguise. Marc was always careful to avoid the plastic surgery and left clear smudges in the make-up.

Riggs expressed the belief that although much of Marc's work was based on mythology or history it had a third level of meaning pertaining to events in their history, although he declined to convey the rational for his conclusion. It is more likely that Riggs is guilty of seeing the poetry from his own agenda and placing a higher level of importance upon their relationship, from Marc's perspective, than existed. Riggs had a profound influence and effect on the young Marc Bolan, but he was far from being the Daisy Buchanan of the pop worlds Jay Gatsby. Bolan had many more influences and loves than Riggs O'Hara and his smudges in the make-up of his writings clearly indicate which works are about Riggs.

Considering how much relevance Riggs placed on his influences upon Marc, he knows surprisingly little about his protégée (in his eyes), but to make valid judgements and analyses the judge has to understand the judged and for anyone to state that Marc Bolan was not interested in music surely proves a blindness of true understanding. Riggs' brief appraisal of Marc's poetry being related to their relationship is, apart from being purely narcissistic of Riggs, giving far to much credit to the ability of Marc Bolan. To write with three layers of allegories is beyond most of the world's geniuses and although the agenda being pursued here is to give credibility to Marc Bolan's words, Riggs' theory would apply the make-up to thickly to adhere to the face.

The true face of this poem is only subtly made-up by Marc and in slight contradiction to the preceding debate, and in irony, it may have a coincidental interpretation linked to their relationship, but one that was, without doubt, unintended. The poem is about steeling, about taking things that are precious, for various reasons, greed or in the guise of learning and this is where the connection to Marc and Riggs' relationship could be made, that Marc, when he had stolen all the knowledge from Riggs that he could, left down the stairs of wind. It is a tenuous link that is not supported by the rest of the poem but one that Riggs can be forgiven for making in his brief reading of the piece. The true face of the poem lies in the tombs of Egypt, more specifically that of Tutankhamen. Tutankhamen means 'Living image of Amun', a name that appeared in the last chapter, reputably the divine father of Alexander the great. Amun is the Egyptian god of air and wind, as his cult developed in the ancient dynasties he took on more roles being linked to Ra and, by the Greeks, to Zeus as he was seen as the king of the gods; Greek/Egyptian references to Zeus-Amun can be found implying that the two were, by some, thought of as the same mythological character. Because the wind is invisible Amun was represented by the colour blue, as it is the colour of the sky seen through the air. The opening lines now become clear…

Down the stairs

Of wind he went,

as the god of the air and sky, Amun descends from above using the wind as a staircase.

Bent with bolt of thunder sword

With spike and shield of Lazuli,

He is armed with a thunderbolt sword, Marc's word play giving the connection to Zeus, the spike or spear and the shield of *Lazuli* a further link to Amun as Lazuli is a precious gem stone, blue in colour, Amun's colour.

To do battle with the elder horde,

The ancient brood

That dig and gnaw

With lust and greed,

Earths' fiery cove

The god Amun comes down to earth to battle with the old tribes who pillage the caves and tombs of the Earth, the tombs of the Pharaohs (who it was believed became gods) that were laden with treasures amassed to assist them in their journey into the afterlife. His battle would probably be seen to take the form of the realisation of the curses believed to be set on their tombs.

With silver beards and grimy hands

They have long robbed the local lands

Of Topaz and stone

The Gods have grown,

The grave robbers have scavenged the local lands for years stealing the gems the gods have made.

On silver nights,

From moony heights

With fingers green

They'd tend and preen

On clear bright nights the gods would, from the skies (Moony heights) cultivate with magic fingers the gems and treasures of the world.

These things were seen

In bygone days

When men had eyes for

Things of wonder.

It should be emphasised that Marc is recounting fairly modern events of grave robbing that have occurred in recent centuries, when the ancient beliefs had died out or given way to less mystical religions, these last lines relating modern man's failing ability to see the magic of the ancient gods and the beliefs that surrounded them.

Now all that remains

Is the vermin

That under the earth

Burrow and rob.

With any respect for ancient beliefs lost all that is left are robbers.

They change and churn

And hope to learn

Of hidden things,

Here Marc changes the nature and motive of the robbing from that of greed to that of the quest for knowledge, but gives no mercy for the apparently 'more acceptable' reason for the defiling of the ancient shrines.

But woe betide

Down deep inside the Halls of Storm,

This is the warning of the curse that was supposed to protect 'the Halls of Storm' referring to the chambers of Tutankhamen's tomb, remembering that he was the living likeness of Amun, the god of wind.

In human form

A lunar prince

It is here that the links begin to connect as the son of Amun and his divine wife Mut was Chons the Egyptian Moon god *(Lunar Prince)*. One of his roles was to slay the enemies of the pharaoh, in a particularly horrific manner, hence he was referred to in Egyptian texts as the 'one who lives off hearts'. The sacred animal of Chons was the baboon, pictures of which can be clearly seen on the wall of Tutankhamen's burial chamber.

With cape of chinz

And battle steel,

Has come to claim

His hero's fame

Chons has come dressed for battle and the revenge he will administer, in the nature of the curse will overshadow the fame of his hero Tutankhamen.

It is the small details that Marc conveys which help confirm the analogies of his work, albeit they still lie slightly hidden in allegories. Egyptologist Howard Carter discovered the tomb of Tutankhamen but he was sponsored by George Edward Stanhope Molyneux Herbert, 5th Earl of Carnarvon. A short while after entering the tomb with Carter, Lord Carnarvon died from blood poisoning as a result of a mosquito bite, at the time of his death the lights were reputed to have gone out over Cairo and back in Britain his dog Susie was reported to have let out a howl before dying herself. Lord Carnarvon was not in the best of health and was seriously disabled as a result of a car accident in 1901. The media of the time exploited his death, embroidering it as the 'Curse of Tutankhamen' and it is believed that a young journalist by the name of Arthur Conan Doyle originally penned the wording of the curse…

'Death shall come on swift wings to him that touches the tomb of the Pharaoh'

which in actuality does not appear anywhere on or around the tomb.

And dispatch all

Would mean to kill.

Who bark and crawl

Refers to Lord Carnarvon's dog, Susie, and Lord Carnarvon himself who had a severe limp.

And steel the things

The Swan Kings

Left for man's elation;

These lines obviously again relate to the stealing of the treasures from the tomb, deposited there to assist the Pharaoh in his journey to the afterlife. *The Swan Kings* associates with Amun, as he was the god of air and the wind he was often depicted with birds in some way, his headdress or crown was usually drawn with two large plumes extending from it, hence 'The Swan King', also the pictures of the kings drawn at the time portrayed them being quite pale with long necks; not forgetting that Tutankhamen means 'the living image of Amun' or more fittingly the living image of the Swan King, hence the plural 'Kings' for the two characters Amun and Tutankhamen.

Things to please his sight

So that they might

Have a bond,

A hold to reach him by.

The beauty of the treasures forms a bond between the god and the Pharaoh assisting his passage.

For the Gods need beauty, purity

Or a fair thought

On which they may enter

The hearts of men.

These final lines conclude and emphasise the previous ideal that the gods need a vehicle upon which to connect with man, which would be things of beauty, such as the treasures in the tomb or good thoughts.

An interesting poem in many respects although it appears to repeat various elements of itself in different guises and would undoubtedly have benefited from a rewrite by Marc it does show how aware he was and how he absorbed knowledge. In order to help confirm the analogy of this poem being about Tutankhamen it should be noted that the British Museum played host to the Tutankhamen Exhibition in 1972 between March 30th and September 30th, there was a great deal of interest and media coverage in anything mummy-like. With Marc's interest in ancient mythologies it is highly likely that he attended the exhibition.

The overall impression is that Marc strongly disapproved of the violation of the pharaoh's graves no matter what the motive, even the academic thieves come under rebuke. He appears to be expressing a criticism that there is no longer respect for the sanctity of ancient cultures and that under the umbrella of intellect and academia their religious sites are desecrated quite casually. This is easily seen in this country when visiting stone circles; parents allowing their children to climb the stones whilst sitting on them themselves picnicking, boys using them as goal posts with no regard for the fact that they are the religious sites of their ancestors, touristic historic voyeurism, acts that would not be seen in a cathedral. He also expresses concern that man has lost the sight for magic and mysticism, something Marc Bolan seemed to have.

His apparent disapproval for the gathering of knowledge holds a strong irony considering his own thirst for it. He had obviously drank from the fountain that Howard Carter turned on or he would not have been able to write such a knowledgeable poem; his almost vampiric approach to ruthlessly obtaining knowledge from others is also in conflict with this disapproval. His hunger for knowledge is one of the most common traits attributed to him, to re-quote Marc's brother Harry "He was a reaper of knowledge".

Marc certainly understood the importance of knowledge but only in the areas that interested him and that he knew he could exploit. From Riggs O'Hara he learnt the importance of gaining the knowledge that gave him substance to his writings and where to get that knowledge. From Simon Napier-Bell he learnt how to manipulate the industry he wanted to work in. From his idols such as Elvis, Cliff Richard, Chuck Berry, the Beatles and many more, he learnt how to perform and understand rock music, forming an amalgamation of movements on stage compiled from those of his heroes. His words and music were much the same, an amalgamation of his hero's styles but all with the extra individual ingredient of Marc Bolan. He sucked knowledge from everyone in some way and from every aspect of life. Riggs even believed that his expedition into drugs was a part of playing the role in order to gain knowledge of the experience, as an actor may take a job as a fisherman in order to understand 'the fisherman' before playing the role. Riggs even expressed the possibility that he could have been emulating Elvis, almost deliberately following the 'Rock Star' agenda to be complete in the part. To place that level of deliberate intent on Marc's role-playing would be to label him with an almost psychotic intensity of determination; that would be unfair, it is more probable that he fell into the same traps as most rock stars and simply lost his way for a while.

Marc's harvesting even extended as far as his wife and later girlfriend. June for her music industry knowledge at a management and PR level and then Gloria for her musical knowledge and capability. There was nobody in Marc Bolan's life that did not contribute in some way, either knowingly or unknowingly, to his acquisitions of knowledge and experience. In a 1972 interview, with specific reference to managers, he said "I work with people I think are good, while they're good. If they're not good, I won't work with them anymore."

He had a naturally inquisitive mind that he focused on the areas of particular interest to him, Harry recounts that he was always ready to debate with people to see what he could learn from them. The acquisitions he made he stored up and used at various points, in various ways, whether it was the theatrical exploitation of bright clothes and make-up to add colour and drama to what had become a mundane rock stage, or a depth and intrigue to his words. As must by now be appreciated by the poetry embodied here, his knowledge fuelled his imagination, the two elements of his mind bouncing off each other, without the knowledge he constantly gathered there would be nothing fresh to spark his imagination, you cannot paint a picture without paint and Marc knew and understood that and thrived on it. When his mind became lost to drink and drugs his imagination suffered, the knowledge he was reaping became numbed, his input was of a negative influence, which became apparent in his output that was shallow and meaningless. The songs became short bursts of inspiration, lacking any real depth or direction. In interviews the articulation began to fail him, he was no longer as astute as he had been. In other artists drugs appear to have induced a surrealistic imagination and freed their creativity, the Beatles and the Stones are obvious and familiar examples of this. The effect on Marc Bolan was the opposite, without the intellectual food to nourish his mind it dried up. If the rich allegoric lyrics of 'Slider' are compared to the empty repetitiveness of 'Bolan's Zip Gun' where he slipped back into the 'Love me do' style of lyricism, there is nothing to echo the magic of 'Ballrooms of Mars' or 'Spaceball Ricochet'. Musically Marc has continued to experiment a little but still partly hid in the shadowy safety of his tested formula.

By the time Marc released 'Futuristic Dragon' it was clear he was on his way back. Although the title and opening introduction held a resonance of David Bowie's 'Future Legend' that opens his 1974 album 'Diamond Dogs', the album as a whole had far more substance and depth, the title alone relays an improved imagination spawned by fresh inspirations and Marc's probable inner realisation that he had sunk as low as he could enabled him from somewhere deep inside his amassed chambers of knowledge to pluck enough to give the songs a hint of lyrical substance, Bolan was cleaning up his act and it showed.

He began to collect knowledge again by extending his reach into television, punk and production, which in turn re-ignited and motivated his imagination. All the disciplines and principles that Marc had learnt early in his journey had returned along with the ambition to reassert himself in the role he had cast for his creation.

If a close examination is made of the threads of thought that flow through the poetry in this book, it can be seen that there are quite deliberate excursions taken by Marc into various realms. There are lines clearly flowing through from Dionysus and Orpheus to Alexander the great and from Alexander the great to Amun and Tutankhamen. There are many threads like this through Bolan's work, encompassing his musical gurus as well as his screen gurus, literary gurus, mythical gurus and 'Metal Gurus', all portrayed at differing levels of symbolism. It would be an extensive exercise to outline all of them which infers the amount of reaping Marc Bolan did to spin those threads; hopefully the examples cited will be sufficient to enforce the realisation of the extent of his knowledge.

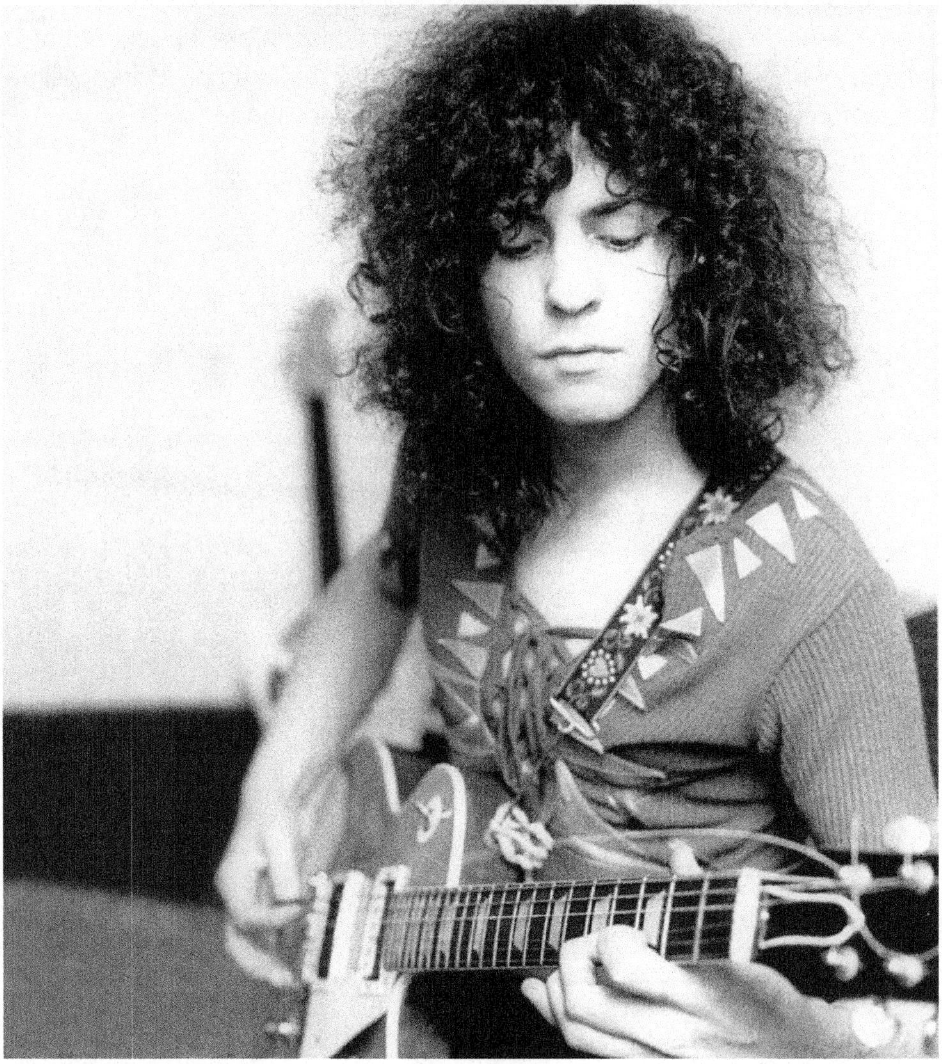

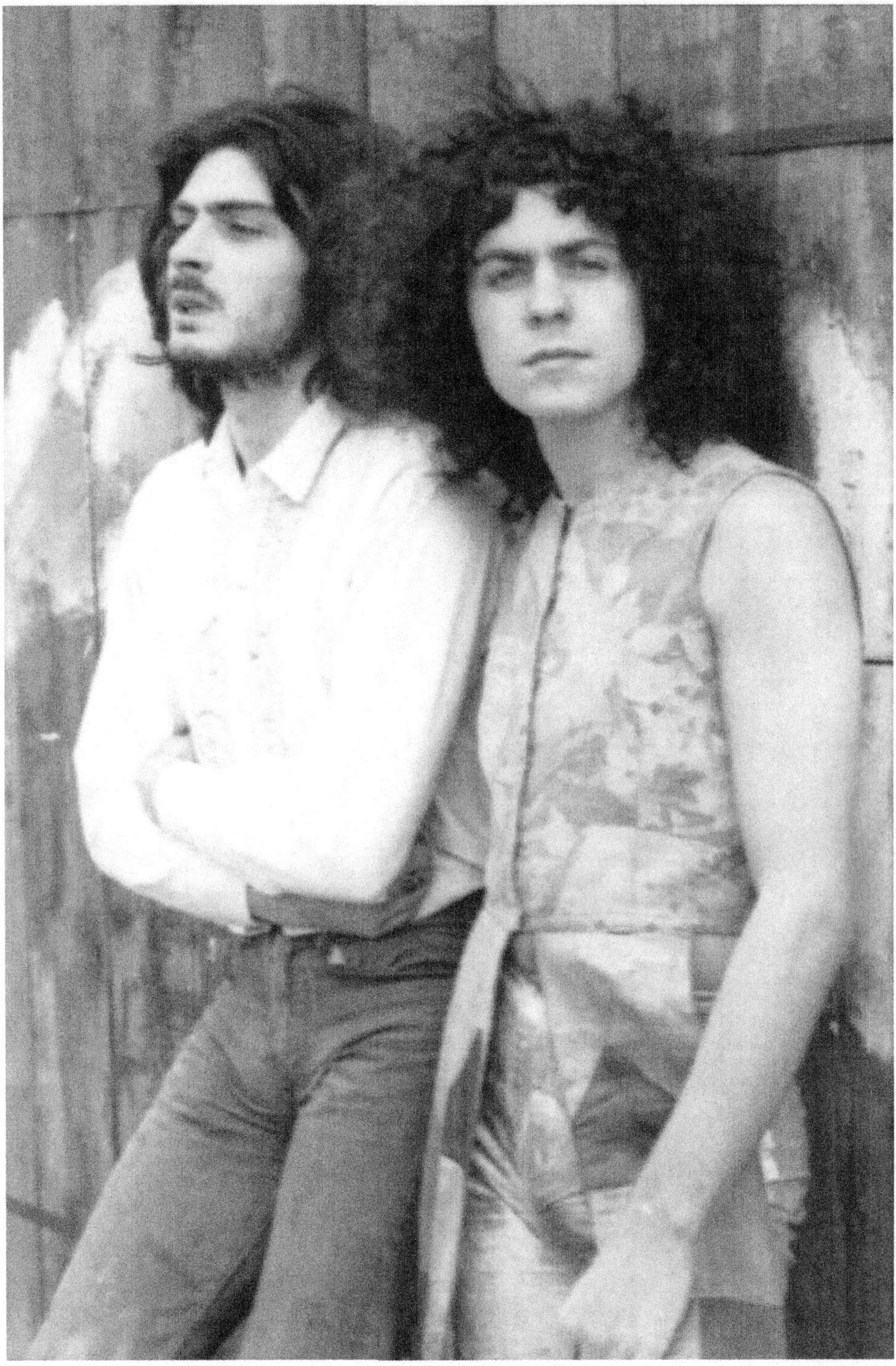

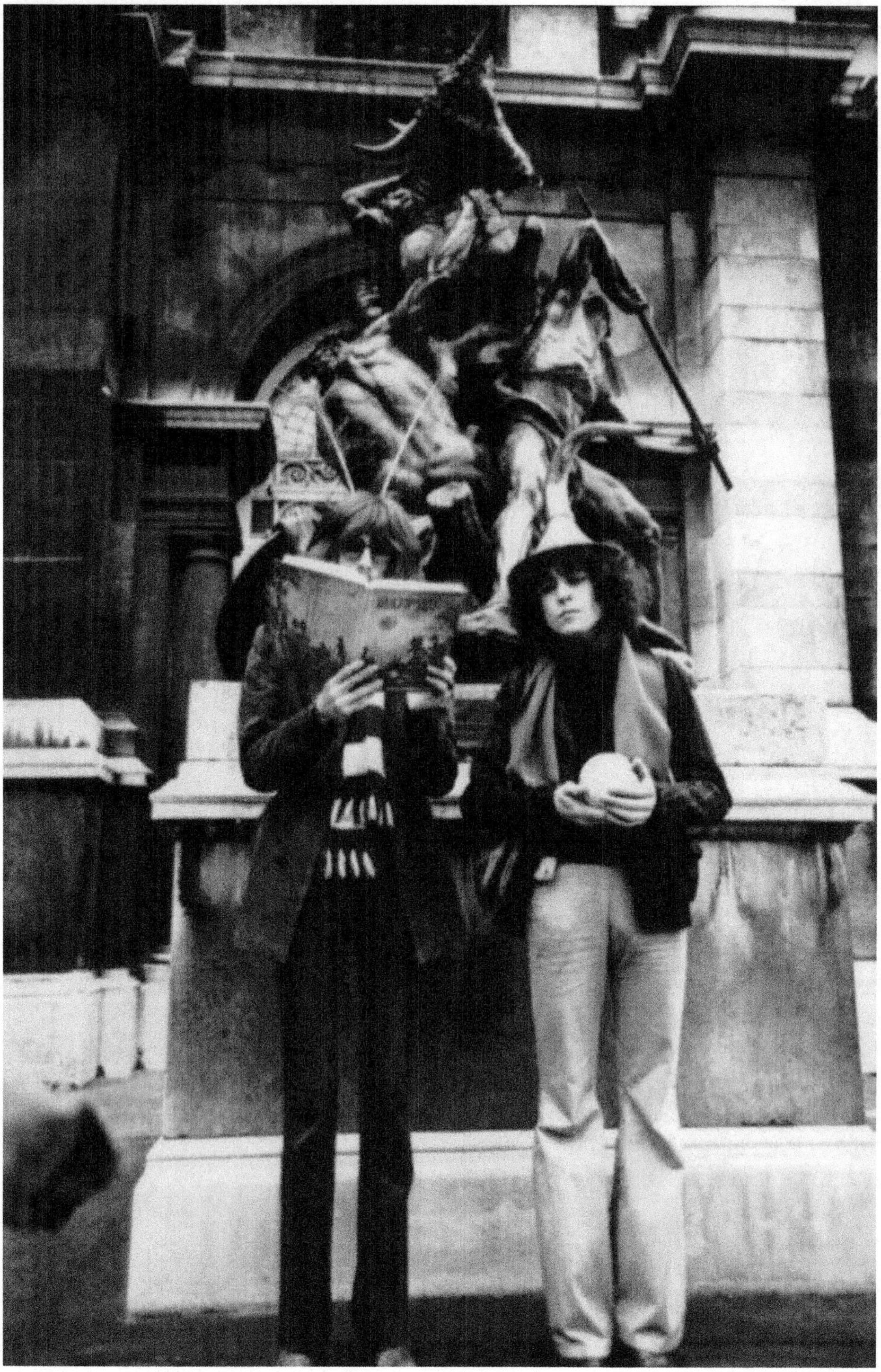

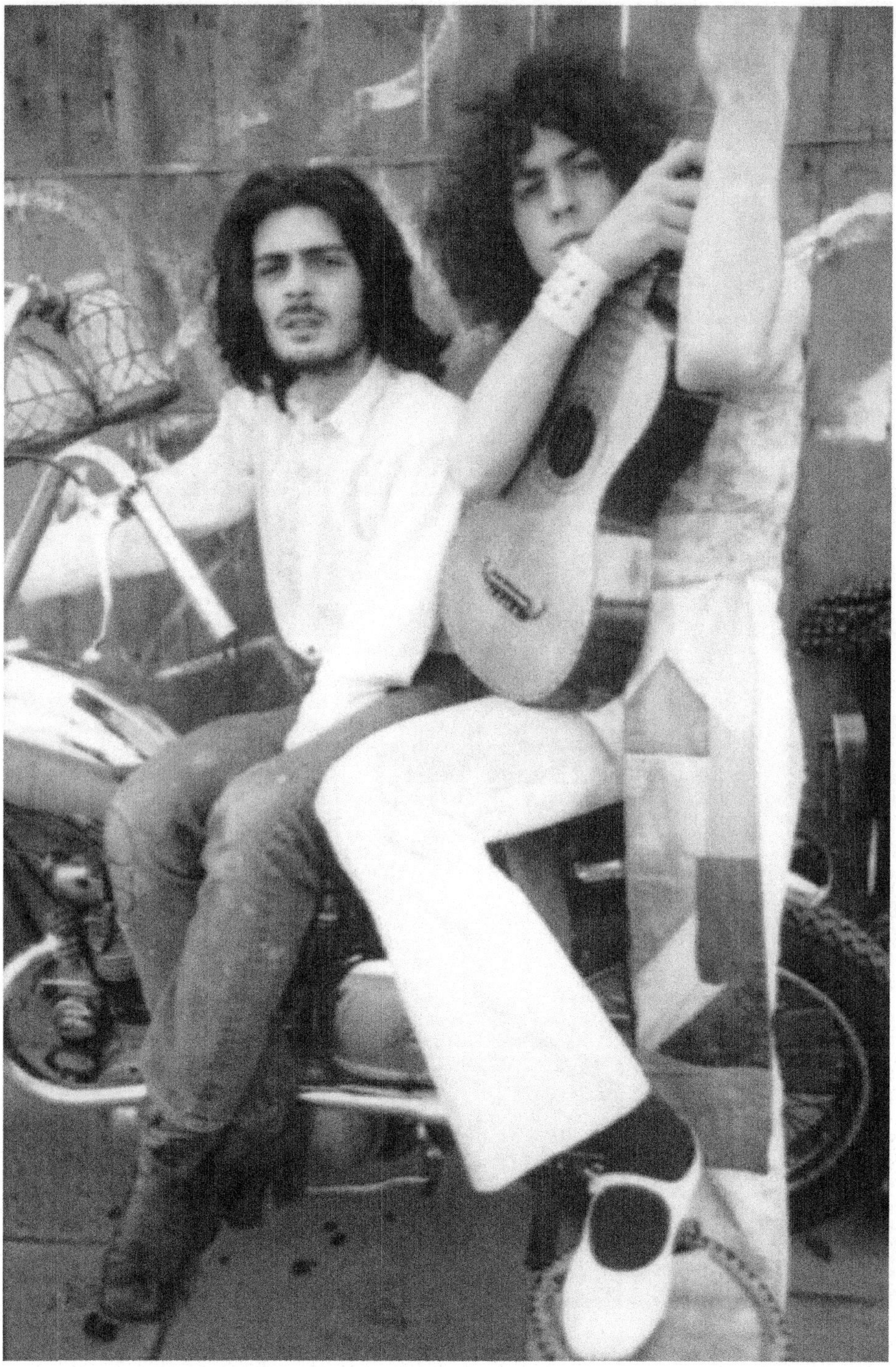

~~past~~ ~~pres~~ ~~seeker~~

the tall man adomanon was blue he belonged ~~into~~ to this world but another. he came as a seeker, a finder of facts an alein archer with a Qiver full of sceince & Wonder it will be small he said in a voice like a mandoline, it will be small & frail & I shall care for it.

he donned a helm of aqua blue & strode from his ship into the park. it was a cold day.

a winter world. black & white & alein ~~conspicuously different~~ looked ~~conspicuously~~ his blue plattened hair & multifaceted eye of a million blue hewes contrasting wildly with the pale landscape of holland park

4

the noise of
the traffic
tore his ears
he was unused
to such distortion
of natures
natural silence,
his world,
the planet
aothos
was a ~~torre~~
land of
~~Quiet~~ peaceful
vibration machines

5

& elemental mastery.
he shivered in ~~england's~~ season
england's cold ~~~~
the blue of
his cheeks, chilly
~~~~ ~~~~
more intense
than on his
arrival only seven
minites prior
his ~~~~ teeth
~~~~ chattered in
his long face
when ~~~~ ~~~~
suddenly

he stood~~~~ still, great waves of calmness penetrated his aqua helm. this brow lightened & the colour of a thousand medeterian oceans filled his goatish face.

the ~~~~ lite girl ~~~~ ~~~~ was pursuing

7

her frisby
when she suddenly
stopped & gasped.

a tall blue man
extened a thin
blue appendicha
which held the
childs toy.

Mathedon bacheno
spoke adomanon
like a cretan harp

the ~~child~~ child 8
looked puzzled
& came a little closer
to the blue man
she motioned for
him to bend
down.
surley ~~my~~ child
of my ~~heart~~, image
so pure, I weep
for your visage
~~said in a ~~

still she motioned
him lower till,
he on his knees,
*she, leval with
his camillion eyes

he trembled prayers
of reverance
~~to~~ to the angel
child * awaited
the flow of
godgiven wisdom
*eloquent prose
that   most surley

how 10

he expected from
the mouth of
the child

a vibration of pain
seered the root
of a daffodil,
nearby geraniums
dyed in there
hundreds,
her fingers proded
& her dirty nails
scared the sweet
tastes from the

bone,

Sandra I wont
tell you again
come on or I'll
give you what
for, coming
mum, the child
kicked the blue
helmet to see
if she missed
any sweeties,
mum ~~brack~~ I found

12

a candy man

what you like
monkey, honest
mum he was
made of blue
~~a~~ toffee, it was
ever so ~~tasty~~ tasty

dont be so spudid
child ~~theres~~ no
such thing as
blue ~~toffee~~ &
whats that

your sucking only a gob stopper mum, give it here, you know you wont eat your dinner

Yes George, that kids got such a vivid imagination.

14

she said she was
eatint a bluetit man,
can you believe it
& then I found her
sucking a gob
set stoper
　　just before
her dinner too.
horrible it was
я george, it looked
　　just like an
did eye it dear?

10. **In The Eyes of a Child**

"I'm in a realm of fantasy; I can do whatever I want to do and get away with it."
Marc Bolan 1972.

Blue Seeker

The tall Adomanon man, was blue,

He belonged,

Not to this world

But another.

He came as a seeker,

A finder of facts,

An alien archer

With a quiver

Full of science and wonder.

"It will be small."

He said

In a voice like a mandolin,

"It will be small and frail

And I shall care for it."

He donned a helm of aqua blue

And strode from his ship

Into the park.

It was a cold day,

A winter world,

Bleak and white.

The alien looked conspicuously different,

His blue platined hair

And multifaceted eye

Of a million blue hues,

Contrasting wildly

With the pale landscape of Holland park.

The noise of the traffic

Tore his ears,

He was unused to such distortions

Of natures natural silence.

His world,

The planet Gothos,

Was a land of peaceful,

Vibrating machines and elemental mastery.

He shivered in England's cold season,

The blue of his cheeks, chilly.

More intense than on his arrival,

Only seven minutes prior.

His teeth chattered in his long face,

When suddenly

He stood still.

Great waves of calmness

Penetrated his aqua helm,

This brow lightened

And the colour of a thousand Mediterranean Oceans

Filled his goatish face.

The little girl

Was pursuing her Frisbee

When she suddenly stopped and gasped.

The tall blue man

Extended a thin blue appendage

Which held the child's toy.

"Mathedon bacheno."

Spoke Adomanon

Like a cretian harp.

The child looked puzzled

And came a little closer to the blue man,

She motioned for him to bend down.

"Surely, child of my heart,

Image so pure, I weep for your visage."

Still she motioned him lower till

He on his knees and she,

Level with his chameleon eyes.

He trembled

Prayers of reverence

To the angel child.

And awaited the flow

Of God given wisdom

And eloquent prose

That most surely

He expected to flow

From the mouth of the child.

A vibration of pain

Seared the root of a daffodil

And nearby geraniums

Died in their hundreds.

Her fingers prodded

And her dirty nails scrapped

The sweet tastes from the bone.

"Sandra, I won't tell you again,

Come on or I'll give you what for!"

"Coming mum."

The child kicked the blue helmet

To see if she had missed any sweeties.

"Mummy I found a candy man."

"What, you little monkey?"

"Honest mum,

He was made of blue toffee,

 It was ever so tasty."

"Don't be stupid child.

There's no such thing as blue toffee

And what's that you're sucking?"

"Only a gob stopper mum."

"Give it here!

You know you won't eat your dinner."

"Yes George,

That kid's got such a vivid imagination.

She said she'd eaten

A blue toffee man.

Can you believe it?

And then I found her sucking a gob stopper,

Just before dinner too.

Horrible it was George,

It looked just like an eye!"

"Did it dear?"

This may not have been intended as a poem but there is not sufficient length to the piece for it to be anything else and the flowery descriptiveness Marc has employed implies poetical form. On initial reading there appear to be no mythological influences present, the emphasis being on 'initial reading' but they are present. It is recommended that the poem be read a number of times before entering into the analogy and that the visible face of the poem is understood.

There is no hidden face here, the poem is a short story relating the tale of an alien from the planet Gothos landing in Holland Park, in Kensington London. He encounters a young child who sees him from her perspective, oblivious to the relevance of his landing and in her innocence she interprets his bright appearance and sweet taste as a sign that he is for eating, a giant toffee man.

She is rebuked by her mother for eating sweets before her meal and whisked off home, where her mother tells the misconstrued tale to her husband.

A peculiar and unusual little story from Marc's imagination, especially when compared to his other poems. On the surface it hosts no rich allegories and there are no mythical secrets to unravel, it is quite clear and obvious in its simplicity, although he cannot help tease the reader by implying a deeper meaning. The key to understanding this poem is not in the mentioning of *Holland Park* but in the apparently casual reference to the alien's home planet, Gothos and also in the awareness of Marc's interest in Science Fiction.

The tall Adomanon man, was blue,

He belonged,

Not to this world

But another.

He came as a seeker,

A finder of facts,

An alien archer

With a quiver

Full of science and wonder.

It is in the opening lines that Marc teases us with possible mythological connections, and indeed there is a link. The name he gives the alien, apart from having an ancient Greek or Egyptian resonance, is a complete pursuance by Marc into his game of wordplay, with many interpretations. Adomanon can be broken down into a variety of possible ingredients, the central one being man. If we remove the last two letters we get *Adoman* a possible derivative from *Adam man* implying the biblical definition of the first man, Adam. It can be taken further, if the two letters either side of 'm' are removed then *Amon* is left, being a possible evolution from the Greek interpretation of the Egyptian god *Amun* which is Ammon. As discussed in the previous chapter, Amun was always depicted as being blue, as Marc has portrayed *Adomanon*. His referral to the alien being a seeker of knowledge, an alien archer, with a quiver full of science and wonder, takes the reader in two directions one of ancient times and one of modern times, of which Adomanon is the joining of those routes, whether he be the source or the destination. This, along with Marc's carefully constructed name for his alien, suggests that he is weaving the possible theory that the gods and the human race are evolved from aliens. If this suggestion had been put forward at the beginning of this book it would have been perceived as an excessively ambitious insight, but having proved Marc's interests and knowledge of the gods, mythology, literature, science fiction, wordplay and more, it surely must hold credence. It is not however Marc Bolan's theory but one he embraces. It is the theory of Eric von Daniken, author of a number of books projecting the hypothesis that man has been influenced many times in ancient history by alien intelligences. His books, 'Chariots of the Gods', 'Gods from Outer Space' and 'The Gold of Gods' were first published in 1968, 1970 and 1972 respectfully and caused a considerable amount of controversy during that period, along with other revelations and theories such as the Dead Sea Scrolls, all combining to spawn extensive scientific and theological debates about man's origins. Again the chronology is perfect for the connection to be made with confidence, along with the evidence that can be clearly heard in interviews, with Marc debating similar topics.

"It will be small."

He said In a voice like a mandolin,

"It will be small and frail

And I shall care for it."

The seeker has come to find a sample or a pet from Earth, one that needs his care and that he can easily control. Marc makes a musical reference, giving the alien an ethereal sounding voice.

He donned a helm of aqua blue

And strode from his ship Into the park.

It was a cold day,

A winter world,

Bleak and white.

The alien looked conspicuously different,

His blue platined hair

And multifaceted eye

Of a million blue hues,

Contrasting wildly

With the pale landscape of Holland park.

Here Marc sets the contrasting and contradicting scene, describing the alien and his futuristic array of blue, the helmet he wears, his hair as being *platined* which is believed to be a wordplay on platinum (as 'platinum blonde'), all in direct conflict with the cold bleak English winter landscape of Holland Park.

The use of 'Holland Park' brings on a sense of reality and normality, Marc was familiar with Holland Park, he had visited it many times with Riggs O'Hara, who, apart from having a friend that lived close to the park, took an interest in the newly developing open air theatre based there and the exhibitions that took place in the

Orangery. It could be that an element of inspiration for this poem may have come from something Marc saw at the park, such as a sculpture, a painting or even a street entertainer working the park but unfortunately there are no records available from Holland Park to help with that possibility. There are other links between Holland Park and Marc Bolan, albeit circumstantial. Holland Park used to be the grounds to Holland House, which was the home of Lord Holland. The house was all but destroyed in a bombing raid during the Second World War and, following the selling of the grounds to the local authorities, the park was opened to the public in 1952. The link, however, goes further back in time to when the house was occupied by Lord Palmerston when regular guests of the house included Lord Byron, one of Bolan's classical icons.

The noise of the traffic

Tore his ears,

He was unused to such distortions

Of natures natural silence.

His world,

The planet Gothos,

Was a land of peaceful,

Vibrating machines and elemental mastery.

More contrasting by Marc, comparing the noisiness and chaos of a central London park and its surroundings to the quiet control of Adomanons home planet, Gothos, where the machines are peaceful and work in harmony with the elements.

He shivered in England's cold season,

The blue of his cheeks, chilly.

More intense than on his arrival,

Only seven minutes prior.

His teeth chattered in his long face,

When suddenly

He stood still.

Great waves of calmness

Penetrated his aqua helm,

This brow lightened

And the colour of a thousand Mediterranean Oceans

Filled his goatish face.

Further emphasis on the effects of the English winter on the alien and more confirmation of his colour, but then he sees something that distracts his uncomfortable reaction to the cold, calming him inside his blue helmet. Marc utilises an intriguing descriptiveness with the use of a *thousand Mediterranean Oceans,* the Mediterranean being the one common element connecting the countries of the mythologies that Marc was most interested in. He then describes Adomanon as having a *goatish face*, a striking feature of the Fauns of Dionysus fame and many other mythological characters, like Pan. It is apparent that Marc is attempting to make subtle connections between his alien character and the ancient personas of the gods.

The little girl

Was pursuing her Frisbee

When she suddenly stopped and gasped.

The tall blue man

Extended a thin blue appendage

Which held the child's toy.

"Mathedon bacheno."

Spoke Adomanon

Like a cretian harp.

The child looked puzzled

And came a little closer to the blue man,

She motioned for him to bend down.

"Surely, child of my heart,

Image so pure, I weep for your visage."

What has caught the alien's attention is a little girl, a child playing with her toy, a Frisbee. Adomanon looks on the child in wonder, beguiled by her beauty, he perceives her as something angelic and pure. She, however, sees him with the eyes of a child, her innocence and childish imagination oblivious to the importance of the meeting. He has caught her toy, and in an act of a friendly 'first contact', offers it to her with a greeting, *Mathedon bacheno*, words that have a definite Greek style. More wordplay, which along with Marc's description of his voice being *Like a Cretian harp*, further enhances the Mediterranean aura being projected by Marc for the alien.

The child does not see him as godly though, and in pure infantile inquisitiveness beckons to him to come closer, when with pure Orphetic charm he declares his love and passion, crying in adoration of her beautiful face.

Still she motioned him lower till

He as on his knees and she,

Level with his chameleon eyes.

He trembled

Prayers of reverence

To the angel child.

And awaited the flow

Of God given wisdom

And eloquent prose

That most surely

He expected to flow

From the mouth of the child.

She beckons him closer still and he kneels before her and awaits the words which he expects to be of a magnanimous nature from such a pure, celestial looking being, but he is to be disappointed, the child is but a child and does not understand or relate to his agenda.

A vibration of pain

Seared the root of a daffodil

And nearby geraniums

Died in their hundreds.

Now the irony becomes apparent as pain is innocently inflicted on the visitor from another world when the little girl, who has seen him as a walking sweet shop, tests her theory.

Her fingers prodded

And her dirty nails scrapped

The sweet tastes from the bone.

Liking the taste of the giant sweet she has found, she eats him. The description of her dirty nails adds to the irony by defiling the purity of the image as discerned by the alien.

"Sandra, I won't tell you again,

Come on or I'll give you what for!"

"Coming mum."

What should have been a momentous occasion has been instantly reduced to a mundane domestic event as the child's mother summons her.

The child kicked the blue helmet

To see if she had missed any sweeties.

In childish greed she looks to see if she has missed anything amongst his remains.

"Mummy I found a candy man."

"What, you little monkey?"

"Honest mum,

He was made of blue toffee,

It was ever so tasty."

"Don't be stupid child.

There's no such thing as blue toffee

And what's that you're sucking?"

"Only a gob stopper mum."

"Give it here!

You know you won't eat your dinner."

The sardonic response of the mother to her child's story of a toffee man enhances the contrast in the relevance of the meeting from the viewpoint of the two parties and is further enhanced when the mother relates the story to her husband...

"Yes George,

That kids got such a vivid imagination.

She said she'd eaten A blue toffee man.

Can you believe it?

And then I found her sucking a gob stopper,

Just before dinner too.

Horrible it was George,

It looked just like an eye!"

Who reduces the relevance of the event even further by patronisingly dismissing his wife's recounting.

"Did it dear?"

An extremely imaginative poem raising a number of stark contrasts and conveying the relevance and meaning of the quote of Marc's used at the beginning of the preceding chapter, "Somewhere one has to decide that everyone has a different head".

A simple and obvious observation, one that is frequently forgotten by everyone, including world leaders. Every individual is working to their own agenda, which is influenced by their culture, personality, intelligence, age and their circumstances in life at the given time.

The alien, Adomanon, came to Earth in search of knowledge, contact and a friendly embracing of galactic culture and intelligence, but his research was not detailed enough to prepare him for all possibilities and he blindly walked into a scenario he was not prepared for. The child, although she could be perceived as the guilty party of a failed alliance between two worlds (a fairly heavy burden), is completely innocent, the encounter was beyond her comprehension, it was no more than a game, a lucky treat to her. In complete simplicity, what Marc is saying, in an elaborate, imaginative way, is that we all see life differently, and we should be aware of that.

As well as highlighting Marc's interest in science fiction this poem also connects that interest with ones of mythology and religion, and indicates the presence of an inner theological debate connecting the two. A debate that Marc Bolan did not have time to consolidate. Early in the evaluation of this poem, reference was made of the key to the poem being the alien's home planet, Gothos. In elaboration of that comment it should be revealed that Marc, with the aid of his furtive imagination, has performed what can be justly described as a 'Jeepster' with the writing of the 'Blue Seeker'. He has taken his inspiration from a previous work and regurgitated it via the Bolan imagination machine. Yet again the chronology plays its part in the evaluation and it has to be remembered what was happening in the period surrounding 1970, in every direction. This poem has its roots in an episode of a cult science fiction series, which was first broadcast on January 12th 1967. It is a series that Marc Bolan is known to have been fond of and, as with all things he admired, he could not resist paying his homage to it, disguised as it may be.

Conversely, it does not wear as much make-up as most of his tributes; he has simply reversed the roles, flipped the game and given it many different twists. He has even involved the parents, in a similar way as the original. The penultimate scene of the poem, where the child brings the invader to his knees to sample the 'sweet taste', is an almost parallel scenario to that of the program.

"To boldly go where no man has gone before" was the agenda set for Captain James T Kirk and his crew of the starship Enterprise by Gene Roddenberry. On stardate 2124 they were interrupted in their galactic gliding by an encounter with the planet Gothos. 'The Squire of Gothos' was the eighteenth episode of Star Trek to be screened, written by Paul Shneider and directed by Don McDougall the plot proceeds as follows; The Enterprise is on its way to Colony Beta 6 to deliver supplies when it comes across an uncharted planet, Gothos. They briefly scan the planet but do not have time to investigate fully so decide to make haste to Beta 6. However, the Captain and Helmsman Sulu vanish from the bridge; the Enterprise is thus forced to orbit the planet while it traces them. When Captain Kirk and Sulu are tracked down it becomes apparent that they are all to be the forced 'guests' of a character who calls himself General Trelane, the self proclaimed squire of Gothos. Trelane is on his home planet so from his standpoint the crew of the Enterprise are the aliens and he has been studying Earth for a while, describing it as his hobby. He has, however, been watching Earth 900 years in its past, as it is 900 light years away, and this is reflected in the environment he has created for them. They are forced to play out a number of charades with Trelane while they find a means by which to escape his control. There is the inevitable final fight between Captain Kirk and Trelane where swords are the chosen weapons and Trelane, believing he has won, tries to force Kirk to kneel, but he refuses. It is here that Trelane describes victory as tasting sweet but Kirk out wits Trelane and breaks his sword. The squire descends into a childish strop accusing Kirk of cheating. Two voices are then heard, from above, calling to Trelane to come in. It transpires that Trelane is no more than a child playing with his pets and the voices are his parents who rebuke him for being cruel to them. The parents then apologise to Kirk for their child's behaviour and set him and the Enterprise free.

The episode weaves a tale of man, as the alien invader, encountering what he regards as an intelligent life form on it's home planet but it transpires to be a child who is merely playing and oblivious to man's glorious agenda to 'explore strange new worlds…to seek out new life and new civilisations'.

Marc has perspicuously absorbed the basic thread of the plot, performing the same process as when he absorbed Howlin' Wolfs song 'You'll be mine' and gave it re-birth as Jeepster. He has taken Paul Shneider's original story line, mixed it up a little in his imagination, adding a few Bolanesque convolutions, and given it a re-birth, his imagination playing its role beautifully in the development of the embryo into a newly formed life.

Marc's imagination was his strongest asset, as previously stated, he was almost pure imagination. The knowledge he amassed acted as the seeds of his creations but seeds will die on dry barren soil, Marc's imagination was the water, the embryonic fluid that fed his seeds' growth enabling them to sprout into fresh new plants. Without the seeds of knowledge there would be no forest, nothing to cultivate, each needs the other for growth. If there are too few seeds and too much water then the seeds will be washed away, a healthy balance has to be maintained. Imagination needs to be able to feed knowledge as much as knowledge needs to be fed and conversely knowledge needs to feed imagination as much as imagination needs to be fed.

Marc's statement that he was living in a fantasy world was true; everything in his life was due to his imagination. Marc Bolan was a creation from the imagination of Mark Feld, he was, quite simply, what he imagined.

At the risk of diverting into a diverse philosophical debate, it is surely man's imagination that sets him apart from other species, not his knowledge, for without imagination man would not have been able to explore ways of gaining knowledge. All animals are born with varying levels of instinctive knowledge, but they do not expand that knowledge to any relevant degree during their life. Man, however, constantly re-invents the tree, shaking things up in his mind to find alternatives, whether it be philosophical, mathematical or artistic alternatives, all of man's inventions were initially forged in the imagination. In actuality we are all living in what was once someone else's fantasy world.

Marc was fully aware of the reality and the importance of imagination, as he relayed in an interview previously referred to, where he debates that the tape recorder being used by the journalist interviewing him would not exist if it had not first been imagined by someone. With imagination a man creates, the stronger the imagination the more creative the man will be. To label Marc Bolan as living in a fantasy world and being self absorbed in imagination is to pay him the highest of compliments because he had an abundance of the one thing that makes mankind special.

It is this asset that made him unique, in every aspect. There are many songwriters but none that write songs like Marc Bolan, there is nothing to compare with the individuality of his style and the content of his lyrics. David Bowie is probably the closest contender for comparison but even he is more aptly described as an efficient chameleon of music than a true innovator, when placed next to Bolan. His approach to lyrics in itself was unique, most songwriters use allegories but Marc allegorised to the extreme, he relished painting the mask of intrigue to the point where everything became symbolic, even Marc Bolan.

It is ironic that his strongest asset was also his failing. The depth of his imagination was so strong that people failed to understand his words and it became simpler to dismiss them as empty ramblings, simple sounds rather than meaningful lyrics and the ingenuity of his carefully constructed songs was overlooked by many, including his peers. For a period this annoyed Marc and June told of how he used to turn up the volume because no one was really listening; this frustration may have been another element playing its' part in his falling into the underworld. He became the 'Blue Seeker' a colourful character from another world, full of imaginative knowledge that he had come to share, but the people he tried to communicate with only saw what they wanted to see, not what was really there, and only took what they thought they wanted, not what he offered.

Adomanon had travelled the galaxies gathering knowledge only to become a child's two-minute toffee treat, and although the child relished the treat it did not due justice to his efforts, his quest was wasted, this could be how Bolan had begun to see himself. The dedication he had given to Rock music was lifelong and life consuming, Tony Howard said he ate and drank music, Bill Legend said that it was his complete motivation and it is yet another of Marc Bolan's attributes that is echoed by everyone who knew him, there are few artists that give as much devotion. He would, therefore, have expected to gain some credibility for his efforts. If he felt that he was being considered as a two-minute treat it would have had a devastating effect on him. He would have become depressed and tried to hide behind a thicker mask of make-up, taking solace by losing his disillusionment in a bottle, or drugs… which he did.

His imagination was strong enough for him to find a route to gain the credibility he needed as the godfather of punk. Whether there is any truth in the claim is irrelevant, the belief gave him the strength to pull himself out of the underworld he had slipped into and position himself for a new journey.

Such is the power of the imagination…

SINGER
FAIRIES
The Prophet
KAHLIL GIBRAN
The Broken Wings
KAHLIL GIBRAN

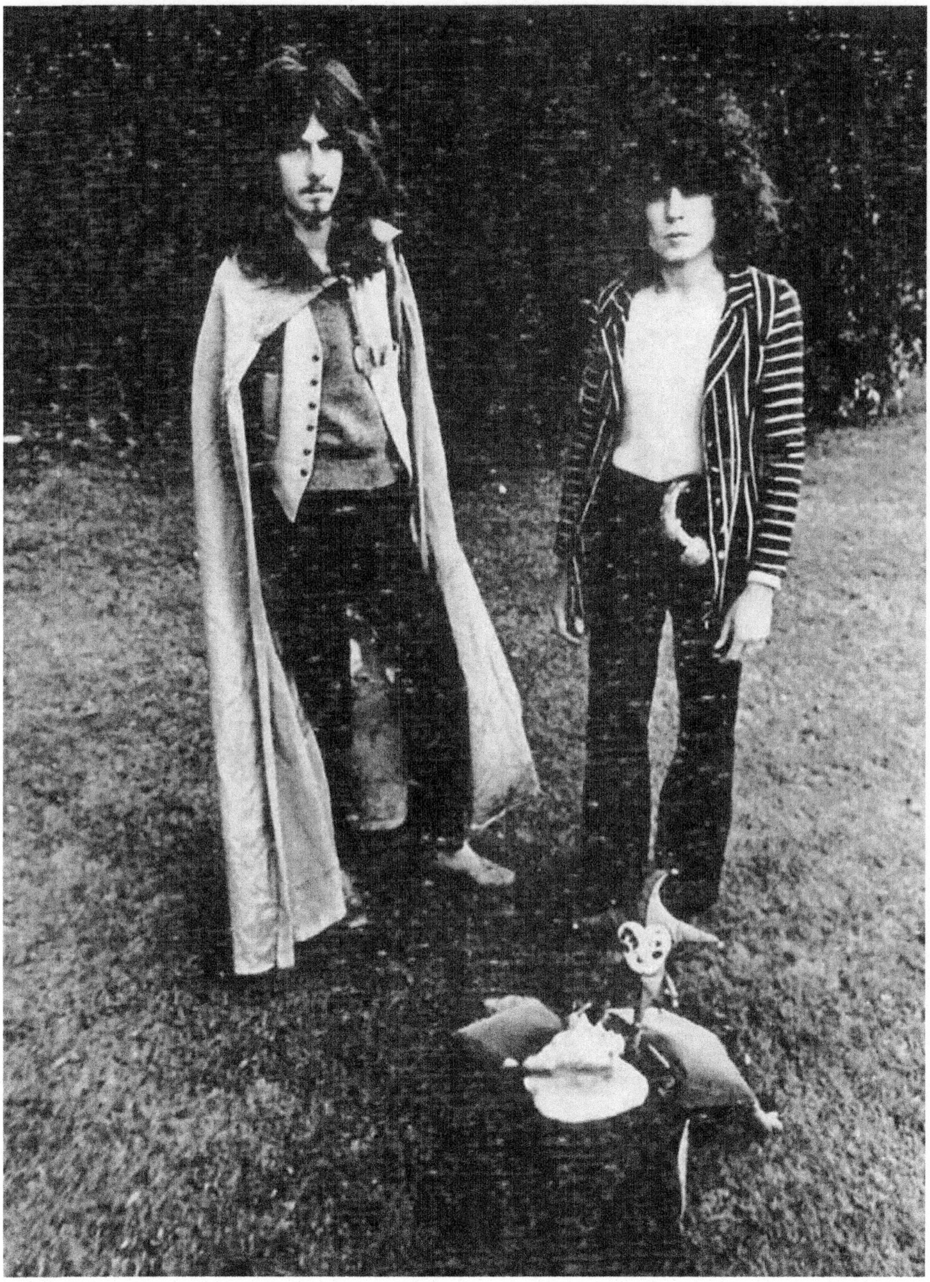

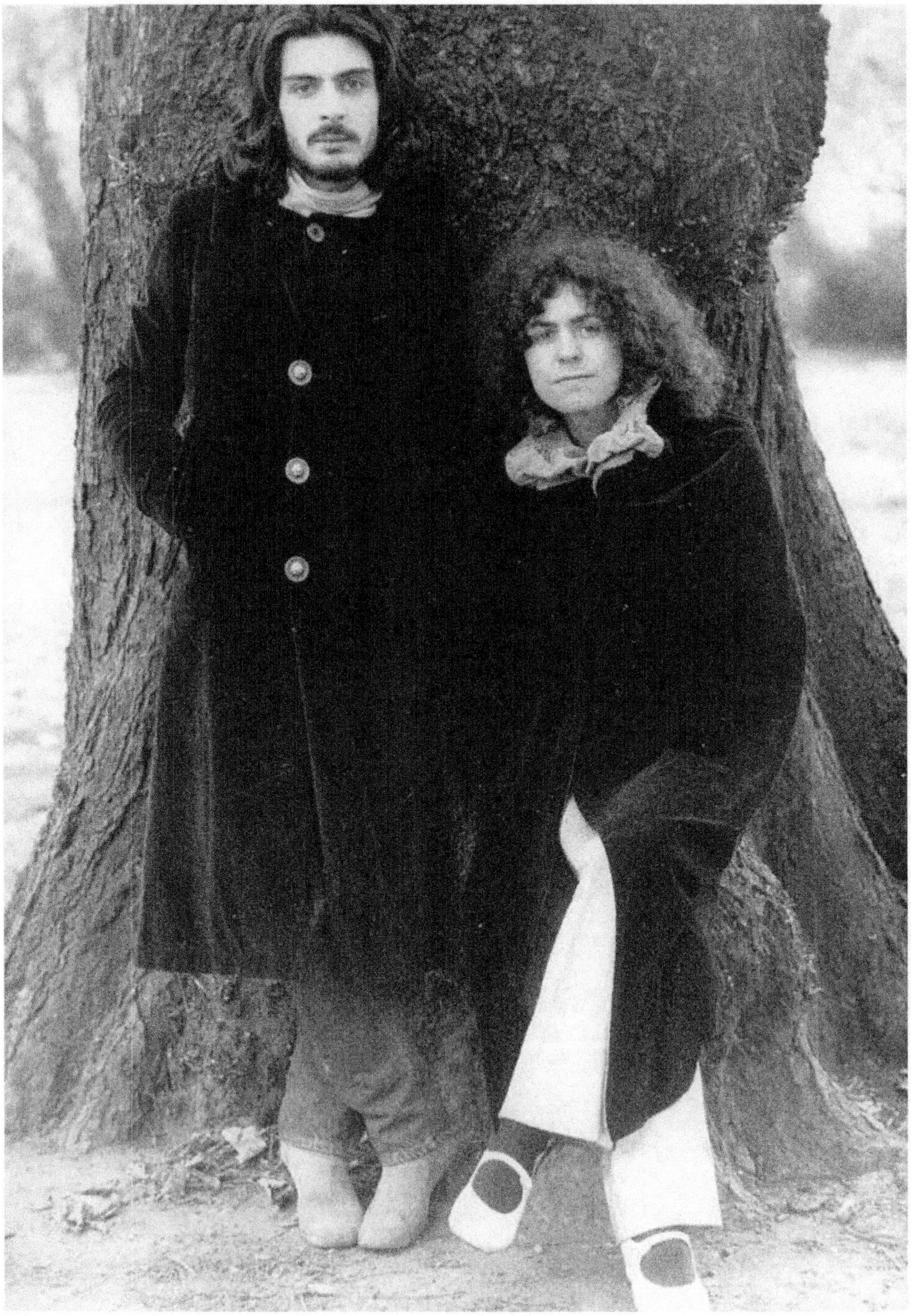

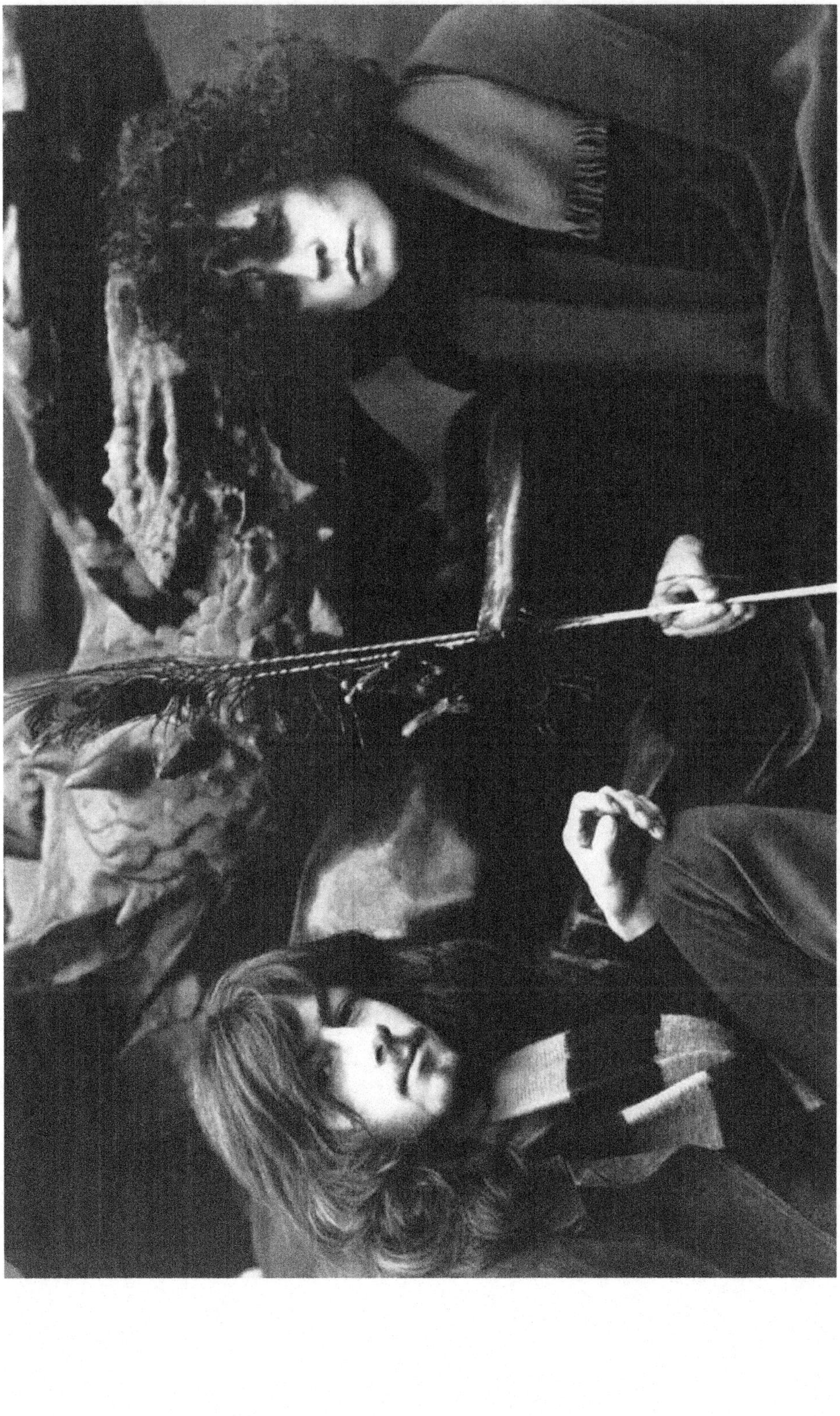

✓ gods & men ✓

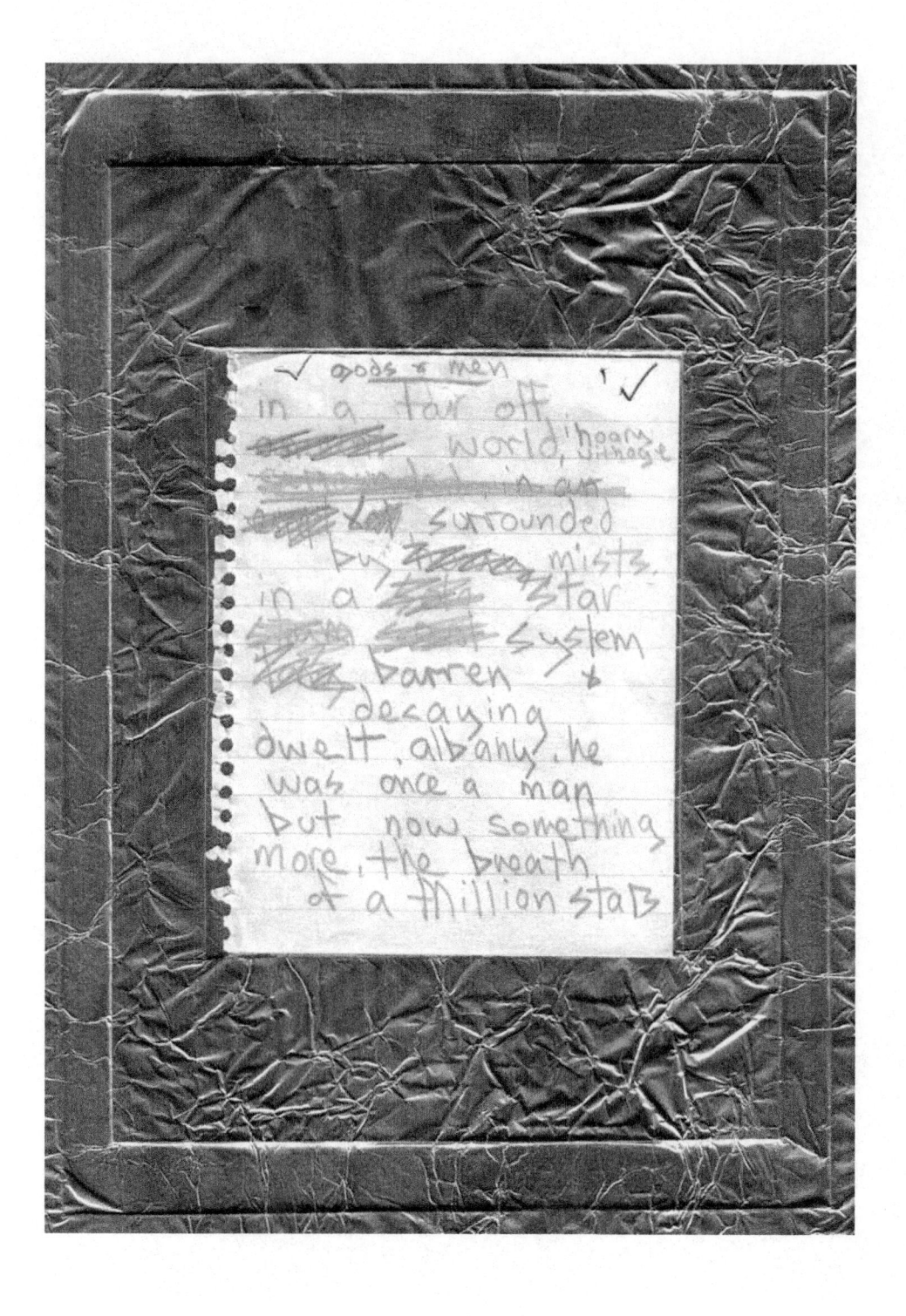

in a far off
~~~~~~~~ world, hoary vintage
~~~~~~~~
~~~~ surrounded
by ~~~~~~ mists,
in a ~~~~ star
~~~~ ~~~~ system
~~~~ barren &
decaying
dwelt, albany. he
was once a man
but now something
more, the breath
of a million stars

had altered
his metabolisim
into the image of
a god, but
what god &
whose. was this
the visage of
the star one
lofty brow punctured
with pores, & green
with molds
and bacteria, legless
but still
walking

eyeballs, orb's
of contradiction
leaning out into
the foggy night
on crimson
stalks, seeing
nothing yet
smelling all
albany the man
it would seem
had long
what remained
what loped
in his misshapen husk of a body

4

thru the mists
of this barren
planet, was it
him, ashemoc
the cursed
curser, the god
who would
 was willing
or tylon the
windy, the multi-
beaked, the
wanderer, or even
yet turna
, the everyman

5

~~xxxx~~ the
changeless
the frozen one

on a dark dawn
in a morning
of ice, a
manship came
from the world
beyond the worlds
#, it landed
on a planet
of ~~xxxx~~ freezing
dust

two earthmen
cowled in
plastics & fish
bowls of glass,
wandered
numb thru
the forests
of white
oaks, they
ran like
children thru
the valley
of the snow

< at last
unkowing they
~~~~ entered
like meat,
the plateau
of the beast

over a cold
smoldering fire
they talked of
earth > tried to
~~keep~~ >ut> the
warmth
they caught

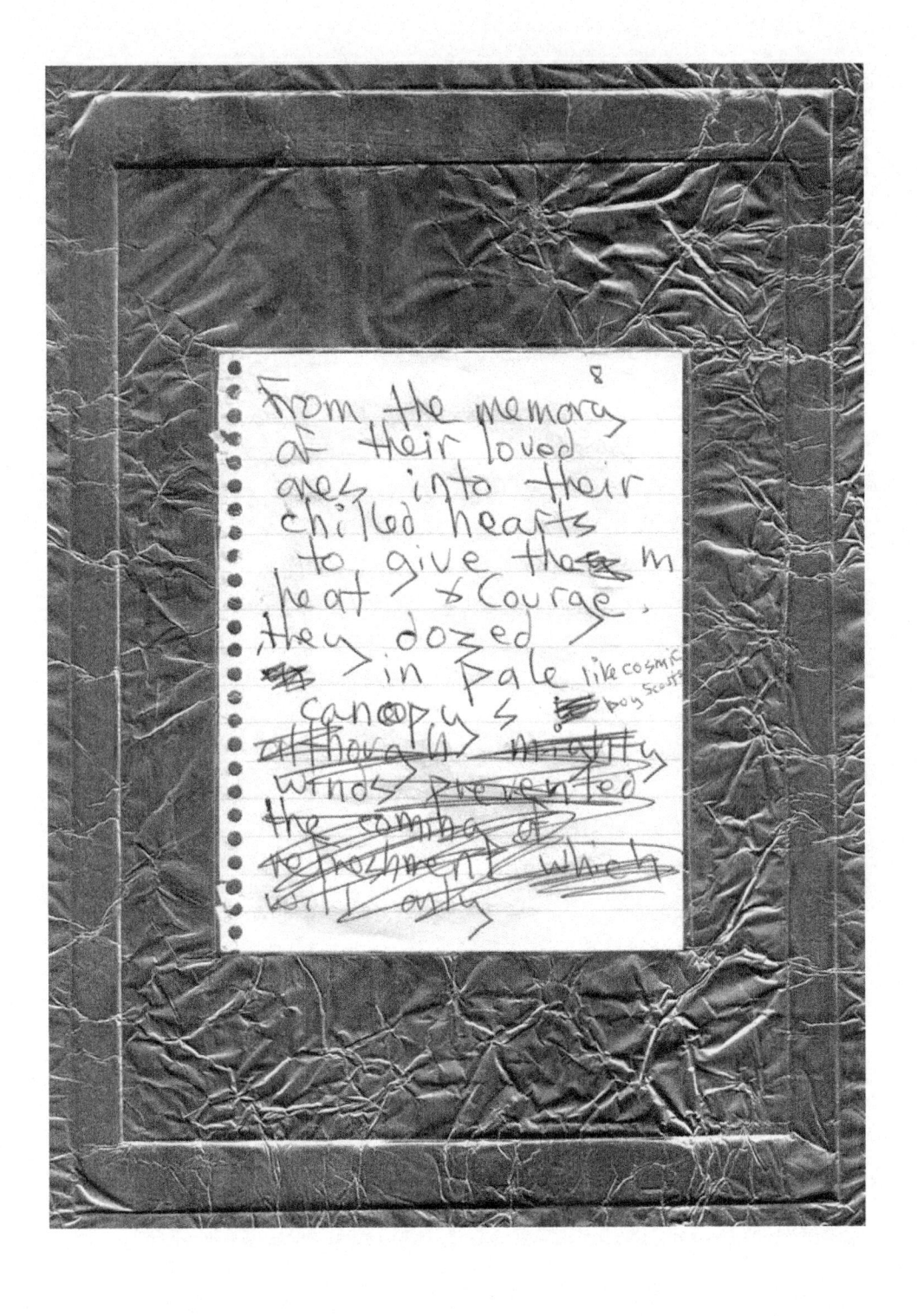

from the memory of their loved ones into their chilled hearts to give them heat & courage. they dozed in pale like cosmic canopy's boy scouts ~~although mostly winds prevented the coming of to freshness which will only~~

they were
awoken at
dawn by wind
which clawed
at their tent
like a lion, &
then he came

~~~~ the first
caress from
his deamon
mind brought
blindness

~~For~~ in his
mind~~sockey~~ mouth
he crunched
the eyeballs
like ~~crackley~~ over
~~easy~~ fried eggs

× then their
limbs, he
sucked the
bones bare
like a ~~mephis~~
tennessee
chicken eater

, the nails &
lips, rare delocoss
, he chomped
 slowly.
the howls of
pain shook
 the foilage
 in the forest
 of white oak
& lastly the
heart. a master
peice by a hated
 master

littered the
floor ~~$~~ making
he gulphs*
magical cosmic
rune talk

12

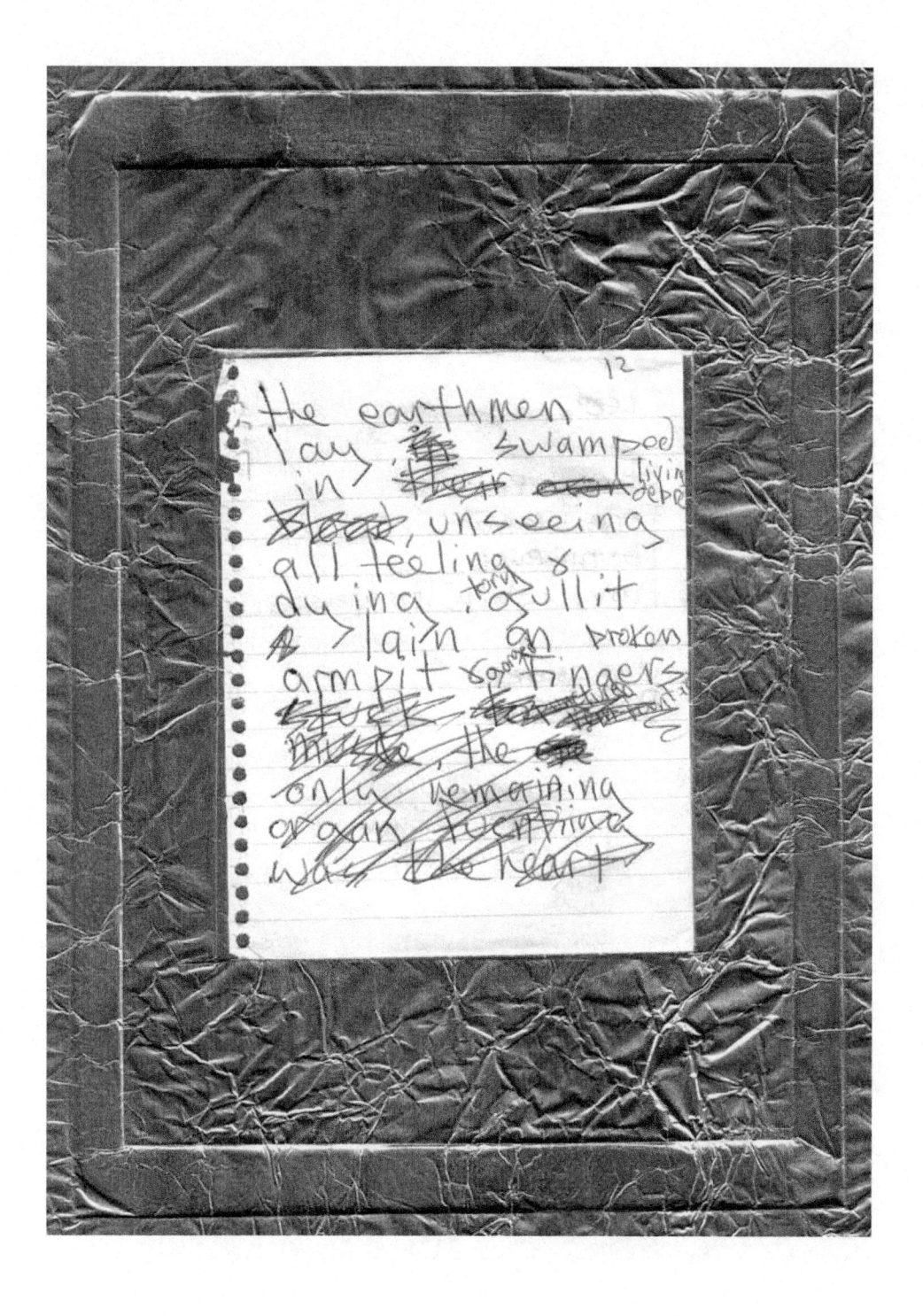

the earthmen lay, swamped in ~~their own~~ livin debr ~~blood~~, unseeing all feeling & dying. tom & gullit >lain on broken armpit ~~sorry~~ fingers ~~stuck~~ ~~for~~ ~~his~~ ~~must~~, the only remaining organ ~~feeling~~ was ~~the~~ heart

13

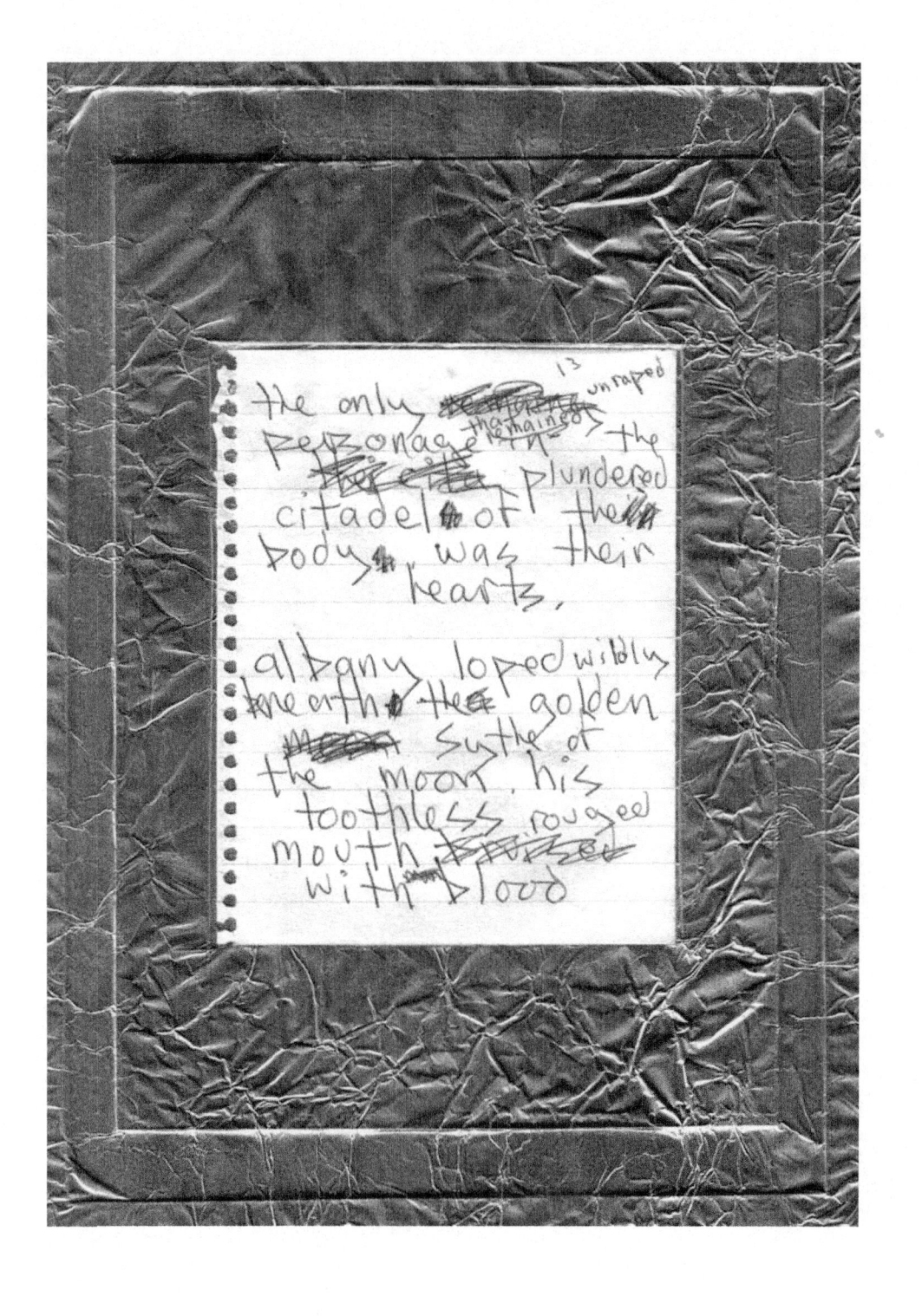

the only ~~remains~~ unraped
personage ~~that remained~~ the
~~first city~~ plundered
citadel of their
body, was their
hearts.

albany loped wildly
~~beneath~~ ~~the~~ golden
~~moon~~ scythe of
the moon, his
toothless rouged
mouth ~~bruised~~
with blood

14

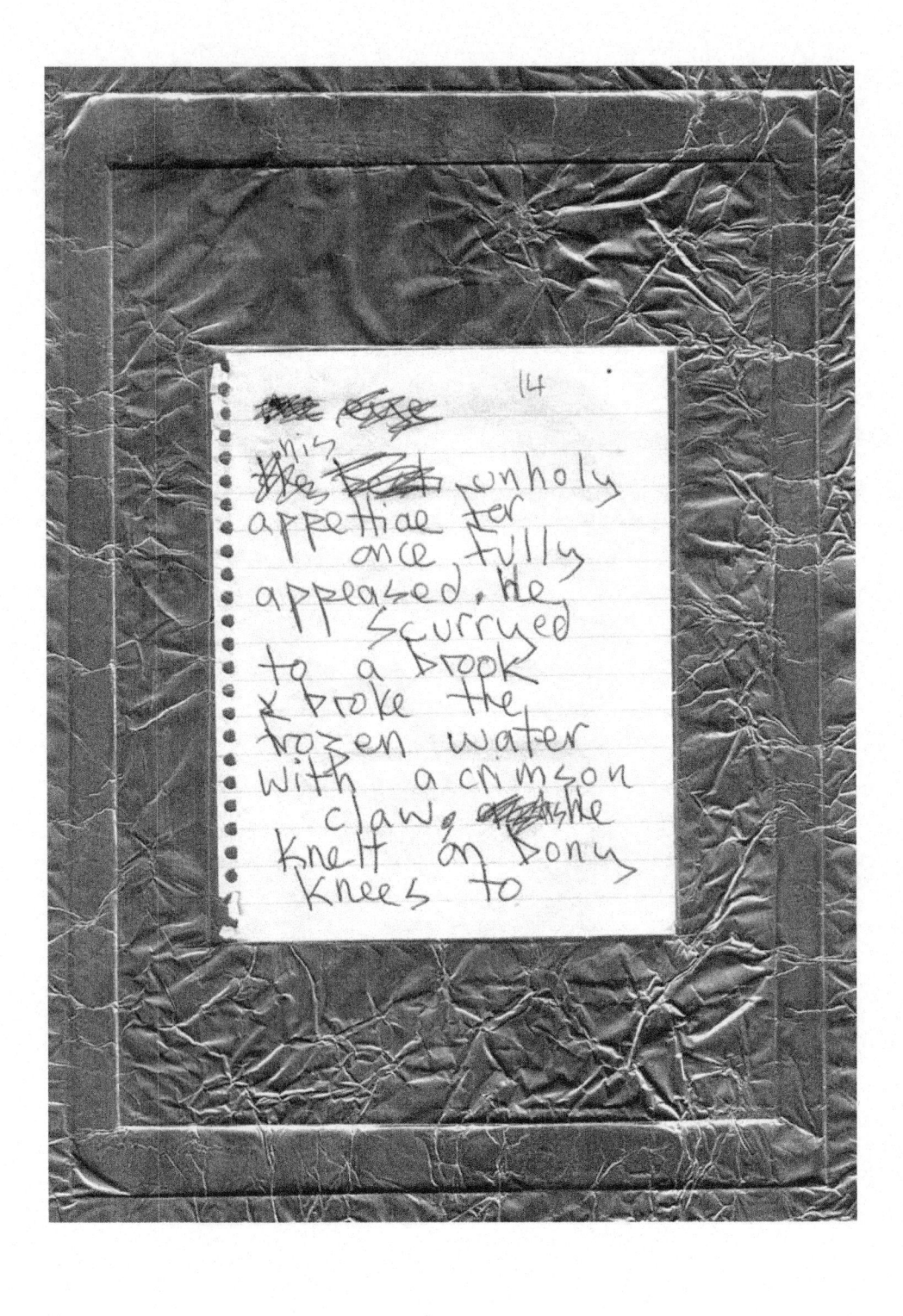

~~his~~ ~~the~~ ~~Rat~~ unholy appetite for once fully appeased, He scurried to a brook x broke the frozen water with a crimson claw, ~~the~~ He knelt on bony knees to

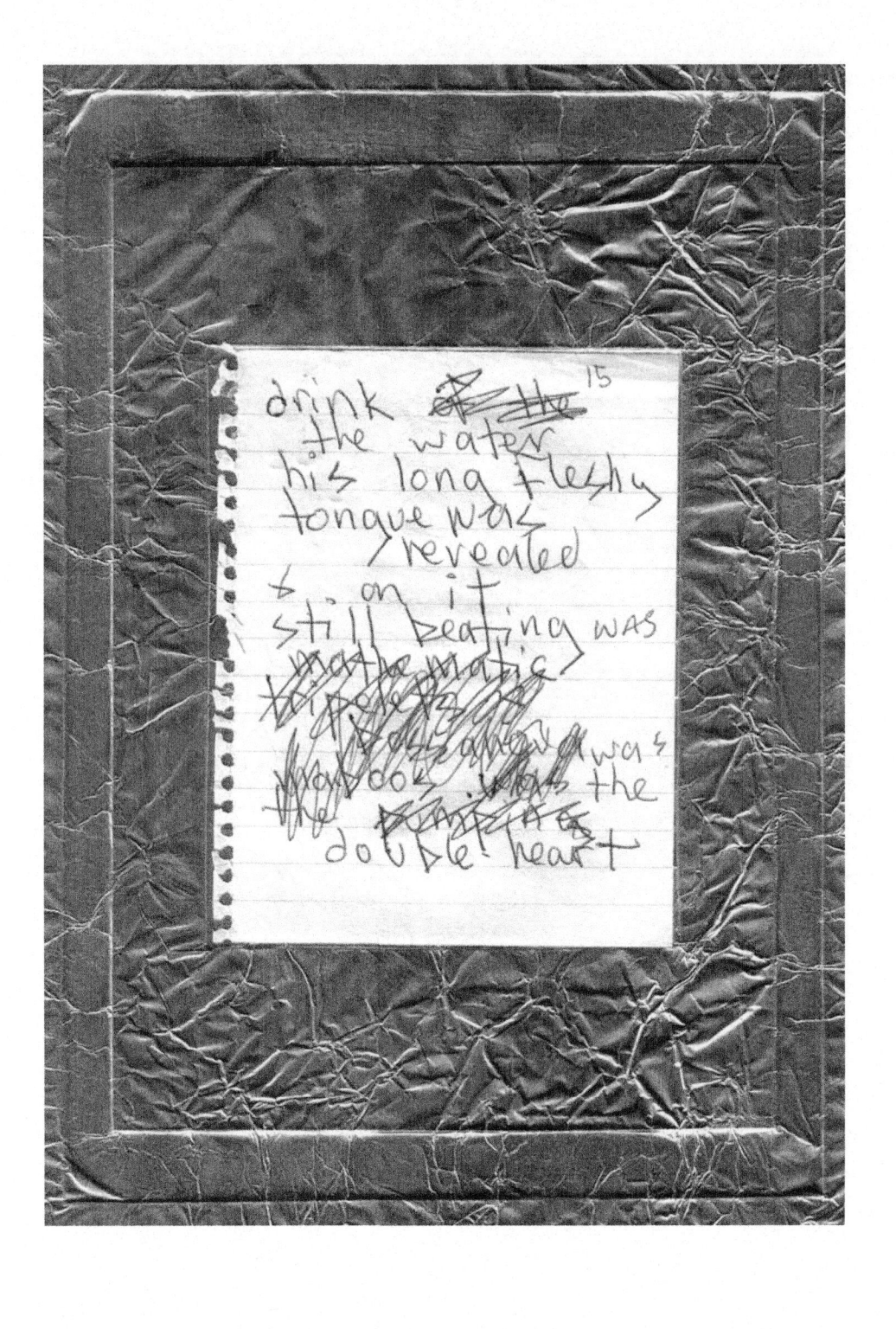

drink ~~& the~~
the water
his long fleshy
tongue was
revealed
& on it
still beating was
~~mathematic~~
~~[scribbled out]~~
~~[scribbled out]~~ and was
~~[scribbled out]~~ the
double heart

11. **Gods and Men**

"He hopes to be alive still" Marc Bolan 1972

Gods and Men

In a far off world

Hoary with age

Surrounded by mists,

In a star system

Barren and decaying,

Dwelt Albany.

He was once a man

But now something more,

The breath of a million stars

Had altered his metabolism

Into the image of a God.

But what God and whose?

Was this the visage of the Star one?

Lofty brow punctured with pores

And green with moulds and bacteria,

Legless but still walking.

Eyeballs, orbs of contradiction,

Leaning out into the foggy night

On crimson stalks,

Seeing nothing but smelling all.

Albany the man,

It would seem,

Had long been dead,

But what remained?

What loped in his misshaped husk of a body

Through the mists of this barren planet?

Was it him, Ashemoc, the cursed curser,

The God who would and was willing,

Or Tylon the windy,

The multi beaked, the wanderer,

Or even yet Purna, the everyman, the changeless, the frozen one?

On a dark dawn, in a morning of ice,

A man ship came from the world beyond the worlds.

It landed on a planet of freezing dust.

Two earthmen, cowled in plastics and fishbowls of glass,

Wandered, numb, through the forests of White Oaks,

They ran like children through the valley of eternal snow

And at last, unknowing,

They entered like meat

The plateaux of the beast.

Over a cold smouldering fire

They talked of Earth

And tried to put the warmth they caught

From the memory of their loved ones

Into their chilled hearts

To give them heat and courage.

They dozed in pale canopies

Like cosmic boy scouts.

They were awoken at dawn

By a mighty wind

Which clawed at their tent

Like a lion,

And then he came.

The first caress from his demon mind

Brought blindness,

In his minds mouth

He crunched the eyeballs

Like crackerly over fried eggs

And then the limbs,

He sucked the bones bare

Like a Tennessee chicken eater,

The nails and lips, rare delicacies.

He chomped slowly,

The howls of pain

Shook the foliage of White Oak,

And lastly the heart.

A masterpiece by a hated master

Littered the floor,

Making hieroglyphics

And cosmic rune talk.

The earthmen lay

Swamped in living debris,

Unseeing, unfeeling and dying.

Torn gullet lay on broken armpit and gorged fingers.

The only un-raped personage

That remained of the plundered citadel of the body

Was their hearts.

Albany loped wildly

Beneath the golden scythe of the moon,

His toothless mouth

Rouged with blood,

His unholy appetite

For once fully appeased.

He scurried to a brook

And broke the frozen water

With a crimson claw.

He knelt on bony knees

To drink the water,

His long fleshy tongue was revealed

And on it, still beating

Was the double heart.

The final poem in this collection raises stark and grotesque issues and comparisons. Again it needs to be read a number of times to understand the face it shows before attempting to delve below its make-up. It is an apt finale and combines many elements of Marc's mind in one. It is very different from all the others, yet similar and copious connections can be readily made.

Although it is well known that Marc was extraordinarily prolific, not only in his music but also in his poetry, little of it remains. He is reputed to have had many boxes of poetry under his bed but in the years since his death it has all gone astray, being either lost, stolen or sold off as single sheets of memorabilia to his fans. In a sense this is a tragedy because as proven, there is much hidden in the labyrinth of Marc Bolan's words, however, to collate hundreds of sheets that have been dispersed around the globe would be an impossible task, although a worthwhile one. This book houses what is believed to be the only complete collection of his poetry, apart from that published in 'The Warlock of Love'. Despite being aware of the possibility that some pieces may not have been finished and have not been prepared or edited for publication by Marc (they may not even be presented in the way he intended), they are all strong, plausible examples of his work. Each poem is completely different and shows how diversely he bantered with differing subjects; he revisits themes, words or subjects he had used before, expanding upon them or reinterpreting them, he constantly shook his mind for fresh permutations of ideas, music and words, but did not neglect the established ones. Although difficult to do it is important to try and view the whole of Marc Bolan, every facet of his life, creativity, knowledge and imagination in order to understand any single piece.

Although it is impossible to know, it would be fitting if this were the last poem Marc wrote, as in some aspects it epitomises his journey.

In a far off world

Hoary with age

Surrounded by mists,

In a star system

Barren and decaying,

Dwelt Albany.

He brings the reader to a distant world, a dying empty planet, Grey with age, misty and bleak in a forgotten and dying star system. It is inhabited by a grotesque being he calls Albany.

He was once a man

But now something more,

The breath of a million stars

Had altered his metabolism

Into the image of a God.

But what God and whose?

Was this the visage of the Star one?

He then begins to debate the origins of the creature, recounting that he was once a normal man who had been changed into a god by the influences of a millions stars, but questions which and whose god he could be.

Was this the visage of the Star one?

Lofty brow punctured with pores

And green with moulds and bacteria,

Legless but still walking.

Eyeballs, orbs of contradiction,

Leaning out into the foggy night

On crimson stalks,

Seeing nothing but smelling all.

He queries whether this creature that has degenerated into such a horrific form could really be the *Star one*, implying a comparison by his description of Albany that the *Star one* would have been the opposite, beautiful, alive, active and aware, seeing all clearly.

Albany the man,

It would seem,

Had long been dead,

What Albany used to be has long gone and is dead.

But what remained?

What loped in his misshaped husk of a body

Through the mists of this barren planet?

Was it him, Ashemoc, the cursed curser,

The God who would and was willing,

Or Tylon the windy,

The multi beaked, the wanderer,

Or even yet Purna, the everyman, the changeless, the frozen one?

Marc continues to debate what and who the creature could be and if there is anything left inside the tortured being of his former self, giving three potential identities or personas for Albany.

On a dark dawn, in a morning of ice,

A man ship came from the world beyond the worlds.

It landed on a planet of freezing dust.

Two earthmen, cowled in plastics and fishbowls of glass,

Wandered, numb, through the forests of White Oaks,

They ran like children through the valley of eternal snow

And at last, unknowing,

They entered like meat

The plateaux of the beast.

On a dark, cold morning a spaceship from earth lands on Albany's planet. There is a Bolanesque description of two astronauts *'cowled in plastics and fishbowls of glass,'* who innocently wander the planet, across the snow covered valley, through the forests until they unwittingly, like wild game, enter the plateaux where Albany lives.

Over a cold smouldering fire

They talked of Earth

And tried to put the warmth they caught

From the memory of their loved ones Into their chilled hearts

To give them heat and courage.

They dozed in pale canopies

Like cosmic boy scouts.

The astronauts make camp and around a fire they reminisce about their families in an effort to relieve the feelings of isolation they have on this cold desolate world, far from home. They then fall asleep in their tents, Bolan likening them to boy scouts.

They were awoken at dawn

By a mighty wind

Which clawed at their tent

Like a lion,

And then he came.

In the morning they were awoken by a raging storm, then Albany came, he had found them.

The first caress from his demon mind

Brought blindness,

In his minds mouth

He crunched the eyeballs

Like crackerly over fried eggs

In the first wave of his attack he tore out their eyes and crunched them in his mouth, like crisp fried eggs.

And then the limbs,

He sucked the bones bare

Like a Tennessee chicken eater,

The nails and lips, rare delicacies.

He chomped slowly,

The howls of pain

Shook the foliage of White Oak,

And lastly the heart.

In the second wave of his attack he sucked the meat from their bones as if he was eating Kentucky Fried Chicken, taking time to enjoy what he considered the delicacies. Their cries of pain shook the leaves of the trees before reaching the heart of the forest.

A masterpiece by a hated master

Littered the floor,

Making hieroglyphics

And cosmic rune talk.

The earthmen lay

Swamped in living debris,

Unseeing, unfeeling and dying.

Torn gullet lay on broken armpit and gorged fingers.

The only un-raped personage

That remained of the plundered citadel of the body

Was their hearts.

Marc compares the horrific mess of blood left on the floor from Albany's attack on the men to a painting of an artist everyone hates and does not understand. The form of expression he has chosen is likened to Egyptian writings that only a few can decipher. All that remains of the men is the messy remnants of their bodies. He has, however, left their hearts.

Albany loped wildly

Beneath the golden scythe of the moon,

His toothless mouth

Rouged with blood,

His unholy appetite

For once fully appeased.

He scurried to a brook

And broke the frozen water

With a crimson claw.

He knelt on bony knees

To drink the water,

His long fleshy tongue was revealed

And on it, still beating

Was the double heart.

Albany, covered in the blood of his meal, which has finally stemmed his hunger, clumsily runs to the stream, he breaks through the ice to drink the water, when Marc reveals that he could not resist and on his tongue he is still relishing the beating hearts of the Earthmen. Albany has finally eaten the hearts of men, those who would have made him a god.

In contradiction to what has become idiosyncratic to Bolan, there is no key to open this poem, no clue, no smudge in the make-up. All the names used are deliberately ambiguous and offer no common link to any mythology, country or person no matter how tenuous. *Albany* is the name of a number of American towns and cities, the most famous of which is the capital of New York State and although a convincing debate could be outlined for the creature being an allegoric representation pertaining to New York, it would have a loose weave. It is also a name Marc had used before on 'Unicorn', the song 'The Misty Coast of Albany' but again there is no significant link. *Tylon*, apart from having a possible link to mythology by being the supposed name of a son from the bonding of Hercules and Omphale, which is not a wide spread or unanimously accepted theory amongst mythologists, is a village in north Wales near Llandwrog and Caernarfon. Although Peter Sanders remembers them regularly frequenting a cottage of Marc's in north Wales at weekends, there is nothing substantial enough to connect with this poem. *Purna* is the name of a revered Buddhist monk, which is more than likely to be coincidental. *White Oaks* is a variety of places throughout the world from log cabin resorts to bed and breakfast guesthouses and obviously numerous areas of woodland. Ashemoc, again is a name Bolan has used before, in a poem in 'The Warlock of Love' where he describes a widow as having 'the illness of Ashemoc'. The only thing that links all these names is Marc Bolan.

The lack of a connecting thread is unusual, as has been shown, Marc was extremely proficient at weaving allegoric threads but surly the lack of one is so conspicuous it becomes the thread. There is a clue in the title, 'Gods and Men' it is dramatically simplistic, a clear profound statement, bold and provocative, it does not hide behind any mask or make-up. Marc has been aloof with his allegories in this poem because he understood exactly what he was doing in the piece. To give a connection with any specific culture, mythology, country or religion would be to singularly attack that specific. He is attacking the concept of divinity as a whole, whether it is Egyptian, Grecian, Roman, Christian or any other dedication to a discerned superior being or cause. 'Attacking' is possibly too strong a verb, it is more fitting to say that Marc was questioning the roots of many of man's beliefs, raising the issue. As Mark Feld had come from a predominantly Jewish community, he would have understood the danger of appearing to target any one group and would avidly avoid doing so. As in his sexuality, in religion he projected an ambiguity, which he strived to protect.

Albany was once believed to be a god, but over the centuries as man's knowledge grows, beliefs change, and what was once a god has become a monster, alone and desolate and given the opportunity, he readily feeds off those who were once his worshippers. Man has been consumed by what he once believed in. It could be read as a warning to be wary of believing too deeply in any one thing, as it will ultimately consume you.

In 'Gods and Men' Marc has dispensed with the lines usually drawn between religion, mythology, science and science fiction and amalgamated them all into one, implying that the truth is a cocktail made up from elements of them all. Remembering this, there is another potential hypothesis.

If Albany is Marc Bolan, he has found himself in a lonely deserted place, a world of music where he is in decline, decaying. Marc Bolan was once an ordinary man but the influences of other stars in the galaxies of Elvis and Cliff turned him into a star, god like, but to whom did he belong? Is Marc Bolan's (Albany's) face the face of the one that was once the number one star? A face that had become fat and is deteriorating, one that used to be alive and aware of everything going on around him, seeing clearly every new trend, in music and fashion? He has now become lost and blinded (by drugs, drink and disillusionment) and is rotting way, but he can still smell the scent of what is around him although the man he once was is long gone! Who was Marc Bolan? Was he the one who was willing and would do anything to succeed, or was he the multi-faced chameleon, who wandered the trends to fit in, or was he the one who was cold and determined, unchangeable in his arrogant self-assuredness?

One day a new trend in music appeared, the men that came with it wore masks made of glass and it was easy to see through their disguise. They wandered aimlessly in a world they did not fully understand, like children they were lost, amateurs in their art. They unknowingly entered the realms of the one giant beast, who was master of his world (Tyrannosaurus Rex). Punk had arrived!

They made their camp in his world, marked out their territory, created their own musical niche. When they felt safe and relaxed in their own world within worlds, he came and fed off them, he nourished himself with their success. He proved himself the master and left his mark in their camp before he strolled back into his domain to refresh himself at the stream, having fed on the heart of punk.

Although this analogy is deeply self-obsessive, in a world of allegoric fantasy, it fits the fingers of Marc's poetic hand like a glove. It would seem to be an ambitious hypothesis if Marc had not entered into the realms of narcissistic biographic verse before, in song as well as poetry. 'The Groover', '20th Century Boy', 'London Boys', 'I Love to Boogie' and many more songs can readily be described as narcissistic and the final poem in 'Warlock of Love' narrates the tale of Blackhat, a wizardly character, who watches with joy as a huge block of ice from a glacier melts and releases the reptile king, the final line 'Tyrannosaurus Rex reborn and bopping' being a blatant reference to the new line up of Tyrannosaurus Rex, remembering that 'Warlock' was first published at the same time as Micky Finn replaced Steve Took and Tyrannosaurus Rex moved in an electric direction with the release of 'A Beard of Stars'. The photographs on the cover of 'Warlock' and 'Beard' are from a similar photo session by Peter Sanders. Marc Bolan had undoubtedly adopted himself within this lingual fantasy.

The second analogy does not outweigh the first as this poem has a number of faces, which evolved from one root idea. Again it is known that Marc frequently redeveloped a previous idea, either expanding on it or reworking it, 'Scenescoff', which was discussed at the beginning of this book, is a prime example. 'Gods and Men' is what could be described as a sister poem to 'The Blue Seeker' from the previous chapter. It has the same basic story line, aliens (albeit earthmen) land on a planet and are eaten by an occupant of that planet, in total disregard for their quest. There is a clear line of development from the original Star Trek story 'The Squire of Gothos' through 'The Blue Seeker' to 'Gods and Men', the story taking on slightly different properties in each stage of development. Marc's buoyant imagination has completely re-costumed the frame of the story.

With the use of a 'Sherlock Holmes' style examination of the original notebook pages it has been easily deduced that Marc wrote 'Gods and Men' immediately after 'Blue Seeker' which was written completely in pencil. The same pencil has been used at the beginning of 'Gods and Men' but Marc changes to black pen two thirds of the way down page four. The pencil parts of both poems have amendments made in the same blue pen and on the back of the last page of 'Blue Seeker', which would have been adjacent to the first page of 'Gods and Men', Marc has written 'Poem 2' in the same blue ink. In further possible confirmation, on the back of the last page of 'Blue Seeker' the rusty mark of a paper clip can be seen, which coincides perfectly with indentations and marks on the first page of 'Gods and Men', although this could have been done at any time since Marc wrote them. These small bites of forensic information may seem trivial but they help to confirm the theory of an ongoing story development.

Marc's first adaptation is almost comical, a whimsical recount of first contact, completely dismissive of its relevance, wrapped in the oblivious innocence of a child. The second, in complete contrast, is dark and grotesque leaving the taste of death in the reader's mouth. Yet Sandra and Albany, the respective diners of each poem, perform the same act but with differing motives and awareness. If the two poems are assessed jointly they can be seen to affirm Marc's assertion that everyone has a different head and sees things from a different perspective, but although both scenarios are viewed through different eyes with differing agendas, the outcome is the same, the death of the alien. They both narrate the death of explorers who have pushed themselves to the limits in the pursuance of knowledge, only to be consumed by that which they seek and their noble efforts nonchalantly discarded with their bones. With the risk of overburdening these poems with yet another dimension of meaning, this could be Marc Bolan's true message hidden in the maze of these sisters, his fear of being forgotten in death, his life being wasted, the realisation that he was in danger of being consumed and casually forgotten by what he had laboured for all his life.

The true meaning that hides within these two final poems is the same as the mind of Marc Bolan, a cocktail of all the elements and theories portrayed, there is truth in each one that blends with the others.

When Marc learnt of Elvis' death on August 16th 1977 he was worried that if he died, Elvis' death would overshadow his and he would pass away unnoticed. Marc died exactly one month later on September 16th and he was not forgotten.

All through his life Marc had expressed a belief that he would die young, when the subject was touched upon in interviews he became uneasy. June had said on occasions he was worried about dying in his sleep before he had finished, and would sit up regularly through the night writing. He purported to believe in reincarnation, which he said 'Cosmic Dancer' from 'Electric Warrior' was about, and told that he remembered being here before a number of times, but this was more likely to be Marc Bolan playing the media than his true beliefs.

His wide interests in various mythologies intimates a searching for some type of meaning, as does his bantering with ideas as he did in these two poems. Marc also had a fascination for legends of every kind, historic, musical, mythical and big screen legends and understood that dying young would most likely secure him a place as a legend, providing his contribution warranted being attributed to a legend. His constant zestful productiveness displayed impatience in time, as if it was running out and he needed to hurry.

Whether or not Marc Bolan feared death is not known, but it is reasonable to concur that he did; it is more probable that he feared being forgotten after his death more. He undoubtedly expressed the desire to be remembered as a legend.

Marc was described by many as being spiritual, Peter Sanders said as much but also said that Marc had put the consolidating of his spirituality on hold. Although he clearly believed in another dimension of existence after death, he obviously had not formulated his final conclusions. Various comments he made through his words clearly depict his considerations and the fact that he could debate so articulately shows that he must have debated the afterlife in his own mind, regardless of how much is attributed to his media manipulation.

From the viewpoint of a spectator it appears that Marc deliberately avoided truly confronting the reality of death and buried himself in the fantasy role of a rock star, which he believed might become immortal. Treading water while he surveyed the options. Despite Marc Bolan's ambiguity of beliefs regarding the afterlife he was completely aware of how to sustain a life, as a legend, after death in this world and legends provoke continued inspiration.

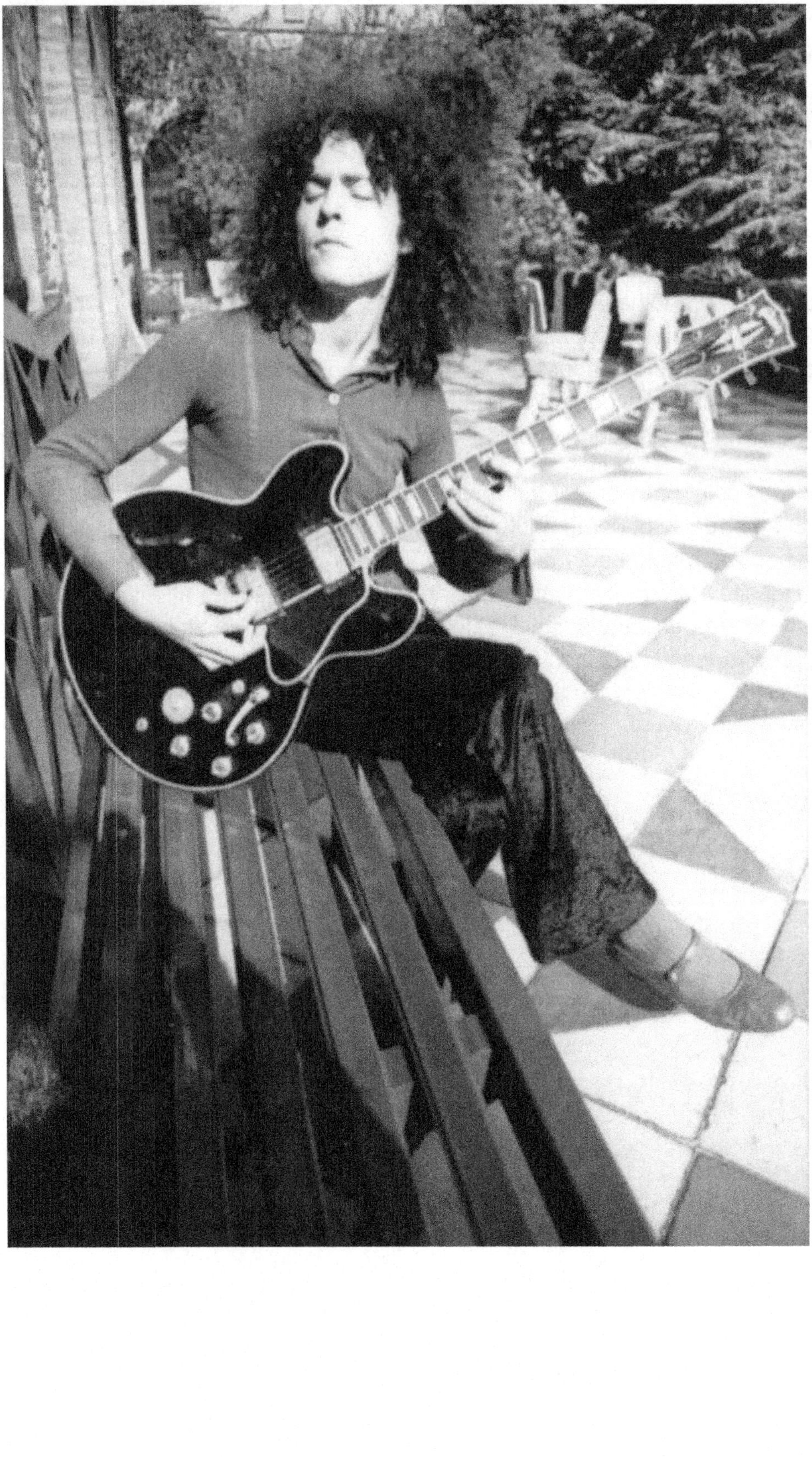

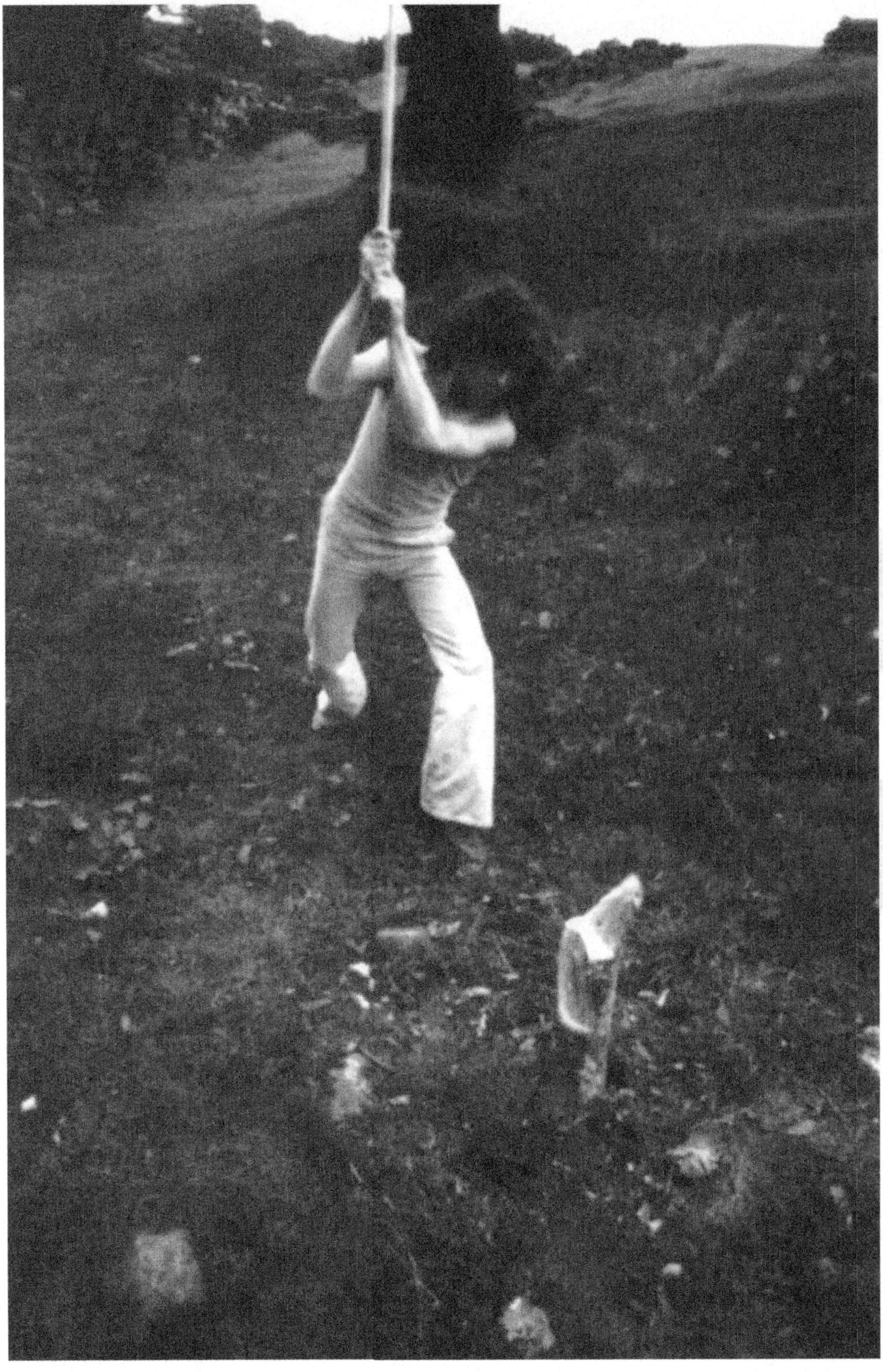

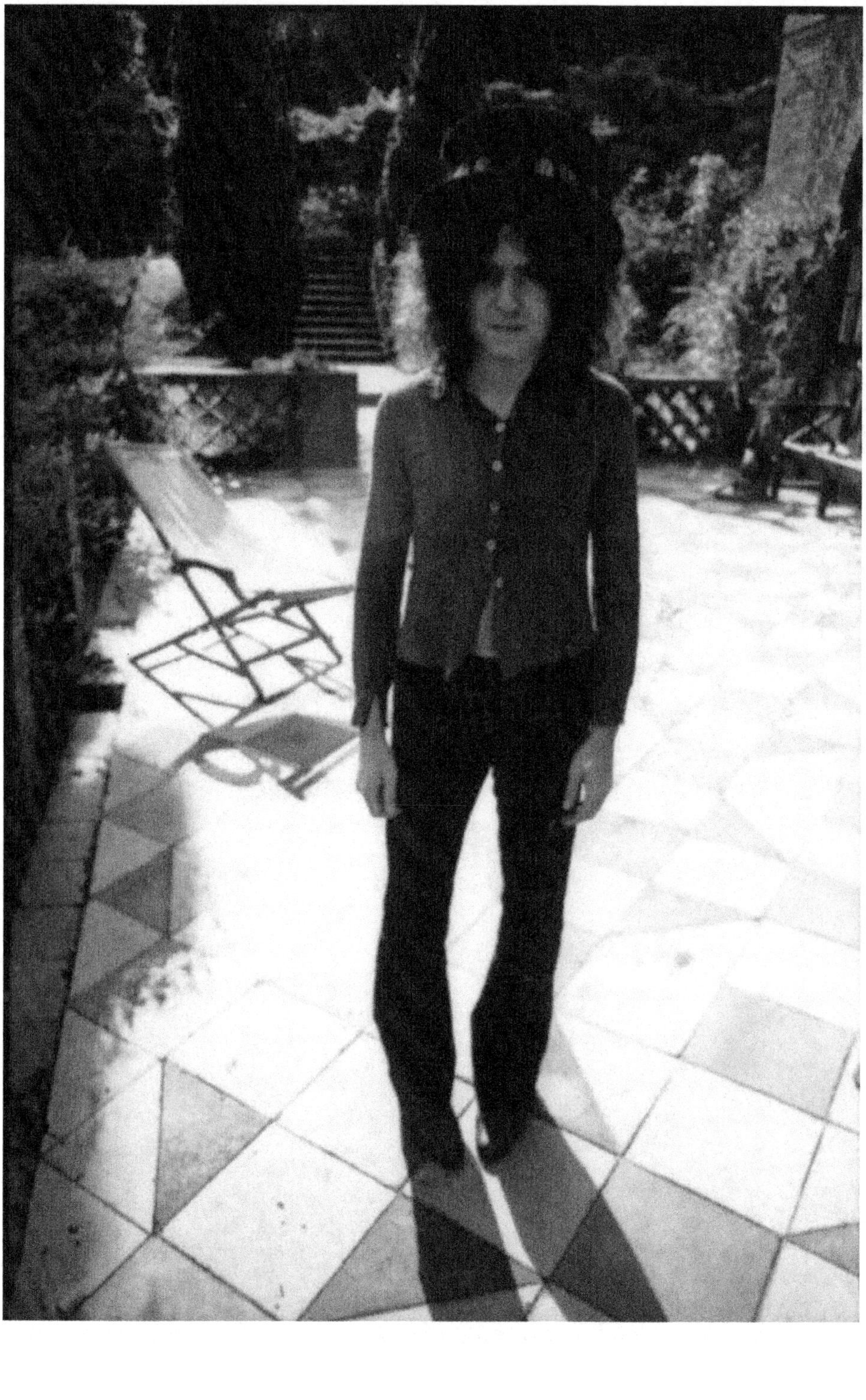

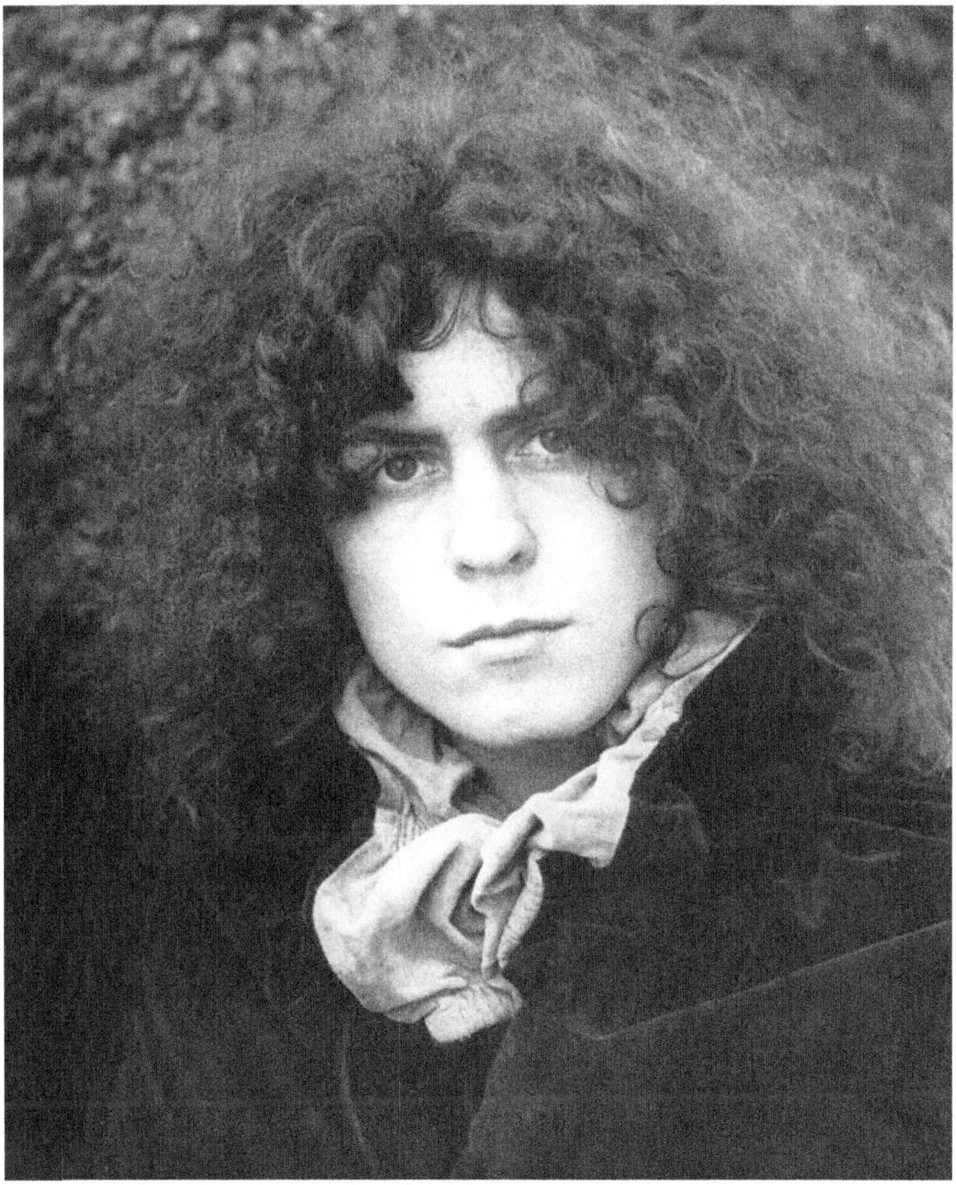

12. **Gurus and Dreams**

"You've got to try and understand the soul of the man who's playing those songs."
Marc Bolan 1972.

Metal Guru is it you

Metal Guru is it you

Sitting there in your armour plated chair.

Metal Guru is it true

Metal Guru is it true

All alone without a telephone.

Metal Guru could it be

You're gonna bring my baby to me

She'll be wild you know

A Rock and Roll child.

Metal Guru has it been

Just like a silver-studded sabre-toothed dream

 I'll be clean you know

Pollution machine.

Metal Guru is it you

Metal Guru is it you?

Have the depths of Marc Bolan's mind been explored well enough to finally unearth the identity of Metal Guru? Surely it is now obvious? There are an abundance of keys in the lyrics to unlock this Bolanesque mystery. In truth it should now be quite transparent. Especially if all the lessons learnt are brought to the table, how he played with words and bantered with peers.

Note should indeed be taken of the messages that the man himself has left us. Firstly that there is a need to understand the soul of the man who wrote these words and the foremost clue he repeatedly gave us, that it is about someone he knew. Also the need to be aware of the chronology of the song, when it was written and what was going on in the world of Marc Bolan at that time, his dreams and aspirations, the things that were of importance to him and the influences that had moulded him. It may be useful to take another short walk down the pathways of Bolanology.

Marc would take a phrase from the song of a musical hero give it a twist of Bolan and then implant it into one of his own songs or use it as a source of inspiration. He would always be honest about this process and pay due homage to the original, should it be known where to look and of course, there being an awareness of the original and the process. As in 'Get it on' with the final line 'Well meanwhile I'm still thinking' as discussed earlier, and also with the song 'Rabbit Fighter' which is full of clear references to Marc's musical heroes. 'Moondog' appears in one of Bob Dylan's most famous songs, a song that was one of Marc's first recordings, 'Blowin' in the Wind'. In Dylan's version it is a reference to Louis T Hardin, a mysterious composer who wore the personification of a wizardly druid and a popular artist with Dylan and his kinsmen in the late 1960s. Bolan's reference is either to Hardin or Dylan. Jo Jo is from the Beatles last album, the song 'Get Back'…with lines such as 'Jo Jo was a man' etc. The dude that got badly burned is undeniably Bowie, who at this particular time in rock history had been ripped off by his management, having been so heavily into drugs as to not notice.

With each subtle allusion Marc Bolan paid his respects to his fellow artists and gurus, placing himself upon the pedestal along side them, which is precisely what 'Rabbit Fighter' is about. The phrase 'Rabbit Fighter' comes from one of the heroes Bolan truly aspired to be the equal of, Elvis Presley. In the song 'Hound Dog' Elvis sings *'You ain't never caught a rabbit so you ain't no friend of mine'* (although it sounds like 'fought a rabbit'). Bolan is clearly proclaiming that he has not only caught rabbits but has fought them, he is a rabbit fighter, he has paid his dues earned his fame, hustled his way to the top, he is 'up there' with the greats…'call me the King Rabbit Fighter' he is saying,' I am up here with you Elvis!'

Marc Bolan is up at the top with Elvis and all the other gurus he had grown up admiring, he had become their equal and in some cases their friend and mentor and Marc Bolan was elated by this. Not only had he achieved the status he had so wholly desired since his childhood, but he actively bantered and parried with the people he admired the most, he was their hero too, they were admiring him. He had gained their respect!

The subtle and not so subtle name-dropping is extremely prevalent on the Slider album, which 'Rabbit Fighter' and 'Metal Guru' appear on, with references to Lennon, Alan Freed, many to Dylan and endless innocuous drops that become clear with concise investigation. This minstrelling banter is not unique to Bolan, many artists take part in this game; Dylan himself was an expert, his first reference to Moondog being an excellent example. Even Ringo's 'Back off Boogaloo' is said to have had inspiration from Marc (who played on the album 'Ringo') and to be about Paul McCartney and the events of the Beatles' break up. That song a statement in itself that Bolan was now a part of the world he had dreamed of.

Marc Bolan had accomplished many of his dreams by the time Slider appeared; he had been a model, a best selling poet and now a successful and respected rock star, a peer to his gurus. Yet he had one dream yet to fulfil, and it was about to be realised.

From an early age, like many, Mark Feld had dreamed of the silver screen, of being glamorised by celluloid. He had been enchanted by the magic of cinema, from his first experiences of 'Mighty Joe Young' and the 'The Wizard of Oz' he had longed to be immortalised in a star-studded cast of famous contemporaries and this dream was about to be born, to be spawned from his collaboration with ex Beatle drummer Ringo Starr.

'Born to Boogie' followed in the footsteps of the Beatles films, a rock and roll indulgence on celluloid, showcasing Marc Bolan. Comprising predominantly of concert footage filmed at Wembley Pool, which is self-explanatory, it is punctuated with surreal scenes that only Bolan would understand. It opens and closes with Marc standing alone jamming with his guitar and amp, no other band members present, a gentle hint that he is T-Rex. The first surreal scene has Ringo Starr dressed as a mouse chauffeuring Marc and being hit with a fly swat, totally subservient to the glam rock king! The portrayal of the ex Beatle as a tiny rodent alongside the reptile king has an ironic humour to it that could be thought of as accidental if not for the fact that Bolan's pawn, the eater of cars (remembering that he has described Tyrannosaurus Rex as the eater of cars many times), suddenly appears having been magically summoned and is then duly hit with the same fly swat, putting him firmly in his place. Marc's statement here is clear, it is that he is the master, he is in control! This may seem arrogant and egotistical but it has already been established that these are both traits of Marc Bolan's personality. The hypothesis is strengthened when Ringo is seen dressed as a clown in the studio scene with stuffed animals, all part of the great rock and roll circus, while Marc is smartly donned in a musical jacket, the ringmaster! There is further confirmation in the 'picnic' scene where Marc is clearly the host, having taken over the role from John Lennon in his own garden (the scene was filmed at his Tittenhurst Park mansion). With Mickey Finn made up as a blood sucking vampire, Marc's wife

June and Chelita Secunda dressed up, holier than thou, as nuns and Ringo, freshly groomed, all predominantly eating from Marc's table while he performed with a string quartet that was forced to mime because Bolan had neglected to inform them about the songs he would be playing. The final touch to this scene, which closes the ruse, is that the archetypal British actor, Catweazle star Geoffrey Bayldon (another of Marc's gurus), is employed as a butler, cooking and waiting on the assembled guests, reciting poetical snippets of Bolan's in reverence to rock and roll, which he has admitted to not understanding. The lord and master of this scene was of course Marc Bolan, although magnanimously humbling himself by performing while sitting cross legged on the floor, he was unquestionably playing the role of the conquering star, he was in the top spot and on Lennon's home turf to! Did no one see the joke being played? Further metaphoric signs of the arrogant assertion is the photo of Marc sitting on the sabre toothed beast, he has tamed the tiger and happily rides it, and at the end of the film he is modestly led off by an elemental child leaving an almost empty scene, which is magically occupied by the eater of cars who feeds on the amp (symbolic of the music), the only thing left behind. If the eater of cars symbolises the monster created by Marc Bolan T-Rex (as previously implied) then this in turn implies that the monster is feeding from what Marc has left it to feed from, his music. It may be thought that this hypothesis is somewhat extreme and maybe an unintended motive to the movie, but it has been shown that Marc was highly intelligent, ingenious and more than capable at playing such a gambit. The fact that he kept the identity of Metal Guru secret when bantered many times for a revelation is surely evidence enough that he was more than able to pull such a scam. He was a true master of his world.

This is not to condemn him for the game, it was not malicious, more mischievous, but to understand and explain the soul of the man. He revelled in the ruses he cast with his words and deeds, from his sexual ambiguity to his lyrical deceptions, he enjoyed the mysteries he wove and loved the banter they caused. Marc knew that these mysteries inspired intrigue and debate and perpetuated the legend, and now the legend would be preserved in celluloid, another dream accomplished! But there was a hole in the plot of this script.

There have been many criticisms of Marc Bolan, his words, lyrics and poetry. Many put downs, not only from critics, but also from close friends and associates, which must have been deeply hurtful to Marc because to him in his imagination the meanings were clear, but no one was on his 'wave length' and all were misinterpreted as meaningless rambles that sounded good. Maybe one day he would have opened the door to his words himself, truly revelling in the revelations and the joke would have been complete, it will never be known. There is, however, a sadness there, because he was so extremely prolific and so incredibly expressive, yet no one got it, how frustrating that must have been for him? How lonely and intellectually isolating. It is not surprising that he took to drink and drugs, despite his apparent triumphs. The mask had become successful but nobody took the time to look beneath it! The ego was truly unleashed but bruised, what better game to play, therefore, than to preserve a peer, an idol in a song forever, making them allegorically subordinate, disguised within the metaphors and wordplay…and nobody would ever know. Unless he told them, but he did not and the identity of Metal Guru remains unresolved.

Should he be uncloaked? Would there be any betrayal to Marc's motives or intentions by the disclosure? With full confidence the analysis of the lyrics can be made, but a doubt lingers as to whether or not it is in some way a breach of confidence. Yet, in truth, it is fitting that thirty years after his death the mystery should finally be unlocked.

Let us start from the bottom…

Pollution machine

Obviously a car, but more than that, Marc saw a car as a work of art, something he revered and admired. He had a love for cars, which he expressed many times through his lyrics and in interviews, despite never being able to drive, possibly that enhanced the image for him, accentuated their mystery. This line has led to people believing that Metal Guru was about a car, which is understandable but misguided.

I'll be clean you know

A simple statement saying that he will be good, perform well, look fantastic, like a real work of art, like a car.

Metal Guru has it been

Just like a silver-studded sabre-toothed dream.

The clues have already been laid out in this chapter. First take the phrase 'silver-studded', it is the amalgamation of the two common film phrases, the 'silver screen' and a 'star studded' cast. Then 'Sabretoothed dream', this is a reference to the tiger Marc was photographed sitting on for the promotion of his film and the relating album, the 'sabre toothed tiger', also the logo of MGM was the roaring lion Leo. 'Dream' relates to it being a dream like film, surreal, as described by Marc himself and of course that it is one of his personal dreams realised. These lines therefore translate thus…

Metal Guru has it been

Like a dream of the silver screen with a star studded cast and with lions and tigers.

The preceding verse to this leads the way to the analysis,

Metal Guru could it be

You're gonna bring my baby to me

She'll be wild you know

A rock and roll child.

It would be an easy mistake to perceive the 'baby' as a girl, a love interest, which it is but not of the human kind. Marc's 'baby' at this point in time was his new venture, his new film 'Born to Boogie' and it was going to be wild, a real rock and roll film!

All alone without a telephone.

Ringo is seen at the beginning of the film sitting in the back of a Cadillac on his own with no phone, while Marc is engaged in an 'important' rock and roll phone call.

Sitting there in your armour plated chair.

An 'armour plated chair' is one surrounded by metal…a car.

Metal Guru is it you.

It should by now be easy to guess the real identity, but let there be a clarifying explanation offered. 'Guru' another word for hero, someone revered, a star…or Starr. 'Metal' is one of Marc's word plays; Richard Starkey was bestowed the nickname of Ringo because of all the rings he wore on his fingers, all the 'metal' he adorned himself with. So Ringo Starr becomes Metal Guru and makes it to number one, pseudonymously.

Ringo Starr is it you

Ringo Starr is it you

Sitting there in your automobile chair

Ringo Starr is it true

Ringo Starr is it true

You're all alone without a phone (while I'm sitting here with one)

Ringo Starr could it be

You're going to make my film for me

It'll be wild you know A rock and roll film

Ringo Starr has it been

A star-studded silver-screen dream

I'll be good you know

A real work of art!

Metal Guru…Ringo Star, someone he knew and admired!

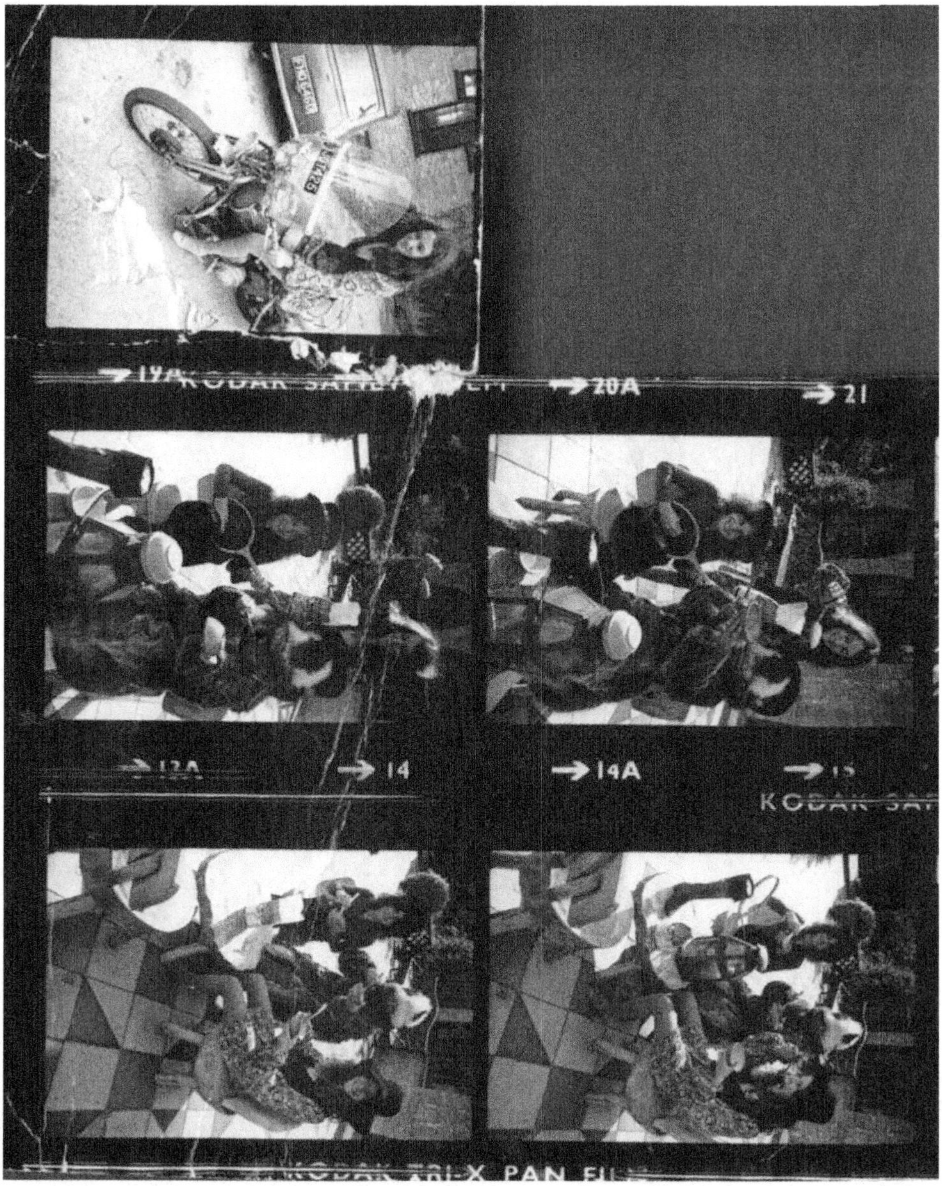
20A
21
14
14A
KODAK

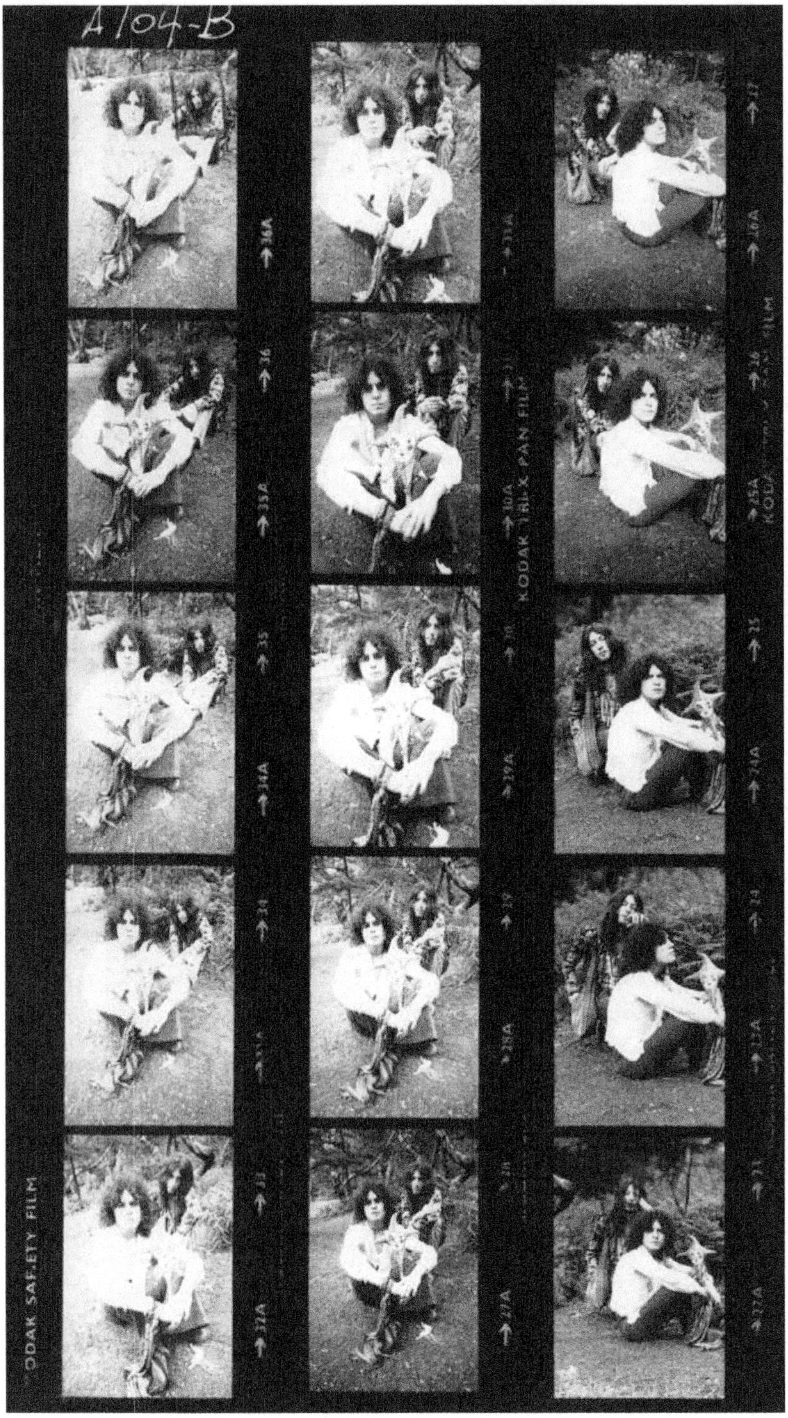
A104-B
KODAK TRI-X PAN FILM
KODAK SAFETY FILM

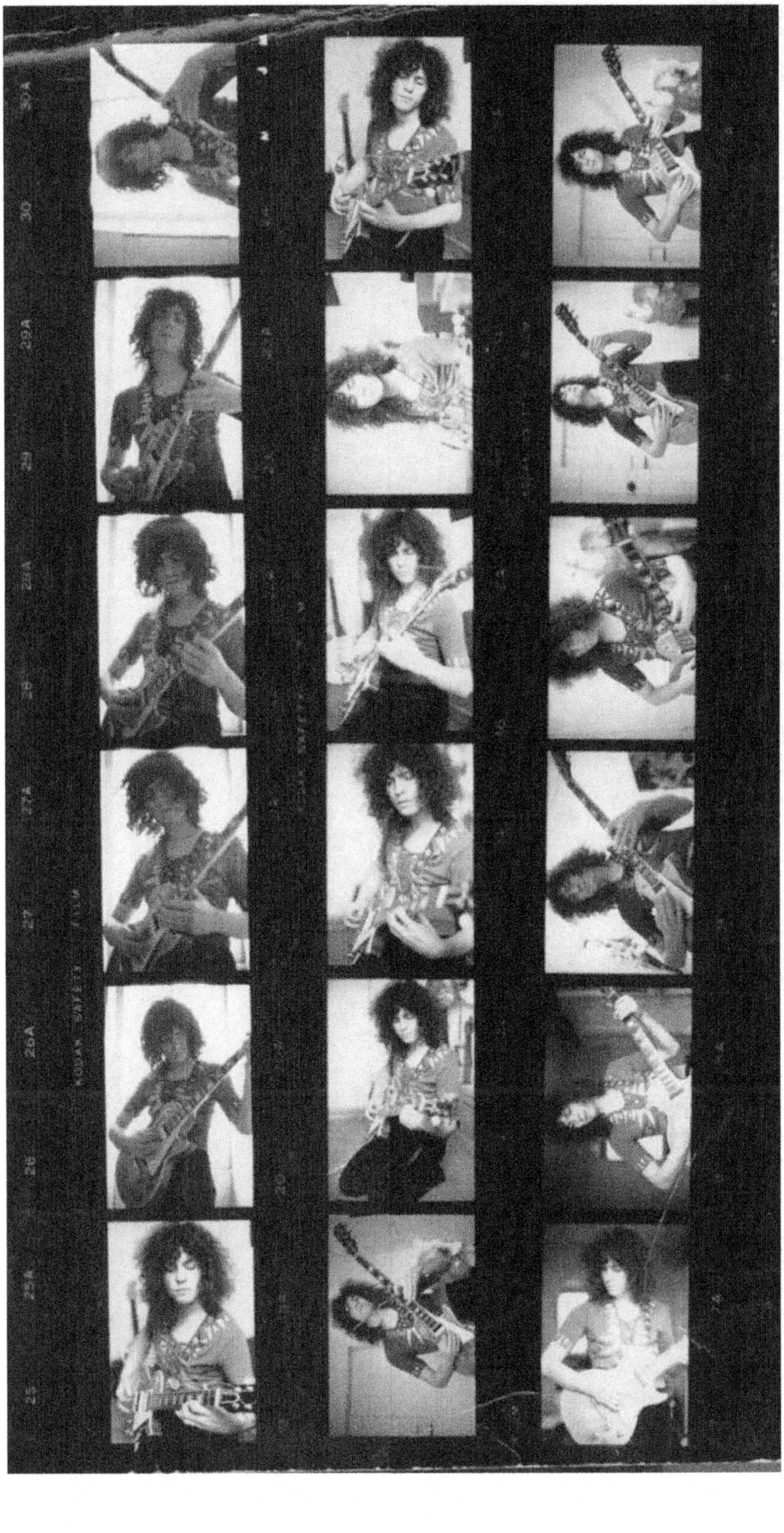

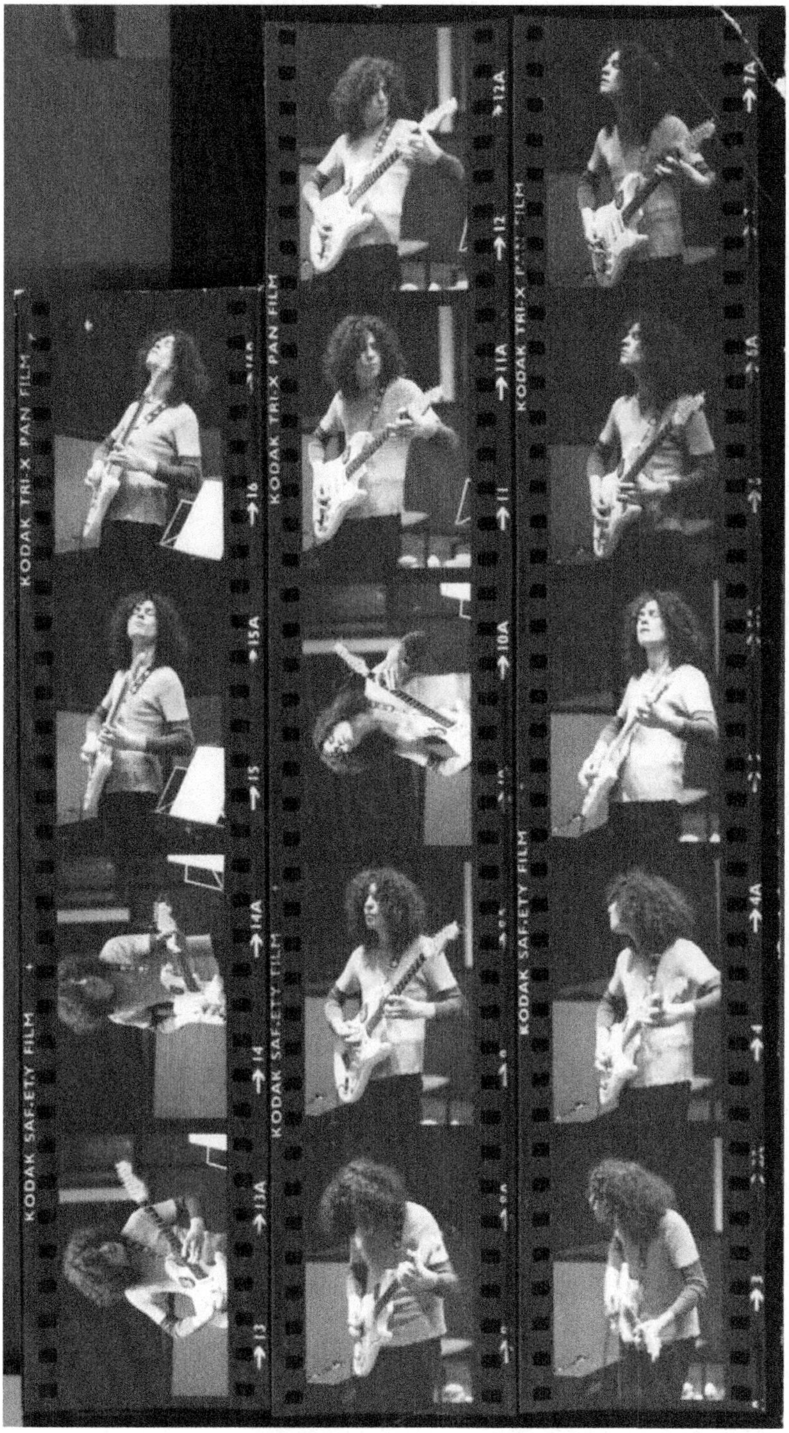
KODAK TRI-X PAN FILM
KODAK SAFETY FILM

13. **In the Shadow of the Wizard**

When I saw T-Rex at the Odeon in Birmingham in 1972, I had just turned fifteen and would have gone with my cousin, Chris Cocking, being my closest friend at the time. I lived in Wolverhampton and Chris near Dudley and I don't recall how we got to and from the gig, I presume one of our parents played the role of taxi driver. My father had driven me to Birmingham months before to queue for the tickets, lecturing me during every stage of the twelve-mile journey to be careful and leaving no doubt in my mind as to how insane he thought I was. All I cared about was whether I would be early enough to get a good enough position in the queue to stand any chance of getting tickets!

When he dropped me off near the front of the theatre in New Street, I could see that the queue had already started to form and had turned the corner down an alleyway at the side of the Odeon but this was only approximately twenty yards, so I wasn't overly concerned. As I followed the line around the corner, my heart sank into a pit of despair as I saw that the queue vanished into the distance, turning another corner at the rear of the cinema, and then further still, stretching out towards New Street railway station, which seemed to be half way across the city. I remember cursing my father for not allowing me to come earlier as I was sure that there was no possibility of getting tickets.

This was a stark difference to when I had bought tickets twelve months previous. T-Rex had played the Civic Hall in Wolverhampton on the 19th May 1971 and tickets for rock concerts at the Civic were handled by the Astra International Agency, which was based in the Club Lafayette just off Broad Street in Wolverhampton. You had to climb three flights of dingy stairs to get to the office at the top of the Lafayette and there was rarely a queue, the only one I recall was for the Rolling Stones. The venue was always sold out by the night of the gig and I saw many acts there, usually sneaking out of school at lunch time to buy tickets for bands like The Who, Queen, The Groundhogs, Hawkwind, Black Sabbath, Deep Purple, Argent, Curved Air, Yes, Led Zeppelin and many more. I lived for music at the time, every penny I earned from a number of jobs, I spent on records, tickets and loons… I had to dress the part too! I remember buying an ex air force overcoat which, in conflict with my teenage ideals, met with strong approval from my father who dubbed it a 'sensible, warm coat', I did not get the same approval when I brought home a pink satin jacket!

I had been hooked on T-Rex from the first time I heard Marc's opening guitar phrase on 'Ride a White Swan', the 'B' side got me to, I loved his version of Eddie Cochran's 'Summertime Blues'. I acquired the 'T-Rex' brown album and the 'Best of T-Rex' on Fly and was enchanted, I had never heard such magically mystical music wrapped up with raunchy rock, Marc Bolan's music was different!

I struggled to find any other albums of Marc's in the shops of Wolverhampton and remember swapping two of my albums with a friend at school, Anthony Flanagan; I can't remember the albums I parted with but I know I gained original versions of 'Unicorn' and 'A Beard of Stars' on the Regal Zonophone label, they were deemed collectors items even then and I was ecstatic with my new prized possessions. By the time I first saw Marc Bolan at the Civic Hall on May 19th 1971 I was a dedicated fan!

The Civic Hall gig held much of the Tyrannosaurus Rex identity and had an air of spiritual musicality; there was a sense of purity and innocence portrayed in the whole aura of the concert, especially when compared to Black Sabbath and The Who. It was an enchanting experience.

On the 24th September I was one of the many who couldn't wait to get his hands on the new album, 'Electric Warrior', I bought it on my way home from school, but for some reason I had had to go to my grandmothers, who did not possess a record player and I remember sitting in my grandfathers old arm chair pawing every inch of the sleeve, reading every lyric, credit and footnote, no matter how insignificant, I lost myself in the maze of George Underwood's inner sleeve drawings and counted the minutes in tortured anticipation. When I finally got home and played it on my parent's precious radiogram I felt like Charlie Bucket when he walked into Willy Wonka's chocolate factory, it was all I had dreamed it to be.

From then on I bought everything Marc Bolan released, and some he didn't. When I heard of the Birmingham concert, through the same school friend who I had exchanged albums with, I knew I had to go but by the time I had finally walked to the end of the queue, I was sure my early morning was in vane. For six hours I stood on the same spot watching the queue get even longer behind me, when finally a murmur came down the line like a Mexican wave that the box office had opened. It was a slow progression as the queue diminished in front of me and I watched with jealousy the faces of those tightly clutching tickets as they made their way home. I remember feeling the tension grow as I rounded the last corner and could see the box office ahead, I was sure that they would run out of tickets before I got there. I was lucky, they didn't and I came away with two orange tickets for July 9th at a cost of 75 pence each (outrageous). I realised just how lucky I had been when just a few places behind me fans saw the box office doors closing on them.

I can only liken the months of waiting for the concert date as to that of waiting for Christmas and when the day finally came I could hardly believe it. The gig, however, was as different to the one of a year previous as it could have been; Marc had taken on the role of pop star and responded to the cries of the hysterical fans with allegoric sexual gestures. Even his stage performances had become symbolic. I will admit to being partly disappointed with the gig, it felt commercially exploitative and lacked the magic that was previously there, apart from a few special moments. Deep inside I knew the decline had already begun and although I went on to buy 'Slider' and relished it, it did not have quite the same impact on me as the album 'Electric Warrior'. I remained a faithful fan and followed Marc through 'Tanx' and 'Zinc Alloy' but then my life began to take over and I fell by the wayside, as I know many others did. I still enjoyed and regularly played Marc's earlier works and kept a casual watchful eye upon him, just in case the magic returned but he had become too 'pop' for my musical tastes and the make-up had become to big a part of the act.

I got married (the first time) just after Elvis died and remember the strong feeling of disbelief that hung in the air, no one could truly accept that Elvis was dead, it seemed impossible. Although I respected him, I had never been an Elvis fan but I still felt a sense of loss. I had a new house, a new role in life and I was now a fully independent adult with a mortgage, so I did not really fall into a vat of grief over the King of rock and rolls death, but I recall it did make me aware of everyone's mortality, after all, if Elvis could die?

When I heard of Marc's death, I was driving along a dual carriageway on my way home, I felt as if I'd been shot and had to pull over. Unlike Elvis, Marc Bolan was a part of my life, his music and words had touched me, he had given me such a lot and I had an overpowering feeling that I had let him down. In my maturity I can assimilate the feeling to those felt by a parent who has lost a child prematurely; they have watched them grow through their childhood and relished the magic of their innocence but lost them for a while during their adolescence; the parent patiently waits for them to return from that rebellious period of life so that they can share in their child's maturity and closeness again, but the child dies in mid adolescence. Apart from the overwhelming grief, the parent is left with a feeling that they have let their child down in some way. That is exactly how I felt. I also had a sense of being cheated, as I felt when my parents both died young and I realised I would never be able to give them back what they had given me, I had been robbed of the opportunity to repay them.

Through the years since Marc's death my life has been busy and turbulent and as my knowledge, intellect and appreciations have grown and developed, I gradually began to see and understand aspects of Marc Bolan's work I had not seen before, as much in his later work as in his earlier work. Despite having an exceedingly broad field of interests, particularly in music, no other artist has had such a significant and longstanding influence on me; it is Marc Bolan who first inspired me to begin writing poetry in 1970.

I have always held a belief that there was more depth in Marc's work than he was accredited with and understood that the glam image did not help to enhance his credibility, so when I found myself with the opportunity to put my theory to the test, I embraced it wholeheartedly. I was only too aware of the large number of books that had already been written about Marc Bolan; Mark Paytress wrote an excellent biography 'Twentieth Century Boy' and has done much since to champion Marc. Cliff McLenehan did an impressive job of collating information to produce a chronological record of Marc's career, and there have been countless 'fanzine' type publications, but I felt that there was something significant missing.

The agenda I set myself with this book was a brave one, to prove that there were meanings in Marc Bolan's words, words that have for years been condemned, even by the loyalist of his fans, as being 'out there'. Not wishing to enter the copyright arena of Marc's lyrics, I chose a batch of his poetry that had never been published, or polluted by a variety of previous analogies. In order to do this effectively I knew I would have to wear Marc Bolan's head, to think what he thought, feel what he felt and attempt to see the world from his eyes. When I have conveyed this objective to the many people I have interviewed who knew Marc at various stages of his life, I received a similar response from them all, after an initial laugh they all wished me the best of luck, but thought it impossible.

Without the advantage of being able to live Marc's life, I feel that I have achieved that goal as closely as is attainable. I hope that I have managed to relay that understanding of Marc's mind through these pages. The insight I have gained has given me a new dimension of appreciation for Marc's poetry and songs, I can now listen to lyrics that once beguiled me and understand them, 'Metal Guru', 'Rabbit Fighter' and even 'Salamanda Palaganda' are no longer mysteries to me.

It has been an arduous journey, and I have found it incredibly frustrating at times to find the source of Marc's inspiration, most of the poems required weeks of untangling before I could finalise any form of true analogy, and I disappeared down many dark dead ends before stumbling on the route home.

Although I believed in my agenda, I was not prepared for where Marc Bolan has taken me; I was not prepared for the depth of his entwining of themes and allegories and the breadth of his knowledge, his extensive vocabulary and wordplay. It is clear that he was extremely well read, sought out knowledge and retained it, bantered ideas and theories in an incredibly imaginative way. I would not have believed at the beginning of this project that I would be researching Alexander the Great, Edmund Spenser, Tutankhamen and episodes of Star Trek, connecting them all through the mind of Marc Bolan. His mask of makeup was too convincing and he fooled us all, even those who did not want to be fooled. It must have been a cruel twist of irony when he realised that he had played his role too well and was not being regarded credibly, and I am certain he would have realised his folly, he has proved to have been far too astute not to have noticed or understood. He must have felt a sense of drowning in his own make-up.

There is no itinerary available that lists all the books Marc read and all the music he listened to, I have had to deduce his influences from his own words and the observations of those who knew him; the only person who really knew all of Marc's intake and influences was Marc Bolan himself. It is indisputable that Marc's absorption of knowledge was considerable; it is evident through the vocabulary he employs and the varied subject matter of his work. Apart from the true, disguised meanings within his words, the symbolism he uses draws from an abundance of varied subjects and fields of knowledge that is almost intimidating. I believe that it has been easier for critics, over the years, to discard Marc's words as meaningless rather than make the effort to really understand them. Although I think that Marc, in his ambiguity, was partly to blame for this, he encouraged the belief by his avoidance to give meaningful explanations. It seems clear to me that he saw it as a game, a challenge for the listener or reader; it gave him a sense of superiority knowing that his lingual puzzles were beyond the comprehension of most mortals. It was an art that he had honed and crafted carefully and painstakingly, continually fuelling his imagination with all it needed to construct a world of real fantasy.

Mick O'Halloran, who spent nine years with Marc as his roadie, told me that Marc was always reading, and that he and June were always buying books, he read whenever he could, on flights and every other opportunity he could find, that is when he wasn't recording, performing, writing, or acting out the role of rock star he had created.

If Marc Bolan had not died on the September 16th 1977 he would have evolved into a mature and respected musician and writer, his self-preparation and deliberately focused growth was unprecedented amongst his peers. According to Bill Legend, Marc was an extremely proficient musician, quick and efficient in the studio and 'knew how to write a good hook'. He would have gone further to re-align his motivation and ambition. He had already begun to emerge from his lowest point, where Mick O'Halloran believes he had become bored, which is understandable. For a head that was so single-minded, to have reached his objective and made his fantasy reality must have been anti-climatic. For Marc Bolan to find himself standing alongside his idols following his lifelong blind devotion to his dream, would have inevitably left a hole in his future that would be difficult, if not impossible to fill. So for him to feel lost, bored, lonely, uncertain and tired would be quite understandable.

The true essence of Marc Bolan was the combination of all his elements, he was not one thing, he was all the parts combined, writer, musician, singer, actor, self-educator and idol but by far the strongest and most powerful ingredient in his make-up was his imagination. It is with that tool that Marc turned everyday events into songs and poems, converting reality into fantasy in the same way as he turned fantasy into reality. Marc could not have given a truer analogy of himself when he said "I'm in a realm of fantasy, I can do whatever I want to do and get away with it".

Everything in and about Marc Bolan was a fantasy come true for Mark Feld; he had become his dream and lived it as reality. Marc Bolan was the mask worn by Mark Feld, everything he wrote and did hid behind allegories and make-up, even his Rolls Royce was a Bentley in disguise!

Most people have not made the effort to see beneath the image he projected and understand that it was a role he played, they are happy to believe in the fantasy but in time the real Mark Feld would have re-emerged; fate, however, did not allow that to happen and we are left to consider the Tutankhamen style mask he left us with, unsure of his true likeness. It is only by understanding the words he left that we can hope to see a glimmer of his true identity, but Marc wore many masks and his real face will always be slightly hidden by glitter and make-up. I would like to believe that I have removed some of his disguise and revealed a new depth to Marc that has not been seen before.

But in reality….The true wizard of imagination that lay beneath the gown and make-up was not Marc Bolan but his creator…. Mark Feld.

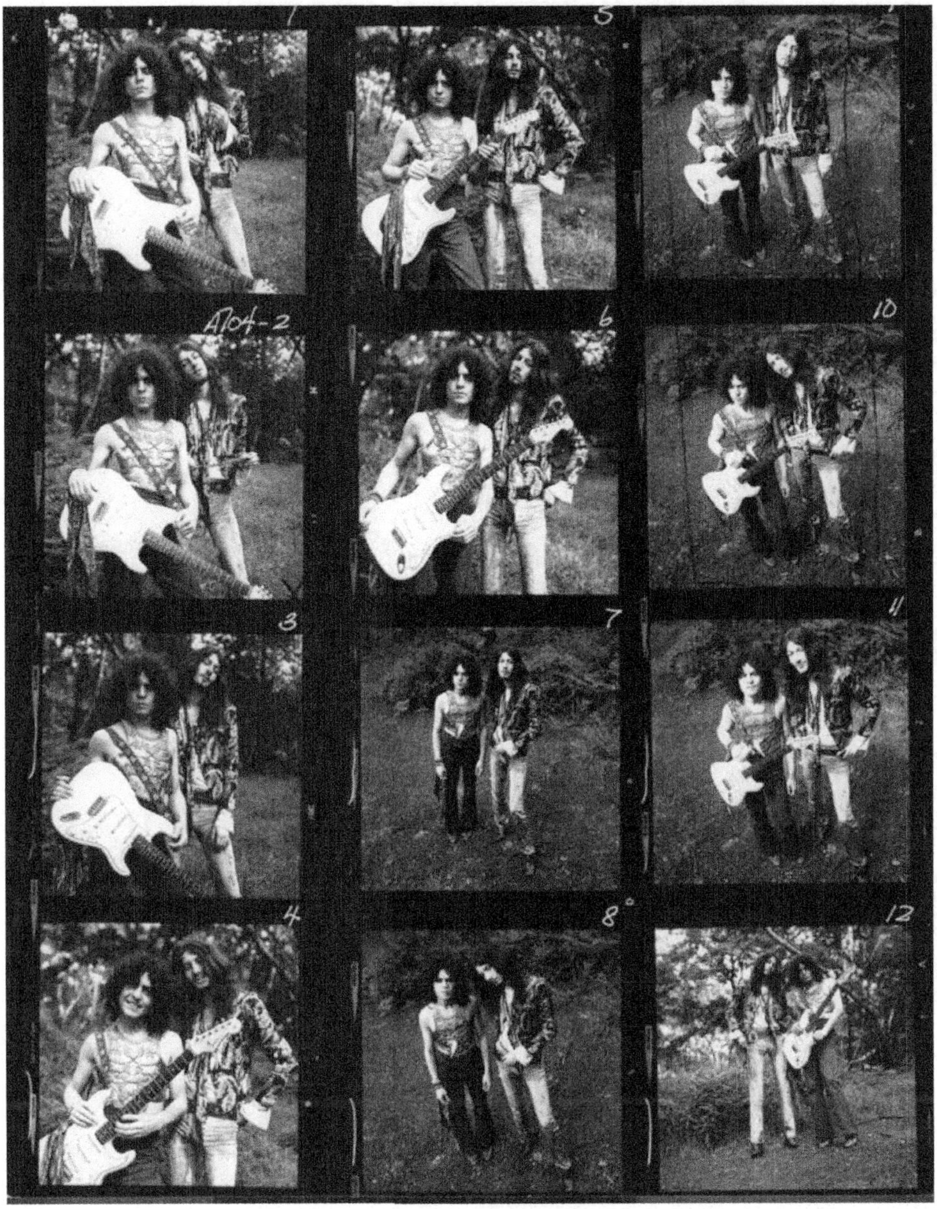

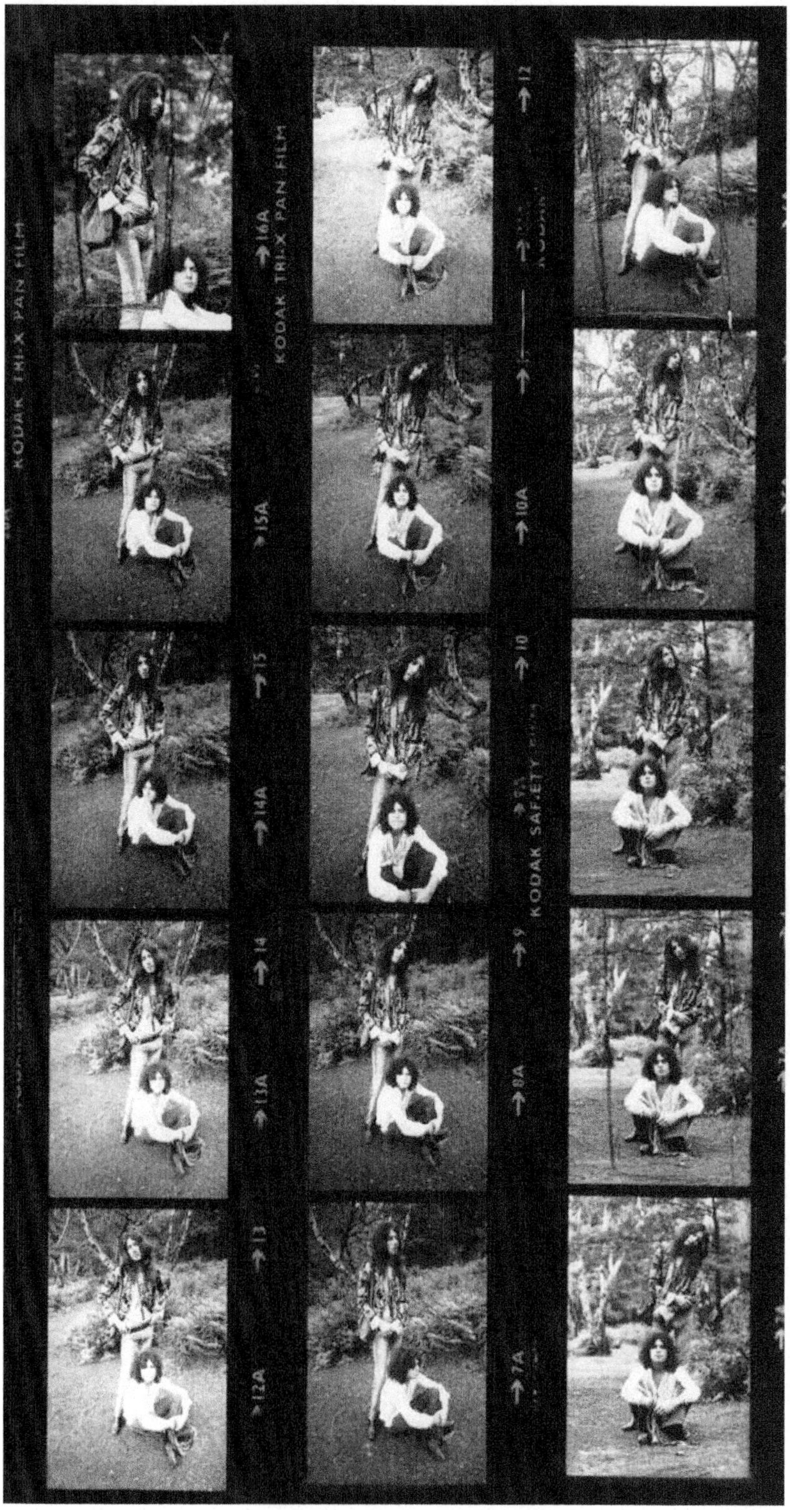
KODAK TRI-X PAN FILM
KODAK SAFETY

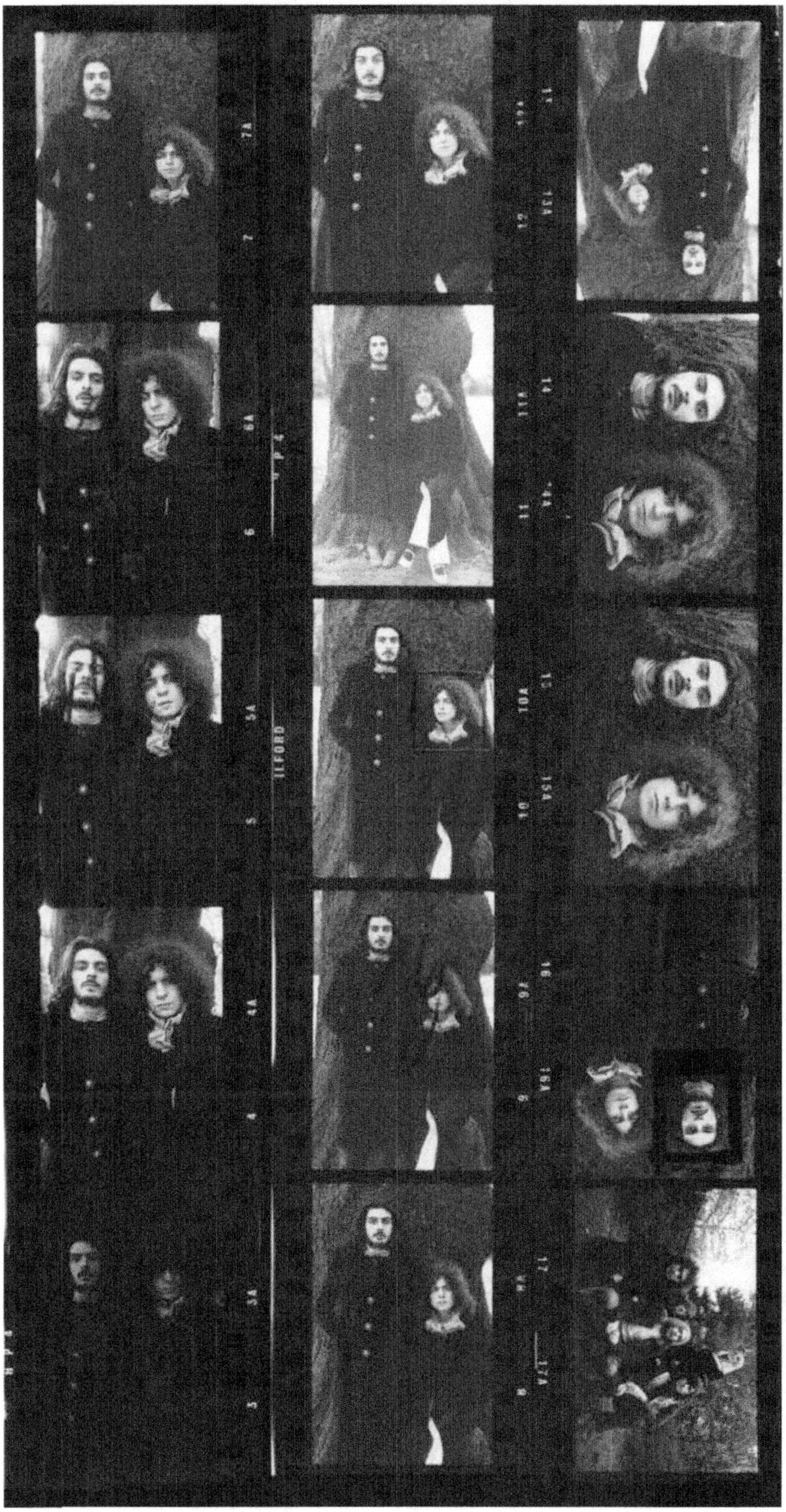
ILFORD

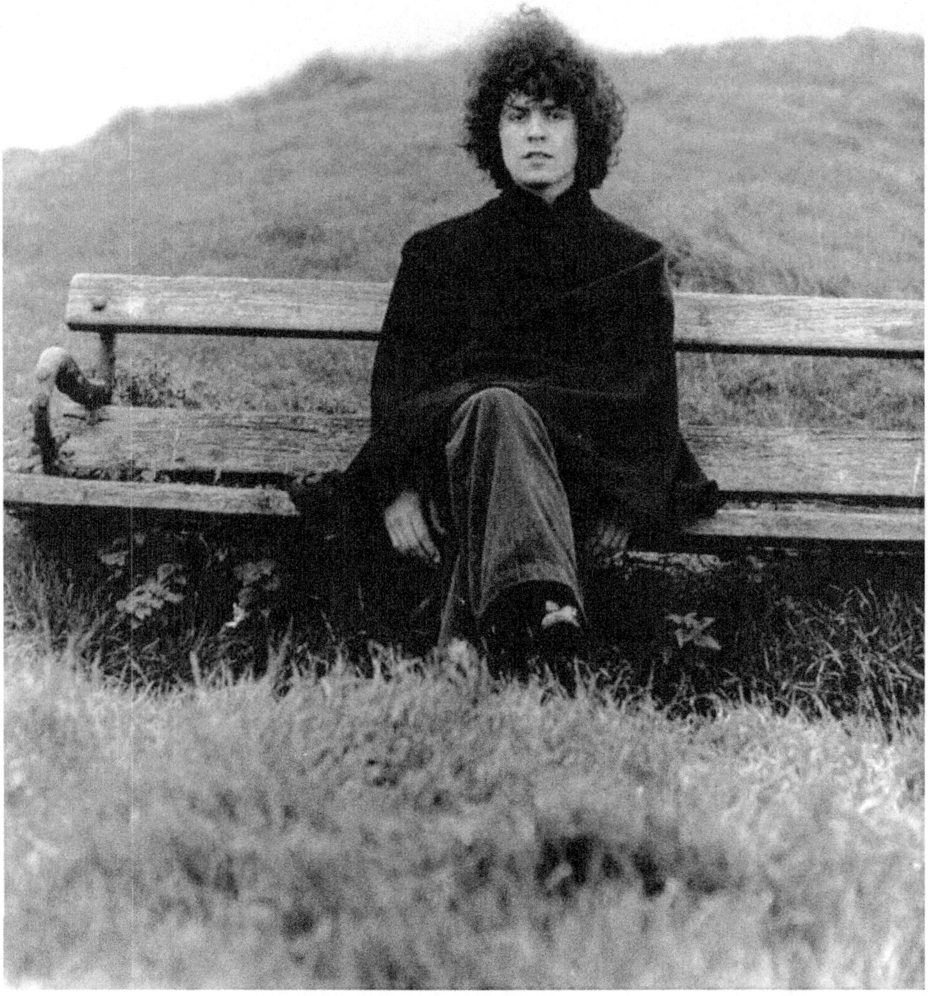

14. The True Inspiration for 'The Wizard'.

INTERVIEW……With Riggs O'Hara

By Tony Stringfellow

WEDNESDAY 14TH JULY 2005

At the opening of this interview, Riggs has been handed a copy of 'Pictures of Purple People' By Marc Bolan. He also reads other writings of Marc's at various points during the course of the interview.

RO   Oh well, these are all scenes, is there any dialogue?

TS   Yes there is a little dialogue, there are two versions of it, when he wrote that he was living with Pruskin.

RO   Mike Pruskin? Oh my god that is around the same time.

TS   And he typed it up.

RO   Pruskin did?

TS   Yes, he typed it up from Marc's notes, its very close.

RO   How interesting.

RO   I still don't see any dialogue, Oh yeah, my goodness.

TS   Basically its about sort of a couple of lads who acquire some purple sweets and go off and get high.

RO   Purple hearts. God, I remember those. But you see, this says Marc Bolan 1966. But he wasn't Marc Bolan in 1966.

TS   No, that's what the publishers have put.

RO   Yeah, Oh I'd have to go through all of this to see, you would really have to turn it into a play, but I bet you could. The Bolan Society. Can you believe it?

TS   Yeah, there is a lot of various society's and fan clubs in the name of Marc Bolan.

RO   Well it keeps it all alive doesn't it.

TS   Well it does to a degree.

RO   What's this?

TS   That, again, it's not complete, but that is a lot more interesting. That is a story he was writing, and that is a section of it, it's part of something called The Children of Beltane, very pagan, Celtic…

RO   Oh well, this is later, because he wasn't into that kind of stuff when I knew him.

TS   He wasn't?

RO   No. I'm supposed to be the wizard you know.

TS   I know.

RO   Quite weird isn't it? I tell you how I discovered all of this nonsense for myself, because I was in a Waterstones, and I saw a picture of him on a book of Poetry and realised he'd written poems to me.

TS   Have you seen them all?

RO   I'm not even sure if I've seen all, but I mean I was quite shocked, and then someone put it together because the things that he said that he and the Wizard did are actually things that he and I did like going to Paris and all of that.

TS   He tells so many people, he told quite a few stories about that period about going to Paris.

RO   Well it was his learning curve, from just being someone who is out there wanting to be famous, I was very… I was a convert idealist to the importance of theatre, so all of my conversations with him were about how important the arts were and how important education was and how important it was to see things and do things. Before that he knew nothing about that.

TS   So how old… when exactly did you meet?

RO   He was about sixteen, I think. I've now put two and two together, this guy who lives in Earl Court who was a friend of Alan Warren, I think, and I have no idea why I went to see this guy who lived in a basement flat. I later found out that he was a pretty hard-core male escort, I never knew that. But when I went there just to sit and chat, Marc was there, and we just got on well together and left together, and I gave him a lift, and we became……he was a wonderful boy, terrific, really terrific, really really terrific. I never forget him sitting in front of the television watching Top of the Pops with all of these young pop stars, young, well he was young too, and him saying to me "Anyone can do that, I can do that, look".

TS   He was supposedly a big Elvis fan, supposedly his idol.

RO   He liked the image, the shaking hips image. He thought that covered up a lot of sins, if you could just, you know, be that kind of sexy, he just knew it, he knew this wasn't something that happened by accident. Nothing, I mean maybe later because I didn't know him then but at the beginning he didn't, nothing happened by accident, he planned everything, he knew what he wanted, he knew how to do it, he chose the ones he should do and not do and whatever…

TS   Songs, you mean or the actual career?

RO   The career? Oh yeah, he chose the pop career because it was the one he thought would be the easiest to get into.

TS   When you first met him he wasn't working?

RO   No.

TS   Was he still living with his parents?

RO   Oh yeah, I used to drive him home. Wimbledon, that area, yeah, they used to live in a pre-fab. You know he taught himself to speak properly, yeah, he taught himself that, by the time I met him he spoke absolutely perfect English – he taught himself.

TS   He didn't do very well at school, he finally got expelled.

RO   Did he? Oh, he never told me that.

TS   I don't think he was officially expelled. He missed a lot of the last year of his education and he spent more time in café/bars, places like that…hanging round.

RO   I can't impress upon you too much that he chose it because he knew how it worked. I mean… he might have chosen something else if he knew how that worked.

   My career has always been something that I can't seem to make money out of, I too much of an idealist. I keep thinking that its about discovering new boundaries to conquer rather than… you know, trying to please the masses or whatever, I just wanted to learn things from it, which is why I'm going to stop doing it in the way I've been doing it once I get this last play on because I'm not learning anything anymore.

TS   I think you have to do a little of both, you have to play to the audience a bit.

RO   Yeah, and I want to write, you see I was brought up in the literary theatre, which is all about writers, and I've always been in awe, you no, the writer was the king, I've been brought up to believe that writing, composing and painting are the only creative arts, the others are all interpretive, and I've put it off and put it off because of the fear, and now I've got a couple of ideas for books and um, I want to do that thing that people do, I keep thinking of Noel Coward, taking 6 months off to go and write a play, I want to go somewhere and write a play, sit on the terrace and look at the Mediterranean and write my book.

TS   I understand exactly what you mean.

RO   And I also… I want to do it by hand, I heard… I get a very different feeling when I do it by hand, I'm really rather good about being objective about writing, very good… I can read something, say "yeah this is great" and then I sit down and fix it. I'm very good at editing. Excellent, maybe too clean, I tend to cut out every strenuous word. I'm a Beckett fan you see, Samuel Beckett; so I think if you can say it all in 3 minutes, why take 10.

TS   Well, yes… I think there are different aspects to that. I think you obviously thought of Marc a lot in that area, there are some of his songs… and I'm looking for the poem actually in here that is absolutely and totally amazing.

RO   This is so amazing you know!

TS   Because in the splurb of my book I put "a lot of Marc's lyrics are what I describe as linguistic paintings", which I think is a very good description, because he literally paints a picture and he is extremely descriptive and almost goes over the top with elaborate descriptions which are beautiful and he creates a mystical look by doing that. But there are some where his lyrics are just one lines. There is one song… have you ever heard of "New York City"?

RO   No.

TS   Well, I've featured this in my book, the line is "have you ever walked into New York City and seen a women carrying a frog in her hand". Now, because I am examining Marc, examining his writing, and trying to understand him as a writer and artist myself, I think I understand where he's coming from. He'd just been to New York with David Bowie and seen a woman carrying a frog in her hand, now the statement…

RO   He wouldn't have made that up, do you think.

TS   Well he probably did, but the whole point of it I think was to show the uncertainties of cities, and that was it, that was all it needed, just that one line to show it.

RO   Yes, it's a great image of New York, even if it didn't happen.

TS   Yes, just that one line to describe the whole absurdity of the big city… you can see it and that was the point… he didn't need to say any more. So he learnt when not saying anything got the message across. Because sometimes it does. I started as an artist, drawing and my father always used to say "it's not always what you do draw, it's what you don't draw".

RO   I once had a discussion with David Hockney, he was always going on about what a brilliant artist Picasso was, and we used to argue about it all the time, because I used to say he was an extraordinary innovator, but for me he didn't have the gift you need, which is he didn't have the gift of colour. He just didn't have that, and I said once to David, "my favourite painter is Matice, because even the space that he didn't use, works".

TS   Well that's the secret of a true artist.

RO   I tell that to my actors all the time – you have to know it before you can cut it. You can't leave it out and not know you've left out, you have to know what you've left it out.

TS   And to know why you've left it out. But Marc, I think developed that art, he definitely got that art, because even right through to his later songs, some of his songs were extremely complicated, musically and lyrically, and others were so simple.

RO   Well I was always very intrigued by the simplicity of words. Always, I mean I would definitely talk to him about that all the time.

TS   He loved words.

RO   I think that's to do with me you know. Because I fell in love with words, I don't come from a highly educated background at all, but I discovered words, and I used to talk about that sort of thing all the time, we'd go to the theatre, and we'd see things and I took him to see Beckett and things like that, who was also another hero of mine, Beckett, Brett and Goldony? That's a combination. That's how I direct my plays you know… as though they are written by all three people. That's how I do it.

TS   Isn't it strange how we are all influenced by certain things, you have to be I suppose though.

RO   I just thought that there has to be a way to combine political drama, classical drama and originality to me the accumulation of originality creates originally. It's nothing new, it's like there's nothing new about a sweater in fashion, there's nothing new about a sweater and a skirt and a pair of shoes, a handbag… it's how a particular designer puts them together that's original. And that's what I felt about these various styles. So the writer that I worked with who had never written a play before, who now thinks he can do everything without me and he can't. Because he didn't hang around long enough. I taught him how to write the sort of plays I wanted to do, so now our plays really, you know the intellectuals who come up afterwards and say "my god there are so many different styles" because that's what I wanted, that spontaneity with the structure and thrust of traditional drama. I wanted to figure out how to do that so that it's not improvisation, although it appears, I can't tell you how many times people have come to see our plays and think they'll never be able to do that twice, but they are rehearsed down to the last move, so of course they can do it for weeks, but it always looks like they just thought of it. Because that's the way we work it, and the narrative side is so strong, it's like a clothes line, you can hang anything on it. I once went to see a Georgio, a production of a play in Paris, and it was about going on holiday, love affairs, and the guy tells her that he loves her and she walks to the front of the stage and says, 'he' the author 'should have written me a speech, but he didn't' and she went back in to do the play, and I thought that was the most wonderful thing, I couldn't believe it, and I've been keen on that thing of using the actors as a bridge for the audience into the narrative, I find that if I create a theatrical reality in the front and behind that I create a theatricality, the theatrical reality will drag the audience into the theatricality without making it look like it's like one of those plays where you're flipping a magazine in a hairdressers, you know, you look at all the pictures, it makes them feel that they are part of it and once they're part of it you can do anything with them. In my work, the audience is very much a part of what goes on on stage because their feelings have to be included. You have to get them on the bus.

TS   That's something that must have affected Marc.

RO   Well, I've always believed it, we were in each others pockets, and I wasn't that much older than him, but I was educated as it were.

TS   So where were you, what where you doing when this was happening?

RO   I was a struggling actor.

TS   And you and Marc obviously moved to London.

RO   Oh, I was living here already yes.

TS   Where do you hail from? New York?

RO   Yes, I came over here for 'West Side Story', and then I stayed.

TS   I presume you've got family in New York?

RO   Oh yes, I'm the baby, so not much of the family left.

TS   You were born in New York?

RO   Yes in Brooklyn.

TS   And so you hadn't gotten to the point when you actually wanted to write yourself then?

RO   No, I thought I was going to be a serious actor, but it just never worked out, because in those days you were hampered by the fact that you didn't have a good British accent, they just didn't include you in anything, but I was never out of the circle, because when I was in West Side, I met some extraordinary people that I got involved with the Royal Court Group, who really taught me everything about the Theatre. In fact my adored mentor, a woman called Jocelyn Herbert, the designer, died last year or something and I think that has a great deal to do with the fact that I don't want to do it anymore, because she's not around to see the work. There's just no point in it for me, just no point in trying to convince people I have no respect for that what I am doing is right, it's awful to say that, but it's the way I feels.

TS   Do you not feel that you are just bowing down and giving in to what they want?

RO   I give them what they want, and it happens to be what I want, I don't give them what they want and separate myself from that. My job is to figure out a way to make them want what I want.

TS   I was talking commercially.

RO   I have nothing against commercialism, I have nothing against it at all, I found now a very extraordinary thing happening, I find there are young people out there copying my work, and I am quite happy about that you know, I am really very pleased about that, I am happy to be at the end of the phone if anyone needs any help or whatever, I do find the one's that copy my work get much better notices that I do, but that because they don't go as far as I do. Like, the new play that I'm doing which is based on an idea of mine and it's written as a melodrama, I've written all the melodrama out, I tried to make it as cold and as hard as possible and now I've got this idea that they are going to come on with this script and they are going to sit in a semi-circle of chairs and they are going to start with their scripts as though it's a rehearsed reading and as the drama gets more and more involved they'll be dropping the scripts, I might put a few bits in so that they pick them back up again but at the end, because I haven't got a last speech, because he hasn't written it… I decided to… and just talking to you now, I realised where it's come from… I've decided to do a version of "here the author should have written something", I'm going to have my leading lady say "where's my last speech" at the end of the play and the others are going to say "it isn't written" – "what do you mean it isn't written, if it isn't written I'm not doing the play" – "but you've already done the play" – "oh, that's not fair". That kind of thing is going to go on. So I like that idea of, never allowing someone to get… it's a kind of mother courage idea, the screen comes down and tells you what's going to happen, which stops you from becoming emotionally involved, and yet you become emotionally involved anyway. You know what is going to happen, you see the scene where it happens and you still become emotionally involved, that's what I find fascinating.

TS   Do you get hooked with the audience?

RO   Oh yeah, I can read a book and say "this is the point where I got 'em", from then on I can do whatever I want. I can read it and know exactly what the point is.

TS   It's like Marc when… and he must have got all this from you… because he went through his hippie days, with Tyrannosaurus Rex where musically he was very acoustic and very deep, and then there is one point where people say he sold out … 'Ride a White Swan' was his first big hit and straight away he was on Top Of The Pops, you know… he was a success and then people said he'd sold out and he wasn't real in his philosophies, and I disagree.

RO   Well anyway, because how long did it last him being a philosopher? It wasn't exactly existentialism was it, it was a kind of bastardised version of existentialism. It's interesting that people still today don't realise how insidious existentialism was. Because we live with it today, with everyone wanting to be an individual and wanting to be free and you have this whole thing that's going on in the world now which is, as far as I'm concerned… it's about stamping out what happened, you know, because it floated around, it became hippiedom, it certainly affected America, it certainly affected New York in the sixties, but people forget that it started with France, that kind of thing, and I think all through the sixties and seventies the conservatives in America have tried to wipe out what happened then and the dilemma for people these days is we still feel that we want to be free and we want to be individuals but everything about what's happening is stopping that.

TS   The thing I find fascinating with the hippie movement like the mods, like the rockers…

RO   He was a mod you know.

TS   Yes, he went through a phase of being a mod.

RO   Well he dressed like it.

TS   But even as a mod he was trying to be different.

RO   Well he was never a real mod because he was never interested in groups.

TS   You mean groups as in groups of people.

RO   In that kind of thing, he was never interested in that kind of thing. He was never interested in mods but he certainly went through a phase… certainly when I met him and as I knew him, he loosened up when I knew him, but when I first met him he was always impeccably dressed like the mods were, and yet he never had any mod friends. He never went to any group meetings, he never went where they went… he discovered that was a style that he liked.

TS   Clothes always seemed to be a big thing for him.

RO   Yeah, I think it had a great deal to do with reinventing himself, from where he'd come from.

TS   It's funny you say that because what I was about to say was that with the mod cultures, the music cultures where they go out to be different, with ten thousand others dressing the same… there is an irony there… they are trying to be so different, and you see it nowadays with the lads walking down the street trying to be different but there is a hundred of them!

RO   Exactly, well it's a different generation… as opposed to England, that's where it spread you see, you see in Paris where it was happening in the late forties and fifties it was about being an individual and not part of a group, and when you did have a group they were intellectuals who were trying to be individuals and then it came across, the idea of being individual suddenly got turned around a bit so it meant "we are separate from the generation before us" rather than "we are all separate". Marc was always separate. He was never a joiner. He was never a party animal.

TS   Yes, that comes across.

RO   He was always interested in learning things. He wanted to know more and more and more. It was as if his whole life was devoted to getting away from his circumstances. Not getting away because he hated it… his parents were adoring.

TS   Did you know them?

RO   Yes. But, it happens all over the place, people leave home don't they, and then they leave everything they came from, and that's what he wanted to do, he wanted to be somebody and it almost didn't matter to him in what area it was, as long as it was somebody.

TS   So you don't feel that the music was really the most important thing to him?

RO   I think the music was the most important thing to him because he felt that was what he could conquer.

TS   He always calls himself a poet.

RO   That's part of the game.

TS   What do you mean by that?

RO   Well, a villain was called a poet wasn't he… it was part of the game. Part of the game was calling yourself a poet, turning the hippie thing into something original because the hippies never wore as much make-up as he did. He certainly never wore it like that when I knew him; I mean he had short short hair. Did you ever see the pictures? Was it Angus McGill for the Evening Standard who did the article on him when he was about fourteen? No it wasn't Angus McGill… it was that guy who died. I can't remember his name

TS   It was about when he was a mod.

RO   Yes, when I met him he was still in that look… the very short hair, combed.

TS   Was he getting into Dylan at all that time?

RO   He was into… this sounds very calculated, but I'm just trying to say how smart he was… he was into anyone who was successful and different, anybody who made it work.

TS   What I've got here… which you did ask to flick through… these here are copies of the batch of poems that I've got… that I own… you are welcome to look through them…… but what I've got here is a selection of writing and as he develops you can see a development, some of it is crap.

RO   Well he was very young.

TS   Precisely, I mean I'm not saying this as a criticism, my interest in it is that you can see it developing from crap until you get to work like this which is really extremely good poetry, but you can see the development, he goes from talking about strange things happening on the sub-way/the tube to all of sudden he's into Ginsburg and stuff like that, so you can see him developing.

RO   Well I think his mind was always developed, you can see, the acquisition of experience, that develops, but his mind – he was always developing, he always wanted to know more, he wanted to know everything. The thing that shocked me more than anything was when I found out he had a drug problem, because he certainly never took anything when I knew him. He was never a drug addict. Never.

TS   He definitely went through the rock 'n' roll drugs scene.

RO   After me, oh he certainly did, that's what I heard. And there's a part of me that really feels terrible that I never got in touch, because I could of saved that – there was always a bit of guilt for me about that, I know I could have saved it.

TS   It's the one period, around 1974, that's the worst period drugs and a bottle of brandy a day.

RO   He never drank.

TS   I know, I know he didn't in the early years, but he definitely went through the...

RO   He was an ambitious kid, he never did any of those things… he was always spot on and focused. Always.

TS   He comes across like that for 90% of his career, apart from the couple of years in the middle when he dropped into drugs and the saddest thing of all is that he'd cleaned himself up and his last album showed that…he was returning back to his original form. I mean there is some video footage… which I don't know if you've seen,

RO   I find it very difficult to watch it.

TS   Which bits?

RO   All of it. I find it very difficult to listen to the music as well.

TS   Why?

RO   Because it ended so tragically, but in a way you know… I have to tell you… that what's happened to him since his death is what he would have wanted. He wanted that.

TS   That's one question I wanted to ask actually, did you ever get the impression that he had any extra sensory type of feeling.

RO   Feeling about whether it was going to… about his destiny? The only thing he felt about his destiny was that he was going to make it, and he wanted to be a legend. That's what he wanted, more than anything else, is he wanted to be a legend.

TS   How about how he would die?

RO   No. He was too young for that and also I think there was a part of him, I don't know, you know, I think that somewhere in his mind there was a part of him that thought that, you know… that kind of thing happens to legends… that's how you become a legend by going out at your peak.

TS   A number of times he's said in interviews that he was going to die in a car crash, yet he couldn't drive.

RO   Well, the interesting thing is that he'd say that to be dramatic… I don't know if he believed it… I think he'd say it to be dramatic. He wanted to be a legend, he didn't just want to be a pop star… he didn't just want to be rich.

TS   Money didn't seem to matter to him.

RO   No… never did.

TS   He wasn't materialistic.

RO   Not at all.

TS   It's strange that because you see his lifestyle, yes he went through a little bit of the excessive lifestyle, but when you see photo's of his flat etc bearing in mind who and what he was…

RO   I'd be very interested to see pictures of his flat, I would like to see if there was anything he did in his flat that he got from his flat.

TS   I might have a couple of his pictures of his flat on my computer, I'll have a look.

RO   Yeah, I'd be very interested to see.

TS   It's a very theatrical looking flat.

RO   As opposed to "pop-star" looking, that's interesting because so was mine.

TS   I've got one very good picture of him.

RO   How interesting… it's interesting to think that you were such an influence on somebody but I didn't set out to be an influence… it's just this is what I believe.

TS   You were a very strong influence on him.

RO   That's why I feel so guilty about not coming back into his life… but I didn't know, you see I left for America in 1975 and I was there for 10 years.

TS 1975. That would be why no one was able to track you down then.

RO I came back in 1985, but they didn't track me down until the nineties. No, I never got involved, it was someone called Martin Barden and he was the one who called me up out of the blue and said "are you… did you know" whatever and then he did that interview with me, but up until then, oh I was just, oh too serious an "artist" to be involved… to be part of a pop-star's history.

TS It must have been rewarding to know that you were such an influence on him.

RO It would have been more rewarding if I could have been there when he needed me. I think I was there at the beginning, but later on, because I remember a friend of mine, Sandra Karen who was a good friend of The Beatles, she was up at Apple one day and he came in and asked her about me, and she told me… and I just thought… oh you know I'm too busy.. let him get on with his life, I can't tell you how many pictures I threw away, Paris pictures, the whole shebang. I had pictures of him and I on the boat that goes around the Seine.

TS Tell me about the Paris trip.

RO We just went for a long weekend. We did all the tourist things, I wanted him to see it, it was the first time… I think… he'd ever been abroad.

TS He didn't seem to travel abroad with his parents at all.

RO No I don't think they went abroad, it wasn't that kind of time you know.

TS He didn't even seem to go abroad much, other than touring, for holidays at all.

RO No he was very… he wanted it bad, he wasn't interested in reaping the rewards of fame, he just wanted the fame.

TS He was incredibly prolific.

RO Well he had… you know…. he'd been thinking since he was a teenager, a young teenager, so you know when the finally open the flood gates, all of that stuff comes out.

TS Did he write much while you knew him? Did he write anything while you knew him?

RO I was never aware of it… I paid for his first demo disc.

TS Can you remember where that was?

RO   No I can't remember where, but it was a studio, we hired a studio… and I can't even remember what the songs were… I do know he made me stand next to him while he was singing.

TS   It wasn't the Joe Meeks Studio?

RO   I wouldn't remember.

TS   Was it on Hollywood Road?

RO   It was a room, a place with rooms.

TS   It wasn't like a converted house?

RO   No, it was a place with rooms and each room was like a little studio, you just hired the studio and did what you wanted to do. I mean, when I knew him he wasn't that proficient with the guitar. He was fiddling around trying to teach himself… I would be very interested to see it.

TS   You can see what his writing was like, it gets worse.

RO   It's so spiky isn't it?

TS   And that's it, there we are… "Riggs O'Hara" in the title.

RO   It's entitled that? Oh my god. When was this written?

TS   This was written around 1967 'ish.

RO   That was just after I stopped knowing him.

TS   I don't know exactly…..

RO   Interesting. What's interesting to me is "up walks a cool looking hipster" I mean, you don't know that that's who you are, when you're in it, but that must have been the image he had of me. This is another one isn't it. That's sweet. How sweet.

TS   He actually wrote a song about you as well… I'm not sure which one it was yet, but I do know that it's safe to say it was influenced by you rather than about you. I mean it starts off …… it is about a wizard. It is definitely inspired by you. There is a song, which I think, is definitely written about you, but I haven't quite narrowed it down to which one yet, so I wouldn't like to run it by you until I know for sure which one it is.

RO   Ok, come with me.

Here I show Riggs a picture of Marc in his flat and he takes me to show me around his… the similarity was amazing!

BREAK

RO … and I still live exactly the same way… I always have… it was always that way.

TS Amazing, as you say, you obviously had a massive effect on him. So you travelled to Paris, you travelled by ferry I presume.

RO Yeah, I think we did, although we could have easily flown. I know where we stayed, I remember it, we stayed at the Hotel Bourgogne Montana on the rue de Bourgogne on the left bank… right by… right around the corner from the Café Fleur.

Showing Riggs Photos of Marc.

TS The one photo on there… some of those I've played with… but there's one there which I did particularly like, I always think is quite sad really which I was going use as the final picture in my book… the one casting the shadow … well I could but ……

RO I only had a few left and a couple of bits of writing that he did and I sold them at auction. I don't know who bought them.

TS When you say writing, what do you mean?

RO Yellow sheets of letters to me and things like that… pictures of him… 8 x 10 pictures of him… one extraordinary one where his fly was half undone, where he was desperately trying to be sexy but he was so young looking… he didn't look sexy at all… or I didn't think so. I never saw that side of him… inside of him… that's why I keep saying that this was created… 'cause inside he was… if he lived… he would have written… he wanted… anything… he would have written books, I mean he wanted that elevation of his talent level. He always wanted more.

TS You should read this, there's not a lot there, that's only a fraction of what has been put together because the one fan club that was run by someone, instead of keeping all his sheets, they got sold off… his written work in notebooks… and they sold it off sheet by sheet.

RO Didn't they even make photocopies?

TS I don't think so.

RO   How bizarre.

TS   The collection of poetry that I've got of Marc's is the only complete collection, most people don't own a complete poem… there's tonnes of it out there but most people don't want to own …

RO   I remember the day that I threw them away, in New York. I remember the day. I had a little counter in the kitchen, the kitchen was here, and then there was this separation wall and there was another little counter and on top of this counter there was a piece of glass and under it I had all these pictures, and when I moved I just chucked them.

TS   You didn't save any?

RO   No, ordinarily I never do. I've got pictures… I've got a trunk full of pictures downstairs that I hardly even got through, but usually I keep everything…

TS   How do you perceive Marc spiritually?

RO   He had a mission. Now you can connect spirituality to that. He believed. He knew he could do it, he knew how to do it, he knew what he had to do to do it… he had this faith… whether it transpired itself into any recognisable religion? He had this faith… he knew it was going to happen you know… he always knew it.

TS   He knew he was going to make a success of it?

RO   Oh yeah, he always knew it.

TS   Did he have any spiritual or religious beliefs at that point?

RO   You mean did he ever talk about God?

TS   Not necessarily God in the classic sense… I don't know what religion he had.

RO   I think what he had was faith.

TS   Faith, what religion are you of.

RO   I am Catholic.

TS   Marc… his father was Jewish and his mother was Christian.

RO   I didn't know that.

TS   Right. He was predominantly brought up in the Jewish world… shall we say.

RO   He never… he was kind of….

I show Riggs one of Marc's poems

TS   I would like you to read that, I've edited that, when I say edited, all I've done is formulated the punctuation and lines. I haven't changed any of the words apart from spelling mistakes. Now, it took me a while to break that, but it's about the reincarnation, the resurrection of Christ.   He's made a mistake……

RO   But you see he could write that from a picture, he didn't have to know anything about religion, he could be inspired to write that by looking at a picture of the crucifixion.

TS   I'm not saying he's done it as a religious poem as such… you have to bear in mind he was brought up as a Jew… they don't believe in Christ… but…

RO   Well they do, they just don't believe that he was the be all and end all, they couldn't, it was they that killed… they don't accept him as the Messiah… Well that was because of the money lenders.

TS   He makes the mistake of saying that he lay for one day, he said 'I lay for one day' as opposed to three days before the resurrection, but apart from that it is undoubtedly… to me… that it's about the resurrection of Christ. But that was one reason for asking, not because I… I just wondered if…

RO   See what I get from this poem and from the one that I read that he wrote about me is that he'll get an image in his head of something or someone and then he just goes with it, and I would honestly say that he would say "one day" because it rhymes with sprayed.

TS   It's interesting though… he's got more confidence in his poetry there… A lot of his work revolves around Greek mythology.

RO   Well, I tell you something else which is very funny, there was a point when I was thinking of taking a lease on a shop in Camden Passage and opening up a little antiques shop, and we went in to see the place, and he fell in love with this little statue of Pan?

TS   Have you seen the pictures on there?

RO   Well I bought it for him. £8… That was a lot of money in those days. And the extraordinary thing is when I went to the stone laying and you know you've got all these guys, you know, all these roadies and things… guys and whatever, and I said "You know what really interests me… I bought him this little statue of Pan? …and I wonder if it lasted". And there was this one guy… an older guy… must have been some kind of roadie or whatever, and he got very nervous like as if I was going to ask for it back, and he said "Oh, I've got it", and I said "Oh, I'm glad, as long as its safe" and he's got it. A very ordinary looking man… Obviously not an ounce of artsy-craftsy in him at all.

TS   Mick O'Halloran?

RO   I don't know.

TS   I think it probably was.

RO   Not that I remember, all I remember of him was the way he clammed up when I mentioned it because he thought I was going to say I want it back.

TS   There is a picture of it on here, with Marc Bolan.

RO   Oh, I think I saw that, I don't think that's the one.

TS   Well let me show you, because he used it on an album cover.

RO   But he was always very interested in that kind of thing you know. He wanted to be a myth.

TS   He wanted to be Orpheus, I think.

RO   He wanted to be a god.

TS   I think he wanted to be the god of music.

RO   No, I think he wanted more than to be the god of music, he just wanted to be a god, more than just of music. He was very interested in mythology, always. In that thing, the thing when they never die, they live forever, if they ever existed in the first place.

TS   Yes. This…

RO   Is that made of…

TS   I don't know what it's made out of… It appears to be gold in colour, but doesn't stand out that well in photos, so I can't tell.

RO   The one we got was like you know that bronze type of metal that goes green.

TS   Right, it could have been, it's metallic in some way but whether its…

RO   It was a heavy little thing… I can't tell how big it was there.

TS   Well Marc wasn't tall, was he?

RO   But that saying it's big… That was different I think, it was exactly the same statue, but it must have been another one… Could have been that one… I don't remember… All I know is that I bought him it… he loved it.

TS   He kept it in his flat as well… so he would ……

RO   Yes, because in those days you see he thought of himself as cheeky like that. I don't know if he ever thought of himself as being Adonis. I really don't think so.

TS   No I don't think so, he wasn't big enough… he saw himself more as an elf.

RO   Yes he did, always. That's the Midsummer Night's Dream thing.

TS   So did you introduce him to poetry, you said you taught him to read.

RO   As I say, I was very literary, so there was always a book going on, but it was mostly about the literary aspect of theatre, and these are very theatrical poems, I think they come from that as opposed to from books, they come from this exposure to the theatre.

TS   Shakespeare?

RO   Oh yeah, I used to see everything.

TS   Do you recall what else you would have taken Marc to see.

RO   No.

TS   He always seemed to have a sense of drama on stage.

RO   Theatricality. That… the understanding… he would have gotten from me. But also, I have to be honest and say he also knew about the theatricality of people like Presley.

TS   You say he taught himself to speak?

RO   Oh yeah… proper English. Have you met his parents? You know his mother used to sell apples in Berry Street Market. That's what he spoke like at home.

TS   When you see him interviewed he's very…

RO   Proper English. He could go into it. He used to every once in a while smile and say, some little cockney phrases, and all that, he knew what he was doing and then he would laugh.

TS   Difficult to keep that pretence up all the time…… There is nothing to say that the poetry that I've got here though is finished… Ready for publication… let's put it like that.

RO   When was this poem written?

TS   Written around… about… between 1969-70.

RO   This is very familiar.

TS   In what way?

RO   This could very easily be about us… Little things, the down the stairs and the…

TS   There are lots of little things in his songs that pertain to your life. There are some that very clearly refer… but then…

RO   See this is you know… 'things to please his' … 'so that they might have a bond or hold to reach him by for the gods'… 'purity or fair thought on which they may enter the hearts of men'. Sounds very much like him and I.

TS   You think so?

RO   Yeah. See he would use the name Sandra, because that was my best friend at the time.

TS   This one I believe ……Awkward when you are analysing from his handwriting. There have been occasions, as well, as I've been analysing …

RO   It's very interesting these poems you know, because I had never realised before that they are so……

TS   These are some of his very early writings…...

RO   A bit of a diary, I like that. You know what, they bring back… I know that people talk about the mythology and all of that stuff, but there are things in all of those poems that remind me… you know there are little quatrains in there that I think "my god, I remember that, that's what happened there?"

TS   Could you pick one out?

RO   I think probably it's easier to… all I can say is that reading it brings back memories of the time we spent together, so there must be something there. Um, it's very interesting, weird, very weird.

TS   These were written much later on.

RO   See, this reminds me, 'down the stairs of winds he went then with bolt of thunder sword… A lunar prince with cape of chintz… battle of steel has come to claim his hero's fame and dispatch all of the ……………' this is very… I remember once… so odd to even think about these things… I'd got a film, and I was very sort of nervous about it, and I was really giving him a hard time, it was the most extraordinary think in the world, I remember I was in the bath and he said "I'm going now", I never saw him again.

TS   You'd got a film part?

RO   Yes, and I got very caught up, you see before that I hadn't been working and so we were just caught up in the sort of quest for fame and glory and work and all of that sort of thing and he just left and I thought… when he did it… I thought to myself what an extraordinary thing…no recriminations, no fights, no 'why are you ignoring me?' nothing, he just went. Interesting that, that's why when I read these things about…

TS   Can I just ask you…if you don't mind…what was the nature of your relationship?

RO   Are you asking me if I was in love with him?

TS   Yes, I suppose so.

RO   No. I loved him, but I wasn't in love with him, there was no question ever in my mind though… you know… that this is something that is going to develop into a life long relationship, I certainly thought that it might develop into a life long friendship, but I think that he became very dependant on me, because I kind of… I guess I still do it now with my actors here now… I kind of took over his life, you know, he was there all the time and so what I did we did together, if I was going out to dinner he came with me, if I was going for a drive he came with me, if I was going to the theatre he came with me. But it was never what you would call a love relationship, I mean I loved him and I think, I'm sure he loved me, but it wasn't that other kind of thing, it wasn't hand holding and gazing into each others eyes, it was about learning and growing and you know trying to make careers and all of that sort of stuff and I've always like passing on what I know and teaching, I've always loved teaching and um, he wanted what I had… had nothing to do with money or anything like that, it just… he wanted what was up here and I was happy to share it.

TS   So, you never had any contact with him again once he left.

RO   Well, no I got on with my life and he got on with his. And I never even bothered to call and say, "Where are you?" It was weird that, it was just the cleanest… in a way; because it was such a clean break it's why we never forgot each other.

TS   He disappeared with no animosity?

RO   None whatsoever, I'm still amazed at his maturity. Because we were in each other's pockets, and he just went off and became a legend while I'm still banging my head against a wall, I should have hung on to the tail of that comet…

   No… I couldn't… I'd never do anything like that, I was thrilled for him but I never understood and I wasn't here when all the fame was happening so I was never barraged with it.

TS   He never really made it in America… I don't think the Americans, at the time, got the glam rock thing.

RO   I think that if he wanted to make it in America, he would have. Because he would have sat down and figured out what they wanted and he would have given it to them.

TS   Well at the time he was trying to do it he was probably hooked in with the drugs ……

RO   Yeah, but if he was hooked in with the drugs at that time it would have made it more exciting for him to be successful in New York. I think what he would have had to do is he would have had to live there to make it work because he was that kind of person he had to know and understand.

TS   He never made it ……

RO   I remember walking in the village and seeing one of those T-Shirt shops and it had a T-Rex T-Shirt in the window with his picture, and I thought "I don't believe this" I just was amazed that I was so pretentious about the "art" that I thought being a pop star was just, you know, a secondary position.

TS   Selling out?

RO   No not selling out, just a secondary position, you know to me it would be terrific to be a pop star if you made it lead to something else. I remember getting him an audition for that film, started with a P, not The Pretenders, The Performance was it? I think it was something that Mick Jagger finally did.

TS   Ned Kelly??

RO   No, it wasn't called Ned Kelly, it was before that. I think it was called "Performance" and I got him an audition and he almost got it you know. That would have changed his life.

TS   You think he would have been an actor?

RO   Well it would have broadened the aspect, you know, broadened his view of what could be done and how it could be done.

TS   You haven't seen Born to Boogie?

RO   No.

TS   It's typical Pop Art of the time, he made it with Ringo Starr, it's just been re-released. Predominantly it is Concert footage… There are a lot of surreal scenes… It's typical surreal pop art of the time, it's quite good, it's entertaining, but it's not, it has no plot, in any form… whatsoever. Very strange… But it's funny you should say that because the writing of this is part of a larger musical project he was working on called the Children of Rarn and there are tapes of Children of Rarn… unfinished, it was a massive project, or potentially a massive project and he was writing the storyline and the music and he never finished it and he also wanted to get more involved in film directing, he wanted to start making films…… So, I think he saw pop star is a step to something else.

RO   Yes, he definitely had ambition. He was cheeky.

TS   Cheeky?

RO   Cheeky, very cheeky.

TS   Do you say that from that or from?

RO   No from memory, I mean he always had this little kind of cheeky little, wickedly little grin whenever he would do something silly or foolish. He was a kid, I mean in his head.

TS   That comes over actually in Born to Boogie, because there is a lot…of joking around going on in the studio and lots of playing around, lying around.

RO   Very interesting, I read these poems of the period and they bring back everything.

TS   I think it's interesting to see them developing…probably from a different prospective. I mean seeing his writing developing and gaining more substance as he progresses.

RO   Gosh. I mean, I don't know whether I …

TS   He goes through various phases…

RO   What's interesting to me is how, to see how he saw me and the time we went together. I would never have previously dreamed of making this kind of connection.

TS   It's over a relatively short period of time.

RO   Couple of years.

TS   Quite a short time.

RO   But it was always very special.

TS   Most writers spill themselves out in their poetry.

RO   I don't want to get into the situation where I think "My god, they're all about us", but they do seem, there are little kind of clicks.

TS   Well these that you are reading at the moment are from that period…… I've found that there are many influences but I'm more interested in what you feel rather than what I see.

RO   I feel, and I don't know whether, I have no reason in the world to make this assumption other than what I feel, and I feel that they are all about, you may think they are about gods and you may use different names or whatever, but I feel they are all about him and I.

TS   Maybe, maybe.

RO   Because I, it's not that I remember particular things, it's just that they are kind of things that I think to myself "Oh my god, yeah".

TS   I'll tell you something… you know his wife June?

RO   Yeah, I've never met her I don't think.

TS   No…she's dead now… It's very strange that, probably shouldn't say this to you, it might worry you, most of the people that were around Marc and in the band are now long gone, most of them have died.

RO   It was probably a good thing that I left.

TS   There is only one member of the band still alive – the drummer Bill Legend. June, his wife …

RO   Because I had a dog you see.

TS   They might all be caricatures then... She said of the one song and I think it refers to you that Marc wrote it about a man he loved now the only problem that I've got is that I'm not sure which one she refers to, it could be one of two…and she says this song was about a man that he lived with when he was about 16 or thereabout… I presume it was you.

RO   Well, I would love to have met her and talked to her about it because it wasn't romantic love, I think he idolised me.

TS   Yes.

RO   Ummm.

TS   I can tell you something funny, but carry on.

RO   Go on.

TS   No, carry on.

RO   I was so busy running, trying to make my own career or whatever, and the memory that I have is of him running with me. That's why when I read some of those poems about people who left and things like that… and I think that when I got the film and I suddenly started to go crazy about, you know, I really got crazy. All the poems that he rights about losing people and all of that and this period about people going and about… I feel a connection with all of those because mentally I left and I think that that's probably what forced him to leave, because mentally I had already left.

TS   He left that quick?

RO   I'll never forget it, I was in the bathroom and he said I'm going now and I knew, I knew, it wasn't "where are you going", there was nothing, there was no "where are you going, when will you be back", there was nothing. It's just, you know how when you are both struggling to do something, or when two people or friends are struggling to do something and then something happens for one of them and they just, there is this comradery when you are both sitting together watching television having the dreams and then one person gets the job and suddenly it's not… you don't have anything to share anymore, because what you were sharing was that neither of you had anything but wishes hopes and dreams and I think he probably felt that I had excluded him.

It's very interesting reading this. But that… what? they are almost too difficult for me to read you know, because I never realised that that's what he thought of me. I never had the feeling that, because if I thought that that's what he thought of me I'd have run a mile.

TS   Really?

RO   Oh yeah, I wouldn't have been able to handle the responsibility. I didn't….

TS   Did you ever know Simon Napier-Bell?

RO   I don't think I ever met him.

TS   You met him.

RO   I did?

TS   I'm not sure you would know, but Simon Napier-Bell is a record producer.

RO   Yeah, yeah yeah

TS   You know of him, and he first signed Marc, and… and I …

RO   Andrew Oldham. Now I remember, what the hell do I remember? I remember Andrew Oldham coming round to the house and then we were all in his car and we were going off because he was looking for a house or something, I can't even remember where the hell we went off, but it was not a scene that I took seriously, the pop world, because I was so caught up in this world of… you know, the serious art of theatre, I just never took that… it was always play time, I never took it seriously. I don't take it seriously today, you know they come and go so fast.

TS   Well you met Simon Napier-Bell, you'll probably laugh at this, and I hope you don't take it the wrong way… Marc and, Simon Napier-Bell says he discovered Marc Bolan, Marc Bolan actually went out and knocked on his door and said "here are some of my songs". Right, so kind of the other way around really, but apparently he was out for a meal with Simon and he talked about you a lot and Simon got this … impression of you being a huge American.

BREAK

RO   You know, you are talking about a time where after 11.00 there was nowhere to go. But then this whole thing started to happen in the sixties, and what happened was… if you were in a certain circle it wasn't defined by the particular business you were in, it was defined by were you in that particular group.

TS   Yeah?

RO   And… my friend Sandra, who is still my oldest and closest friend…her sister was Alma Cogan. And they used to give these extraordinary parties in their flat on High Street, Kensington, and everybody was there, everybody from Ethel Merman to the Beatles. Everybody who was in town because it was… everywhere you would go would close, people would go to the theatre or they go out to dinner or whatever and then you would go down High Street Kensington and you would stand outside because it was one of those block of flats where the bottom was always locked and you would throw pennies up at the window and they would open the window and throw the keys down. And I was there night after night after night until 3.00 / 4.00 in the morning; he could easily have been part of the people that you remember from then, because I was very close to the family, the whole Cogan family. But I was always very involved with the Royal Court group.

TS   Right… It must have been an incredible time.

RO   It was a most extraordinary time ever. One day I'll have to sit down and write a book. Because I once found myself in a position where everybody who was anybody was starting out and we were all there together so you are sat there watching Albert Finney doing Sunday night performances of Twelfth night… at the Royal Court… just one performance – it wasn't very good though. I was very upset, I thought "why do people complain about my accent, when he's never changed his?" How can you say Shakespeare with an accent like that? I was so puritanical!

TS   It's like Sean Connery, he never changed his accent.

RO   Oh god, I remember Sean Connery in a play called Judas, when he was palling around with Adrian Corey. God, Adrian Corey educated him.

TS   Educated Sean Connery?

RO   Yeah, he educated him.

TS   It was Bond that really made Sean Connery.

RO   Oh yeah. And that was luck you know, because he was a joke as an actor, he really was.

TS   What was the film, by the way?

RO   Which one?

TS   The film that you got the part in.

RO   I think it was called "Promise Her Anything", with Warren Beatty. And he was producing it… it was the first film he ever produced.

TS   You did the part?

RO   Yeah, and he did, it was a film about a guy who made soft porn movies and one of them becomes hailed as a work of art, it was with Leslie Caron, when he was first dating her, when he had first taken her away from Peter Hall, and there was mighty …….

TS   And you were in that film?

RO   Yeah

TS   How many films did you do? I know you said you did Virgin Soldiers,

RO   Yeah, and I did that one and I did Becket, a film called Becket.

TS   Oh yeah.

RO   I played the young king, Henry III or something. They were big things for me at the time, The Victors……

I just got caught up in this learning thing you see, 'cause I came over here in Westside as an all singing all dancing chorus boy, well there were no chorus really in that show, I had a part in it as well. When I got caught up with the Royal Court group, I started to take everything seriously, much more seriously than they did in fact, I called myself a convert idealist, and I just didn't take any of these other things seriously unless there was art. I remember being offered a record contract myself by EMI and I turned it down because I didn't think it was good enough for me, sophisticated, you know. I didn't want to be, I mean the minute I left Westside I stopped wanting to be a dancer, I wanted to be serious actor; I mean I really went the whole hog... Screwed up really.

TS   You are obviously very well read yourself, so were you well read at that time?

RO   I was learning all the time. All the time I was learning.

TS   So you were at a similar stage to Marc?

RO   In a way, and I had my mentors and I was just passing it all on.

TS   I was in Wordsworth's house at the weekend.

RO   Ohhh.

TS   Didn't get to sit in his chair though. Do you know that Marc went to the William Wordsworth School?

RO   I don't know anything about that.

TS   He was very, very ……

RO   These are just amazing. Makes me laugh that she would say that I was in love with him.

TS   No, that he was in love with you.

RO   That's what she said?

TS   Yes. Very much in love with you.

RO   I never knew that.

TS   I mean it's got to be you.

RO   Well, I can't imagine that it would be anybody else, because there wasn't anybody else in his life… that had, you know, we were like two halves of the same coin for all that time, I mean we just did everything together, we just went everywhere together, it was just "come on, we're going" or you know, and he followed along, he never really said, "why don't we go here" or "why don't we do that". Never.

TS   Would you describe him as a loving, caring person?

RO   Oh he cared about me, I knew that…

I remember I had to go to New York once for about three weeks and when I came back was the first time I realised that he actually missed me when I wasn't there. Because he made that very plain to me! I never… as far as I was concerned we were just pals that, you know that just… you now how it is when you are young and you… well, we were always together, always… But I love it you know, (sound of children shouting/screaming) I have to tell you, I just love it, it's a nursery and the idea of getting up in the morning to the sound of those kids is just fabulous and when I look out my window I can see them all playing, I just love it… I was too self involved to realise the influence I was having on him, I was just passing these things on, I wasn't passing them on because I was aware that I was passing them on, this was how I lived and this is what I did, there were always tonnes and tonnes of books in the house and, just every thought was about creating something, every single thought was about that.

TS   One of the most common descriptions of Marc is that he always had an aura about him…

RO   The thing that I remember about him the most was that if you knew something he didn't know, he stayed until he knew it.

TS   Right.

RO   I was never aware of an aura, I just knew that he was going to make it because it was what he wanted, I mean now when I think back I think probably, I mean if he had stayed around he might have taken second place to what I was doing, because I really… I very… I have no memory of sitting down and saying "would you like to do this", I only have memories of saying "come on, we're going here" or "we're going there" or "we're going to the theatre" or, you know, always remember that, but I don't ever remember. I don't have any memory of romance, none whatsoever.

TS   With most of his relationships ……

RO   But did he have other relationships? Who with?

TS   He had a relationship with a girl called Terry Mosaic, as he called her, and then it was his wife June, he had number of other relationships along the way. And then with Gloria, who was driving…

RO   I thought it was the wife that was driving.

TS   No…Gloria… but what I was about to say… and again with friendships… he was very close to John Peel…

RO   Oh yeah, he did a lot for him.

TS   Yes… he was very close to John Peel. But the strange thing is, you're saying about how he just went, that seemed to be a pattern with him with all relationships, because with John Peel as soon as he had got all that he needed out of John Peel …

RO   You see, I think that the problem with… his need to go was not because… when I read that poem about um… the one about …

TS   'Down the stairs'…

RO   Yeah, when I read that I could see him realising that he had stopped being the focus of my passing on knowledge or sharing my life, he stopped being my focus because my focus was now on the job, but I can… this is what is so amazing to me when I read these poems I think to myself, he never… I don't know how to explain it… it was never a break-up you know, there was never a "he's got as much as he could and now he's gone"… it was never like that at all. It was about me moving on and him not really wanting to hang about if, you know the whole relationship changed because when the two of us were sitting around doing absolutely nothing for months and months and months and months at a time, it was suddenly different, he wasn't doing anything and I was hysterical in those days, you know, absolutely hysterical so it was like this all the time I always thought I was so much more important than the rest of the world thought I was.

TS   We all do that…

RO   So it was certainly not a situation where he felt he got as much as he could and then left, and if from reading those poems it seems, all of those years afterwards, it seems to me that obviously it was something that never left him.

TS   I don't know, I think if……

RO   I opened doors for him, not so much professional doors, but mental doors. That's what I did, I opened mental doors for him, but I wasn't aware, I mean I do the same thing with my company now, I mean it's like one of my actresses who I've been working with for years said to me the other day, "you don't understand, you don't just direct us in plays you change our lives". You know, I get a street writer to sit down and listen to Bach. Or I take six of them to see Gina Ravera in Chicago because I wanted them to see what that was about. I've always been that kind.

TS   Did you ever introduce him to Ginsberg?

RO   No. I always thought that those guys were of their time… Kerouac. I always thought they were of their time and they really weren't what I was about at all. I was running around with the great writers of the day, learning about the great directors of the day and that was the kind of… I flirted with the hippie movement because I liked the flowered shirts and the beads.

TS   It's a nice theory…

RO   No, I… what the hippie thing?

TS   Yeah…

RO   Only because the world won't let it be… because they won't leave you alone.

TS   But some of the earlier …

RO   I would say he got into some of that through Bob Dylan.

TS   There are some poems in there where you can see the influence of Jack Kerouac and Ginsberg… But then he loses it completely.

RO   But they told me at this memorial thing that he turned gay?

TS   Marc…

RO   I can't image that.

TS   I think he …

RO   Marc was one of those boys who was never really that interested in sex you know.

TS   Never?

RO   No never really that interested in it.

TS   He, this is difficult because there is no one to ask…

RO   Well that's what all the roadies and that say, I didn't believe it.

TS   I think he went through that phase, he definitely went through that phase.

RO   There's a difference between having experience… Listen, they were very free times, everybody was doing it, everybody.

TS   I think he definitely went through that phase, but I don't think he… he is quoted as saying 'I've tried it…but I prefer women'… one of his quotes but…

RO   I never knew him to be interested in anybody, I mean I never, I cannot remember him ever looking at anybody, male or female, and saying "oh, that's hot".

TS   Really?

RO   Ever, ever.

TS   Strange. Especially for a lad of that age, because he would have been you know… my son is 18 and he's…

RO   Did you happen to see that Gordon Ramsay show last night?

TS   No.

RO   He was so funny, there was this chef that was just useless that was #### to the restaurant. And he says to him "you are supposed to be beating that, look at the way you're beating that, you've got no energy, you're 21 years old, you should be getting ten hard-ons a day, you're not getting one a month".

TS   That's true! What is strange about Marc is that a lot of his songs are extremely sexual.

RO   Yes, that I realise now from the poems as well, so obviously it made some impression on him, but I was never aware of that.

TS   A lot of his poems and songs are extremely sexual, I mean Get It On for example is an extremely sexual song.

RO   But I think that was part of the business.

TS   Well, yes.

RO   No, I think that was part of the business that he understood how to do that.

TS   And the image he portrayed at the time was sexual in both ways, I mean the image he portrayed …

RO   Ambivalent.

TS   Yes.

RO   About sex?

TS   Yes.

RO   And that's what he always was.

TS   He went both ways.

RO   Well I would …

TS   I've got one quote, which is one, which is taking the pee basically where he says "I'm tri-sexual".

RO   Try anything…that used to be an old joke around the times then. But he wasn't really very sexual.

TS   His image portrayed blatantly ……sexuality.

RO   I think that was all part of the image.

TS   I don't think, he was certainly very ….

RO   He wasn't running around picking up girls and banging them and making them pregnant, and he certainly wasn't running around the gay bars or anything. He was interested in people's minds, he was not interested in their bodies.

TS   Did you ever meet Harry his brother.

RO   Yes.

TS   Very different.

RO   Always was.

TS   Harry described him to me as a reaper of knowledge.

RO   Yes, yes!

TS   Which I thought was a very good description…

RO   And when I got to that point where I was so self involved I wasn't passing anything on, that's when he left.

TS   But now that takes me back to the point I was just talking about where every relationship was almost like that, even to cruelly… what I know of the relationship and I don't know about the relationship with June his wife, and I feel sorry for her the way he treated her to be truthful because it was almost as if… June worked at a record company secretary and he would call…… and they got married very quickly and she managed him through most of his career, so she managed all the day to day running of a rock star so as he had support, so he had time, because of that to concentrate on his writing and music.

RO   Oh it was very difficult for him to do anything without support.

TS   But as soon as he had got where he needed and…

RO   He left her.

TS   Yes.

RO   Well I feel…

TS   From the outside though, that's what it seems like.

RO   Well, reading the poems and by reading the fact that years after we had seen each other he is still writing about me, I guess it must have devastated him.

TS   I don't think it did.

RO   It must have devastated him, and it could easily have laid the ground work for this "I'll never get close to anyone again because…"

TS   Well it can do, it was early in life.

RO   I had no idea you know, reading these things, it brings the whole period back.

TS   You are giving me your prospective? To look at some of these lyrics…

RO   Well all the things that I have read today, I don't know the lyrics, all of the things that I have read today, the best way I can put it is "I feel I'm there", so whatever magical influences and inferences that people put on them, I don't see that, I see them as disguising him and I.

TS   Have you read Warlock?

RO   What's the title?

TS   'The Warlock of Love.'

RO   Warlock?

TS   'The Warlock of Love.'

RO   You see, I say to myself, when you say things like that, I think "It must be me".

TS   Why?

RO   Because, when I read about the way he felt about me and, you know calling me the Wizard, calling me the magician, to me it immediately says "The Warlock of Love" and I suddenly realise, and then she says he was in love, it immediately makes me think that well, he must have thought of me…

TS   It's interesting actually, the title "The Warlock of Love", I mean most of his earlier work is very ethereal, very ethereal… very wizardly, very mystical etc etc and even "Ride a White Swan" is all about the people of Beltane, druids and all that sort of thing… The later stuff becomes a lot more raunchy, a lot more pop rock…

RO   He would, he would…

TS   But you can still see things disguised meanings…

RO   I had no idea I had that influence on him and the interesting thing is that when my gang now tell me how much influence I've had on their lives I think well maybe that's what I do. But I had no idea.

TS   Well you definitely did have an influence, even his wife said.

RO   Well to hear the wife say. Because it couldn't be anybody else but me.

TS   I know it's not, because of the chronology.

RO   It couldn't be anybody else, I've no idea.

TS   He lived with you, then he went back to his parents for a while, then he moved out again and lived with somebody else.

RO   Well, he never actually moved in, but he was there all the time. But he never packed a little suitcase and brought it round, but he was there day and night for months, months and months, you know, every once in a while he would go home, or I would drive him home or drop him off and he would come back the next day, but he never, the idea that anybody would have, hey, maybe he thought so, but the idea that anyone might have that it was roses round the door and hand holding and walks through parks, never. It was… I mean I had a tremendous amount of time for him because he was so smart and so focused and so perceptive. He wasn't that articulate when I first met him.

   I mean I've done the same thing with my nephew, a painter, I met him when he was a kid and I discovered he had talent and sent him to art school and generally supported him, I still do in fact, he's got a place where he lives that I've given him and he's just found out that he's a father and he's going for custody because the mother's not capable of looking after him and they didn't even know she was pregnant, and… you know that's just the way I am. I just say yes, he must go for custody and I'll help him in every way I can. But I don't, I don't ever take that kind of thing in that other way,

TS   Yeah… I mean Marc was obviously very in awe of you.

RO   For me the realisation is not really as romantic as the image about us. I'm not romantic, and yet I am, but I'm just not romantic in my life, I'm romantic in my thoughts. I obviously can't avoid a certain amount of sentimentality, but er, I have a wonderful friend who's a painter, dead now, who said to me "sentimentality is a middle class emotion" and then I read something recently which was absolutely wonderful "sentimentality is for people who want love without the risk". Good that isn't it. There is a risk to romance. The only thing with sentimental love is that the risk is not as high.

BREAK

I'm the bull in the pen you know. As long I know what's mine I'm fine, I don't want to share it. My little pasture is mine, if you tell me that corner of the room is yours, that's fine with me as long as this is my corner. That's why I have all this open plan kind of thing, no walls. The people who live on the top floor, because I know that I'm basically reclusive, and if I didn't force myself into an open situation I would sit and stare at the wall and dream and think and imagine, and I have this dreadful thing of if I imagine it, if I can visualise it as far as I am concerned it's done, I'd rather do it, because to do it means you are doing it so someone else will approve and I can't be bothered with anyone else's approval.

TS   That's strange though as an actor.

RO   Oh, I've changed though. When I was an actor I wanted to be loved by everyone. But when you read all these things and you say to yourself how obviously important I was to him, the fact that he never called again, and I never called again is very interesting.

TS   It's almost as if he realised …

RO   It's only by reading these poems I realised how important I was to him – I had no idea. It was a wild and crazy time, because at that time when they started opening up after hours places, coffee bars, and um, then there was a friend of mine called Eric who suddenly started taking over these various kinds of bars/nightclubs and putting on shows that we always went to, but it was a wild and crazy time where anything goes. It was an amazing time.

TS   In my research, I've learnt a lot about Marc's life… obviously he became a famous rock star…

RO   He never swore you know, not when he was with me. And not because I said don't swear, he was so polite, never, I mean when I see these words in these poems, he never used these words, never.

TS   He made thirteen studio albums.

RO   You're kidding.

TS   But, that is just scratching the surface.

RO   But that tell's you everything you have to know… don't you. Work came first.

TS   Oh, absolutely, he lived to write.

RO   Yeah, the work came first, but you see, this thing about calling it some kind of… he knew it was a job, he really did, this is not some mad spirit that was just… he knew the job, he knew what he had to do to get it. It was work, the work, I think in these days you would call it a workaholic.

TS   He was only actually successful, he was only there at the top for 10 years.

RO   That's a long time you know. No… but I mean it's a long time for a pop star. He never wore jeans. Never. But then again, very few people did then, it was a very different time. Listen, the other thing that happened at that time was suddenly, the commercial world realised that young people had money, because they were getting out of school at 14 and they had jobs in the afternoon and they had money and so they were all buying clothes, they were all buying trousers and suits, shirts and sweaters, things were being imported but it was about being well dressed, it wasn't about the jeans. I don't ever remember him in a pair of jeans, I don't remember him having a pair of jeans.

TS   I have seen him in denim dungarees.

RO   You see, this to me is… I wouldn't know when this was written… This "Gods and Men". This to me is like why he left. "The breath of a million stars that altered his metabolism", and I tell you, I had gotten this movie and "into the image of a god but what god and who's was this visage of the star one ….." and all that stuff and it just goes on. See when somebody reads this "on a dark dawn on a morning of ice a man ship came from the world beyond the worlds" that seems to me, to me it invokes how we met.

TS   How you met?

RO   Yeah, this is very hard for me to read.

TS   That's…

RO   Yes, too personal. Yes, they… when he wrote that poem about me and said I promised I would never mention his name, I would never have allowed him to say those kind of things, they are too close. I always, I wanted nothing to do with that part of the world, you know, one of the reasons I never got in touch with anybody and said "hey, I'm the guy" because I did not want to be a footnote in the life of Marc Bolan, I just, you know, walked away from it, the idea of being … nothing in it, not for me, when I read these things they are terribly personal.

TS   Not to…

RO   Other people, yeah well I never read them before and I find them very personal, I find them too close to the mark.

TS   I found things … are personal and I would write the same sort of poetry.

RO   He is very close to the mark there, as far as I am concerned, because only he and I would know these things. I just, only he and I would know these things, there is no way anyone else would know these things, whatever interpretation anybody puts on them, I can smell it, I can feel it, I know, I can see him walking from room to room, I can, I wouldn't, if he had showed me one of those, I would have said "you can't say that" and I suppose if he felt strong enough at the time he would have said "but no-one will ever know anyway". But… They're a little close to the mark.

TS   I must admit I've wondered… But there is only you who would know.

RO   You know… it's very difficult for me to know how far to go. It is very very difficult, it really is, it's very hard for me, because I had no idea that it was that important to him. It is very hard for me to know – I mean I grew up in a world where you are discreet about things… it's just that it's very hard for me to, some of the things are very close to the mark.

TS   From my perspective…

RO   This is very difficult for me, you realise that don't you? You must appreciate that this is very difficult for me, I'm not a grandstander, I'm not someone who wants to find their picture in The Sun saying "this is the man that, whatever" you know, I prefer to be anonymous. In life as well.

TS   My perspective of this book is to understand Marc Bolan not to muck rake…

RO   To understand him, I can tell you everything about understanding him that you want to know.

TS   Can I say my reason for that? My reason for that is because most of the critics… have labelled his words as nonsensical, nobody has ever…nobody's ever analysed his lyrics.

BREAK

RO   He stops himself from going to far. But he… without… he makes the people involved, into mythical figures, in order to protect me.

TS   He does? There is actually an interview where he says as much, not about you but about his writing, he will make the bad manager into a chrome stallion… or something like that.

RO   But the poems that I read about the split, all those poems that he writes about people leaving and having different things on their mind and being caught up in the glamour and the glory, and I think, "oh my god", it really effected him, he obviously was… much more involved on a personal level than I was, and that is not to say that I didn't adore him, but I adored him as a kid who had talent and was going to go places. It's just… they're very scary to me, very scary indeed, very scary.

TS   There is one song on his last album that is very close to David Bowie, they moved in the same circles at one point, right from very early days.

RO   I would have thought, right from the very early days he would have been more interested in David Bowie than he was in Elvis or any of the other guys, but he would mention Elvis and Bob Dylan because they were iconic names.

TS   But he and Bowie played at the same clubs.

RO   But he would be more interested in that thing of showmanship first. I mean, he was… his whole attitude was about this is a show and you have to do this, that and the other, I remember him jumping off the sofa that night, I was telling you about it, jumping off the sofa and wiggling his hips and saying "anybody can do that, look, all you have to do is this". You know, I am one of those people who never really thought that Elvis moved with much grace, it was suggestive for the time, but there was no grace involved in it, and I was brought up as a dancer, so you know, the odd shoving out of a hip, unless the line was right, means nothing to me. And I remember sitting there and being amazed that someone, this age, saying anyone can do that, all you have to do is this, and getting up and doing it.

I think he developed… I have a theory about it you know, I have a theory that he got to the end of his knowledge and there was no one around to teach him anything different.

TS   You may be right.

RO   Yeah, he got to the end, it would be very interesting to me to see, or hear the lyrics of the last album to see whether they are still involved in the same kind of thing that he was, or whether they are breaking new ground.

TS   The title track of the album is called 'Dandy in the Underworld'…

RO   So he hasn't left… he didn't leave it there.

TS   He portrays himself, supposedly as Orpheus on the title track.

RO   We watched the film you know, the Cocteau film, we watched it together.

TS   This is very interesting, because all the things that his key characters are doing in the poetry… that he mentions you saw… you did together.

RO   Yeah, that's why I'm saying that I think he actually got to that point where so many pop stars do that it's, however big they are, as big as Jagger or Paul McCartney, or whatever, they are just re-visiting old ground, there's nothing new happing, they are not taking it to another level and… my guilt comes from, if I was there he would have taken it to another level because I would have wanted more… You know, I'm the sort of person who would have said to him, well if you are going to do a show lets get Josef Svoboda the designer from Czechoslovakia who invented the Laterna Magika and let's get so and so to direct it, I mean, I've always had major ideas, big ideas, that's the thing that bothered me most, actually I don't feel as bad now that you tell me he wasn't a drug crazed freak, because that's the way they were portraying him.

TS   He got lost in it for a while. But he pulled himself out of it.

RO   He was very straight laced you know.

TS   Was he?

RO   Oh yeah, he wasn't a hooligan; he wasn't a predator in any way, shape or form.

TS   Well no, that doesn't come across in anything.

RO   It's evident about what you've told me about the wife… there she as a receptionist of a recording studio, naturally he's going to get her. And when he needs her to do all the work, naturally he's going to get to her and the minute he doesn't need her anymore he's out of there because it's about… there was no-one around him to learn from, he had no-one to learn from anymore, he was surrounded by people who either thought he was gods gift and could make no mistakes, or were in the same business and were thinking about where's the hit coming from. There was no one about him to say… if no one's offered to do a film, lets develop the script. You are big enough now, come-on lets develop the script, there's no one around.

TS   He did one film with Ringo Starr, they were just playing… it was just rock stars playing… that's what it was.

RO   So that kind of… you know… I just had no idea. Until all of this stuff has come up, because as I said, I discovered there was a poem.

TS   Have you seen that one about you…

RO   I can't remember if I saw that one, but I saw one that was dedicated to me and I was astounded, I mean the first thing I did was I saw a book and I picked it and said poems by Marc Bolan or whatever and I'm giggling to myself saying "I don't believe this" you know, I mean this little kid that I knew has suddenly got a book of poems published, lets get real here for a minute. And when I opened it up and realised that I was in it and then a year later, when I found out, because I know nothing about all this wizard stuff.

TS   It's his first song, the first one he wrote.

RO   I never heard it, I don't think I ever heard it. I have no idea what the lyrics are.

TS   It's, you would probably…like you've done with that poetry, find something personal in it , but outwardly it's……

RO   Well, when they first found me, the one thing that shocked them is they thought he'd made it up, they thought he'd made this person up.

TS   That would be because of the way he told the story.

RO   And also he did exaggerate, he did say evidently, he did say I think I read somewhere he said he spent six months in Paris with a wizard, well it was a long weekend. But, what I'm saying is that when I read those things I know what's personal and where he's gone off into some kind of phantasmagoria thing, I know, I can read between the lines and it scares me, it scares me because I had no idea and it also shocks me, because we never had those kind of conversations. I mean those kind of explicit conversations; we never talked about things like that.

TS   Sometimes in relationships thought things don't get said though and you never know what's going on in the other persons mind.

RO   But you see it is the world and him that has made it a relationship, I had no idea he was having a love affair. I had no idea.

TS   Because you don't know what's going on in the other persons mind.

RO   It wasn't something I was even prepared to entertain, I wasn't interested in that.

TS   But that's the problem with relationships.

RO   I don't know, how do you call a relationship and do you don't call a relationship, you know, who says it's a relationship just because you spend time together?

TS   Well it's a relationship of a type isn't it.

RO   Well, I tell you, if you are asking me about a feeling about him, I would have to say that I respected him and I admired him, and I'm not going much further than that. You know, it's difficult for me, it really is, it's very difficult for me, I mean one day maybe, but not now.

TS   That one's quite interesting…

RO   You see this just, this Swan King…

TS   That's my title for that chapter.

RO   But I mean, this particular poem is just…

TS   I've got ten poems and I've based it on one poem per chapter...

RO   You see, when he says things like "things to please his sight so that they might have a bond or hole to reach him by" immediately, in my mind I change the 'they' to 'I' that he is writing about, so that he is writing it personally saying "that I might have a bond or hole to reach him by".

You see when he says, "Albany the man, that would seem had been long dead" I think of myself, did he sense that I was pulling away? "The manship came from the world beyond the world and landed on the planet of freezing dust" which to me immediately is him landing on the planet of freezing dust. "The two earthmen covered in plastic and fishbowls of glass wandered numb through the forest of white oaks they ran like children to the valley of eternal snow and glass unknowing they entered like meat the plateaux of the beast", it's like our meeting…… Gosh, he was really upset, wasn't he? He really was, "a masterpiece by a hated master", I had no idea, I feel so awful, if only I'd known, I was so self absorbed though.

TS   I ……

RO   The one's that bother me are the one's that are really dirty.

TS   I think that was really……

RO   I can't find it now.

TS   him just experimenting…

RO   I don't know about that, I feel like they were about me, but I feel, but I can't find them. It's a printed one, not a written one.

TS   It's within this section.

RO   This section? But I remember reading it… it was a typed one.

TS   The typed ones are the one's that I am publishing, they are the one's that I own. These are one's that other people own.

RO   Yeah, but I mean I just read it here… it was a typed one.

TS   The one that starts off 'From… No it's not one of these. It's quite neatly written.

RO   What's it called? It's very scary.

TS   From what I have learnt, a lot of his experiences and feelings are hidden in a lot of his work.

RO   Not so hidden to me.

TS   They wouldn't be to many, I managed, just from my perspective, to get inside…he was very close to David Bowie, well David Bowie went through a very blue time, career wise, he got ripped off as most rock stars do at some stage… and struggled, and Marc, at that time Marc was at the height of his success and he gave Bowie a hell of a lot of help in that period… right, but then Bowie turned his back on Marc in various ways and there is one line in one of the verses on his last album where Marc takes a pop at him and that is something that is common knowledge so you can spot it, but anybody else that didn't have that little bit of knowledge and know that, you wouldn't pick that verse out as being about Bowie.

RO   They're all very extraordinary, very very extraordinary.

TS   He didn't… there's very few of his lyrics or poems that use any bad language.

RO   He never used any type of bad language at all when I new him. He just wasn't that kind of kid, he was so proper.

TS   There are tapes of him in the studio, tapes of what's going on in the studio where he swears. But it's almost part of the atmosphere.

RO   Part of being a pop star.

TS   Yeah, it doesn't seem to come out of his mouth naturally.

RO   No…he worked all of his life to make sure it didn't.

TS   Going back to the point I made earlier with relationships…his friendship with John Peel… The reason that their friendship went awry is because John Peel really championed Marc Bolan at first, but as soon as he went electric, he didn't like it and John Peel didn't play any more after that and Marc took offence to that and they went their separate ways, but after that…

RO   He was a wonderful boy, really a wonderful boy. But there was no way that I saw making a life with him, I mean there was just no way I saw that, it never entered my head.

TS   That's not your fault though, so don't crucify yourself over it.

RO   If I had known...?

TS   If you'd have known he thought that much of you would it have made that much difference?

RO   Yes.

TS   What would you have done?

RO   I'd have said "look, I realise I'm behaving badly, I need some time". That's all, just a little time, just let me get this job out of my system then everything will be fine. I'd have probably called him if it wasn't a job and we would never have split up if it wasn't a job, but the point is we split up on the Friday and I started work on the Monday. And I was on it for weeks and I was in my element, you know I was getting the director of the film tickets for the theatre that he couldn't get. I got him tickets to see Olivier in 'Othello'. He couldn't get them. I was just up there at the top table.

TS   …There are many people we pass in our lives that we have influence on and we don't realise…

RO   Well I'm aware now of the influence I have on people, I'm certainly aware of that, because I influence them to my way of thinking, but then again you have to say…

TS But what you are doing now is typical of catholic upbringing, and I can say that because I had a catholic upbringing. It's the guilt thing…

RO Catholic guilt…That's why I go to mass every day, every morning… 8.20?

TS It is the catholic upbringing. I did the same, I'm not a practising catholic, I was taught by nuns and then I was taught by monks…says a lot… but I was so over indoctrinated to the point of saturation by the time I was thirteen or fourteen, I'd had enough you know? But you were still indoctrinated with that…

RO Oh yeah, it's like the Jesuits would say "give me a child until he's seven and we have him for the rest of his life".

TS Yeah, and the guilt trip is always there. The first person I ever blame is myself.

RO Me too, I call it taking responsibility.

TS Yeah, but you can't take responsibility for things you have no control over.

RO Oh, but I'm a control freak.

TS Not in everything.

RO Tell that to me.

TS I crucified myself when my last wife left, because I adored her but she didn't deserve it…

RO …. Your adoration?

TS No.

RO I feel that nobody deserves mine, I give it anyway but I'm always wandering around thinking "you don't deserve this". I find it very difficult to convince myself to make a decision as based solely on what I want. I have to convince myself that I'm doing it for someone else.

TS You may have to be more honest with yourself…

RO I may have to be after today. I may just have to be.

TS I've kind of done that in my life, I've gone through my life doing things for other people and only in recent years have I started to do things for myself. I want to do this so I do it.

RO   In the past few months, the break-up with my writer has altered me. I've now realised that it's about time that I was allowed a little freedom and I'm having a difficult time dealing with it, I am struggling to get the door of the pen open, I really am, but I have decided this…

This has been very enlightening for me, this has been odd, this has been very enlightening for me.

TS   Well hopefully it will be more so when you read my book.

RO   I don't know if any of that is of any interested to your book, it's certainly of interest to me.

TS   I would like you to, I have a strange felling about this project, because, I was close to Marc from a different prospective, I never met him, I don't know him as a person but what I've tried to do is what someone who knew him should do, but you've got to know his music and know his lyrics to do it, as well, you see, I want to give him credibility and put him where he belongs or where I feel he belongs and a lot of people do… and nobody's ever done anything, there have been a lot of books out there about him and nobody's ever done exactly what I am doing which is analysis his music, his lyrics and poetry.

RO   I think though if you've got anything out of today… I'm chain smoking, you realise that don't you? I go through five or six cigarettes a day, I've now gone through ten and it's only 3.40 pm… You can't be frivolous, if you take on the responsibility of other people you can't be frivolous about it. I was young…

TS   Do you take on responsibility?

RO   I thought I did. When I read those things and I realise that it was with him, the pain was with him forever.

TS   He chose to be there with you…

RO   I'm not talking about that, I'm talking about leaving, how could I be so cruel? I'm not a cruel person, how could I not even think I was being cruel, if I said to myself then "I'm being selfish and that's the way I am" maybe I could have accepted it, but I had no idea I was being selfish until I see these things and I realise what went on.

TS   You weren't being deliberately selfish, you just…

RO   Tennessee Williams said it best, in 'A Street Car named Desire' he has Blad say "deliberate cruelty is the only unforgivable sin". I have never been deliberately cruel and I haven't been, but you have to take a certain amount of responsibility if you have been cruel, even if it's not deliberate.

TS	While I've been writing this, I feel that I have been guided through this, very strange, because every time I've needed something or got to a point where I've thought, "where am I going with this", it seems to land on my lap. Now I wanted to write, for a foreword in this book, a poem, in Marc's style rather than a long boring foreword, and I would like you to read it, because, it's not particularly long, but for me it says what I want to say and when I tell you that I woke up at 2.00 in the morning with this in my head, just there, and yes I've tweaked just a few lines, but the basic structure of it was there in my head and I don't know where it came from, I wasn't actually thinking about it at the time, I was asleep and I woke up with it complete!

RO	You don't mind if I edit this as I go down, I hate runes, I wish it was the other, 'ruins'.

	It is lovely.

TS	It's only a short poem.

RO	No it's lovely, the ruins of time, it sounds to me (here's my editor hat on) it sounds clever.

TS	It was supposed to.

RO	I suppose that is what he would have done.

TS	That's what I was saying earlier, I wanted it to be in his style.

RO	See if I was there when he was writing it I would have said to him 'ruins'.

TS	There is just one other book, actually, which I should have brought, he only had himself in his life one book of poetry published which was 'The Warlock of Love', there is no dedication as such apart from to the woods of knowledge which was probably to influence sales by appealing to his fans…

RO	I think… deeply, I think he was obsessed with knowledge.

TS	Obsessed with knowledge?

RO	Oh yeah, he wanted to learn, it was all about bettering himself. It was what was so attractive about him, for somebody like me who wanted to pass on all of this stuff that I was getting to somebody else it also made it more real for me to be able to pass it on, but he was obsessed with knowledge.

TS   Not just for the rock star purpose, generally?

RO   No I think if he had of stayed with me there is every possibility that he would never had been a pop star. Well if I had known how much he liked to write, I would have encouraged the writing.

TS   Did you know he was the best selling poet in this country? Mainly because he was a rock star but …

RO   Those poems have had a tremendously powerful effect on me, I think if anything the fact that they are so personal makes them better than if they are just flights of fantasy.

TS   Well yes, it does, poetry is written from a personal perspective. I don't think always…

RO   Well it's a very personal thing isn't it.

TS   I can go for months without writing poetry, but I have to try and force myself, if I haven't got the emotion that I need to write that particular poem it doesn't work, but if the emotion is there to propel that thought, whatever that thought is, then it flows but the emotion has got to be there to do it.

RO   And I am a lateral thinker you see, so I never take a step without checking out everything on the left and everything on the right.

TS   That's a trait that comes through in Marc…

RO   I was never aware of him as a thinker.

TS   You weren't?

RO   No, never.

TS   DO you think it's fair to say that he was…

RO   I was never aware of that.

TS   Because…

RO   He was just a kid on the scene… He got what he wanted in the end. He got what he wanted.

TS   He wanted to be a legend…

Riggs looks again at 'Pictures of Purple People'

RO   I'd love to have a read of those, they are screen plays, there's not enough there for anything else. But you could take those scenes and try to figure out a way to… figure out a way to … shorter than Beckett. I've been working on "Not I" which is what, three minutes long, that is so packed that you need an hour just to get off it. Be interesting to work on. Let me just look at the… because you're saying the second one is more interesting.

TS   Totally different.

RO   These are very well put together aren't they.

TS   Well these were put together by fan clubs, these were.

RO   Very well put together though.

TS   This is totally ethereal (Krakenmist), whereas this is very streetwise, street orientated (Purple People).

RO   Let me read a bit of the other one, I think this is much more of a child's piece.

TS   That is just part of a complete work.

RO   But it's much more of a child's piece to me than the bit of this that I read.

TS   Oh definitely. I don't think they would stand up on a stage well.

RO   See, these have a kind of child like imagination, a childlike innocence, I'm not aware of that boy. When I knew him there was no childlike innocence, when I knew him there was no child like fantasy at all.

TS   Really.

RO   He was focused, determined, there was no magic, he didn't believe in magic when I knew him, he believed in 'this is how you do it'.

TS   That's interesting because, so much of what he's sold is based on the theory of magic.

RO   He had no interest… None whatsoever.

TS   So you've never really listened to much of his music.

RO   No. I'm interested in hearing the things that are personal. When he goes off in his little fantasy lands, to me, like when I read that, to me all I see are the practical problems, how do I do this, how do I do that. I would have to strip it down, look at all the bare bones, get all the fantasy out, what is this about.

TS That's basically about kids getting high and the wizard character……

RO I don't know, I don't know why he's always got wizards and everything, I don't understand how that influence is just in everything.

TS The wizard character in this, is the supplier…

RO I don't ever remember us having a drug filled evening, ever, ever, I don't ever remember it. He didn't smoke… he didn't drink. I don't ever remember the two of us taking pills then going out, we never went out, I mean we went out to the theatre, we went out to dinner, but we never went out clubbing or anything like that, never.

TS But I mean, purple hearts was a culture of the time wasn't it?

RO Oh yeah.

TS Very big in the mod culture as well.

RO Oh yeah. Oh I remember the old days, we used to go to these coffee bars that were open after 11.00 in the basements and whatever in Chelsea and we would take these purple hearts and at the end of the night when the place closed at 2.00 we would go to the Laundromat because it was the only place… thing… open. And everybody would take off an item of clothing and put it in the washing machine because if they came in, if they found you in there, a whole bunch of kids in there, they would chuck you out, but they couldn't chuck you out if you were doing your laundry. And we would sit in there with one of those little radios, listening to Radio Caroline. But it was a once a week thing, well for me a once a week thing, it was never, I couldn't handle the amount of energy all that speed gave me. I just bothered me, I don't want to run around like that, I wanted to think, I didn't want my mind to be concentrating on moving about and getting things done, I wanted to think about things.

TS I would say that that is about a life that Marc …

RO When you tell me that it's about a group of guys that get high, my first reaction to that is – that's superficial. That's it's not really about that at all.

TS Probably not, but that's what the bare bones are about.

RO But that's not what it's about in his mind, when you read the first things about… the things that hit me are his attitude of the wizard giving him things and they are not really what they seem, it hit's me very personally.

TS He's saying they're sweets, but they aren't they're purple hearts…

RO   Exactly.

TS   When you take the sweets and absorb them…

RO   So, I have an entirely different reading of it you see, I think the sweets are bits of knowledge and they are not really sweets, because knowledge is a killer, certainly destroys instinct doesn't it? That's why actors have to dumb in order to be good… because their instincts are so much more important than their knowledge. I've known the greatest actors this country has ever produced and none of them are very bright. None of them, none of them are very bright, well when I say very bright, I mean they are not deep thinkers…they are not philosophical thinkers/actors.

TS   I see that.

RO   They understand the instinct.

BREAK

RO   They get very confused when they do that. I tell my actors that the character's more important than they are, the character is more real than they are. That they have to have a full rounded character even if there are bits of character that are rounded and not used, they still have to know it's there. Most actors only want to deal with what's there. Most Directors only want to deal with what's there.

TS   But that's like the character in a book, the writer has to have the whole character...

RO   Whether you use it all or not. I mean that's my little ditzy thing about a book, I decided I would start the easy way, by writing a detective novel. I love detective novels… they are all I read. Well, it's so, what's going on in my head, because, and the reason I can't put a pen to a piece of paper is because I have to know everything, it's not just about knowing little bits, knowing what you need, I have to know everything. I have to know how they feel; I have to have the rhythm of how their mind works. It tells me how they speak.

TS   I'm trying to do that with Marc…

RO   I think that what you are trying to do is really terribly interesting though I mean. You are trying to legitimise it. What on earth makes you decide to do that.

TS   I have always admired him, for his individuality, there was something so individual about his music and creativity, there isn't another rock star another musician that is as individual, imaginative…but Marc was…

RO   They were very old fashioned, we knew that then, I remember Alma (Cogan) saying when Ella Fitzgerald recorded 'Ticket to Ride' she said "she's no fool, she knows it's an old fashioned song".

TS   This sums it up really, and it's in my opening chapter right, at the time when the charts were full of 'Love me do' pop songs, Marc gets to Number 2 with a song about druids and the Beltane, that sums it up.

RO   But it's very popular now though I bet, with all this Harry Potter and hobbit stuff. But I would have thought somebody should have re-released it.

TS   It's out there.

RO   Now tell me something, did the kid ever get the money?

TS   No.

RO   They just lost it.

TS   It's still lost, he's still fighting the battle but it's still lost. As far as I know.

RO   And who are the administers of the estate?

TS   The administrators are a firm of accountants in London.

RO   And do they have anything to do with the son?

TS   No. They are answerable to somebody.

RO   To who?

TS   I don't know.

RO   Well the obviously haven't told the boy either. So the record company is just paying the estate.

TS   They pay royalties to the estate… and they obviously pay royalties to somewhere…

RO   The record company's getting it?

TS   I don't think so. Marc set up an offshore company before he died, Wizard Bahamas? it all goes there, all goes to Wizard Bahamas but nobody knows where it goes from there…

RO   They can't find out.

TS   Somebody somewhere must know obviously.

RO   Does anybody know what's in there?

TS   A lot of money.

RO   Does anybody know how much?

TS   Somebody must know.

RO   But what I am saying is, it's not public knowledge.

TS   No.

RO   So that means there might be nothing there. Because whoever is in charge of the Estate might have taken it out.

TS   It's all very strange. June was his only legal heir when he died, but she has since died…

RO   But she is the boys' mother isn't she?

TS   No.

RO   The boy is the son of Gloria? So you think that June just took the money and…

TS   No, I don't think she did take the money…

RO   But who though?

TS   They don't know.

RO   Has Roland got any talent?

TS   Yes, he's a musician… Gloria was Jamaican so Roland is half-cast.

RO   I've met him.

TS   You've met him? He's, you can tell he's Marc's son…

RO   He's too laid back.

TS   Yes, he's very laid back. His mother was a singer, so yes he's got beauty and he's got talent, and he's an artist in his own right…

RO   But he can't challenge the Estate?

TS   He's trying to. I believe he gets a little amount… The film Billy Elliott, that was all Marc's music in that film.

RO   Oh, I didn't know that, haven't seen the film.

TS   There are couple of songs that aren't Marc's, but a good 70% of the music in the film was Marc's. 'I love to boogie', that's in there. And there's a 'Robinson's' advert on at the moment, Robinson's squash, where it comes on and there's a glass and a few drops of squash drop into the glass and it starts to dance, it starts to dance to 'I love to boogie' which was Marc's last hit.

RO   I don't even know it.

TS   Well, next time you see the squash advert.

RO   I remember the levi's one. What was that one song called?

TS   '20th Century Boy'…

RO   And when I heard that I thought "that's fabulous".

TS   Elton John on Live8 – did a Marc Bolan song.

RO   What did he do?

TS   'Children of the Revolution'. He made a tribute to Marc and he said this is a song from an old friend of mine, Marc Bolan, who died back in 1977 and he was one of the greatest rock 'n' rollers this country has produced…

RO   All I caught of Live8 was bits, cause I couldn't care about those old people, when I turned on and I saw Elton John doing that stuff and all those thirty something's out there rocking, I thought, "sorry, I am not there anymore, I have moved on and wouldn't it be nice if you did".

TS   I loved it for the music I must admit and when I saw The Who and Roger Daltry looking like a business man in a suit, it kind of went out the window a bit…

RO   I couldn't handle any of those old fogies, entertaining each other, I couldn't handle that. I couldn't be bothered with it. Move On. You know, just move on for goodness sake. It certainly wasn't for the younger generation was it. It was all for those thirty something's who are their fans, they have all left their kids to go to their mothers to go to this thing.

TS   Haha… I mean…

RO   I was always a Motown freak, I was never interested in The Stones or The Who or anybody like that, I was only ever interested in Marvin Gaye, The Supremes, Gladys Knight, oh my god, Martha and the Vandella's to this day, 'Dancing in the Street' gets me on my feet.

TS   Smokey Robinson? The first Motown number one…

RO   'I Second That Emotion'?

TS   No…

RO   'Tears of a Clown'? You know, in those days I had a little Triumph convertible and had a record player in it. It would take 45's.

TS   With the needle bouncing across it.

RO   No… perfect. It fitted right in, you just slipped them in and played them and I used to wait in front of the record shops the day it was coming out, buy it, drive straight to Carnaby Street, park the car and play the song all day and go in and out of the shops. I knew all the kids who worked there. God all those kids are all gone too, they're all dead. It's not the same as it was, but then it was the only place. It was the only place.

TS   I bet it's all changed now, all shops now…

RO   So that's where I was at. I quite liked some bubblegum stuff, you know 'Young girl, get out of my mind' all that kind of stuff, but it was definitely Motown and still today, you just can't stop that beat can you.

TS   I like most music, so long as it's good…but I don't know what it is…I just want to give Marc some serious credibility…

RO   Well, I think part of the credibility you can give him is that this was not all just imagination, that this came from the soul and came from personal experience. That it wasn't just fantasyland. He dressed it in fantasy clothes but, from what I can read, there are very serious emotions in there, very personal emotions in there.

TS   He dressed everything up…

RO   He had a funny shaped body you know. His legs were quite long and he had a very short waist.

TS   You don't get that image of him…

RO   He had a very odd body, he was built kind of like Tom Cruise, except Tom Cruise is dressed now so that you don't show it but, he was high waisted with a short back, long legs and kind of broad in the hips in a funny kind of way.

TS   He was very slim…

RO   He had a lot of baby fat when I knew him.

TS   He wasn't very tall, just…

RO   Oh no, he was more than that

TS   He was only supposed to be about 5'2"..

RO   He wasn't tall, but he was more than 5'2". He was never a midget.

TS   He always portrayed himself as elflike.

RO   Yes, but that was the impish thing that he liked, but he was, had to be about 5'6" or something, he was not shorter than I was, he was not shorter than I was but I'm not tall, but he was not shorter than I was, I don't remember that, maybe an inch but he was only 16 at the time, must have grown.

BREAK

…handled the witty remark where they try to be serious. He's the only one that took abstraction of external objects and made it abstraction of internal objects. He's the only one who made paintings that you can't possibly replace with a camera. And they can't handle that. It's a weird country, a very weird country. They want everything to stay the same. They don't… my theory is… I'll explain the difference between America and England, American's want more, the English want enough. They find it very difficult to cope with people who want more. How happy was England when we had that great big stock market crash and all those yuppie kids were suddenly having to sell their BMW's and had nothing left, I remember somebody saying to me "I can hear the filofax's burning from here. They loved it, they were thrilled. Because they replaced class with money and you can't do that in this country, in this country they have this just absurd idea that money is vulgar. Try living without it, in all fairness I think this is what did Margaret Thatcher in. She tried to change society into thinking that money was the most important thing, and they didn't like it and they still don't like it.

TS   It's not the most important thing, but you can't live without it.

RO   But they want enough, they don't want more than enough. There is a generation out there now, but they are mostly ethnic, that want more.

TS   I find it difficult to eat without money so I'm quite happy to take more.

RO   It's like what I say about living in London, you either have to have nothing so that the state pays for everything, or you have to be a zillionaire, you can't be middleclass in London, it's too expensive…

TS Must have been scary…

RO   With the bombs? They love the idea that they are going to soldier through, you heard them, the people on the television saying "we lived through the second world war, this is nothing", I mean, you've heard them say it, last week they were saying it, I mean they just love that Triumph over adversity…what was it my friend used to say "snatching victory out of the jaws of defeat". They love it. I mean, the whole thing about, what was it called? When they all had all these ships that went over and got all the soldiers out of France before the Germans were there? You know when they sent all the boats over, the one they made the film about.

TS   Dunkirk?

RO   Yeah, I mean, we were losing, isn't it presented as a victory? We were retreating and it was shown as a victory. I find the country very perverse, it's only in the last six months that I have realised that, they will never be able to handle me… they have no idea how I work, how my mind works, what happens, they have no idea and they don't like it, they really don't like it, I've had terrible problems with councils, I can't get an arts council grant for love nor money, seven times they've turned us down and we do plays that are sold out. The audiences love the work, you get these little twelve year olds who are running all these fringe theatres because they are taking 'art administration' course, trying to tell me what theatre is about and sometimes I lose it.

TS   Where do you put your plays on?

RO   Well, we are going to go to the Oval House, before when we were at the old Post Office we used to put them on there, we got a big grant, I didn't get a grant, but the writer mostly got it, we suddenly decided that we did our plays other places so it became a quest to find a theatre every time and I'm one of those people you know, I want a home, but I bought this place so that we could do plays in that room, but I never got any encouragement to spend the money that I needed to spend to have it fixed so I thought "why the hell should I"? Now I just want out. I just want out, I've had enough. I have an idea in my head, I would like to have an evening of Becket plays, but with a black cast, never been done, I've been working on bits and pieces with some of my actors for years now and they are ready. That's something I would like to get out from under my belt.

I've got to get this play done first, called 'Whistling Maggie' TV presenter, interviewer kind of cross between Jeremy Paxman and Kirsty Walk? Only interviews presidents and Prime Ministers. He is about to interview on television the man who is tipped to become the next Prime Minister in six weeks and basically you find out that he molested her when she was twelve years old, and she is about to expose him on national television and so the press machine, the political press machine sets about destroying her life, and they destroy the affair she is having, they destroy her marriage. You find out that her mother was involved, you find out that the guy who did it then paid for her education, sent her through University, fixed all of the first jobs that she had, in whatever, it was what the mother wanted, the mother wanted a better life for her. So, he wrote it so melodramatically, I've cut it to the bone. I came back from holiday with the idea, I then had to structure the whole play, scene by scene, who's in it and what it's about. He then went away and wrote it, he brought it back, I then had restructure it and edit it to within an inch of its life and start to change things but it didn't work. I still don't have a last scene, but I have it in my head. I know what I am going to do, and I don't need him, well I hope he doesn't turn up.

TS   Writing is difficult some times.

RO   Especially when you don't pay attention. He is writing by numbers now. I've got an hour tomorrow, I'll do some work on it – sorry, not good enough.

TS   I have to write when the inspiration's there, I find it difficult to write, even writing factually when… if the inspirations not there, you've got to sometimes block it and go away and walk around or go and do the shopping or something like that while you straighten your head out, and then sometimes you have something come into you head that you have to get down now and it might not pertain to what you are working on.

RO   But don't you find that once you are on a roll you shouldn't stop?

TS   Oh yeah.

RO   He stops, because he's busy writing something else. Now he wrote this little sketch for this girl, this director girl at the Oval House who is trying to put together this devised piece which makes my laugh so much because she is only trying to do this because she's seen my work. Even goes so far as, I sat down and said to her, because she's the one that booked us in, I sat down and said to her I decided how to do the play, I'm just going to have five chairs and, because my whole theory is the work in work in progress is the interesting work, and I find out from somebody the other day that she has decided she is only going to use chairs. It makes me laugh and then he wrote a sketch for her and I went to see the thing, well I didn't know which one he had written and when I found out which one he'd written I was so embarrassed, it was so terrible, so boring and so bad and then they tell me "oh well, now they are doing sketches where people interact with the audiences and then they go back into the scene "well thank you very much folks", and Carol said to me "well maybe that's the way Courtier is writing it", I said "who the hell taught him to write like that, let's get real here for a minute". He only knows what I told him and I have so much more. I mean he has no idea how to structure a three act play, no idea, I wanted him to do an adaptation of a Chechov,

I wanted him to do it for years, I finally found someone else I could work with on the adaptation of 'Three Sisters', I had this idea of being placed on one of the islands, wanting to get to London and now I find out someone else is doing it. I've been after him for years to do something that, I wanted him to do a musical charting the people who came over on the Windrush, three generations, one generation each act representing each generation by the change in the style of the music, someone else is doing it – they are not doing it as well as we would have done it, but it's in the West End now. It happens, I've been begging him to do these things, it happens all the time. He is talented but he stopped. He refuses to think about things that are not relevant. But my theory is that a great play is a great play and it is always relevant what we have to do is make it accessible to a generation who don't think of it as relevant.

TS   Well…

RO   Please, it's been crazy and neither one of us have eaten..

TS   I'll grab a sandwich.

RO   Well, if you want anything else, let me know.

TS   You've given me a great perspective, insight, which is what I was looking for. I was looking for exactly the way Marc was, you know inside… I just hope this hasn't been too emotionally disturbing for you.

RO   It has, it has. I feel so guilty about not loving him as much as he loved me. I had no idea.

TS   I'm sure there are people out there who have loved me that I don't know.

RO   That you don't know?

TS   The thing to remember is that it became what it was.

RO   There was never, whatever went on went on, but there was never that, you know how you see somebody that you… you meet them and you start a relationship or whatever and you are drawn together by some sexual chemistry, it was never there, never, it was never about that. Other things might have happened, you know, but we all know the difference between someone who turns you on and somebody who doesn't.

TS   It might not have been that way for you, but it might have been for Marc.

RO   I don't think even with Marc I don't think that was the main objective, I really do not, not for one second do I think that was the objective. I would love to be able to believe it, but I'm sorry I don't, there is no way that he took one look at me and thought "oh wow" there is just no way, it was what I said, what I thought, what I believed was important. That's what formed the basis of our relationship. There wasn't the other thing at all.

TS	Well we are all passionate about our ideas…

RO	He just wanted to learn, he wanted more, always wanted to learn things to know things, if anything at that age, whether the experience at the time was as deep as it later became, I don't know.

TS	Maybe he romanticised, exaggerated…

RO	Well I guess that maybe that's what he did. It's nice when you read the poems, he didn't sentimentalise his memories. I just never knew I had that effect. Obviously it helped make him who he is, so that's okay, that's something good about it, but I just wish I was there more often later on, as a friend to say "what the hell are you doing?" and "how's this going".

TS	Well, as I said earlier, we all have our own agendas and everybody has their agendas.

RO	Well, I always believed that my agenda was other people.

TS	You are not necessarily wrong, but you can't be responsible for everybody else's agendas.

RO	But if you change somebody else's agenda my theory is… if you are prepared to break the plate, you have to be prepared to pick up the pieces. I had no idea I had broken a plate. If I had known that I would have picked up the pieces.

TS	I don't think you did that.

RO	No I guess not. I just wish I was there. I really do wish with all my heart that I was there, just at the end of a phone to say "congratulations, what they hell are you doing now? Why aren't you doing this?"

TS	Why weren't you? Was it because you just didn't think of it?

RO	No it was just, I don't remember a moment of remorse, not a moment. Not a moment of loss, not a moment of sadness, I don't remember it at all.

TS	You obviously thought a lot of him, because of your initial reaction when I spoke to you.

RO   Oh yeah, you don't forget someone of that age who wants so much and knows how to get it, and went out and got it. I was always aware of his knowledge of how to make things work.

TS   Even at that age.

RO   Even though I never lived his life, I lived mine. Never lived his life. I never met a friend of his, never, never met a friend of his. I was never aware that he had any.

TS   He wasn't a social person…

RO   He didn't have any when I knew him. He never once said, "I'm going to meet a friend, I'll be back later". Never once. He never came back with a friend saying "this is so and so", never once.

TS   I mean he didn't have a lot of friends…Marc didn't have that, he didn't appear to have that, he'd got friends, two friends that were still close to him… but they lost communication in the middle somewhere…

RO   And who were they? What did they do?

TS   Jeff Dexter is in the music business as well.

RO   And did what?

TS   He is still in the music business, used to be a DJ.

RO   Used to be a DJ?

TS   Yes.

RO   Again, nobody who couldn't give him anything. Well, you know what I mean by that. Push him further into different areas.

TS   Yes. You mean guidance and knowledge.

RO   A groupie.

TS   Jeff was quite involved with Marc… around about the time… It's quite funny because Jeff Dexter tells a story, he was very close to John Peel… Jeff Dexter was, and John Peel says to him one night "you've got to come and meet this incredible new singer I've met, he's absolutely brilliant, a guy called Marc Bolan". Well of course Jeff Dexter knew him as Mark Feld, so he said alright, they went and met him at Hyde Park I think on a bench and it was Mark Feld and they had been quite close friends in school, but there are just two or three people like that but mostly the people in his life…

ROI bet they did all the work. Keeping the friendship, I bet they did.

TSHe strikes me as not wanting to admit he needed people…

ROI don't think he needed to admit anything, not in terms of personal things, unless he got his fingers burnt with me, it's clear to me from reading what I have read today that he needed me, I wasn't aware of it, but maybe that just did something.

TSI'm not sure what.

ROI just don't know.

TSWhat?

ROI know the boy that I knew. I know that there was no surprise to me that he did what he did. The boy that I knew, knew that he was going to do it, it wasn't some weird and magical thing that happened, he knew how to do it and he knew what he had to do in order to get it.

TSAny emotional ties …

ROHe had none. As I said… I never met a friend of his, never. He met all my friends. He lived my life.

TSEverybody that's known him has said that he was very amiable, very friendly, very kind, one of the nicest people they've met. But he didn't have what I would call…normal casual friends, all the people around him were part of his world…

ROYou know, he was always on the move, but he never made me feel as though he was on the move. Never. Not for one second did I ever feel as though I was being used, not for one second. Never, never.

TSIt might not have been conscious…

ROI wouldn't have known the difference, of course I wouldn't. You know what… he never took advantage, never asked for anything.

TSHe just learnt…

RO   All the time, because of the life I led. It was about going to the theatre, it was about going listening to music it was about reading books and all that sort of thing.

TS   It was the impression that you get from my perspective is that he did go out to use people… in a way, what I am saying is that partly you get the impression that he did go out to… but then you speak to people, like you just said, they never felt they were being used.

RO   Well, I can honestly say, I've been with people who have used me in the past, they had none of those attributes. None whatsoever.

TS   June describes him as a sponge, a sponge for knowledge. His brother, the reaper of knowledge…and you get the other extreme, Tony Visconti, Record Producer … which… strange quote from Tony Visconti, although he also produced others, like Bowie, although most of his career and his work was with Marc… but there are quotes where has turned around and said Marc Bolan couldn't read.

RO   That's not true.

TS   I know that, that's blatantly obvious, and you get quotes like that and you think "why make a quote like that when it's so blatantly untrue". Because he was in fact very well read.

RO   Marc was more interested in the actual information rather than the art of reading. So you could tell him what something was about and he would be more interested in your giving him a summary of what it is about than actually sitting down, he wanted to be taught.

TS   But he read…

RO   I have no memory of coming in and finding him sitting in a chair reading a book. But then again, there was so much art going on around him that.

TS   But he read Gibran, Ginsberg…

RO   Oh yeah, I could see him, once it all got started, I could see him getting involved with all that stuff. Searching, searching, looking for a way to know more, reading those kinds of books, to me would mean to him that he was trying to find someone to give him the key, teach him how to be autodidact… But he knew it when he saw it...

        Well. Gosh what a day……

TS   Sorry about that…

RO   It's Ok…

AUTODIDACT: - SELF TAUGHT PERSON!

END

Legends

We should walk the lands of the ancient ones

To see what they once saw.

We should touch their minds with ours

                                            So we may learn some more.

We should stand inside their castles

And examine every stone.

We should clean the dust away

From what was once their home.

For

We cannot ask them questions.

We cannot touch their skin.

We cannot share their feelings.

And

We cannot feel their sin.

But

We can read the signs they left us

And colour between the lines,

We can understand their motives

And dig within their mines.

We can give their lives true meaning

If we care to take a look,

And ride their swans of glory

To write within their book.

By Tony Stringfellow.

Acknowledgements

Travelling through the mind of Marc Bolan has been a strange journey and I was not prepared for the places and adventures I found there. It has been similar to the journey in the 1966 science fiction film 'Fantastic Voyage', a comparison I know Marc would have approved of. I had a planned route, but was thrown off course many times by unexpected twists and discoveries. I have seen endless wonders that I did not expect to be there and I have emerged bewildered and fascinated. It is a journey I could not have made without guidance from many people who Marc Bolan touched in his life. Although this book was never intended to be a book of copious biographical facts and events, they are obviously relevant to the processes of deduction and I have been fortunate in being assisted by many people who have indulged me with their time and memories and although they may not have appreciated the contributions they have made themselves, all of them have been of invaluable assistance in guiding me through the labyrinth of understanding I have travelled.

My first handshake of gratitude must go to my special friend at the time Chris Bromham and his wife Anna Marie, without whose support I would have stumbled very early in the journey. Secondly to Peter Sanders for his outstanding photographic contribution and affectionate memories. Then to Bill Legend and Mick O'Halloran for their first hand insights.

I spent a long time with the wizard himself, Riggs O'Hara and his eccentric recollections were both entertaining and revealing, I am very grateful for his time and frankness. Simon Napier-Bell, on two levels, firstly his patience with my continued pestering of him with questions that I'm sure he did not see the relevance of and secondly for the valued reference material in his revealing two books, 'You Don't Have to Say You Love Me' and 'Black Vinyl, White Powder'.

Marc's brother Harry Feld was very open and amiable to my personal intrusions, as was Marc's cousin Caroline Feld, they both gave me valuable viewpoints and I thank them both. Although we didn't manage to formally meet as I would have liked, Jeff Dexter, Marc's lifelong friend still managed to guide me with his donation, for which I am grateful. For Bolanesque technical guidance the encyclopaedic mind of Barry Smith has been invaluable as was Dave Reginald's contribution of Marc's early handwriting. Thank you to Mary and Chris Payne from the Radio London appreciation society for their work and Jo Kapella for her expert opinion on Marc's handwriting.

I am grateful to Christopher Chittel for taking time off from his training for the London Marathon and Emmerdale to give me insights into Marc's last years at school. I was also very grateful to Wendy Wichenski, Daralyn Gold, Carol Shaw, Joy Faulkner and Roy Vincent for their reminiscences of a young Marc Bolan. Thanks to the Hackney Council Archive dept and Debbie Saum of the Hackney Gazette for their help in tracking down people who knew Marc as a child. A hearty pat on the back to a confused Marcel from the British Museum who could not see the connection between Marc Bolan and Egyptology but still patiently indulged me.

I must acknowledge the excellent works of Mark Paytress and Cliff McLeneham, 'Twentieth Century Boy' and ' Marc Bolan 1947-1977 A Chronology' without whose efforts I would have been lost, and the people of the Tyrannosaurus/Marc Bolan Appreciation Society who put together a number of unofficial publications that were of great assistance.

I must exclaim a much overdue thank you to Anthony Flanagan for parting with his albums so readily and my cousin Chris Cocking for accompanying me to so many gigs. And a general thanks to everyone I have spoken too who has helped point me in the right directions of research and everyone who has written and reported anything on Marc Bolan, because I'm sure I must have read all your works at some point.

And finally the most important thank you, to Rachel for being there.

Thanks to you all…including of course Marc Bolan.

Marc Bolan by Tony Stringfellow 2005.

On reflection....

My motivation for writing this book was to address the perceived opinion set out by the music critics (both professional and amateur) that Marc's lyrics were nonsensical and that he was some sort of fraud. As a poet and creative myself, I had always had the gut feeling that there was so much more to Mr Bolan! As a teenager I lacked the knowledge of my convictions, but as the years passed, I began to make intellectual connections, as I fell over common inspirations. When I began my research and started to outline the book, I was overwhelmed by what I found, it far surpassed my expectations and I was constantly surprised by the revelations that I was uncovering...daily.

Since 'putting the book to bed' and with my newly gained awareness of Marc's brain and the way it worked, I have found continued reaffirmations of his intellect...and his awareness of the creativity around him...one example would be, in an interview during the early seventies, he referred to a Chrome Stallion, I didn't make the link before, but on recently hearing a Dylan song where he clearly sings about a Chrome Stallion, I made the connection, Dylan, as we know, being Marc's hero...there may be more to write about the mind of Mr Marc Bolan....

TS.

Printed in Great Britain
by Amazon